LIBRARY IN A BOOK

PRIVACY IN THE INFORMATION AGE

Revised Edition

Harry Henderson

Facts On File

An imprint of Infobase Publishing

PRIVACY IN THE INFORMATION AGE, Revised Edition

Copyright © 2006, 1999 by Harry Henderson

Facts On File, Inc.
An imprint of Infobase Publishing
132 West 31st Street
New York NY 10001

Library of Congress Cataloging-in-Publication Data

Henderson, Harry, 1951–
    Privacy in the information age / Harry Henderson.—Rev. ed.
        p. cm.—(Library in a book)
    Includes bibliographical references and index.
    ISBN: 0-8160-5697-8 (hardcover)
    1. Privacy, Right of—United States. 2. Data protection—Law and legislation—United States. I. Title. II. Series.
KF1263.C65H46 2006
323.44′80973—dc22   2005037387

Facts On File books are available at special discounts when purchased in bulk quantities for businesses, associations, institutions, or sales promotions. Please call our Special Sales Department in New York at (212) 967-8800 or (800) 322-8755.

You can find Facts On File on the World Wide Web at http://www.factsonfile.com

Text design by Ron Monteleone

Printed in the United States of America

MP Hermitage 10   9   8   7   6   5   4   3   2   1

This book is printed on acid-free paper.

To my brother, Bruce Henderson, 1953–1997,
Computer pioneer, techie supreme,
and all-around family person

CONTENTS

PART III
APPENDICES

PART I

OVERVIEW OF THE TOPIC

CHAPTER 1

INTRODUCTION TO PRIVACY IN THE INFORMATION AGE

Privacy, like most abstractions, can mean different things to different people. It can mean seclusion—a place where one need not fear prying eyes. But it can also mean the ability to control access to our personal information. Robert Ellis Smith, editor of *Privacy Journal*, combines the two definitions, speaking of "the desire by each of us for physical space where we can be free of interruption, intrusion, embarrassment, or accountability and the attempt to control the time and manner of disclosures of personal information about ourselves."[1]

In 1928 Supreme Court Justice Louis Brandeis saw privacy as woven into the very fabric of our national life:

> *The makers of our Constitution . . . sought to protect Americans in their beliefs, their thoughts, their emotions and their sensations. They conferred as against the Government, the right to be left alone—the most comprehensive of the rights of man and the right most valued by civilized men.*[2]

However, it must be noted that Justice Brandeis was expressing the minority opinion of a Supreme Court whose literalistic interpretation of the Fourth Amendment had found nothing unconstitutional about the police tapping a phone line without a warrant.

When the Court revisited the issue in *Katz v. United States*, almost 40 years had passed—years that had seen the anticommunist crusade of Senator Joseph McCarthy, the gathering of dossiers on thousands of Americans by FBI chief J. Edgar Hoover, and the establishment of an elaborate national security apparatus. In a world of hidden microphones and radio transmitters, the Court now declared that people have a reasonable expectation of privacy at home and with regard to certain activities. Most Americans agree with this principle, at least in broad terms. For example, we expect that a letter will get to its destination without being opened and read. Likewise, no one should be able to listen in secretly on our phone calls without a court order. And if the police suspect someone has committed a crime, they must go to a judge and obtain a warrant before searching her home.

3

Besides protecting specific places and activities, privacy can also mean protection for intimacy and family life, and indeed, the right to make decisions about whether to have a family, without interference from government.

Legal scholars make a distinction between the "decisional privacy" that was affirmed in the Supreme Court's *Griswold* and *Roe v. Wade* cases, and "informational privacy." The latter, as described by Columbia University law professor Alan Westin, is "the claim of individuals, groups, or institutions to determine for themselves when, how, and to what extent information about themselves is communicated to others."[3]

However, as Americans go online in search of shopping, entertainment, and social contact, that sense of control over information seems to be missing, and thus privacy seems to be not a firm guarantee but at best an uncertain promise. Thus, according to writer Jeffrey Rosen,

> . . . *as thinking and writing increasingly take place in cyberspace, the part of our life that can be monitored and searched has vastly expanded. E-mail, even after it is ostensibly deleted, becomes a permanent record that can be resurrected by employers or prosecutors at any point in the future. On the Internet, every Web site we visit, every store we browse in, every magazine we skim, and the amount of time we spend skimming it, creates electronic footprints that increasingly can be traced back to us, revealing detailed patterns about our tastes, preferences, and intimate thoughts.*[4]

During the past decade or so Internet users have gradually come to realize that the computer screen is not a sign or a mirror but rather, a window. As the user searches for information and makes selections, data about that person is flowing outward, where it is accumulated in databases. These "electronic footprints" make the consumer himself or herself into a product that can be bought and sold.

While informational rather than decisional privacy is the focus of this book, there is no absolute distinction between the two types of privacy. In a society where communications and information technology are central to economic and even social life, many privacy advocates feel that the right of persons to control how information about them is obtained and used is deeply intertwined with the experience of autonomy and liberty. Without control over their personal information, how can people feel confident about making important decisions? And in a world where cyberspace so often intersects physical space, how can one secure life's private spaces?

PRIVACY ISSUES

As important as the right of privacy is to so many people, it is clearly not the only consideration in making decisions about how society will be organized. What makes privacy issues so often contentious and hard to resolve is the inevitable conflict between privacy and other important goals, such as business efficiency, law enforcement, and, particularly in recent years, fighting terrorism. Because hardly anyone is against privacy in the abstract, privacy issues generally involve one side saying that privacy is being threatened and the other side saying that the threat is minimal and is justified by important social, commercial, or governmental interests.

Privacy issues are found in virtually every activity and institution of modern life. Today some of the most prominent ones include

- What should happen to the information consumers provide when they buy something in a store or online?
- Is it acceptable for web sites to track users if it enables them to provide a more "personalized" and relevant selection of goods?
- Should companies have to ask permission before they distribute customer information—or is it up to the customer to say no?
- If information can be collected only if the consumer allows it, will the availability of credit and other services decline, and costs go up?
- Who should have access to a person's medical information? Should insurers be allowed to turn down persons who have genetic risks of disease? What role, if any, should medical records play in employment decisions?
- Should employee use of e-mail, chat rooms, and web sites be monitored to avoid potential lawsuits?
- How can children be given access to the rich resources of the Internet without compromising their or their family's privacy?
- Should all e-mail and other Internet activity be digitally traceable? Would the ability to find and punish spammers, hackers, or online predators outweigh the loss of anonymity that might protect vulnerable people or whistleblowers?
- Would the use of a universal ID card, biometric passports, airline passenger screening, and integrated databases make the nation safer from terrorism? If so, would it be worth the cost in privacy and the ability to move freely without having to be accountable to a largely unseen and unknown security apparatus?
- Is it a good idea to have surveillance cameras in major public places? Does it deter crime but also deter people from associating freely? Should any restrictions be placed on the ubiquitous web cams and camera phones that allow anyone to capture images?
- Are we becoming a "surveillance society"? Should we admit that privacy is a lost cause, or give people the technical and legal tools to "watch the watchers"?

Before considering these and other conflicts over privacy, it is useful to look more closely at the idea of privacy and how it has emerged in the development of modern society.

THE IDEA OF PRIVACY

Throughout history most societies have been organized with an emphasis on communal living. In medieval Europe, many tribal societies throughout the world, and even in the America of the first colonists, people generally lived together as extended families under one roof (often in one room). The idea of a person having a private bedroom was virtually unknown. Under such circumstances, there was little that people did not learn about one another.

On the other hand, there was little need to keep track of details about individuals outside the immediate group. Written records were not generally kept, except perhaps for the church's records of birth, marriage, and death, and records pertaining to the few people who owned land. Rulers generally had little interest in the details of the lives of ordinary people.

EMERGENCE OF THE INDIVIDUAL

The Industrial Revolution, which began in the late 18th century, created a tidal wave of change in living conditions for people in Britain and Western Europe. It brought thousands of people to work together in factories and offices in huge, teeming cities. As increasing numbers of people began to change from a rural, subsistent, agricultural way of life to urban wage labor, extended families tended to break into smaller units. A young person who left a rural home in search of work in the city was likely to find a marriage partner there and raise a "nuclear" family that was likely to be out of touch with the extended family.

This more mobile but in some ways more isolated life created new social needs. The medieval world had imposed rigid social classes but offered some security in providing everyone with a well-defined status, a "place in life." The industrial world and the growth of the middle class broke down rigid barriers and offered new opportunities for upward mobility, but it also created insecurity and tensions as people from different backgrounds and with different customs were thrown together and had to find ways to live comfortably with one another. The need to enable individuals and families to establish boundaries of personal space found expression in the idea of a right to privacy. For example, the act of visiting another person's home became more ritualized, and wealthier people started to devote a special room in their house for such visits.

The emerging need for privacy also reflected cultural and even psychological changes. According to privacy expert Robert Ellis Smith, from the point of view of the individual, "The right to privacy includes a sense of autonomy, a right to develop a unique personality and living space, and a right to distinguish one's own persona from everyone else's."[5] But this is a sentence that would have made little sense more than a couple of hundred years ago.

Just as lines in a geometric polygon define an inside and an outside, the existence of a sense of self is what gives rise to the idea that some things are interior, personal, and private, while others are public, belonging to the world as a whole. To modern people, it seems quite obvious that we have an inside and an

6

outside—and that protecting and nurturing what's inside is of special concern. But when one looks at the literature and art our ancestors have left for us, it seems that the emergence of a modern sense of self was a gradual process. As literary scholar Alastair Fowler has noted:

> . . . *Medieval literature knew almost nothing of individual personality: its introspection proceeded along rigidly casuistic [formally logical] lines. During the Renaissance subjectivity began to stir, particularly in dramatic literature, where the feelings associated with decisions were displayed, and in sonnets, which did much to explore one range of private emotions. The 17th century epigram did more. And the inquiries of [Robert] Burton and [Thomas] Browne (in their very different ways) enlarged the possibility of self-consciousness. But it was only in the 18th century that literature made a sustained attempt to express the individual feelings of those with the leisure to discover themselves.*[6]

As art and literature began to depict the world in more realistic detail, the textures of individual personalities became a major focus of novels such as those of Jane Austen. Turning toward the 19th century, the romantic poets, such as William Wordsworth, Samuel Taylor Coleridge, and William Blake, looked at universal ideas through the bright, sharply focused light of the individual imagination.

While few people in the early 1800s had the leisure or talent to become poets or novelists, the new focus on the self in high culture reached middle-class readers, who could participate through the fashionable new practice of keeping a diary, a private space in which one could assess one's daily experience and express one's hopes and fears.

A POLITICS OF INDIVIDUALITY

At the same time people were starting to define new social customs that protected privacy, the political philosophy of thinkers such as John Locke was starting to emphasize the rights and even the sovereignty of the individual in interaction with the government. In the medieval world, rights were attached to social status (most of the rights in the British Magna Carta of 1215, for example, referred to the nobility, not the common people). But 18th-century British statesman William Pitt declared in a speech before Parliament:

> *The poorest man may, in his cottage, bid defiance to all the forces of the Crown. It may be frail, its roof may shake; the wind may blow through it; the storm may enter; the rain may enter; but the King of England may not enter; all his force dares not cross the threshold of the ruined tenement.*[7]

Privacy, like freedom of speech and the press, emerged as rights that could be asserted against the government. Meanwhile the political reformers of the late 17th and 18th centuries replaced the idea of absolute monarchy with the growing power of a Parliament that represented the people (although admittedly only males with a certain degree of economic status were truly represented).

The colonists who came to America from England shared the regard for privacy and individual rights of the English political reformers. For example, the Rhode Island Code of 1647 stated that "a man's house is to himself, his family and goods as a castle." On the eve of the American Revolution, colonist John Adams told a jury that "An Englishman's dwelling House is his Castle. The law has erected a Fortification around it."[8] Indeed, one cause of the friction that led to the American revolt was that officers of the Crown frequently broke into colonists' homes to seize papers, having only the authority of a vague "general warrant."

The U.S. Constitution that came into effect in 1789 was primarily a blueprint for the organization of government, with Congress, the executive branch, and the judiciary branch each being given specified powers. While such a structure may have implied that rights not given to the federal government remained with the states or the people themselves, a keen awareness of abuses that had been suffered under British rule had led to demands for explicit guarantees of individual rights. The result was the adoption of 10 amendments, called the Bill of Rights, in 1791.

Several of the amendments have something to say about privacy. In particular, the Fourth Amendment states:

> *The rights of the people to be secure in their persons, houses, papers, and effects, against unreasonable searches and seizures, shall not be violated, and no warrants shall issue, but upon probable cause supported by oath or affirmation, and particularly describing the place to be searched, and the persons or things to be seized.*

This language gives specificity to the "your home is your castle" idea, declaring a fundamental right of privacy that officers of the state can overcome only by having sufficient reason ("probable cause") to believe that a crime has been committed, and that the place to be searched is likely to contain specified evidence relating to the crime.

Other amendments of the Bill of Rights also touch upon privacy. The Third Amendment prevents the government from taking over private homes to house soldiers during peacetime. Of more relevance today is the Fifth Amendment, which includes a provision that no person "shall be compelled in a criminal case to be a witness against himself." In other words, the information locked inside a person's brain is private and cannot be forced out and used against that person.

PRIVACY IN INDUSTRIALIZED SOCIETY

America at the time of the Constitution's framers was a primarily agrarian society. By the early 19th century, however, an industrial revolution was underway, reshaping daily life and the land itself, and creating new technologies that had unpredictable social impacts. To many artists and literary romantics at the dawn of this revolution, industrialization and technology threatened to turn emerging selves into interchangeable parts of some vast and relentless machine.

In America, a land that celebrated both limitless growth and individual freedom, transcendentalist philosopher and author of *Walden* Henry David Thoreau retreated to the woods, and essayist and philosopher Ralph Waldo Emerson protested that "Society everywhere is in conspiracy against the manhood of every one of its members. . . . The virtue in most request [demand] is conformity. Self-reliance is its aversion. It loves not realities and creators, but names and customs."⁹ This restated the romantic vision: the creative power of the individual versus the deadening power of conformity. In America, at least, the apparent boundlessness of the land could postpone for a time the regimentation that would characterize emerging European states such as Prussia in the latter part of the 19th century.

Just as industrialization was threatening individuality, so too was an emerging science challenging the idea of an autonomous self. A Newtonian explanation of the mechanics of the universe had already led to the suggestion that if the paths of planets could be predicted by exact mathematics, perhaps nature and human life itself were equally determined by a clockworklike interaction of forces. If accepted, such a picture of the universe threatened to make privacy irrelevant. (And thus, the romantic poet William Blake had portrayed Isaac Newton as a demonic figure of fearful power.)

At first the incredible complexity of biology seemed to resist mechanistic explanations. Biologist Louis Pasteur demonstrated that even microscopic life always comes from preceding life, rather than being generated from some mysterious "vital force." In the middle of the 19th century naturalist Charles Darwin introduced an elegant, powerful, and controversial explanation of evolution by natural selection. When Darwin examined the "human animal" and its position in the scheme of all things, he concluded that

> *The great difference in mind between men and higher animals . . . is certainly one of degree and not of kind. The senses and intuitions, the various emotions and faculties, such as love, memory, attention, curiosity, imitation, reason, etc., of which man boasts, may be found in an incipient, or sometimes in a well-developed condition, in the lower animals.¹⁰*

Two other great explainers of the 19th-century scientific revolution were Karl Marx and Sigmund Freud. Marx attempted to demonstrate that the conditions of human life and culture arise not from the individual will but from inexorable economic and historical forces. One might say that at least in the things that mattered, people did not make history; history made people. In this view, the inner self was peripheral, not primary.

Freud, on the one hand, actually made the private self more important. He made dream interpretation, free association, and the systematic examination of memories and feelings the key to freeing the individual from mental illness. On the other hand, Freud, like Darwin and Marx, was a determinist. He said that human behavior was determined by forces of which the individual was usually unconscious—forces that acted according to laws not unlike the hydraulic behavior of fluids. While exploring the private self was given new importance, its privacy, its harmful secrecy, would be seen as a barrier to be pierced by the light of analysis. (Later, 20th-century behavioral psychologists would attempt to dispense with the inner world entirely, working directly on observable behavior through stimulus, response, and reinforcement.)

The Victorian individual thus lived in a world of rapidly growing complexity. Science and technology offered explanations and new capabilities—even new leisure for some people to explore their private selves. But science and technology also threatened to make the self obsolete or irrelevant—and perhaps to annihilate privacy. Thus in 1890, in a landmark law journal article on the right of privacy, Samuel D. Warren and Louis D. Brandeis noted:

> *The intensity and complexity of life, attendant upon advancing civilization, have rendered necessary some retreat from the world . . . so that solitude and privacy have become more essential to the individual; but modern enterprise and invention have, through invasions upon his privacy, subjected him to mental pain and distress. . .*[11]

THE ALL-SEEING EYE

Around the turn of the 19th century, a British social reformer and philosopher named Jeremy Bentham developed a theory of utilitarianism, which viewed life as a kind of balance sheet of pleasure and pain. For Bentham, the object of a scientific, rational society was to maximize the former and minimize the latter, crafting social policies that would create "the greatest happiness for the greatest number."

For the reformation of individuals who broke the laws designed to secure their happiness, Bentham designed a new kind of prison he called the "Panopticon." This circular prison would be carefully arranged so that its inmates could be watched everywhere and at every moment by guards, who themselves could not be seen. It was not that every prisoner would be continually observed. Rather, Bentham thought that a prisoner who *could* always be seen and thus, at any time, *might* be under observation would have no choice but to behave "rationally" and gradually be transformed into a productive, happy citizen.

No Panopticons as such were ever built, but just as 19th-century science began to put the self into troubling new perspectives, late 19th- and early 20th-century technology would change what it would mean to hear and be heard, see and be seen. The telephone, introduced in 1876, seemed magical at first but soon became indispensable. The ability to talk to people without meeting them made it possible to sustain a much larger web of business and social relationships at a much faster pace than the daily rounds of the mail carrier.

10

But besides being disembodied, phone conversations were not necessarily under the sole control of their participants. Besides the operators needing to connect early phone calls and the common use of party lines, according to technology writer Erik Davis, "The mere *possibility* that unknown and unseen agents are bugging your line is enough to puncture the psychological intimacy afforded by a phone call, transforming your humble handset into an insidious tentacle of unwanted and invisible powers."[12] As early as the late 1870s, telephone inventor Alexander Graham Bell's assistant, Thomas Watson, was confronted by a man who was convinced that enemies had connected his brain to a telephone circuit so they could implant fiendish suggestions. (Each new technology seems to offer an image to be seized by paranoids: Later some would wear tin foil hats to block mind-control radio waves; in recent times, some have claimed that they are under the control of implanted computer chips.)

Until the 1930s, though, most people who were not spies or gangsters—or paranoids—did not spend much time worrying about phone tapping. But the powerful new totalitarian systems of fascism and communism used the telephone to pierce privacy and coordinate oppression, and used the invention of radio broadcasting to try to mold opinion on a vast scale. World War II demonstrated weapons of unparalleled physical destructiveness, but it also suggested the effectiveness of the increasingly sophisticated technology of social control.

BIG BROTHER

British novelist George Orwell responded to communication and technological developments by publishing in 1948 his famous novel *1984*, which seemed to be the summation of all that people had learned to fear about the use of technology to destroy liberty and even individuality itself. In Orwell's world a still newer technology, television, would realize the vision of Bentham's Panopticon. No citizen would escape the eye of Big Brother. Even the very idea of having a self separate from Big Brother would become "thoughtcrime."

Indeed this ultimate dictatorship aimed not merely to punish crime but also to render it impossible. As *1984*'s protagonist Winston Smith is informed, the media of television and the press would be used to mold minds through a specially designed language, Newspeak:

> *Don't you see that the whole aim of Newspeak is to narrow the range of thought? In the end we shall make thoughtcrime literally impossible, because there will be no words in which to express it. Every concept that can ever be needed, will be expressed in exactly one word, with its meaning rigidly defined and all its subsidiary meanings rubbed out and forgotten. . . . The whole climate of thought will be different. In fact there will be not thought, as we understand it now. Orthodoxy means not thinking—not needing to think. Orthodoxy is unconsciousness.[13]*

In the world of Big Brother, privacy cannot exist because, without consciousness, there is no sense of self.

LITTLE BROTHERS?

More than half a century after 1948 (and two decades after 1984), Orwell's vision of totalitarianism may seem as primitive and simplistic as the huge dams and power plants beloved by the leaders of the defunct Soviet Union. The "telescreen" (an early name for television) indeed became ubiquitous, but in the 1950s it showed not Big Brother but *I Love Lucy* and the resplendent wonders of modern kitchen appliances.

Social critics of the 1950s and 1960s began to see the threat to the individual as coming not from the focused propaganda of a single Big Brother but from the pressures for conformity in the corporate workplace, in schools, and in the consumer culture with its relentless display of TV commercials. Now the self could be eroded by homogenizing the individual, masking the unique inner self with a bland construct of images and desires. If privacy depends on identity, loss of any unique identity might make privacy irrelevant.

Popular culture has continued to reflect this theme. In Hollywood, for example, the 1998 movie *Pleasantville* used the metaphor of color versus black-and-white to portray a rebellion against the conformist 1950s world. However, the ultimate expression of this theme can be seen in the *Matrix* film series, where what we perceive as reality is actually a virtual-reality construction operated to serve the needs of hidden conspirators.

"The Big Brother Society that was imagined in 1970," one critic notes, "depended on coercion and fear. The society we are developing appears to be more [Aldous] Huxley-like than Orwellian. It is a Brave New World dominated not so much by tyranny as by a deadening political and cultural phenomenon that Ralph Nader calls 'harmony ideology.'"[14] Linguist and radical critic Noam Chomsky refers to this phenomenon as "the manufacture of consent." In other words, people are given a superficial individuality (defined mainly by possessions and lifestyle) and an illusion of having an inner self.

As television continued to evolve, it created increasingly immersive substitutes for community, with sitcoms giving way to the oxymoronic "reality TV." (The movie *The Truman Show* takes the trend to its logical conclusion, where a person's life is unknowingly a reality-TV broadcast.)

At the same time, the news media invades and feeds on the revelation of the private life of public people, from football player and actor O. J. Simpson, Princess Diana, and President Bill Clinton's sex life in the 1990s to pop singer Michael Jackson and Terri Schiavo in the first years of the new century. Many lesser celebrities are fed into the maw of trials as entertainment.

Perhaps people who identify with beleaguered celebrities are vicariously experiencing their own concern about their privacy as they worry about personal information being stolen by criminals or diverted, sold, or abused by institutions such as insurance companies, stores, and government agencies. As the boundary between public and private has become fluid in the media and the culture as a whole, for many people the fear is that, according to Simson Garfinkel, "The future we're rushing toward isn't one in which our every move is watched and recorded by some all-knowing Big Brother. It is instead a future of a hundred kid brothers who constantly watch and interrupt our daily lives."[15]

THE GROWTH OF INFORMATION TECHNOLOGY

Accompanying television as postwar high tech, the mainframe computer was also seen as an ominous threat to individuality. Science fiction writers began to visualize Big Brother in a new guise as the ultimate computer. (As an old joke went: When the huge room-filling machine was asked "Is there a God?," it blinked and whirred a while and then announced, "There is one *now*.")

The ancestor of modern information technology was the card-sorting machine invented by Hermann Hollerith and first used successfully in the 1890 U.S. census—just as Warren and Brandeis were sounding their warning about new technological threats to privacy. Card tabulators grew increasingly sophisticated through the 1920s and 1930s. World War II brought the first electronic digital computers, giving the capability not only to sort information but also process it into new information.

Computers of the 1950s and early 1960s had several characteristics that suggested an unsettling threat from these new "electronic brains." They were large and complicated-looking, their method of operation was unknown to most people, they were tended by a white-garbed "priesthood" of operators, and they were too expensive for anyone except big corporations and the government. The punch card soon became a symbol of an individual life reduced to a pattern of holes. Increasingly, decisions about everyday life seemed to be coming not from a human clerk one could talk with but from a machine animated by mysterious programming.

The three big TV networks and IBM thus became emblems of a power that dazzled and disturbed, promised and threatened, seeming to point at the same time to the ultimate in modern lifestyle and an emptying out of the inner self. TV seemed to replace the stuff of life with manufactured images. The computer might complete the abolition of privacy by turning the uniqueness of life into mere data. But the technology would prove to be both much more fertile and more ambiguous than the doomsayers could have imagined.

INSIDE THE WEB

Just as the early 19th century had spawned a cultural rebellion against industrialization, the new managed society of the 1950s and its information machines provoked a new flare of romanticism in the 1960s. The counterculture rejected both the computerized, managerial State and the blandishments of consumerism on TV. But the rebellion did not reject science and technology entirely: Indeed, much of it was fueled by electric guitars, a growing sophistication in electronic sound and visual effects, and hallucinogenic chemistry.

Privacy in the Information Age

At the same time that the 1960s cultural and political movements were getting underway and targeting government institutions and their technological trappings, one loosely knit group of explorers and activists were seeking not to destroy the computer but to reinvent it. Their name for themselves, "hackers," today has come to mean people who break into computers to destroy them or to steal valuable information. Originally, though, the hackers were brilliant though obsessive programmers who took advantage of a new generation of smaller, transistorized machines called minicomputers. They created the first video games, generated electronic music, and in general stretched the capabilities of the machines to the limit.

By the mid 1970s experimenters had shifted their attention to the microprocessor, or computer chip. They built primitive desktop computers and wrote about their revolutionary possibilities. One such visionary, Ted Nelson, proposed

> a screen in your home from which you can see into the world's hypertext libraries . . . offer high-performance computer graphics and text services at a price anyone can afford . . . allow you to send and receive written messages . . . [and] make you a part of a new electronic literature and art, where you get all your questions answered.[16]

Today we know this system as the World Wide Web. Even while the personal computer was being born, the 1970s also saw the creation of what would become the Internet. In the early 1990s Tim Berners-Lee invented the protocols for linking and transmitting text over the growing networks. By the middle of the decade, graphical browsing software such as Netscape made it possible for users of ubiquitous personal computers to participate in the Web.

While the economic possibilities of e-commerce took center stage at the end of the century, the social effects of the Internet have been at least as important. The primitive bulletin boards and commercial online services of the 1980s gave way to chat rooms and instant messaging. Millions of young (and not so young) people began to play in elaborate game worlds where a person's character or alter ego could build a house, carry on a profession, and even "marry" and raise a family. Meanwhile e-mail became ubiquitous at home and in the office. In the online world a person can take on many roles: a character in an elaborate game, a parent or a child, an employee, a customer, a patient, a citizen. In each of these roles information is exchanged with others, sometimes explicitly, sometimes implicitly, behind the screen as it were.

Cyberspace is a far cry from the Panopticon or the world of Big Brother's dictatorship. Big Brother projects his wishes into minds that have been so formed that they can hold nothing else. Television has been accused of being an instrument for imprinting conformity on millions of passive eyeballs. But in coining the word *cyberspace*, science fiction author William Gibson conveys a different vision. In the world of his novel *Neuromancer:* "The sky above the port was the color of television, tuned to a dead channel."[17]

Cyberspace is "inside" the TV set: There are no watchers, only characters. The choice of whether to be active or passive lies, as in "real life," with each individual. For Gibson and the other authors who created this postmodern science fiction, cyberspace is an exciting but not necessarily healthful place. In "cyberpunk" fiction, cyberspace is filled with violent conflict, techno gangsters, and the exploitation of the slow or unlucky by the fast and efficient. The world of cyberpunk, like the real information society it portrays, is a place where privacy and identity can be quite precarious.

INFORMATION PRIVACY AND THE DATA EXPLOSION

Back in the present-day world, the gathering, processing, and reuse of information continues to grow as the storage and processing capacity of computers and networks has steadily increased.

Our modern economy depends on massive exchanges of information, such as the details found in billions of checks and credit card charges. Most people would probably think that such details should not be accessible to the government without a court order. However, in *United States v. Miller* (1976) the Supreme Court ruled that checks and bank records were not private because they flow between banks as a part of commerce, and many people will have legitimate need to see them. The same has been held to be true of phone numbers, whose impulses must travel through many parts of the phone network. In other words, if something has to be seen by a number of people, it cannot really be private.

At minimum, one is faced with the question of how privacy principles should be applied to each new technology of communication, information processing, or surveillance. Constitutional scholar Lawrence Tribe has proposed a constitutional amendment that would read as follows:

> *This Constitution's protections for the freedoms of speech, press, petition, and assembly, and its protections against unreasonable search and seizures and the deprivation of life, liberty, or property without due process of law, shall be construed as fully applicable without regard to the technological method or medium through which information content is generated, stored, altered, transmitted, or controlled.*[18]

However, coping with the privacy implications of the "data explosion" is a formidable challenge. Just as developments in telecommunications and the processing of transactions have caused struggles over information privacy, so has the development of new ways of collecting, analyzing, and integrating data. The explosive growth of computer databases beginning in the late 1960s has particularly increased the threat to privacy by creating large amounts of information about the details of peoples' lives while providing little control over how this information might be used.

At first, much of the growth in databases came from government agencies that both needed and could afford huge mainframe computers for processing records for tax, Social Security, and a growing number of welfare programs. Large banks and insurance companies soon followed suit. Computerization offered governments the ability to manage an increasingly complex system of regulations and entitlements, while private business sought cost savings by replacing labor-intensive manual record-keeping systems with automated ones.

Public concern about an electronic Big Brother grew during the 1970s. But while the popular image was of a giant government computer stockpiling every scrap of data about every person, the real threat was more complex and subtle. In 1977 the U.S. Privacy Protection Study Commission warned that "The real danger is the gradual erosion of individual liberties through the automation, integration, and interconnection of many small, separate record-keeping systems, each of which alone may seem innocuous, even benevolent, and wholly justifiable."[19]

In other words, the most likely threat was not Big Brother but a swarm of "little brothers" who spend 24 hours a day gossiping with one another. The development of the personal computer and the Internet would vastly increase the number of ways in which information could be collected and shared.

In 1972, when the personal computer did not exist and networking was still confined to a handful of researchers, the Advisory Committee on Automated Personal Data Systems to the Secretary of the Department of Health, Education, and Welfare proposed some basic principles for protecting privacy in the new Information Age:

1. There must be no personal data record-keeping systems whose very existence is secret.
2. There must be a way for an individual to find out what information about him/her is on record and how it is used.
3. There must be a way for an individual to correct or amend a record of identifiable information about him/her.
4. There must be a way for an individual to prevent information about him/her that was obtained for one purpose from being used or made available for other purposes without his/her consent.
5. Any organization creating, maintaining, using, or disseminating records of identifiable personal data must guarantee the reliability of the data for their intended use and must take precautions to prevent misuse of the data.

These are still the guiding principles for privacy advocates today, and they have been embodied in important legislation such as the Privacy Act of 1974, the Electronic Communications Privacy Act of 1986, and earlier in the Freedom of Information Act of 1966. However, the struggle to get government and business use of personal data truly to conform to these principles has been long and complex.

PRIVACY IN THE MARKETPLACE

Of all the transactions involving personal identification and information, the vast majority involve individuals in their role as consumer. After all, the average person deals only occasionally with a health care provider or a government agency, but he or she makes dozens of purchases each week. Many small purchases are anonymous, such as putting a quarter into a rack and taking out a newspaper or buying a quick latté at a local Starbucks. But most purchases involving more than a few dollars are accomplished with a check or, much more often, a credit card.

Until after World War II, credit cards were issued by a particular business such as a department store or an oil company, and could be used only for purchases from that vendor. In 1949, however, Diners Club introduced the first general-purpose credit card, which could be conveniently used by travelers at a variety of restaurants, hotels, and other establishments. By the 1950s the Carte Blanche and American Express cards had been introduced, and the 1960s brought Bankamericard (later Visa), and Master Charge (later MasterCard). With the 1970s came the debit card in the form of the automatic teller machine (ATM) card and, later, debit cards for use in stores.

Cash purchases require no information except a simple receipt. Checks are more complex, but essentially the only requirement is a way to verify the identity of the check writer and, if necessary, the sufficiency of the bank balance. Use of credit cards, however, represents an open-ended series of loans. People who make loans want to make sure they will be repaid, and that means keeping track of information such as the following:

1. *Identifying information:* name and spouse's name, Social Security number, address, and telephone number
2. *Financial status:* amount of income (past and present), employer (present and past), occupation, sources of income
3. *Credit history:* previous type, extent, and sources of credit granted
4. *Existing lines of credit:* payment habits, outstanding obligations and debts, extent of current lines of credit
5. *Public record information:* lawsuits, judgments, tax liens, bankruptcies, arrests [in some cases], and convictions
6. *Prior requesters:* names of subscribers who requested information on the individual in the past[20]

Only an extensive computer network has the capacity to track these details and others for millions of borrowers in almost "real time," over a telephone or data network that enables merchants to accept the credit card and receive instant credit verification. This is only possible because the network taps into huge databases maintained by the major credit agencies: Experian (formerly TRW), Equifax, and Trans Union, which collectively maintain more than half a billion records on about 200 million people.

There are two significant vulnerabilities to the credit network, however. The first is that it depends on accurate identification—the person requesting the credit has to be the actual owner of the account. In recent years identity theft[21] has reached near epidemic proportions. The earliest route to illicit

17

credit card use was by stealing mail with Social Security or account numbers or a dishonest waiter or clerk copying down a card number for later use. However, starting in the later 1990s, a wide variety of techniques have been used to find personal information online or to trick users into revealing it to a fraudulent web site. Some thieves deal not in single accounts but obtain thousands by posing as legitimate users with a need for the information.

The same convenience that allows online purchases using only a card number (not the card itself) also affords cyber-thieves an easy way to take advantage of illicitly obtained credit information. The real prize for any data thief is the Social Security number. Besides retrieving credit records directly, the Social Security number can also be used to pull together all the records on a given person from a variety of public and private databases, many accessible via the Internet. (Ironically, Social Security cards, until the 1970s, carried a warning that read "For Social Security Purposes—Not for Identification.")

Identity theft for financial gain is not the only intrusion to which databases make people vulnerable. The personal information of politicians and celebrities is fair game for opponents or the tabloid media. When today's high-tech private investigators want to track someone down, they use a keyboard or a mouse, not shoe leather. Carole Lane, the author of a book about finding personal information online, boasts:

> *In a few hours, sitting at my computer, beginning with no more than your name and address, I can find out what you do for a living, the names and ages of your spouse and children, what kind of car you drive, the value of your house, and how much you pay in taxes on it. From what I learn about your job, your house, and the demographics of your neighborhood, I can make a good guess at your income. I can uncover that forgotten drug bust in college.*[22]

Even an ordinary person can fall victim to a stalker or abusive spouse who can use a Social Security number or other identifying information to get the target's address—or simply hire an illicit "data broker" or hacker to obtain the information. There are, of course, legitimate reasons for police and private investigators to use databases to track down individuals, such as to determine a person's assets in a divorce or in some other legal action, or to get someone to pay child support. The main problem is that there is little to stop the illegitimate user from accessing the same data resources. The sources of data and the ways to obtain it are many, and the existing regulations and safeguards, although slowly improving, remain far from comprehensive. Data in a networked computer is only as secure as the weakest link in the chain of users, a fact exploited every day by the creators of computer viruses, deceptive e-mail, and spyware.

As the world becomes increasingly wireless, new vulnerabilities have emerged. Cordless telephones are actually low-power radio transmitters, and calls on them can be picked up several hundred feet away. Cell phone calls can be picked up by scanners, although digital encryption now offers considerable protection. The wireless (Wi-Fi) networks now popular in homes, businesses, and public places have only limited security, which is often left disabled.

The second vulnerability of the credit system is that like all databases, it is only as good as the accuracy of the information it contains. Surveys have shown that about a third of all credit records contain mistakes. Sometimes credit information for two people with similar names can become intermixed. Errors can have serious consequences, ranging from failure to obtain a home mortgage to being turned down by a prospective employer as a "deadbeat."

Recognizing the seriousness of this problem, federal law as of late 2005 requires that the three major credit reporting agencies provide one free credit report per year. Privacy and consumer advocates urge everyone to check their record at least this often, both to correct erroneous and potentially harmful information and to spot signs of possible identity theft. The credit-reporting agencies are also required to accept and verify corrections of erroneous information.

DATA BREACHES

In recent years there have been a number of cases where personal data stored in the computer systems of financial institutions or even universities has been obtained by hackers or by criminals operating under false pretenses. These "data breaches" have aroused considerable anxiety and anger on the part of the public.

For example, in February 2005 ChoicePoint, a company that holds an estimated 19 billion consumer records, revealed that a ring of identity thieves had bought 144,000 records by posing as legitimate marketers. Apparently, though, the only reason the breach became public was that one state, California, had recently passed a law requiring disclosure of such incidents.

The records in question included information gleaned from public records including marriages, property transactions, and arrest records—all organized by Social Security number. Even ChoicePoint itself declared that it was in favor of tighter regulations that would balance the commercial value of information against privacy rights. There are many other stories of lost or stolen data, ranging from the loss by Bank of America of a tape containing account information for 1.2 million Americans, the loss of more than 300,000 LexisNexis records to hackers, and even the theft of a laptop containing data about University of California, Berkeley, students. These stories have fueled public anxiety and led to demands for legislation requiring stricter security practices and prompt disclosure of data breaches.

If it is hard to deal with the consequences of domestic data breaches, some observers have pointed to the even greater risks when data is processed outside the jurisdiction of the United States. In recent years many activities such as billing and customer support have been outsourced to workers in countries such as India, where well-trained, English-speaking workers are available for much less cost. Although there is little evidence that personal information is at greater risk of illicit diversion abroad than it is at home, when a breach of privacy does occur, U.S. federal or state regulations cannot be applied. Because of growing unease and a few well-publicized cases (such as one where a worker in India held some American records "hostage" in a wage dispute), Congress and more than 40 state legislatures have pending proposals to restrict the outsourcing of personal data. Some bills would allow consumers to opt out of having their data sent overseas.

Meanwhile, at home, the "outsourcing" of personal-data processing to a growing prison industry has also resulted in litigation. When a woman learned that a stalker who seemingly knew everything about her including her favorite magazines had received that information while working in prison for the data-profiling company Metromail, she successfully sued Metromail to stop the practice.

AN APPETITE FOR INFORMATION

Credit records are far from the only personal information generated in the modern economy. Anyone who belongs to a popular supermarket "savings club" creates a record of every item purchased, combining the information from the bar codes on the items scanned with the person's identifying information in the store's computer. The supermarket can use this information to create coupons instantly to entice someone who likes Kellogg's corn flakes to try the house brand instead. The information can also be used to target the customer for direct-mail campaigns. This same process can occur at a visit to a "big box" store, an auto dealer, or any time a consumer fills out a product registration or warranty card.

Why is so much information collected about everyone's daily purchases? Because, as one observer has noted, "Laws on privacy may vary from country to country, but the laws of economics do not. The laws of economics in the information age say that information has value—it is a product that can be sold, just like socks, cars, and toothpaste."[23]

Marketers suggest that by analyzing buying habits and making better fits between advertisers and consumers, both benefit:

Consumers benefit from receiving information that is targeted to their interests, as well as from not receiving information that is not of interest to them. Apartment dwellers don't want information about aluminum siding, for example, and childless couples don't need to learn about infant formula specials. Similarly, marketers have an interest in not sending messages to consumers who aren't interested.[24]

In turn, according to correspondent and free-market advocate Declan McCullagh, the market as a whole will become more efficient and productive:

It's easy to complain about a subjective loss of privacy. It's more difficult to appreciate how information swapping accelerates economic activity. Like many other aspects of modern society, benefits are dispersed, amounting to a penny saved here or a dollar discounted there. But those sums add up quickly.

Markets function more efficiently when it costs little to identify and deliver the right product to the right consumer at the right time. Data collection and information sharing emerged not through chance but because they bring lower prices and more choices for consumers. The ability to identify customers who are not likely to pay their bills lets stores offer better deals to those people who will.[25]

Just about every shopper likes bargains. Designers of targeted advertising (starting with the first specialized mail-order catalogs) have argued that the more advertising can appeal to a person's particular interests, the more enjoyable and useful the ads will be. But with that, there is also a growing unease about loss of privacy.

Privacy concerns are most aroused because the information gathered from one type of transaction is often sold to other businesses or to agencies that package it and sell it to other direct-mail marketers. While the compiling and use of mailing lists is not new, modern database technology makes consumer information a much more valuable product because it can sort, select, and customize it in so many ways. For example, a mail-order catalog company can target just those women who might be interested in a new line of larger-size clothes. However, data from supermarket loyalty cards has also occasionally been sought in criminal or civil cases. An activist group called CASPIAN (Consumers Against Supermarket Privacy Invasion and Numbering) has sought to publicize potential abuses and argues that supermarket cards yield little in the way of real savings for consumers.

The reselling of personal information first came to public attention through a few high-profile cases in the late 1980s and early 1990s. The LexisNexis database company, for example, admitted that it paid credit bureaus for Social Security numbers and credit information on millions of Americans, which they packaged and sold to direct marketers. LexisNexis was sued in a consumer class action suit and was required to remove the Social Security numbers, as well as remove anyone from their database on request.

In 1991 software developer Lotus Development Corporation and Equifax, a major credit bureau, announced plans to market a CD-ROM database called Households that contained names, addresses, and marketing information on 120 million consumers. But after 30,000 people wrote or called demanding that their names be removed, the companies abandoned their plans.

The marketing of personal information, however, usually goes on below the surface. For example, New York State investigators discovered that the credit bureau TRW had been taking the records it received from American Express transactions and reselling the information to direct mailers. Such undisclosed reselling of information has become a major focus for regulatory action and legislation.

THE MALL IS WATCHING

Visualize this scene from a not very distant future:

> *Johnny Q. Consumer walks into a national chain store, picks up diapers, pays in cash. He does not walk alone. One store camera captures his face, while another network of cameras traces his stroll through the aisles. The pressure-sensitive floor panels note how he lingers and nervously shifts his feet while browsing in the diaper section.*
>
> *At the store's national headquarters, perhaps a thousand miles away, a machine quietly notes in Johnny's file that he may be a new father. That bit of data goes into an algorithm that a few days later cross-references birth records and finds that, indeed, Johnny has just become the proud father of twins. A card is sent out and special discounts will be offered the next time he enters the store.*[26]

All the pieces for this scenario are coming into focus: cameras, face-recognition software, and data-mining algorithms. So far, no store has implemented all these features, but it may be only a matter of time. In the movie *Minority Report*, there is an even more advanced (albeit fictional) version of this system: A shopper walks through a mall. He is instantly recognized by the computer system and advertising holograms appealing to his particular interests are projected into the air as he passes by.

Meanwhile, radio frequency identification (RFID) tags are beginning to be used to track merchandise in warehouses and during shipping—Wal-Mart began to use them in April 2004. The tags contain stored information (such as tracking numbers) that is transmitted when the package is scanned with an appropriate device. That device only needs to be brought within a few feet rather than requiring a close-up hand scanner as with bar codes.

Besides increasing shipping efficiency and reducing theft of goods by employees, RFID tags may also help stores monitor their displays and perhaps remove expired or recalled products. Privacy advocates fear that the ability to identify someone's possession could easily be abused. For example, private detectives or government agents might use RFID scanners to learn whether a person has bought a pornographic book, a radical Islamic text, or a bomb-making manual. Supporters of RFID suggest that reliable signals can only be received within a short distance of the object, reducing the ability of someone to scan surreptitiously.

RFID may be just the beginning of a future world in which all objects have embedded information and even "intelligence," communicating with one another over what Internet pundits have called "an Internet of things." For example, futurists point to packages of meat that can alert the refrigerator they have reached their expiration date—the refrigerator might then dispose of the item and order a replacement from an online store.

E-COMMERCE AND PRIVACY

In many ways the Internet is a shopper's dream come true. By surfing the Web, a consumer can obtain detailed information on just about any product or service, even using a variety of services that automatically compare prices and identify the best deals. Items can be ordered with a credit card number and a few keystrokes. (There is little risk in dealing with a known company that uses a secure web server that encrypts credit card information, but information can be stolen by bogus sites or when sent by e-mail.)

As the 1990s ended, it seemed that e-commerce would supplant virtually all existing businesses, even the local grocery store. And although the "dot-com boom" was followed by a "dot-bust" in 2000–01, online stores and services that offer real value are here to stay—indeed a survey by market research firm Jupiter Research reported that total e-commerce sales during 2004 reached $66.5 billion, up 26 percent from the preceding year. Although this still represents only 4 percent of total retail sales, the impact of e-commerce is disproportionately greater because it involves some of the newest, fastest-growing business models. Further, it was estimated that another $355 billion in retail sales involved goods purchased in physical stores by customers who had previously researched their purchase online.

But the Internet and Web also adds another way to scoop up huge amounts of information from and about consumers. Many web sites store a small identification file called a "cookie" on a user's hard drive. They can then combine that information with the web server's log of all the web pages the user views. The result is a detailed profile of what the user has bought and is likely to be interested in. The use of cookies can save the user time (by making it unnecessary to resubmit credit card and address information for each order) and can also be used to customize the site with the user's preferences and to offer shopping suggestions. (Amazon.com, for example, has an elaborate system for offering recommendations based not only on what books one has bought before but also on what books have been bought by other people who bought those same books.)

Recently Google, the world's premier search engine, developed a free e-mail service called Gmail. The service is free because it is supported by advertising. To sell that advertising, Google ensures that it is targeted to the interests of each Gmail user. It does this by a process called "content extraction," in which the user's incoming and outgoing e-mail is scanned for keywords that might indicate an interest in particular types of products or services. The keywords are then used to generate targeted advertising.

Google has made it clear that no human actually reads the e-mail: The extraction is done completely automatically. However, privacy advocate Chris Jay Hoofnagel in testimony before Congress pointed out some troubling aspects of this technology. If the practice is routinely accepted, does it mean that e-mail users will no longer have an expectation of privacy under the Fourth Amendment? This could make it easier for police to use evidence from e-mail. Hoofnagel argues that "if companies can view private messages to pitch advertising, it is a matter of time before law enforcement will seek access to detect criminal conspiracies. All too often in Washington, one hears policy wonks asking, 'If credit card companies can analyze your data to sell you cereal, why can't the FBI mine your data for terrorism?'"[27]

REGULATION AND CERTIFICATION

The Federal Trade Commission (FTC) has been increasingly active in going after businesses with questionable information practices. The first well-publicized case came in 1998 when the FTC settled a complaint with GeoCities, a popular web-hosting service that offered free e-mail and web pages to individuals and families. As part of the settlement, GeoCities agreed to post a clear privacy settlement to explain its policies, and it also agreed to obtain parental consent before collecting information from children under 12 years of age.

Reacting to growing calls for explicit regulation, industry groups began to call for voluntary privacy standards. The best-known organization, TRUSTe, certifies web sites that provide clear privacy statements that explain what information is gathered and what will be done with it, as well as what a consumer can do if he or she is not satisfied.

Unfortunately, surveys have suggested that most Internet users do not understand privacy policies posted on web sites, nor use them effectively. In one survey,

- Fifty-seven percent of U.S. adults who use the Internet at home assumed that the existence of a privacy policy for a web site automatically meant that it would not share information with other companies.
- Forty-seven percent of users think privacy policies are "easy to understand," but about two-thirds of those users actually misunderstand the meaning of privacy policies.
- Sixty-four percent have not used the Web to get information about how they can better protect their privacy.
- Eighty-six percent would like to see regulations that standardize the format of privacy policies to make them easier to understand.[28]

Industry advocates have pointed out that the market has responded in some cases to privacy concerns of consumers by discontinuing unpopular practices. For example, America Online canceled plans to sell users' phone numbers to telemarketers, while Yahoo! removed a reverse-number look-up feature that could have been used by marketers. Perhaps the best-known case occurred when Internet advertising company DoubleClick ended its plans to combine information from web cookies with a large database called Abacus—which would have, in effect, data-mined Web users.

IS PRIVACY GOOD BUSINESS?

One approach to strengthening privacy is to use regulation (or the threat of regulation) to get companies to change their practices. But some experts suggest that protecting privacy can actually bring business advantages to companies that get out in front on the issue, such as by agreeing to use information only if they receive permission from the customer. According to Ann Cavoukian and Tyler J. Hamilton,

An opt-in marketing strategy does more than simply earn the trust of consumers. By allowing consumers to control the uses of their personal information, permission marketing increases the likelihood that the customer data being collected and used is accurate and up-to-date. Both consumers and businesses suffer when data is full of errors. When an individual's personal profile is inaccurate or incomplete, there is a greater likelihood of that person being judged out of context or treated unfairly. Meanwhile, there is a high cost to businesses when their customer databases are riddled with errors.[29]

Libertarian free-market supporters have suggested that the ultimate solution is for companies and customers to negotiate individual privacy agreements. A free-market contractual approach would rely on accurate privacy statements to inform consumers who would then decide whether to do business with a given marketer. Some marketers might choose to offer a range of "privacy plans," with consumers who are willing to let their information be shared receiving lower prices or other benefits. However, according to legal expert Jerry Kang, the individual

would face substantial research costs to determine what information is being collected and how it is being used. That is because individuals today are largely clueless about how personal information is processed through cyberspace. [Companies] do not generally provide adequate, relevant notice about what information will be collected and how it will be used. What is worse, consumers' ignorance is sometimes fostered by deceptive practices.[30]

Kang proposes that personal information be considered to be property belonging to the individual. This would mean that if a company wants the information, it must negotiate with the customer, rather than the customer having to stop unwanted use of information.

Other advocates see privacy as more like the inalienable rights proclaimed in the Declaration of Independence. According to Katrin Schatz Byford, "since the [property] model treats privacy as a quasi-material possession external to the individual, it cannot take account of privacy's function as an inalienable precondition of personal identity and social existence."[31] If privacy is an inalienable right (as life and liberty are inalienable), it means that no one can negotiate away their privacy.

In practice there is likely to be a mixture of approaches: regulations to prevent abuses that the majority find to be unacceptable, industry certification, the use of privacy assurances as a marketing tool, and consumers deciding for themselves whether the benefits of a company's policies outweigh the disadvantages.

PRIVACY AND THE HEALTH CARE SYSTEM

In recent years we have learned that privacy problems can be just one more thing wrong with America's troubled health care system. Consider these examples based on actual or potential cases:

Privacy in the Information Age

A man goes into the hospital for treatment of prostate cancer. A month later he receives mail from a drug company touting their cancer treatment drug.

An employer searches employees' pharmacy records looking for expensive prescriptions that might indicate fraud or drug abuse. He finds that someone has a prescription for Retrovir, a drug used only to treat AIDS.

A woman's genetic testing reveals that she has a gene that indicates a high risk of her developing breast cancer. What happens if the test results are seen by her insurer? Her employer?

Employers provide most private health care and thus have a strong incentive to reduce what seem to be spiraling medical costs. One way is to try to have healthier employees in the first place. According to a 2004 survey by the American Medical Association, nearly 63 percent of U.S. companies require medical testing of current employees or new hires. This figure, however, is down from 70 percent in 2000, which may suggest that regulations and public pressure may be having an effect.

According to a recent survey reported by the Institute for Health Care Research and Policy's Health Privacy Project,

- One in every five people believes their health information has been used or disclosed inappropriately.
- One in six people tries to protect their privacy in some way, such as paying out of pocket for health care using multiple providers to try to avoid creating a single unified health record.
- Two out of three U.S. adults don't trust private health plans or government programs to maintain confidentiality all or most of the time.[32]

Clearly there is a high level of anxiety and distrust on the part of the public where privacy and the control of one's medical decisions is involved.

WHOSE MEDICAL RECORD?

Since ancient times doctors have professed a code of ethics that goes back to the Hippocratic Oath: "Whatsoever things I see or hear concerning the life of men, in my attendance on the sick or even apart therefrom, which ought not be noised abroad, I will keep silence thereon, counting such things to be as sacred secrets."[33]

The doctor-patient relationship is central to this ethic, which assures people that they can seek medical treatment without having the details of their medical condition revealed to other parties. Today, however, the doctor is only one of a large number of people and institutions involved in the delivery of health care. The tremendous growth in the cost of medical treatment has resulted in third parties—employer and insurance companies or the government—paying for most health care. This in turn means that a bewildering variety of nonmedical personnel are also involved in viewing or reviewing medical records.

The flow of information is crucial to health care today. Doctors and pharmacies believe that access to comprehensive medical records is essential for providing better care and for protecting patients from taking dangerous combinations of prescription drugs. The managers of the government-run Medicare program need to track medical records to ensure quality of care and to prevent fraud. Insurance companies and health maintenance organizations (HMOs) claim they can use information systems to improve efficiency and hold down costs by eliminating wasteful and unnecessary treatments.

Further, uniform medical records and integrated databases offer a cornucopia to medical researchers. Recently the Mayo Clinic and IBM announced a pilot project combining the clinic's extensive patient database with IBM's data-mining technology to create the Mayo Clinical Life Sciences System. This would allow researchers to view at a glance every treatment and outcome for a patient in order to better understand how people with a given condition respond to a specific treatment. And when combined with the growing amount of genetic knowledge, Nina Schwenk, a doctor and chair of the clinic's information technology committee, notes:

> *When I see someone with high blood pressure, I have a choice of 20 to 30 drugs that I can choose from. There is some literature out there that will say, "If you're diabetic, this drug is better than that one." But most of the time, the only way you can tell for sure is to start the patient on the drug. It's almost trial and error to see how well it works for an individual and whether there are side effects. Not so far in the distant future we'll know the various types of genetic difference that cause people to metabolize drugs in different ways. So I know that if you try drug X, it's not going to work on you, and drug Y will have a heightened effect, while drug Z will have side effects. We'll be able to know all that up front.[34]*

As a result of both payment systems and the needs of medical research and quality control, so many people have joined the chain along which medical records pass that one writer suggested revising the Hippocratic Oath to read as follows:

> *Whatever I see or hear in my attendance on the sick or even apart therefrom will be divulged to physicians, nurses, aides, surgeons, anesthesiologists, dieticians, physical therapists, admitting clerks, billing clerks, utilization review personnel, discharge planners, records coders, medical records filing staff, chaplains, volunteers, performance evaluators, insurers, medical transcriptionists, accrediting agencies, public health officials, other government officials, social workers, and employers. AND to whomever else requests them for whatever reason.[35]*

The principal clearinghouse for medical records is the little known Medical Information Bureau (MIB), which has a role similar to a credit-reporting agency. The government also runs its own huge database for Medicare patients.

The Clinton administration proposed a single national databank in which every person would have a "universal healthcare identification number." But the existence of a single central database accessible by a single key number would put all a person's privacy eggs in a single potentially vulnerable basket. Although privacy concerns led to the proposal being withdrawn, there is continuing pressure to tie together all medical records and make them electronically accessible.

FROM HIPPOCRATES TO HIPAA

Passed in 1996 but not implemented until 2003, the Health Insurance Portability and Accountability Act (HIPAA) primarily seeks to make it easier for workers to retain their insurance when changing jobs. However, the law also includes some significant privacy protections. Most people learned about the law when they went to their doctor's office for a routine visit and were asked to sign forms allowing their medical records to be disclosed for certain purposes. The law also gives patients the right to see their medical records and to submit corrections.

Free-market critics argue, however, that HIPAA and other regulations mainly miss the point. They believe that

> *true health privacy relies on empowered patients choosing among options made available to them by providers competing to serve them. This happens in hearty markets, where sellers vie with one another to discover and deliver whatever consumers want. But the American health care system is not well. Concerns about health privacy are a symptom of a much larger disease.*[36]

Given the complex, highly regulated nature of modern health care, however, it is not clear how a true free market could develop in which most people have meaningful choice between competing providers. Most employers offer only a limited number of options, and choices for the self-employed are even fewer.

Adoption of a single-payer, government-run health care system like that found in many other industrialized democracies might remove some privacy issues by eliminating the role of private providers and insurers. However, the government itself would then be both provider and guarantor of privacy.

GENETIC PRIVACY: THE NEW FRONTIER

For many people the deciphering of the human genome announced at the beginning of the 21st century marked a tremendous achievement—the biological equivalent of NASA's Apollo project. However, the growing ability to identify hereditary health problems and risks has lent a new urgency to the struggle for health privacy.

Nancy Wexler, a leading genetic researcher studying the inherited degenerative condition called Huntington's disease, has warned that "All of us have something or other in our genes that's going to get us in trouble. . . . We'll all be uninsurable."[37] What adds to the poignancy of her observation is that Wexler's own mother had Huntington's.

What does genetic testing mean for workers? If everyone has a susceptibility to some disease or another, one expert asks,

> *Do we want employers to be able to rely on dicey predictions about future health, to search for only perfectly healthy employees, and as a by-product keep Americans from their rightful place in the workforce? Such is the specter of genetic testing in the workplace—invasions of privacy, discrimination, and unwarranted control of individual conduct.*[38]

There are two potential sources of legal protection from genetic discrimination. The Americans with Disability Act (ADA) may apply to otherwise healthy people who have a genetic background that leads employers to view them as disabled, but the case law is mixed and the Supreme Court has yet to make a direct ruling. (In February 2001 the Burlington Northern Santa Fe Railroad agreed to settle a case where they had secretly tested workers for a genetic predisposition to carpal tunnel syndrome, a repetitive stress injury to the hand and wrist.)

The other possible legal protection comes from HIPAA, which forbids employer group insurance plans from denying insurance based on preexisting genetic conditions. However, employees or employers who are self-insured are not covered, and companies are not prevented from charging higher rates on the basis of genetic information.

Fundamentally, genetic information (together with more sophisticated medical testing) threatens to unravel the system of private medical insurance. Insurers traditionally put people in broad categories such as by age and a few other factors such as smoking. Rates were based on the overall average risk of medical problems for the group. However, to the extent an insurance company can learn about individuals, it has an incentive to "skim the cream" of healthy patients by offering them lower rates. People at higher risk would be turned down, accepted at much higher rates, or accepted only with the exclusion of preexisting conditions or risks. Although regulations can help protect against misuse of genetic information, it may be that only a fundamental restructuring of the health care system could truly solve the problem. (And, it must also be noted, if the government ran the health care system, the government itself might have an incentive to discover and misuse genetic information.)

PRIVACY AT WORK

After health and family, work is probably the next highest priority for most people. In the work force, though, many of the same driving forces—such as cost reduction and efficiency—are driving employers to monitor employees in ways that raise serious privacy concerns.

Questionable practices often begin before a person even enters the workplace. Most people would consider it reasonable that claims of education, employment history, and references on résumés are subject to verification. Potential criminal records are also a concern—employers want stable, reliable employees and try to weed out potential "problem hires" who might expose them to legal liability. (For example, a store would not want to hire security guards who have a record of violent incidents.)

However, other types of inquiry can raise privacy concerns. Should a potential employee be screened out because civil court records show she has sued a previous employer for sex discrimination or harassment? (As noted earlier, screening for actual or potential health conditions is also a concern.)

Psychological tests or "personality inventories" are often given in an attempt to judge the suitability of an employee to a given position, or to detect proclivities for dishonesty or violence. But some tests can ask questions about religious beliefs and sexual practices that have no connection with job duties. (Some of these tests were attempts to replace the use of polygraphs, or lie detectors, which have been banned for most kinds of employment.) Psychological tests have generally been upheld in the courts, although antidiscrimination laws do regulate collection and use of information relating to protected status such as race, gender, disability, and in some jurisdictions sexual orientation.

MONITORING E-MAIL AND THE WEB

Once on the job, workers who talk to the public on the phone (such as airline reservation agents or technical support specialists) often have their calls monitored for "quality control" purposes. Sometimes, however, personal phone calls are also listened to by supervisors. Video surveillance of employees such as store clerks is also common.

Most workers today use desktop computers connected to an internal network (LAN) and to the Internet. Some workplaces install software that can keep track of how fast clerical workers type and how long they let the machine sit idle. In many offices software also makes a record of what locations users visit on the Internet.

Many employers see monitoring as a way to reduce theft, embezzlement, or sabotage by employees. Indeed, most misappropriation of computer data comes not from outside hackers but from disgruntled or greedy employees. (Ironically, laws intended to protect customer privacy and the response to recent data breaches may add impetus to the use of computer-monitoring systems.) In other cases employers may simply want to reduce the amount of work time lost to online shopping, chat, and playing of online games.

Most such monitoring is legal, but it may have a negative effect on the morale of workers who feel they are "living in a fishbowl." Unions have sometimes made workplace privacy an issue in contract negotiations.

E-mail raises particularly thorny issues. The ubiquitous use of e-mail has replaced the telephone for many purposes. Back in the early 1990s, when Epson employee Alana Shoars discovered printouts of her e-mail on her supervisor's desk, she sued Epson America for breach of her and her fellow workers' privacy.

She argued that she had an "expectation of privacy," the key test used by courts. She said that since workers had to use private passwords to access the e-mail system, it was reasonable for them to think that their messages would be kept private. Epson, on the other hand, argued that its e-mail system was just another business tool like a phone or a copier. Since it was provided only for business purposes, workers had no reason to assume they could use it for private personal messages. In July 1992 the court agreed with Epson's position and threw out the lawsuit. This decision was in keeping with the general trend in workplace privacy issues: Generally, workers do not have an expectation of privacy in the office, and employers can monitor activities (including e-mail) as long as the monitoring has a reasonable, business-related purpose.

Many employers point to the legal system itself as the reason they need to monitor employees' e-mail and Web usage. Employees have been held liable for sexual harassment or "creating a hostile workplace environment," such as when some employees print out or display pornographic material from the Internet. Additionally, a harassing e-mail sent by one employee to another might turn into a million-dollar liability problem for the employer. (Many companies may also be concerned about revelation of proprietary or "inside" information in e-mail.)

Roger Matus, CEO of Audiotrieve, a company that makes e-mail-filtering software, reports that his company had studied e-mail retrieved during the Federal Energy Regulatory Commission's investigation of Enron Corp. The study found that "one out of every 25 messages contained offensive or inappropriate content. Nearly one in five was personal in nature. I read many of these messages and a few of them were quite amazing." Matus further observed that "Already, 30.7 percent of companies with more than 1,000 employees employ staff to read and monitor employee e-mail. This is a fascinating area because employees seem to have no idea that e-mail does not provide any privacy."[39]

One possible defense to such suits is to show that the employer has been duly diligent in discovering potential abuses and correcting them. But the same practices that may prevent harassment claims may also become the subject of a lawsuit for invasion of privacy. Employers can make the best of a difficult decision by making sure their monitoring activities are related to legitimate business needs, are fully disclosed to employees, and assuring employees that any information gathered will not be disclosed to other parties.

In turn, employees should make sure they understand their employer's policies, ideally refrain from using the employer's equipment for personal messages, and, in general, avoid including any information in e-mail that might cause trouble if disclosed—keeping in mind that "deleted" e-mail is not truly gone and can be recovered by system administrators or computer forensic specialists.

PRIVACY AND YOUNG PEOPLE

As most parents know, children seem quite comfortable with high tech and the information society—more so perhaps than most adults. Junior high and older kids keep in touch with each other with rapid-fire instant messages, download and share music files for their iPods and MP3 players, and confidently search the Web for information for school assignments when they are not online chatting or playing games. However, like many adults most children give little thought to privacy or worry about what might be done with the information they disclose online.

MARKETING TO CHILDREN

Although one wouldn't think children would be a major target of online marketers, older children often have access to the family's credit card numbers—or could persuade their parents to buy things for them online. Further, web sites that collect information from children can sell it to other marketers. In 1999 the web-hosting service GeoCities was stopped from collecting information from children without parental consent. Although there was no law against the practice at the time, the FTC was able to rule that the company was engaging in "deceptive acts or practices" in violation of federal law.

In 1998 Congress enacted the Children's Online Privacy Protection Act (COPPA). Since the enabling regulations were enacted in April 2000, web sites that wish to contact children have had to post a privacy policy that explains how information will be collected and used, and obtain explicit information from parents before accepting any information from their children. A year later the FTC found that most web sites were posting the required privacy policy, but only about half were properly notifying parents of their right to review, delete, or refuse the further collection or use of their children's personal information. In February 2003 the FTC imposed civil penalties on Mrs. Fields Cookies and Hershey Foods for failing to obtain parental consent before collecting information from children.

LIMITED PRIVACY AT SCHOOL

For at least the first 18 years of their lives, children spend a good many of their days in school, and whether it be middle school or college, educational institutions have their share of privacy issues. These include

- drug testing
- monitoring or filtering Internet use in schools
- administration of possibly intrusive psychological tests or surveys

Drug testing and Internet monitoring or filtering have generally been upheld by the courts, which have ruled that children have only limited Fourth and First Amendment rights compared to adults. However, intrusion into family information by school personnel has been limited by the Family Education Rights and Privacy Act of 1974 (FERPA), which limits schools' disclosure of student records outside the educational context (with exceptions such as for subpoenas from law enforcement agencies). Parents also gained the right to see and correct their children's school records.

Since the Columbine High School shootings in 1999, there have been a number of cases where diaries, e-mail, and web sites created by students have been identified as containing alleged violent threats. In the aftermath of each tragedy, it is always asked why school officials had seen no signs of the impending attack. On the other hand, much of the threatening material would probably be protected under First Amendment free-expression rights if it had been created by adults, and overreaction is always a danger.

The most intimate and delicate privacy issue comes between parents and their children, and here laws and public policy can be of little help. Children indeed face some serious dangers online, including harassment and even sexual exploitation. Some parents have installed software to monitor their children's Web surfing and e-mail. Children who discover the monitoring are likely to react to it as a betrayal, a lack of trust, and a denial of privacy just at the time when they are discovering what it means to have a private self. Whatever parents decide, it is best done openly after discussion with the children, with an explanation and agreement on the "ground rules." As one child psychologist and media expert suggests:

> *Somewhere between the two extremes is the prudent parent. For example, a parent shouldn't go off the deep end if their 15-year-old son visits a porn site. But if he starts spending hours at porn sites and chat rooms, they need to know about it.[40]*

As young people transition to adulthood, they will find that universities are an Internet-rich environment. Student records, like other personal records, are vulnerable to hacker attacks and criminal diversion. An additional issue arises from the subpoenas requested by the Recording Industry Association of America (RIAA) in an attempt to identify students who have illegally shared copyrighted music files. Some schools such as the Massachusetts Institute of Technology (MIT) have declined to hand over the requested information, citing FERPA.

PRIVACY, LAW ENFORCEMENT, AND NATIONAL SECURITY

Some of the most crucial privacy issues arise in connection with the government itself—particularly with regard to law enforcement, where liberty and even life are often at stake. The government is in a paradoxical position with regard to privacy. On the one hand, legislatures and courts have provided a growing number of privacy guarantees in some areas. On the other hand, the government itself is the largest gatherer and user of information about individuals, and its own practices have long been a concern of privacy advocates. As the Privacy Protection Study Commission reported back in 1977:

> *Accumulations of information about individuals tend to enhance authority by making it easier for authority to reach individuals directly. The voracious appetite*

of investigators for information causes [authorities] to collect and retain virtually any personal data uncovered unless the collection or retention is clearly illegal. This attention to avoiding what is improper, rather than accomplishing only what is necessary and proper, leads investigative agencies into abuses of citizens' rights.[41]

As with commercial information gatherers, the threat to privacy does not come only from isolated abuses but from the pervasiveness of the system as a whole and the lack of built-in safeguards. Many bureaucrats themselves see the systems as being unmanageable. The problem of keeping up with the information needs of government agencies has a tempting solution in the creation of a giant, centralized database for all information about an individual that could be constantly updated and placed at the disposal of each government agency for its own particular needs. In 1965, still back in the mainframe era, a limited version of this idea, the federal Data Service Center (also called National Data Bank), was proposed as a means to correlate all government data to allow for statistical research.

GOVERNMENT DATABASES AND INVESTIGATIONS

Such proposals have always been met by strong opposition. During the 1960s and 1970s, the FBI conducted secret but extensive counterintelligence programs (or COINTELPRO) that spied on Martin Luther King, Jr., and other civil rights and antiwar leaders. The Watergate scandal revealed that the Nixon White House was routinely using government agencies ranging from the CIA to the IRS to spy on or coerce political opponents. Such events made many people suspicious of any further centralization of government record keeping.

In 1972 Supreme Court Justice Lewis Powell noted in a ruling:

Security surveillances are especially sensitive because of the inherent vagueness of the domestic security concept, the necessarily broad and continuing nature of intelligence gathering, and the temptation to utilize such surveillances to oversee political dissent. We recognize, as we have before, the constitutional basis of the President's domestic security role, but we think it must be exercised in a matter compatible with the Fourth Amendment.[42]

The tendency to "federalize" crimes and social problems nevertheless continued to lead to expansion of government information systems and thus of threats to privacy. Examples have included the cross-matching of state and federal records to find persons who have failed to pay child support, verification and investigation of firearms purchasers, and investigations of Medicare or welfare fraud. In each case proponents have argued either that there was no true privacy problem or that the goals of the legislation justified a minimal invasion of privacy. Privacy advocates, however, remained concerned that the accumulation of seemingly minor intrusions on privacy would reach a point where the individual would lose confidence in both privacy and the ability to hold the government accountable.

THE PRIVACY ACT OF 1974

The privacy concerns of the Watergate era culminated in the passage of the Privacy Act of 1974. The act embodied fundamental principles that were intended to make government agencies disclose their information-gathering and distribution activities and to give citizens the ability to learn what information had been collected about them and to correct any errors. But over the past three decades privacy advocates have pointed to what they consider poor implementation and enforcement of this law. Since the act did not appropriate any funds for privacy enforcement, most major government agencies did not at first appoint anyone to oversee implementation. Without an enforcement mechanism, agencies were essentially the judges of their own compliance. As ACLU legislative director John Shattuck remarked during congressional hearings in 1983, "the rule disclosure of personal information without the subject's consent has been all but swallowed up by its exceptions, particularly the broad exception for 'routine uses.'"[43]

Nevertheless, the Privacy Act did provide citizens who suspect the government has inaccurate or inappropriate information about them with a useful if cumbersome tool. The citizen can try to determine which agency may have the information and file a request for it. Information involving law enforcement or intelligence activities, however, may be blocked from disclosure.

THE FREEDOM OF INFORMATION ACT OF 1966

One effective defense against government invasion of privacy is the ability to find out what the government is doing with the information it collects. The Freedom of Information Act (FOIA) of 1966 has allowed intrepid reporters, activists, and ordinary citizens to uncover important information about controversial government activities such as medical experiments and the handling of radioactive waste. The FOIA does allow the government to refuse to release information related to national security, intelligence activities, criminal cases, and other areas. As a result documents obtained by FOIA requests sometimes arrive with many areas blacked out. Critics of the FOIA point to frequent delays in obtaining information and the difficulty of appealing when requests are refused.

PRIVACY AFTER SEPTEMBER 11, 2001

The devastating terrorist attacks of September 11, 2001, brought shock, fear, and a resolve to uncover what appeared to be an extensive and deadly international terrorist network. In this atmosphere, at least at first, the warning cries of civil libertarians and privacy advocates seemed to be drowned out. As former FTC commissioner Robert Pitofsky noted, the dominant feeling was that "September 11 changed things. Terrorists swim in a society in which their privacy is protected. If some invasions of privacy are necessary to bring them out into the open, most people are going to say, O.K., go ahead."[44]

The USA PATRIOT Act was passed by Congress only six weeks after September 11, with little deliberation. A number of its provisions potentially weakened privacy protections. Section 215 allowed for the searching of books, records, or documents if government agents believed they might be related to an intelligence investigation. The agents did not have to provide specific grounds for their suspicions as with a normal criminal subpoena. Given that the Federal Intelligence Surveillance Act (FISA) already established secret courts for granting such subpoenas, the combination of secrecy and lack of strict standards has greatly alarmed civil libertarians, privacy advocates, and the library community.

Another USA PATRIOT provision, Section 213, allows for so-called sneak and peak warrants where the police can conduct a search without notifying the suspects and giving them a chance to contest the subpoena in court. The only requirement is that the judge agrees that there is reasonable cause to believe the secret search is necessary to protect the safety of police or bystanders or "the integrity of the investigation."

Generally, advocates of these provisions have argued that they are necessary because of the particular nature of terrorism investigations where suspects operate in secret and have potentially deadly capabilities. However, civil libertarians have pointed out that these USA PATRIOT provisions are already being used in some cases for crimes such as money laundering that are not believed to be linked to terrorism. At the same time, government officials have been hard-pressed to name even a few terrorism suspects who were apprehended using the more controversial provisions of the new law.

During 2005 a number of key provisions of USA PATRIOT are coming up for renewal. The administration has tried to minimize fear about abuses. Attorney General Alberto Gonzales has declared: "The department has no intention of rummaging through the library records or medical records of Americans. We do have an interest in records that help us catch terrorists."[45]

Going on the offensive, Gonzales notes:

> *Libraries currently are not safe havens for criminals. Neither should they be safe havens for international terrorists or spies, especially since we know that terrorists and spies have used libraries to plan and carry out activities that threaten our national security.[46]*

Meanwhile, FBI director Robert Mueller has assured Congress that the agency has not actually searched any libraries. However, many privacy advocates and perhaps a growing number of people in Congress are not willing to accept such assurances. The Security and Freedom Enhancement (SAFE) Act has been introduced as a modification to USA PATRIOT. It would require that agencies provide specific reasons to justify sneak and peak warrants or to allow searches of library or bookstore records.

THE NATIONAL ID DEBATE

In many respects the requirement for identification has become a normal part of modern life. Identification is needed to cash a check or (in most cases) to check into a hotel or rent a car. In this country, driver's licenses already serve as de facto universal identifiers, but their format varies from state to state, and many are fairly easy to fake.

One of the proposals for fighting terrorism is to develop a secure national identification system that might make it harder for terrorists to penetrate and move within our society. More than a hundred countries (including most of the European democracies) already have national identification systems. Besides its potential value against terrorism, a national ID might also help the nation get a handle on immigration, particularly if the system included a way to regularize the status of undocumented immigrants.

Culturally, identification, however, has long been a symbol of regimentation, of everything un-American. "Show me your papers" (often in a bad German accent) is a staple of World War II movies. As one observer notes:

> *The need to identify oneself may be intrinsically distasteful to some people. For example, they may regard it as demeaning, or implicit recognition that the organization with whom they are dealing exercises power over them. Many people accept that, at least in particular contexts, an organization with which they are dealing needs to have their name. Some, however, feel it is an insult to human dignity to require them to use a number of a code instead of a name. Some feel demeaned by demands, as part of the identification process, that they reveal information about themselves or their family, or embarrassed at having to memorize a password or PIN.[47]*

Another commentator offers a cultural critique:

> *For the purposes of a national ID card, identity is a unique, unchanging set of distinguishing characteristics: the flecks in one's iris, the ridges of one's left thumb. It's what sets us apart from others and from the mass. As Americans, though, we have a higher identity: free agent, self-legislator, citizen. It's a common identity held individually. It's what allows us to bond and make a nation or, if necessary, dissolve our bonds. This identity can't be captured on a card, but there is a risk it could be supplanted by one.[48]*

What is the relationship between identification and privacy? Two writers think they are closely intertwined:

> *There is an inherent tension between authentication and privacy, because the act of authentication involves some disclosure and confirmation of personal information. Establishing an identifier or attribute for use within an authentication system, creating transactional records, and revealing information used in authentication to others with unrelated interests all have implications for privacy.[49]*

But when is identification truly necessary for security? Recently cyber-activist John Gilmore has challenged the requirement that airline passengers show ID before boarding. Although he lost the first round of his legal challenge and seems unlikely to prevail, Gilmore points out that the combination of rather easy-to-fake IDs and a hidden "terrorist watch list" of dubious accuracy seems unlikely to be an effective deterrent to terrorists:

> There is good reason to believe that any list of "known terrorists" contains "suspected" terrorists, not actual terrorists, and is full of errors besides. Particularly when the list is secret and neither the press nor the public can examine it for errors or political biases.
>
> "Johnnie Thomas" was on the watch list because a 28-year-old "FBI Most Wanted" man, Christian Michael Longo, used that name as an alias. But Longo was arrested two days after joining the "Most Wanted" list for murdering his family. After he had been in custody for months, 70-year-old black grandma "Johnnie Thomas" gets stopped every time she tries to fly.[50]

Nevertheless, few people believe there is something inherently wrong with having to show ID before entering a sensitive area such as an airport. Ken Scheidegger of the Criminal Justice Legal Foundation points out that: "The Fourth Amendment forbids not searches that you don't like, it forbids unreasonable searches. Nothing could be more reasonable at this time than to know who you're flying with."[51]

Public support for a national ID peaked shortly after the September 11 attacks, when a poll by the Pew Research Center showed 70 percent of respondents supporting the idea. Only a few months later, though, a survey by Gartner Inc. showed only 26 percent in favor. However, support varied with the proposed use of the ID: A majority supported the use of IDs and databases in airports, but much fewer supported using the national ID to access routine services such as banking and health care. This suggested, according to Julia Scheeres, "that people would only support a national ID for very specific, very limited purposes and that they're suspicious of what government agencies will do with their information,"[52]

This idea of a universal ID with a carefully limited application may seem paradoxical. But a closer look might lead to a more flexible system that provides security with a minimal intrusion on privacy. According to Jim Harper.

> We need to take the focus off of identification and move it to authorization. Systems are available that could communicate, "This person is OK to enter your building" or get on your plane or whatever, without saying "This is Joe Smith." Through a diverse array of privately issued cards, people should be able to access goods, services, and infrastructure that they are qualified to access without giving up identifying information.[53]

DNA Databases

In recent years science and technology have continued to offer new technologies for identifying people. One of the most familiar today is the use of

DNA in criminal investigations. While the matching of suspects' DNA to that found at a crime scene does not seem to involve widespread privacy concerns, the compilation of DNA databases is more problematic to many privacy advocates.

The first such efforts are focusing on violent felons (or all felons), sex offenders, drunk drivers, and other persons who have already entered the criminal justice system. In 2004 California passed a ballot proposition allowing for collecting DNA from arrested felons. However, the law has been challenged because it lacks a clear procedure by which an arrested person who is not charged (or is acquitted) can have his or her DNA removed from the database.

Biometrics: The New Face of ID?

Biometrics is the use of physical characteristics to identify individuals uniquely. While fingerprints are thus a form of biometrics, most recent attention has been focused on such technologies as facial scanning and recognition. Systems using eye (retinal or iris) scanning have also been in use at high-security installations.

A number of programs in development will bring large numbers of people in contact with biometric scanning and databases. By 2004 most major countries had incorporated scannable fingerprints, facial recognition, or other biometric features in their passports in response to pressure from the United States—although not without some opposition. In turn, the U.S. government has begun compiling a database of visitors' fingerprints as part of the US-VISIT program. By 2005 this program was already in use in 115 airports and 14 seaports in the United States. The program integrates 20 existing databases into a system that compares entrants' fingerprints, digital photographs, and other particulars with stored biometric, biographical, and travel data to determine who should be allowed to enter the country. Together with the database screening program being developed for use with domestic airline passengers (CAPPS II, now called Secure Flight), it is likely that the majority of people who travel will soon find information about them stored in vast government databases.

Critics of the widespread use of biometric and other data in such screening databases believe that all such systems must satisfactorily answer the following questions:

Storage: How is the data stored, centrally or dispersed? How should scanned data be retained?

Vulnerability: How vulnerable is the data to theft or abuse?

Confidence: How much of an error factor in the technology's authentication process is acceptable? What are the implications of false positives and false negatives created by a machine?

Authenticity: What constitutes authentic information? Can that information be tampered with?

Linking: Will the data gained from scanning be linked with other information about spending habits, etc.? What limits should be placed on the private use (as contrasted to government use) of such technology?

Ubiquity: What are the implications of having an electronic trail of our every movement if cameras and other devices become commonplace, used on every street corner and every means of transportation?[54]

Many critics believe that programs such as Secure Flight fail under a number of these criteria. Concerns about the quality of the data used were exacerbated for many civil libertarians when the TSA initially denied that it had quietly obtained passenger data from a number of airlines for test purposes. (It turned out the agency had obtained at least 12 million records without passengers' knowledge or permission from six airlines.)

Security expert Bruce Schneier believes the database is likely to generate two kinds of errors: "the Ted Kennedy problem, [in which] I'm not on the list but my name is or a name similar to mine is," and "the Cat Stevens problem, [in which] I'm on the list, but we have no idea why."[55]

The Transportation Security Agency argues it cannot release details about how the database works because of the fear that terrorists will be able to "game the system." However, without assurance that the data is accurate and without a specific way for innocent persons to be removed from the list, the ACLU and a number of critics in Congress continue to oppose the system.

Smart Cards and Chips

Another possibility for identification is to carry it in one's body rather than on it. For some time one has been able to have an identification chip implanted in one's pet to aid in its recovery at animal shelters. However, some humans are also starting to get "chipped." VeriChip is about the size of a grain of rice and is implanted in the arm. It is read using a special scanner. Starting in March 2004 a nightclub in Barcelona, Spain, began giving its VIP customers VeriChips they could use to bypass entry lines and keep track of their bar tabs. Developers see future uses for VeriChip as a means for making secure credit card and ATM transactions as well as for entry into airports, government buildings, and other secure areas.

The concerns about VeriChips are similar to those for "smart cards" and the previously discussed RFID chips—misuse of the data by its collector or misappropriation by other persons.

A SURVEILLANCE SOCIETY?

Most of the systems discussed so far are used (at least ostensibly) for specific, well-defined purposes such as commercial transactions, entry into secure areas, or travel. But another set of privacy concerns arise through the ubiquitous use of cameras to watch people in public or sometimes private places.

CAMERAS EVERYWHERE

At home, surveillance cameras at entryways and around the perimeter are a popular option for security-conscious upscale homeowners. Parents concerned that their child's sitter is being neglectful (or worse) can install "nannycams." Their use seems legal, as with other forms of workplace monitoring. In a 2003 survey by *Parenting* magazine, 82 percent of respondents said they would install cameras only if they had reason to suspect their children were being abused.

Out on the street, public surveillance cameras have been used in Great Britain for a number of years. There is now about one camera for every 14 citizens. The reason given is normally public safety—in particular, reducing crime. However, most studies have so far failed to show that the cameras are actually effective in reducing the crime rate. A recent study by the British Home Office of 14 camera systems throughout the country found that only one was associated with a significant fall in the crime rate. Cameras may make people near the cameras feel safer, though perhaps more self-conscious.

Defenders of camera surveillance such as policy analyst Eugene Volokh suggest that the technology, by removing the human element, might reduce police harassment of individuals:

> *The camera . . . saw only what any passerby, and any police officer who might have been at the intersection, could lawfully see. I avoided any possibility of being pulled out and frisked, or my car being searched. I didn't have to wonder if I had been stopped because of my sex or race or age.*[56]

However, Volokh admits that if the cameras are connected to face-recognition software and the resulting recordings are stored indefinitely in a database, there would be a potential for abuse.

Critics such as libertarian columnist Jacob Sollum see intangible but significant social and psychological costs to the widespread use of camera surveillance:

> *. . . knowing you are being watched by armed government agents tends to put a damper on things. You don't want to offend them or otherwise call attention to yourself. . . . People may learn to be careful about the books and periodicals they read in public, avoiding titles that might alarm unseen observers. They may also put more thought into how they dress, lest they look like terrorists, gang members, druggies, or hookers.*[57]

There is an important distinction to be made between camera systems that work in more-or-less real time, with persons monitoring them and dispatching police where indicated, and systems that store images for later comparison to digital photographic or biometric data. The combination of cameras and face recognition software offers the potential of identifying persons without any cooperation on their part. An experimental system was first used in the 2001 Super Bowl. Such systems raise the question of when the line between crime prevention and the possibly chilling surveillance of lawful activities (such as political protests) might be crossed.

The bomb attacks on the London transit system in July 2005 brought renewed attention to the possible value of public surveillance cameras in the fight against terrorism. Proponents of the cameras pointed out that within days of the attacks a review of camera footage had identified the bombing suspects. Critics, however, have suggested that the cameras would be unlikely to actually deter such attacks. A would-be suicide bomber, after all, would presumably not care if he or she might be identified after the attack. As for non-suicidal terrorists; they might simply seek other targets that lack camera surveillance.

TURNING THE CAMERAS AROUND

Today one does not have to be a big corporation or a police agency to conduct video surveillance. Cyberspace pundit Howard Rheingold notes that "You can bug people the way spy agencies used to do 20 years ago—really cheap now. The Orwellian vision was about state-sponsored surveillance. Now it's not just the state, it's your nosy neighbor, your ex-spouse and people who want to spam you."[58]

Thousands of webcams in a wide variety of settings now beam their pictures to web sites. Most ubiquitously, camera-equipped cell phones now provide more than a way to show one's friends what one's doing. They can also be used to surreptitiously capture images, whether to help catch criminals or terrorists or to further an enterprise such as blackmail. Futurist Paul Saffo notes that:

> *There are two dangers to being an amateur snoop. The first is, you'll find out something that you really would have been much happier not knowing. The second is, what happens when the subject finds out that you have been snooping? My advice is: Think twice before you do it. You may really regret it.*[59]

While surveillance technology in citizens' hands can of course be misused, it does offer a potential way to hold authorities accountable for abuses such as police brutality. For example, a camera could be set to capture images continuously and beam them wirelessly to a secure site on the Internet. In such a case, even if a criminal (or the police) seizes and destroys the camera, that very act becomes part of a record of evidence that has been placed out of reach.

WE KNOW WHERE YOU ARE

One of the fastest-growing technologies combines geographic information systems (GIS) with location systems (Global Positioning System, or GPS). These technologies are undoubtedly very useful. They make it possible to select a destination and get a route with just a few clicks, complete with detailed driving directions. Companies can route their delivery trucks more efficiently and track the movement of valuable goods from warehouse to destination. Government agencies can generate maps showing the best disaster response and evacuation routes, or use computer models to predict the likely extent of a toxic spill.

However, when the movement of people rather than that of goods is the object of a tracking and monitoring system, how does that effect privacy—or the sense of privacy? So far the people who have been tracked have been those who for different reasons are generally viewed as having diminished rights. For example, it was proposed that public school children in Sutter, California, wear RFID tags around their necks, but parents objected—though children in Osaka, Japan, have had similar tags for some time. However, one does not have to wait for school: Individual parents can buy GPS/radio "kid trackers" for about $200.

Many people may not realize their location is already being tracked continuously. Originally GPS capability was added to cell phones to make it easier to find people who have made a 911 call, but some companies have required that their workers carry them. Now the manager can tell at a glance where construction crews are working—and whether a worker has snuck home early. Of course, there are other uses, as Greg Shields, proprietor of the Spygear Store in Cincinnati, notes: "I would say that 60 percent of my sales are to women who say, 'I think my husband is cheating on me.'"[60]

Soon new cars may come with built-in trackers and recorders. The National Transportation Safety Board has proposed that event data recorders (EDRs) be installed. The devices, much like the "black box" recorders in aircraft, would maintain a record of a car's speed and driving characteristics. Stolen cars could be tracked, as with the already used "Lo-jack" devices. Already services such as OnStar (now becoming available in midrange cars) feature the ability to call for help to someone who will be able to tell police or ambulance services exactly where the driver is located. The car can also be unlocked remotely—a boon to someone who has lost his or her keys.

Such devices raise privacy concerns. Could law enforcement officers or cruising hackers listen in on a driver's calls? At any rate there is already a case where a federal appeals court told authorities they couldn't install a wiretap in the car systems of a suspect. However, the judges rejected the request not for privacy reasons but because of the possibility that the wiretap would prevent the driver from being able to obtain emergency service.

The growing desire and ability to track peoples' movements has given rise to a new term: "locational privacy." As one policy analyst notes:

While one must expect to surrender some privacy in public spaces, location surveillance and processing technology has the potential to invade an individual's privacy to such a degree that even maintaining anonymity becomes impossible. To attempt to understand what the reasonable expectation of privacy in the case of location-tracking technology, one can ask these three questions: (1) Would it have been possible to obtain the same information without using the technology in question?: (2) If so, would it have been possible to use the data without additional computer processing?: and (3) If the alternate means of obtaining this information had been employed, or if the additional data processing had been performed, would either have constituted unreasonable surveillance?[61]

PROSPECTS AND ALTERNATIVES

The growing sophistication and pervasiveness of identification, surveillance, and tracking systems may suggest that the effort to preserve privacy is doomed to failure in the long run. However, there are a number of tools and technologies that may prove helpful for privacy protection. But how do Americans feel about their alternatives?

PRIVACY AND ACCOUNTABILITY

One important strategy to protect privacy is to enhance the ability of people to know what the government is up to. This means access to the information the government generates about its own activities. A survey by the American Society for Newspaper editors reported in 2001 some relevant public attitudes:

- Six in 10 Americans see public access as "crucial" to good government.
- Sixty-one percent are "very concerned" about personal privacy; 28 percent "somewhat concerned."
- Thirty-eight percent very concerned about government secrecy; 34 percent somewhat concerned.
- Forty-eight percent believe there is too little access to government records; 30 percent "just the right amount."

The same survey suggests how people might want to balance the right of access to government information and the privacy of government officials and employees themselves: 30 percent believe laws guaranteeing public access to government records should be strengthened, even if it means Americans may lose some privacy in the process. However, 54 percent believe that laws guaranteeing personal privacy should be strengthened, even if it means Americans may lose public access to some records held by the government. About half of respondents agreed that citizens have "no control" over how personal information about them is used by the government and that consumers have no control over how personal information about them is used by private companies.[62] These results suggest an ongoing deep concern with loss of control of personal privacy but less consensus on what to do about it.

PRIVACY TOOLS: ENCRYPTION AND ANONYMITY

Technology itself offers powerful tools to protect privacy. One important tool is encryption, which makes information unreadable except by its owner or intended recipient. Until the 1990s, the use of encryption was pretty much restricted to the government and to certain businesses with powerful computers and special communications systems. A much more user-friendly encryption system was offered in 1991 by a programmer-activist named Phil Zimmermann.

He released a program called Pretty Good Privacy, or PGP. This program uses a kind of coding called public key cryptography in which the decoding keys come in pairs that have a special relationship: Text encoded using one of the keys can only be read using the other key.

A user can distribute one key in the pair, called the public key. Anyone can use the public key to encode a message that can be read only by the person holding the corresponding private key. The private key itself need never be sent anywhere, so it is hard to steal. Further, if one receives a message encoded with a person's private key, one can be sure that it was sent by that person. The private key can thus serve as a "digital signature" that verifies the identity of the sender.

Throughout the 1990s a battle raged between activists such as Zimmermann and self-proclaimed "cypherpunks" and government agencies who did not want powerful encryption to get into the hands of foreign nations. Law enforcement agencies were also faced with a problem: What good was a search or wiretap warrant if the message seized was encrypted and couldn't be read?

Federal authorities first tried to use export restrictions to prevent the distribution of PGP and similar programs. It soon became clear that nothing could stop the spreading of computer code through the worldwide Internet. (Later, another programmer, Daniel Bernstein, would win a court decision overturning the export regulations concerning computer code.)

The government then suggested a compromise: have all computers and communications equipment include a device called the Clipper Chip. This device would provide powerful encryption, but with a catch: The government would retain a key that it could use to read any message encrypted by the device, presumably after obtaining a court order. Privacy advocates, however, argued that there was no independent proof the proposed encryption system was secure, and no way to make sure the government did not abuse its ability to read the code. Further, industry observers questioned whether people would use a government-provided encryption chip in place of software such as PGP.

Eventually, the government dropped the Clipper Chip in favor of a proposal to allow users to employ the encryption software of their choice provided that they deposited a copy of the encryption key with a third-party "escrow" agency. The government, after obtaining a court order, could then obtain the key from the agency. This proposal, too, failed to win public or industry support.

Today encryption is routinely and seamlessly used for online transactions and to protect wireless networks (to some extent). Individuals can also use PGP and other programs to encrypt data on their hard drives.

While encryption hides the data, anonymity conceals the identity of persons involved in communications or transactions. Anonymity can be harder to find than encryption, because people leave so many "tracks" online that could be used to identify them. This is particularly true, as we have seen, when "profiles" of individuals are created and databases accumulated. Thus, according to Catherine Crump,

Data retention aims to change the context of Internet activity. The context change that data retention renders makes it easier to link acts to actors. Data

retention "rearchitects" the Internet from a context of relative obscurity to one of greater transparency. This manipulation of context influences what values flourish on the Internet. Specifically, data retention, by making it easier to link acts to actors, promotes the value of accountability, while diminishing the values of privacy and anonymity.[63]

There are some tools that promote anonymity, such as the use of "digital cash," services that allow payments to be authenticated without passing identification information, and the use of services that allow e-mail to be sent without address information that can identify the sender. However, these tools are relatively obscure and not widely used.

There is an inherent conflict between anonymity and accountability: If people can act anonymously, how can they be identified and held responsible if they do something wrong? Law enforcement agencies want access to the records of Internet Service Providers in order to be able to investigate online crime, for example. And some experts suggest that the only way to address the scourge of spam is to redesign the e-mail system so that each user will be identified and authenticated before being allowed to send messages. Yet our courts have recognized a right to anonymous activity that traces its roots in the pamphleteers of colonial times. Anonymity can protect the right of the vulnerable to speak out without repression.

RETHINKING PRIVACY

The struggle between competing interests of privacy, anonymity, security, and accountability is likely to be with us for the foreseeable future. Perhaps, though, some new ways of thinking about privacy might allow for better solutions.

Privacy was first tied to place (such as one's home) and then to reasonable and customary expectations. There has remained a sense, however, of privacy as being all or nothing: In a given situation one either has it or not. But Justice Thurgood Marshall, dissenting in *U.S. v. Miller*, suggested a different approach. He noted that just because

a phone company monitors a call for internal reasons, it does not follow that they expected this information to be made available to the public in general or the government in particular. Privacy is not a discrete commodity, possessed absolutely or not at all.

In this view privacy is a dynamic concept: It requires that one look not simply at whether one can expect in a given situation never to be observed or to have one's information used but also at what happens when that observation or information is taken out of context and used for another purpose.

Another voice from the legal community urges that the complexity of the information society requires an equally sophisticated notion of privacy:

Privacy in the information age is best conceived as the maintenance of metaphorical boundaries that define the contours of personal identity. Identity is complex; different circumstances reveal different aspects of our nature. Each of us wears many masks wherein each mask reflects a different aspect of who we really are. We do not want our entire natures to be judged by any one mask, nor do we want partial revelations of our activities to define us in a particular situation as other than who we want to be. In short, we want to choose the masks that we show to others; any such loss of choice is painful, amounting almost to a physical violation of the self. When we are secretly watched, or when information that we choose to reveal to one audience is instead exposed to another, we lose that sense of choice.[64]

As difficult as it might be, the protection of privacy seems to require that we develop a way of thinking about social interaction and the use of information that is at least as sophisticated as the technology we have embraced. This may involve a number of efforts such as:

- using regulation to create "firewalls" around the most serious forms of misuse of private information,
- where people might reasonably choose to trade privacy for convenience or other values, allowing them to do so by ensuring they have accurate knowledge and can hold businesses accountable to keep their part of the bargain,
- encouraging technologies such as the Platform for Privacy Preferences that allow users to screen for web sites that meet their privacy expectations,
- trying to ensure that identification and database systems used to protect infrastructure and national security are used only for those purposes,
- making such systems as transparent and accountable as possible, at minimum ensuring that Congress has continual, vigorous oversight over them, and
- encouraging a robust, ongoing debate on the privacy implications of new technologies and programs while there is still time to shape their implementation.

If these and other efforts are pursued, the result might be, paradoxically, a world in which although we may have to give up more of our abstract privacy because of the increasing interdependence and fragility of our society, we may have greater assurance of privacy where it counts. In the words of Travis Charbeneau,

A simultaneously more open and open-minded society [that] enables us to shrink our respective privacy spheres. A smaller, more manageable privacy sphere, safeguarding only those issues that remain genuinely sensitive, [that] means more certain protection irrespective of technological advance.[65]

The complexity of privacy issues and the inevitable presence of compelling, conflicting concerns make achieving a comprehensive solution to all privacy concerns unlikely. However, society may be able to reach a consensus on certain principles and create mechanisms to ensure that they be applied as each new technology emerges.

[1] Robert Ellis Smith, *Ben Franklin's Web Site.* Providence, R.I.: Privacy Journal, 2000, p. 6.

[2] Lewis Brandeis, dissent in *Olmstead v. United States* (1928).

[3] Alan F. Westin, quoted in Fred H. Cate, *Privacy in the Information Age.* Washington, D.C.: Brookings Institution Press, 1997, p. 22.

[4] Jeffrey Rosen. *The Unwanted Gaze: The Destruction of Privacy in America.* New York: Random House, 2000, p. 7.

[5] Robert Ellis Smith, quoted in David Brin, *The Transparent Society.* Reading, Mass.: Addison-Wesley, 1998, p. 77.

[6] Alastair Fowler, *A History of English Literature.* Cambridge, Mass.: Harvard University Press, 1987, p. 184.

[7] William Pitt, quoted in Philippa Strum, *Privacy: The Debate in the United States Since 1945.* Fort Worth, Tex.: Harcourt, 1998, p. 116.

[8] John Adams, quoted in Strum, *Privacy,* p. 116.

[9] Ralph Waldo Emerson, "Self-Reliance," *The Works of Ralph Waldo Emerson.* Available online. URL: http://www.rwe.org (link under Complete Works/Essays).

[10] Charles Darwin, quoted in Jack Meadows, *The Great Scientists.* New York: Oxford University Press, 1987, p. 167.

[11] Samuel D. Warren and Louis Brandeis. "The Right to Privacy." *Harvard Law Review,* vol. 4, December 15, 1890, p. 193ff. Also available online. URL: http://faculty.uml.edu/sgallagher/Brandeisprivacy.htm

[12] Erik Davis, *Techgnosis: Myth, Magic + Mysticism in the Age of Information.* New York: Harmony Books, 1998, p. 67.

[13] George Orwell, *1984,* quoted in Harold Bloom, ed., *George Orwell.* New York: Chelsea House, 1986, p. 136.

[14] Cited in Simon Davies, *Big Brother.* London: Pan Books, 1996, p. 53.

[15] Simson Garfinkel, "Privacy and the New Technology: What They Do Know Can Hurt You," *The Nation,* vol. 270, February 28, 2000, p. 11ff.

[16] Ted Nelson, quoted in Vince Juliano, "Computer Lib (& Dream Machines) by Ted Nelson: A Review." Available online. URL: http://cla.uconn.edu/reviews/cmptrlib.html. Posted in November 1996.

[17] William Gibson, *Neuromancer,* excerpted in Larry McCaffrey, ed., *Storming the Reality Studio: A Casebook of Cyberpunk and Postmodern Science Fiction.* Durham, N.C.: Duke University Press, 1991.

[18] Lawrence H. Tribe, "The Constitution in Cyberspace." Available online. URL:.http://www.epic.org/free_speech/tribe.html. Posted in 1991.

[19] Quoted in Robert B. Gelman and Stanton McCandlish, *Protecting Yourself Online.* San Francisco: Harper/Edge, 1998, p. 35.

[20] From the Federal Privacy Commission, quoted in American Civil Liberties Union, *Your Right to Privacy.* Carbondale: Southern Illinois University Press, 1990, p. 119.

[21] For extensive coverage of identity theft, online frauds and scams, and other information-related crime, see the Library in a Book volume *Internet Predators,* by Harry Henderson. New York: Facts On File, 2005.

[22] Carole A. Lane, *Naked in Cyberspace: How to Find Personal Information Online.* Wilton, Conn.: Pemberton Press, 1997, p. 3.

[23] William Wresch, *Disconnected: Haves and Have-Nots in the Information Age.* New Brunswick, N.J.: Rutgers University Press, 1996, p. 93.

[24] Paul H. Rubin and Thomas M. Lenard, *Privacy and the Commercial Use of Personal Information.* Boston: Kluwer Academic Publishers, 2002. Also available online. URL: http://www.pff.org/issues-pubs/books/010701privacyandpersonalinfo.pdf. Posted in July 2001.

[25] Declan McCullagh, "The Upside of 'Zero Privacy,'" Reason Online. Available online. URL:http://www.reason.com/0406/fe.dm.database.shtml. Posted in June 2004.

[26] Erik Baard, "Smile, You're On In-Store Camera," Wired News. Available online. URL:http://www.wired.com/news/print/0,1294,54078,00.html. Posted on August 8, 2002.

[27] Chris Jay Hoofnagel, "Privacy Risks of E-mail Scanning," Electronic Privacy Information Center. Available online. URL:http://epic.org/privacy/gmail/casjud3.15.05.html. Posted on March 15, 2005.

[28] For more survey material, see Joseph Turow, *Americans & Online Privacy: The System Is Broken.* University of Minnesota Annenberg Public Policy Center, June 2003. Also available online. URL:http://www.asc.upenn.edu/usr/jturow/internet-privacy-report/36-page-turow-version-9.pdf. Posted in June 2003.

[29] Ann Cavoukian and Tyler J. Hamilton, "Privacy Payoff: Better Customer Data," *Computerworld,* March 15, 2004, n.p. Also available online. URL: http://www.computerworld.com/printthis/2004/0,4814,90126,00.html.

[30] Jerry Kang, "Information Privacy in Cyberspace Transactions." *Stanford Law Review,* vol. 50, 1998, p. 1193ff.

[31] Katrin Schatz Byford, "Privacy in Cyberspace: Constructing a Model of Privacy for the Electronic Communications Environment," *Rutgers Computers & Technology Law Journal,* vol. 24 (1998), p. 1ff.

[32] "New Federal Health Privacy Regulation: Questions and Answers." Available online. URL:http://www.healthprivacy.org/usr_doc/Q&A2000.pdf. Downloaded on April 4, 2005.

[33] Quoted in Electronic Privacy Information Center, "Medical Records." Available online. URL:http://www.epic.org/privacy/medical/. Updated on July 8, 2004.

[34] Nina Schwenk, quoted in Steven Johnson, "Trading Privacy for Health," *Discover,* vol. 25, December 2004, n.p. Also available online. URL: http://www.discover.com/issues/dec-04/departments/emerging-technology. Posted in December 2004.

[35] Dale Miller, quoted in Beth Givens, "Ten Privacy Principles for Health Care," Privacy Rights Clearinghouse. Available online. URL: http://www.privacyrights.org/ar/privprin.htm. Posted on November 6, 1998.

[36] "Health Privacy in the Hands of Government: HIPAA Privacy Regulation—Troubled Process, Troubling Results," Privacilla.org. Available online. URL: http://www.privacilla.org/releases/HIPAA_Report.pdf. Posted in April 2003.

[37] Nancy Wexler, quoted in Lauren Picker, "All in the Family," *American Health,* March 1994, p. 24.

[38] Christine Godsil Cooper, "Your Genes or Your Job: Genetic Testing in the Workplace," *Employee Rights Quarterly,* vol. 3, Fall 2002, pp. 1ff.

[39] Roger Matus, quoted in Andrew E. Taslitz, "The Fourth Amendment in the Twenty-First Century: Technology, Privacy, and Human Emotions," *Law and Contemporary Problems,* vol. 65, Spring 2002, p. 125ff.

[40] Quoted in Anne Kandra, "Should Parents Become Big Brother? New Software Allows Parents to Control Virtually Everything Children Do Online," *PC World*, vol. 22, January 2004, p. 59ff.

[41] Quoted in Strum, *Privacy*, p. 148.

[42] *United States v. United States District Court*, 407 U.S. 297, 320 (1972).

[43] John Shattuck, quoted in Strum, *Privacy*, p. 154.

[44] Robert Pitofsky, quoted in K. Curran, "War on Terror Worries Privacy Advocates," NewsMax.com. Available online. URL: http://www.newsmax.com/archives/articles/2001/10/30/162113.shtml. Posted on October 31, 2001.

[45] Alberto Gonzales, quoted in Edward Epstein, "White House Willing to Scale Back Patriot Act," *San Francisco Chronicle*, April 6, 2005, pp. 1, 11.

[46] Alberto Gonzales, quoted in Epstein, "White House Willing to Scale Back Patriot Act."

[47] Roger Clarke, "Human Identification in Information Systems: Management Challenges and Public Policy Issues," *Information Tech and People*, vol. 7, December 1994, pp. 6–37. Also available online. URL: http://www.anu.edu.au/people/Roger.Clarke/DV/HumanID.html. Posted in December 1994.

[48] Walter Kirn, "The Mother of Reinvention: The Real Reason Americans Detest the Idea of a National ID Card," *The Atlantic Monthly*, vol. 289, May 2002, p. 28ff.

[49] Stephen T. Kent and Lynette I. Millett, eds., *Who Goes There? Authentication Through the Lens of Privacy*. Washington, D.C.: National Academies Press, 2003, p. 6.

[50] John Gilmore, "Gilmore v. Ashcroft—FAA ID Challenge FAQ." Available online. URL: http://cryptome.org/gilmore-v-usa-faq.htm. Posted on July 20, 2002.

[51] Ken Scheidegger, quoted in Richard Willing, "Airline ID Requirement Faces Legal Challenge," USA Today.com. Available online. URL: http://www.usatoday.com/news/nation/2004-10-10-privacy_x.htm. Posted on October 10, 2004.

[52] Julia Scheeres, "Support for ID Cards Waning," Wired News. Available online. URL:http://www.wired.com/news/print/0,1294,51000,00.html. Posted on March 13, 2002.

[53] Jim Harper, "A National ID: Government Initiatives and the Private Sector," Privacilla.org. Available online. URL: http://www.privacilla.org/releases/CDIA_Remarks_01-27-05.html. Posted on January 27, 2005.

[54] "Biometric Identifiers." Electronic Privacy Information Center. Available online. URL:http://www.epic.org/privacy/biometrics. Updated on March 30, 2004.

[55] Bruce Schneier, quoted in Kim Zettner, "A CAPPS by Any Other Name," Wired News. Available online. URL: http://www.wired.com/news/print/0,1294,67015,00.html. Posted on March 25, 2005.

[56] Eugene Volokh, "Big Brother Is Watching—Be Grateful!" *Wall Street Journal*, March 26, 2002, p. A2.

[57] Jacob Sollum, quoted in Barry Steinhardt, testimony before the Committee on the Judiciary, Council of the District of Columbia, Washington, D.C., December 12, 2002. Available online. URL:http://www.aclu.org/Privacy/Privacy.cfm?ID=13505&c=130. Posted on December 12, 2002.

[58] Howard Rheingold, quoted in Janet Kornblum, "Prying Eyes Are Everywhere," *USA Today*, April 14, 2005, p. 1D.

[59] Paul Saffo, quoted in Kornblum, "Prying Eyes Are Everywhere," p. 10.

[60] Greg Shields, quoted in David Colker, "Go Ahead, Just Try to Disappear," *Los Angeles Times*, December 27, 2004, p. A1.

[61] James C.White, "People, Not Places: A Policy Framework for Analyzing Location Privacy Issues," Terry Sanford Institute of Public Policy, Duke University. Available online. URL: http://www.epic.org/privacy/location/jwhitelocationprivacy. pdf. Posted in Spring 2003.

[62] For these and other results of public opinion surveys on private issues, see Electronic Privacy Information Center, "Public Opinion on Privacy." Available online. URL: http://www.epic.org/privacy/survey. Updated on July 15, 2004.

[63] Catherine Crump, "Data Retention: Privacy, Anonymity, and Accountability Online," *Stanford Law Review*, vol. 56, October 2003, p. 191ff.

[64] Andrew E. Taslitz, "The Fourth Amendment in the Twenty-first Century: Technology, Privacy, and Human Emotions," *Law and Contemporary Problems*, vol. 65, Spring 2002, p. 125ff.

[65] Travis Charbeneau, "The Future of Privacy: Moot?" ItmWeb.com. Available online. URL: http://www.itmweb.com/f010501.htm. Posted on January 5, 2001.

CHAPTER 2

THE LAW OF PRIVACY

A SURVEY OF IMPORTANT PRIVACY LEGISLATION

Federal legislation, rather than state or local legislation, is more important for issues involving privacy in computer systems and computer communications, since electronic data often travels across state lines. State law, however, can both supplement and strengthen federal protections. State law takes over when interstate commerce and federal constitutional guarantees are not involved. State constitutions can also provide stronger protection than the federal law in some areas.

In the following survey, privacy legislation is categorized by general topic. Under each topic the federal legislation is summarized first, followed by a brief summary of the general trend in state legislation.

Consumer Privacy

FAIR CREDIT REPORTING ACT (1970)

The Fair Credit Reporting Act (15 U.S.C. § 1681), or FCRA, as amended in 1992, begins with a justification for the need for regulating the preparation and distribution of credit reports:

(1) The banking system is dependent upon fair and accurate credit reporting. Inaccurate credit reports directly undermine the public confidence, which is essential to the continued functioning of the banking system.
(2) An elaborate mechanism has been developed for investigating and evaluating the credit worthiness, credit standing, credit capacity, character, and general reputation of consumers.
(3) Consumer reporting agencies have assumed a vital role in assembling and evaluating consumer credit and other information on consumers.
(4) There is a need to insure that consumer reporting agencies exercise their grave responsibilities with fairness, impartiality, and a respect for the consumer's right to privacy.

The law begins by describing legitimate, permissible uses for credit reports, such as responding to a court order, providing information directly to the individual named in the report, and a variety of "legitimate business needs" such as a person using a credit card or applying for credit, insurance, or employment. The law also prohibits "information brokers" from disclosing credit information without it falling under one of the legitimate purposes.

Credit bureaus and agencies are required to notify one another when a consumer disputes information in a report. The credit agency must have an effective procedure for reviewing and correcting information.

FAIR CREDIT BILLING ACT (1975)

The Fair Credit Billing Act (15 U.S.C. § 1666) states that if a consumer tells a merchant about a problem or dispute concerning a bill, the merchant may not report the account as delinquent to a credit bureau or other agency. Installment credit and commercial credit are not covered by this law.

FAIR DEBT COLLECTION PRACTICES ACT (1977)

The Fair Debt Collection Practices Act (15 U.S.C. §§ 1692–1692o) addresses public concern about the often abusive and excessive practices of agencies that are hired to collect debts owed for consumer purchases, medical care, and other services. The law prohibits debt collectors contacting consumers at unreasonable hours (usually before 8:00 A.M. or after 9:00 P.M.) or places, or from coming to the debtor's place of employment if the collector knows that the employer disapproves. Debt collectors may not threaten violence or harm against "person, property, or reputation." They cannot publish a list of debtors (except to a credit agency).

Debt collectors cannot misrepresent themselves (such as by claiming to be an attorney), misrepresent the nature or the amount of the debt, misrepresent the nature of papers (claiming they are legal forms when they are not, or vice versa), or threaten that they will take actions that are in fact not legal to take. Various other similar practices are prohibited.

The debt collector must honor a request by the debtor to stop contacting him or her, though the collector can notify the debtor of consequences such as legal action. If the debtor claims the debt is not in fact owed, the collector must also stop pursuing the claim unless proof of the debt can be supplied.

DEBT COLLECTION ACT OF 1982

The Debt Collection Act of 1982 (public law 97-365, as amended) allows federal agencies to exchange information about recipients of government loans or grants, and to give such information to private collection agencies. It also gives the Internal Revenue Service the ability to obtain records showing the address of debtors, as well as requiring a Social Security number from every loan applicant.

TELEPHONE CONSUMER PROTECTION ACT (1991)

The Telephone Consumer Protection Act (47 U.S.C. § 227) requires that marketers maintain a nation-wide list of consumers who do not wish to receive sales calls. Before making calls, the company must consult the list. If a person on the list is called anyway, he or she can receive damages. Recorded messages cannot be unsolicited (so marketers generally have a live person ask whether it is OK to play the recording). Sending of unsolicited faxes is also prohibited.

TELEMARKETING AND CONSUMER FRAUD AND ABUSE PREVENTION ACT (1994)

The Telemarketing and Consumer Fraud and Abuse Prevention Act (15 U.S.C. §§ 6101–6108) provides further protections against unwelcome or dishonest telephone sales pitches. It directs the Federal Trade Commission (FTC) to develop regulations that prohibit deceptive telephone advertising offers, calls that are repeated so that a reasonable person would feel harassed by them, and calls made at unreasonable hours. Callers must begin by clearly identifying the purpose of the call.

FEDERAL CREDIT REPORTING ACT AMENDMENTS (2003)

In 2003 the FCRA was amended to require credit bureaus to provide one free credit report to consumers per year upon request. The requirement will be phased in regionally, with the entire United States covered by the end of 2005. Consumers must also be provided access to any credit scores. Some additional requirements are that consumers must be notified by retailers before negative information is reported to credit bureaus. Credit bureaus must also notify consumers via a "fraud alert" if there is evidence of identity theft. While strengthening consumer rights, the amendments also potentially weakened protections for some consumers by preempting similar state laws.

STATE LAWS

Most state laws are similar to the federal statutes in their general principles and the commercial practices they regulate. Many state laws provide protection against merchants asking for (or writing down) addresses, phone numbers, or credit card numbers for the purpose of accepting checks. State laws generally require that consumers be given accurate copies of their files. Some state laws also regulate "credit doctor" services that offer to fix people's credit problems (many of these services charge high rates for obtaining information or making changes, things the individual has a legal right to do without charge).

The following states have laws relating to credit cards and credit investigations: Arizona, Arkansas, California, Colorado, Connecticut, Delaware, District of Columbia*, Florida, Georgia, Iowa, Kansas, Kentucky, Louisiana, Maine, Maryland, Massachusetts, Minnesota, Montana, Nevada, New Hampshire, New Jersey, New Mexico, New York, North Carolina, North Dakota, Ohio, Oklahoma, Pennsylvania, Rhode Island, Tennessee, Texas, Utah, Vermont, Virginia, Washington, and Wisconsin. Some example provisions include the following:

- **California:** adds to federal law the right to inspect visually actual files, and the right to sue for invasions of privacy by investigative consumer-reporting agencies.

- **Delaware:** like a number of other states, prohibits merchants recording credit card numbers on checks unless the credit card issuer is guaranteeing the check.

- **Massachusetts:** bans use by credit agencies of arrest records over seven years old or bankruptcies over 14 years old.

- **Montana:** ties its consumer credit laws directly to guarding "an individual's right to privacy guaranteed in . . . the Montana constitution." A credit record is declared to be "a property right with full constitutional protection."

- **Oklahoma:** requires that credit agencies preparing a credit report for a merchant first provide a copy of the report for the consumer to review.

- **Vermont:** requires that companies obtain the consent of a consumer before obtaining a credit report.

Driving Records

DRIVER'S PRIVACY PROTECTION ACT (1994)

The Driver's Privacy Protection Act (18 U.S.C. § 2721) was passed in response to the murder of actress Rebecca Schaeffer by a stalker who apparently obtained her address through the California Department of Motor Vehicles. The law prohibits state DMVs from releasing personal information about license holders but makes many exceptions (such as for government agencies, insurance companies, and private investigators). The law is thus unlikely to prevent anyone who is willing to pay from obtaining information.

Existing protections seemed to be insufficient to head off abuses. In early 1999, three states—Florida, South Carolina, and Colorado—agreed to sell a combined total of 22.5 million driver's license photographs to Image Data LLD, a private antifraud company in New Hampshire. The company said it would use the photos to create a photo database that merchants could use to stop use of fraudulent ID for check cashing. But privacy advocates reacted quickly to the announcement, pointing out that none of the license holders had given permission for their photos to be used by a private company, and that the states had no right to market the pictures. State officials soon began to back away from the plan.

---

* For this purpose, the District of Columbia is a "state."

Financial Privacy

In *U.S. v. Miller* (1976), the Supreme Court ruled that an individual has no constitutional "legitimate expectation of privacy" in the records of financial transactions, such as deposits, withdrawals, checks, and funds transfers. However, in response, a number of laws have been passed that do provide real, though limited, privacy protection for financial records.

BANK SECRECY ACT (1970)

The Bank Secrecy Act (12 U.S.C. §§ 1951 and 31 U.S.C. §§ 1051) is not, as the name might suggest, a law requiring banks to keep certain financial information confidential. Actually, it requires that banks keep track of a variety of kinds of transactions and report them to the federal government in an attempt to stop money laundering, drug-related transactions, or other illegal activities.

For example, transactions involving the movement of funds, currency, or credit in the amount of more than $10,000 out of the country must be reported, and individual travelers must report cash transactions of $3,000 to $10,000. ("Unusual" domestic currency transactions of more than $2,500 must be reported to the Internal Revenue Service.) Banks must also hold records of bank statements, checks over $100, and other transactions for at least five years. Banks must obtain Social Security numbers from customers for identification at the time an account is opened. In 1995, amended regulations (reflecting the Anti Money-Laundering Act of 1992) required additional tracking of wire transfers and other transactions.

Privacy advocates have objected to the widespread tracking of individual finances mandated by the Bank Secrecy Act. In *California Bankers' Association v. Schulz* (1974), the law was challenged on the constitutional grounds of freedom of association (First Amendment), unreasonable search and seizure (Fourth Amendment), and the right against self-incrimination (Fifth Amendment). The Supreme Court, however, upheld the law's constitutionality. The Electronic Funds Transfer Act of 1978 and the Right to Financial Privacy Act of 1978 (both discussed below) in part represented Congress's attempts to provide some privacy protection via regulation.

ELECTRONIC FUNDS TRANSFER ACT (1978)

The Electronic Funds Transfer Act (15 U.S.C. §§ 1693–1693r) regulates the use of the electronic banking systems that have largely replaced the traditional tellers and paper checks. Transactions included are those involving an "automated teller machine (ATM), point-of-sale terminal, automated clearinghouse, telephone bill-payment system, or home banking program."

All transaction systems by definition involve the transfer of information to parties other than the individual; however, an institution must inform the customer about circumstances in which financial information will be disclosed to a third party "in the ordinary course of business." Institutions are also prohibited from issuing unsolicited credit or ATM cards except as replacements or renewals for existing cards.

RIGHT TO FINANCIAL PRIVACY ACT OF 1978

Under the Right to Financial Privacy Act of 1978 (12 U.S.C. §§ 3401–) federal investigators must use proper legal process or "formal written requests" to obtain records of an individual kept by a financial institution such as a bank or credit card company, or financial records held by brokers, attorneys, or accountants. The affected individual must also be given notice in time to challenge the request for access. The Internal Revenue Service, in particular, is required to give 14 days' notice for any "administrative summons" to see financial records; during this time an individual can appeal to a federal judge to deny the summons.

The law also makes it illegal for an unauthorized individual to obtain information from a computer belonging to a financial institution, credit card company, or consumer reporting agency.

GRAMM-LEACH-BLILEY ACT (1999)

The Gramm-Leach-Bliley Act (GLBA; 15 USC § 6801), also known as the Financial Services Modernization Act, was intended primarily to make it easier for banks, investment brokers, insurance companies, and other financial institutions to merge as desired. But because the sharing of customer information is an inevitable consequence of most mergers, the GLBA also provides certain consumer privacy protections.

Financial institutions must securely store and maintain personal financial information. They must advise consumers on their information-sharing policies and give consumers the right to opt out of some sharing of personal information. The information regulated is called "nonpublic personal information" and includes such items as credit and account applications, account histories, and identifying information such as addresses and Social Security numbers.

The law makes a distinction between affiliate companies (those under the same ownership or control) and unaffiliated third parties. Consumers cannot prevent information sharing with affiliated companies. On the other hand, companies cannot transfer their customers' account numbers or access codes to unaffiliated parties, except to credit-reporting agencies. Other personal information can be transferred without customer permission to unaffiliated third parties if necessary for performing services or for marketing purposes, but the information cannot be further transferred. (In general, the number of exceptions and general latitude of these provisions means they are considered too weak by privacy advocates.) The GLBA also prohibits "pretexting" or the use of false identities or representations in order to obtain personal information.

STATE LAWS

Some states have enacted laws relating to banking privacy, with some stricter than federal laws. The following is a list of states with laws relating to bank records: Alabama, Alaska, California, Connecticut, Florida, Idaho (through court decisions), Illinois, Iowa, Louisiana, Maine, Maryland, Massachusetts, New Hampshire, North Carolina (through court decisions), Oklahoma, Oregon, Utah, and Vermont. Some example provisions include the following:

- **Alaska:** declares bank records to be confidential and not to be revealed except by court order or under applicable federal or state law, or to the holder of the negotiable instrument. Following the *United States v. Miller* decision in 1976, it added a provision that depositors must be notified of any request for records unless made under a search warrant.
- **Florida:** requires that banks with electronic funds transfer systems inform consumers about their privacy policies, including "protection against wrongful or accidental disclosure of confidential information"; prohibits use of Social Security numbers to identify individuals in electronic banking systems.
- **Maryland:** banks may not disclose financial records unless customer has authorized disclosure or records are subpoenaed. The subpoena must be given to the bank and the customer at least 21 days prior to disclosure.
- **New Hampshire:** requires that state and local investigators seeking financial or credit information about a bank customer describe the desired information "with particularity and consistent with the scope and requirements of the investigation."

Identity Theft

The crime of identity theft represents an extreme case of loss of privacy in personal information. The great increase in incidence of identity theft, largely facilitated by the growth of the Internet and e-commerce, has led to new federal and state legislation in this area.

IDENTITY THEFT AND ASSUMPTION DETERRENCE ACT (1998)

This law, amending 18 USC § 1028(a), makes it a federal crime when anyone: "knowingly transfers or uses, without lawful authority, a means of identification of another person with the intent to commit, or to aid or abet, any unlawful activity that constitutes a violation of Federal law, or that constitutes a felony under any applicable State or local law."

IDENTITY THEFT PENALTY ENHANCEMENT ACT (2002)

This amendment to 18 USC § 1028(a) essentially adds an additional sentence of two years in prison for crimes in which identity theft plays a part. Concern about identity theft as a tool for terrorists prompted a special higher five-year penalty for such cases.

FAIR CREDIT REPORTING ACT AMENDMENTS (2003)

The aforementioned FCRA amendments include a provision that requires that major credit bureaus issue a "fraud alert" when requested by identity-theft victims. Credit information resulting from fraudulent activity must be (and remain) deleted from a customer's credit report.

STATE LAWS

All states now have laws relating to identity theft, although they vary in scope. Some examples follow:

- **California:** includes a provision requiring a debt collector to stop collection efforts for a debt when the alleged debtor furnishes a police report and other information indicating identity theft. (California has also passed a separate law requiring the disclosure of data breaches that might affect personal information.)
- **Vermont:** requires credit agencies to place a "security freeze" on credit reports when requested by consumers; requires local and state police to accept complaints about identity theft.
- **Washington:** requires that an entity disposing of personal records "take all reasonable steps to destroy, or arrange for the destruction of, personal financial and health information and personal identification numbers."

Government Records

PRIVACY ACT OF 1974

Growing concern about the misuse of the burgeoning government databases of information about individuals led to agreement on some basic principles for privacy protection. For example, the HEW (Health, Education, Welfare) Advisory Committee on Automated Personal Data Systems in a July 1972 report summarized these principles as follows:

1. *There must be no personal data record-keeping systems whose very existence is secret.*
2. *There must be a way for a person to find out what information about the person is in a record and how it is used.*

3. *There must be a way for a person to prevent information about the person that was obtained for one purpose from being used or made available for other purposes without the person's consent.*
4. *There must be a way for a person to correct or amend a record of identifiable information about the person.*
5. *Any organization creating, maintaining, using, or disseminating records of identifiable personal data must assure the reliability of the data for their intended use and must take precautions to prevent misuses of the data.*

The Privacy Act of 1974 (5 U.S.C. § 552a) attempts to implement these principles. In general it prohibits the release of federal information about an individual, but has a variety of exceptions including records used in the routine performance of the duties of an agency, use by the bureau of the census, statistical use when individuals cannot be identified from the records, historical records (the National Archives and Records Administration), and for law enforcement when properly requested. In 1983, the Privacy Act was amended to allow the government to give information about people who owe money to the government to credit agencies.

The "routine use" exception has been criticized as amounting to a major, loophole in privacy protection. According to the ACLU, the law suffers from other defects that make it a weak guardian of privacy and one often ineffective in restraining the actions of government agencies.

In general, a federal agency must keep accurate track of any authorized disclosure of a record, and it must supply an individual upon request with any records pertaining to that individual, and provide the opportunity to correct erroneous information. However, records pertaining to law enforcement or intelligence activities may be withheld. The Freedom of Information Act, however, provides an alternative way to obtain some records.

FREEDOM OF INFORMATION ACT

The Freedom of Information Act (5 U.S.C. § 552), or FOIA, was enacted in 1966 and amended in 1974 and 1986. While the Privacy Act focuses on an individual's right to obtain records pertaining to him or herself, the FOIA attempts to make information about a wide range of government activities available to anyone willing to make the effort to request it. (In practice, there is considerable overlap between the laws, so a person seeking to find out what the government knows about him or her would ordinarily use both.)

Nearly all federal (but not state or local) agencies are subject to the provisions of the FOIA. However, there is no central clearinghouse where one can search for information; the person making the request has to determine which agency or agencies is likely to have the desired information, and issue a separate request for each agency. Agencies are required to respond within ten working days, indicating whether they will provide the information. In practice there is often a backlog of requests and thus considerable delay.

The government does not have to provide information if doing so would endanger national defense or foreign policy, reveal classified or confidential information, or if releasing the information would harm the privacy of another individual. There is a process for appealing a decision not to release all or part of the information requested; appeals are often necessary.

ELECTRONIC FREEDOM OF INFORMATION ACT (1986)

The Electronic Freedom of Information Act (5 U.S.C § 552, amended), or EFOIA, attempts to update the FOIA by responding to the vast growth in the use of computer databases and information systems by the federal government since the FOIA was enacted in 1966. The EFOIA requires that computerized records be made accessible in a way similar to paper records and that agencies reasonably accommodate requests to obtain records in computer-readable format.

COMPUTER MATCHING AND PRIVACY PROTECTION ACT OF 1988

Besides the sheer growth in the size of databases, another concern of privacy advocates has been the ability to match or correlate records from several agencies in order to investigate a particular individual in depth. The Computer Matching and Privacy Protection Act of 1988 (5 U.S.C. § 552, amended) requires that agencies involved in computer record matching programs develop policies and procedures that must be approved by an Agency Data Integrity Board. If an adverse action is to be taken against an individual, the individual must be notified and given the opportunity to correct erroneous information. If government benefits are to be denied to an individual based on data found in a computer match, the agency must independently verify the data first.

STATE LAWS

Most states have their own versions of the Freedom of Information Act. A similar concept is the "sunshine laws" that require many kinds of meetings to be held in public where people can find out how their government makes decisions.

The following is a list of states with laws relating to government use of databases involving personal information: Alaska, Arizona, California, Colorado, Connecticut, Florida, Georgia, Hawaii, Illinois, Indiana, Kansas, Kentucky, Maine, Massachusetts, Minnesota, Mississippi, New Hampshire, New York, North Carolina, Ohio, Oklahoma, Utah, Virginia, Washington, and Wisconsin. Some example provisions include the following:

- **Alaska:** has a set of protections in keeping with Fair Information Privacy principles. Each state agency must notify citizens from whom information is collected or sought: (1) what law allows the government to collect a given set of information, (2) what happens if the citizen refuses to provide the information, (3) what the government expects to do with the information (including to whom it may be disclosed), and (4) how the citizen can apply to correct information believed to be inaccurate.

- **California:** adds the right to sue a person for invasion of privacy if that person intentionally discloses information that he or she should have known came from a state or federal agency in violation of law.
- **Kentucky:** requires that any person shall have access to "any public record relating to him or her" in which he or she is specifically named.
- **Massachusetts:** requires that each state agency designate an individual responsible for its personal data systems and enact regulations involving outside access to information and the right of the individual to correct errors.
- **Minnesota:** Its Data Practices Act was the first comprehensive state privacy act. It includes telling individuals the purpose and intended use of information collected, the consequences of failing to provide it, and how to make corrections. Individuals must be given an opportunity to challenge information developed from "computer matching" before any action is taken.
- **Utah:** includes the federal Fair Information Practices standards in its state law. Categorizes personal information as public (accessible to anyone), private (involves personal information presumed confidential), confidential (medical and psychiatric), and protected (trade secrets or proprietary business information).

Medical Records

OCCUPATIONAL HEALTH AND SAFETY ACT

The Occupational Health and Safety Act (29 U.S.C. § 657), which became law in 1970 and has subsequently been amended, allows workers to examine their occupational health records, but also requires that certain records be disclosed to the federal government when requested. Other laws such as the Rehabilitation Act (29 U.S.C. §§ 793–794) and the Vietnam Era Veterans Readjustment Act (38 U.S.C. § 2012) limit the disclosure of certain employee medical records.

The Privacy Act of 1974, which generally requires disclosure of federal records about an individual to that individual, includes medical records, but provides special procedures for releasing records to a physician instead of the individual in cases where the information may be harmful (such as to an individual's mental health).

Federal agencies, such as the Department of Health and Human Services and the Public Health Service, as well as federally funded mental and substance abuse treatment centers, all have strict rules for disclosure of health information to third parties, with certain exceptions.

HEALTH INSURANCE PORTABILITY AND ACCOUNTABILITY ACT OF 1996

Commonly referred to as HIPAA, the Health Insurance Portability and Accountability Act of 1996 (45 U.S.C. §1320d-2(b)) is primarily intended to ensure that employees can retain medical coverage when changing jobs. However, the law also includes some important though limited privacy protections. Patients must generally give consent before their medical information can be released except as necessary for treatment, payment, or health care operations, with certain other exceptions as provided by law, such as for reporting child or elder abuse. Patients have the right to examine their medical records. States are allowed to have more stringent laws if they are compatible with HIPAA regulations.

STATE LAWS

State laws tend to be strict about disclosure of individuals' medical records with certain exceptions. Patients generally have the right to examine their records, unless doing so might endanger their mental health. Many states provide special protections for confidentiality involving HIV/AIDS and the results of genetic testing.

The following is a list of states with laws relating to the handling of medical records: Arizona, California, Colorado, Connecticut, Delaware, Florida, Georgia, Hawaii, Illinois, Indiana, Iowa, Kansas, Maine, Maryland, Massachusetts, Minnesota, Montana, Nevada, New Hampshire, New York, Ohio, Oklahoma, Oregon, Rhode Island, Vermont, Virginia, Washington, and Wisconsin. Some example provisions are the following:

- **California:** full right of individual access to records except where a mental health professional refuses on grounds disclosure may harm the individual's health; in that case, the individual may designate another professional to examine the records. "No requester shall acquire medical information regarding a patient without first obtaining [written] authorization from that patient." (There are some exceptions including legal proceedings, law enforcement, medical research, and peer review.) AIDS test results are anonymous and must not be disclosed, even through subpoena. Employers are restricted in their use of employees' medical records.

- **Colorado:** defines medical records information as a "thing of value," and links it to the law against theft: "Any person who, without proper authorization, knowingly obtains a medical record or medical information with the intent to appropriate [it] to his own use or the use of another, who steals or discloses to an unauthorized person a medical record or medical information, or who, without authority, makes or causes to be made a copy of a medical record or medical information commits theft."

- **Florida:** health care providers must provide copies of medical records to the patient upon request, and may not disclose records to others without permission, except under subpoena.

- **Maryland:** allows doctors to report medical information to the state motor vehicle administration if it indicates the individual's driving may be impaired; requires that insurance claimants or applicants be given copies of their records (except those provided by a doctor, which are not available for five years, except with the doctor's consent).

- **Ohio:** makes doctor-patient relationship privileged, but requires disclosure of child abuse–related information to authorities. Provides that "No person shall be liable for any harm that results to any other person as a result of failing to disclose any confidential information about a mental health client, or failing to otherwise attempt to protect such other person from harm by any client."
- **Tennessee:** declares hospital records to be the property of the hospital, but requires access by the patient upon "good cause."
- **Washington:** requires that medical data collected by the state's health care financing system be used only for that purpose; requires that any state health ID be more secure (unique and accurate) than Social Security numbers.

School Records

FAMILY EDUCATION RIGHTS AND PRIVACY ACT (1974)

The Family Education Rights and Privacy Act (20 U.S.C. § 1232g) applies to all school districts and colleges that receive federal funds (which most of them do receive). It guarantees students 18 years and older (and the parents of younger students) the right to see their school records. Each school system must have a procedure for challenging and correcting erroneous records.

The law also restricts the disclosure of school records to persons other than the parent or student, but there are many exceptions, including normal procedures that reflect a "legitimate educational interest." A 1994 amendment permits disclosure of records to the juvenile justice system; school officials are also by this amendment prohibited from revealing that records have been subpoenaed. School records can also be disclosed by the Department of Education to credit bureaus in cases of default on student loans, and statistical information can be compiled from student records for reporting crimes on campus.

ELEMENTARY AND SECONDARY EDUCATION ACT OF 1978

Many conservatives have viewed the growing use of psychological testing and psychological exercises in public schools as educationally inappropriate and often as a form of propagandizing. This opposition led to an amendment in the Elementary and Secondary Education Act of 1978 that states, among other provisions, that "No student shall be required, as part of any [federally funded school] program, to submit to psychiatric . . . or psychological examination, testing, or treatment, in which the primary purpose is to reveal information concerning political affiliations; mental and psychological problems potentially embarrassing to the student or his family; sex behavior and attitudes; and illegal, anti-social, self-incriminating and demeaning behavior . . . without the consent of the student, or in the case of an unemancipated minor, without the prior written consent of the parent."

STATE LAWS

Schools are largely regulated by states and school boards, not the federal government. While the federal constitution does apply to schools, and federal agencies can use their "power of the purse" to coerce states into following mandates, specific policies about the use and disclosure of student information vary considerably.

The following is a list of states with laws relating to school records: Arizona, California, Colorado, Connecticut, Delaware, Florida, Idaho, Illinois, Iowa, Kentucky, Louisiana, Maine, Maryland, Massachusetts, Michigan, Minnesota, Mississippi, Montana, Nebraska, Nevada, New Jersey, New York, North Carolina, North Dakota, Ohio, Oklahoma, Oregon, Rhode Island, South Dakota, Tennessee, Texas, Vermont, Virginia, Washington, Wisconsin, and Wyoming. Some example provisions follow:

- **California:** extends the state constitutional right of privacy to students in public institutions of higher education; gives parents an absolute right to examine their children's records in both private and public schools.

- **Maryland:** allows disclosure to the student or education officials of information concerning a student's academic achievement, biography, family, physical or mental ability, or religion.

- **Michigan:** prohibits disclosure by teachers, counselors, or other school officials of pupil information received in confidence, even in legal proceedings.

- **Ohio:** prohibits release of student files for any profit-making activity; allows release of mailing lists of high school students to military recruiters unless a parent or student objects.

- **Rhode Island:** makes it a misdemeanor to circulate without official permission any survey or questionnaire that is "so framed as to ask the pupils of any school intimate questions about themselves and/or their families, thus trespassing on the pupils' constitutional rights and invading the privacy of the home."

Video Rentals

VIDEO PRIVACY PROTECTION ACT (1988)

Judge Robert Bork's nomination to the Supreme Court in 1987 became controversial in part because Bork did not believe that the language of the Constitution implied a right of privacy as declared in cases such as *Griswold v. Connecticut* and *Roe v. Wade*. Ironically, Bork's own privacy was invaded when a newspaper reporter obtained video store records that suggested Bork liked to watch pornography. Many members of Congress, while disagreeing over Bork's fitness for the Supreme Court, agreed that the titles of videos rented by an individual should be private information, as with the records of books borrowed at a public library. In response, they passed the Video Privacy Protection Act (18 U.S.C. § 2710).

Under this law, a video store cannot disclose the titles or descriptions of the videos rented or purchased by a customer. If it does so, the customer can sue. The store may rent customer lists (without title information) if the customer has had the opportunity to remove his or her name from the list. Also, lists or compilations of titles or viewing preferences can be created for purposes of market surveys or other research provided that any information that could be used to link identifiable individuals to the records is removed.

Personal information can be disclosed "if the disclosure is incident to the ordinary course of business of the videotape service provider"—this is intended to allow for normal transaction processing. Personally identifiable information, however, must be destroyed not later than one year after the information is no longer necessary for the purpose for which it was collected.

Wiretapping, Surveillance, and Encryption

WIRETAP ACT (1968)

The Wiretap Act (Title 3 of the Omnibus Crime Control Bill) codified the Supreme Court's *Katz* decision by extending the protection of the Fourth Amendment against unjustified search and seizure to information traveling on a telephone line. It established the basic requirements for a search warrant for government interception of telephone communications. Recording calls by private individuals is not allowed unless all parties to the call give their consent.

ELECTRONIC COMMUNICATIONS PRIVACY ACT OF 1986

In 1985, the congressional Office of Technology Assessment reported that "many innovations in electronic surveillance technology have outstripped constitutional and statutory protections, leaving areas in which there is currently no legal protection against ... new surveillance devices." For example, the original wiretap law did not cover computer networks or data as opposed to voice communications. The ECPA (amending various sections of 18 U.S.C.) fills in this gap, covering radio-paging devices, electronic mail, cellular telephones, private communication carriers, and computer data transmissions (but not cordless phones).

Law enforcement agencies in turn became concerned that they would not be able to intercept computer transmissions using newer technology, particularly when encryption (coding) made the data unreadable. In 1994, the Clinton administration proposed the Communications Assistance for Law Enforcement Act (CALEA), which would require telephone companies to make sure their hardware would allow federal agents to conveniently tap into transmissions. Although FBI director Louis Freeh insisted that the government would not abuse this access by increasing the number of taps, that number continues to rise rapidly and privacy advocates strongly oppose the CALEA and similar proposals.

USA PATRIOT ACT OF 2001

Passed quickly in response to the terrorist attacks of September 11, 2001, the Uniting and Strengthening America by Providing Appropriate Tools Required to Intercept and Obstruct Terrorism (USA PATRIOT) Act of 2001 includes a number of provisions that expand government powers to investigate terrorism suspects and to obtain information. Relevant provisions of the law include the following:

- Section 204 allows stored voice mail communications to be obtained through an ordinary search warrant rather than the more stringent wiretap orders. Interestingly, recorded messages on answering machines are not covered by this provision.

- Section 206 is an important change that expands the Federal Intelligence Surveillance Act's provisions to allow for "roving wiretaps" that can be applied without having to specify the particular telephone, computer, or other communications facility to be used. Privacy advocates are concerned that this expanded surveillance power could potentially sweep the communications of large numbers of innocent persons into the government's net.

- Section 210 expands the types of information about electronic communications that can be obtained by subpoena to include, for example, temporary Internet (IP) addresses and the means or source of payment for service.

- Section 213 is another important change: it expands the use of so-called sneak and peak searches, where the subject of the search is not informed until after the search has been completed. This means that the subject has no opportunity to contest the search order before it is executed. Law enforcement agents need only show "reasonable cause to believe that providing immediate notification may have an adverse effect." Previously, this type of search was allowed only in limited circumstances such as electronic surveillance involving a national security or terrorism investigation. Section 213, however, allows the searches in any case involving evidence of any federal criminal offense.

- Section 215 allows the FBI to request the production of "any tangible things." This provision has aroused considerable controversy because of its applicability to business, educational, medical, and even library records without a showing of probable cause. An amendment was added before passage that prohibits the investigation of a U.S. person "solely on the basis of activities protected by the First Amendment."

- Section 216 expands the use of trap-and-trace and pen register devices to include not only telephone numbers but also Internet routing addresses, presumably including e-mail headers. This removes any legal ambiguity in earlier FBI use of Carnivore and similar technologies for recording e-mail and other Internet addresses. In related provisions, Section 214 removes the requirement that the target be "an agent of a foreign power" or terrorist, but can simply be "any investigation to gather foreign intelligence information." Also sections 216 and 220 allow for nationwide court orders for telephone and Internet traces (previously court orders were limited to the jurisdiction of the court involved).

Many of the above and other provisions were originally scheduled to expire December 31, 2005. Following temporary extensions, Congress is expected to renew most provisions, though perhaps with added safeguards.

STATE LAW

State law varies with regard to private parties recording phone calls: 38 states allow any party to a conversation to record it without the consent of the other parties; 12 states require that all parties be notified and must give consent. A small but growing number of states also prohibit photography or video surveillance in places such as employees' locker rooms and store dressing rooms.

The following is a list of states* with laws relating to wiretapping or other forms of electronic surveillance: Alabama, Alaska, Arizona, Arkansas, California, Colorado, Connecticut, Delaware, District of Columbia, Florida, Georgia, Hawaii, Idaho, Illinois, Indiana, Iowa, Kansas, Kentucky, Louisiana, Maine, Maryland, Massachusetts, Michigan, Minnesota, Mississippi, Montana, Nebraska, Nevada, New Hampshire, New Jersey, New Mexico, New York, North Carolina, North Dakota, Ohio, Oklahoma, Oregon, Pennsylvania, Rhode Island, South Carolina, South Dakota, Tennessee, Texas, Utah, Virginia, Washington, West Virginia, Wisconsin, and Wyoming. Following are some example provisions:

- **Arizona:** It is a felony to intercept a wire or other oral communication without consent of one party or a court order based on probable cause.
- **California:** It is illegal to tap without consent of all parties, except in the case of telephone companies. A person may tap his or her own phone if a conversation relates to serious criminal activity and can be admitted at trial later. It is a felony for anyone except the parties involved in a telephone conversation to disclose it without permission. Cellular telephones and digital pagers are also covered. A device for "observing, photographing, recording, or amplifying" may not be installed in any place without consent.
- **Georgia:** It is illegal to "observe, photograph or record the activities of another which occur in any private place and out of public view" without consent of one party.
- **Louisiana:** Surreptitious videotaping for a lewd purpose is illegal.
- **Massachusetts:** "No person who owns or operates a retail establishment selling clothing shall maintain in a dressing room a two-way mirror or electronic video camera or similar device . . . "
- **Oregon:** Tapping by law enforcers without consent of both parties requires a warrant, which must show probable cause that a crime "directly and immediately affecting the safety of human life or the national security has been committed or is about to be committed."

---

* For this purpose, the District of Columbia is a "state."

Workplace Testing

EMPLOYEE POLYGRAPH PROTECTION ACT (1988)

The Employee Polygraph Protection Act (29 U.S.C. § 2001) prohibits most polygraph tests by private employers (or imposes conditions that make the tests generally impracticable). Some exceptions are made for companies in the security (guard) business or in businesses involving drug manufacturing or sales.

STATE LAWS

Most states prohibit or heavily restrict the use of polygraphs in employment, either when applying for a job or later. Most states permit some drug testing but with restrictions such as notification and the provision of treatment for employees who turn out to have a drug problem. There are generally restrictions on disclosure of test results outside the company. The following is a list of states* with laws relating to employment records: Alaska, California, Colorado, Connecticut, Delaware, District of Columbia, Florida, Hawaii, Illinois, Iowa, Maine, Massachusetts, Michigan, Minnesota, Nevada, New Hampshire, New York, North Carolina, North Dakota, Ohio, Oregon, Pennsylvania, Rhode Island, South Dakota, Tennessee, Utah, Vermont, Washington, and Wisconsin.

The following is a list of states* with laws relating to polygraphs or other forms of testing: Alabama, Alaska, Arizona, Arkansas, California, Connecticut, Delaware, District of Columbia, Florida, Georgia, Hawaii, Idaho, Illinois, Iowa, Louisiana, Maine, Maryland, Massachusetts, Michigan, Minnesota, Mississippi, Montana, Nebraska, Nevada, New Jersey, New Mexico, New York, North Carolina, North Dakota, Oklahoma, Oregon, Pennsylvania, Rhode Island, South Carolina, Tennessee, Texas, Utah, Vermont, Virginia, Washington, West Virginia, and Wisconsin. Some example provisions of these laws are as follows:

- **Connecticut:** Employees have the right to inspect their records and either correct mistakes or file a rebuttal for disputed information; companies may give "truthful statements" that discredit an employee, but may not "blacklist" employees to prevent them from working in their industry. Urine tests for drugs can be administered only if there is "reasonable suspicion that the employee is under the influence of drugs or alcohol, which adversely affects or could affect such employee's job performance." Any positive result must be confirmed by two tests.

- **Louisiana:** A polygraph examiner must inform the person being tested that testing is voluntary and that refusal to take the test may not be grounds for termination. Examiners who fail to do so can lose their license.

---

* For this purpose, the District of Columbia is a "state."

- **Maryland:** Employers must include in application forms a notice that "an employer may not require or demand any applicant for employment or prospective employment to submit to or take a polygraph, lie detector, or similar test or examination as a condition for employment or continued employment."
- **Massachusetts:** Psychological "honesty tests" may not be administered in connection with employment.
- **Nevada:** Employers may not discriminate because an employee "uses a lawful product outside the premises of the employer." An employee may not be dismissed based on information provided by a "spotter" without a hearing or opportunity to confront the spotter.
- **North Carolina:** An employer may test for AIDS as part of an annual physical exam, and employees with the HIV/AIDS virus may be fired if there is a risk to others.
- **North Dakota:** All testing for HIV/AIDS must be confidential and by consent.
- **Rhode Island:** Urinalysis and blood testing for alcohol or drugs is permitted only when there are "reasonable grounds."
- **Tennessee:** The law states that "No employer may take any personnel action based solely upon the results of a polygraph examination." Questions may not ask about sexual behavior or orientation unless (a) the question is relevant to the purpose of the exam, (b) the examinee gives written permission, and (c) the examinee has the right to explain any problematic results. Exams may not ask about religious, political, labor, or racial matters or anything that took place five or more years earlier, except for felonies and drug violations.

Genetic Discrimination and Testing

The following states prohibit discrimination in employment-related decisions based on genetic information: Arizona, Arkansas, California, Connecticut, Delaware, Hawaii, Illinois, Iowa, Kansas, Louisiana, Maine, Maryland, Massachusetts, Michigan, Minnesota, Missouri, Nebraska, Nevada, New Hampshire, New Jersey, New Mexico, New York, North Carolina, Oklahoma, Oregon, Rhode Island, South Dakota, Texas, Utah, Vermont, Virginia, Washington, and Wisconsin. About half of these states go further and prohibit requesting, requiring, or even performing genetic tests.

International Privacy Laws

UNITED NATIONS

The United Nations Universal Declaration of Human Rights (1948) is the philosophical basis for much of modern international law. It has the following privacy-related provisions:

Article 3: *Everyone has the right to life, liberty, and security of person.*

Article 8: *Everyone has the right to an effective remedy by the competent national tribunals for acts violating the fundamental rights granted him by the constitution or by law.*

Article 12: *No one shall be subjected to arbitrary interference with his privacy, family, home or correspondence, nor to attacks upon his honor or reputation. Everyone has the right to the protection of the law against such interference or attacks.*

EUROPEAN UNION

The European Union has emerged with one of the strongest and most comprehensive sets of privacy laws. The document has many "whereases" and details of implementation. The core of the legislation can be found in the following articles.

Article 6 describes the basic principles to be implemented in the EU's data policies:

Member States shall provide that personal data must be:

(a) processed fairly and lawfully;

(b) collected for specified, explicit and legitimate purposes and not further processed in a way incompatible with those purposes. Further processing of data for historical, statistical or scientific purposes shall not be considered as incompatible provided that Member States provide appropriate safeguards;

(c) adequate, relevant and not excessive in relation to the purposes for which they are collected and/or for which they are further processed;

(d) accurate and, where necessary, kept up to date; every reasonable step must be taken to ensure that data which are inaccurate or incomplete, having regard to the purposes for which they were collected or for which they are further processed, are erased or rectified;

(e) kept in a form which permits identification of data subjects for no longer than is necessary for the purposes for which the data were collected or for which they are further processed. Member States shall lay down appropriate safeguards for personal data stored for longer periods for historical, statistical or scientific use.

Article 7 specifies the requirements for the gathering and processing of personal data:

Member States shall provide that personal data may be processed only if:

(a) the data subject has given his consent unambiguously; or

(b) processing is necessary for the performance of a contract to which the data subject is party or in order to take steps at the request of the data subject entering into a contract; or

(c) processing is necessary for compliance with a legal obligation to which the controller is subject; or

(d) processing is necessary in order to protect the vital interests of the data subject; or

(e) processing is necessary for the performance of a task carried out in the public interest or in the exercise of official authority vested in the controller or in a third party to whom the data are disclosed; or
(f) processing is necessary for the purposes of the legitimate interests pursued by the controller or by the third party or parties to whom the data are disclosed, except where such interests are overridden by the interests or fundamental rights and freedoms of the data subject which require protection under Article 1(1).

Article 10 specifies what must be disclosed to the individual about whom information is to be gathered:

Member States shall provide that the controller or his representative must provide a data subject from whom data relating to himself are collected with at least the following information, except where he already knows:
(a) the identity of the controller and of his representative, if any.
(b) the purposes of the processing for which the data are intended.
(c) any further information such as
— the recipients or categories of recipients of the data;
— whether replies to the questions are obligatory or voluntary, as well as the possible consequences of the failure to reply;
— the existence of the right of access to and the right to rectify the data concerning him insofar as they are necessary, having regard to the specific circumstances in which the data are collected, to guarantee fair processing in respect of the data subject.

Article 25 deals with the interface between the EU and other countries. Its main concern is to ensure that data not be shared with countries that do not have similarly strict protections in place, since doing so could lead to improper disclosure or other abuses and ultimately defeat the purpose of the legislation:

1. *Member States shall provide that the transfer to a third country of personal data which are undergoing processing or are intended for processing after transfer may take place only if, without prejudice to compliance with the national provisions adopted pursuant to the other provisions of this Directive, the third country in question ensures an adequate level of protection.*
2. *The adequacy of the level of protection afforded by a third country shall be assessed in the light of all the circumstances surrounding a data transfer operation or set of data transfer operations; particular consideration shall be given to the nature of the data, the purpose and duration of the proposed processing operation or operations, the country of origin and country of final destination, the rules of law, both general and sectoral, in force in the third country in question and the professional rules and security measures which are complied with in those countries.*

In 2002 the EU promulgated additional regulations with regard to the Internet and other data communications services. Among other things, the regulations deal with the obligation of providers of Internet services to safeguard the security of their systems and to inform subscribers of any breaches or special risks that arise. Data being transmitted should not be stored unnecessarily and should be removed when no longer needed. In general, the use of personal information in operating communications services should be kept to a minimum.

CANADA

The British Columbia, Canada Freedom of Information and Privacy Act has provisions that are similar to a combination of the U.S. Freedom of Information Act and the Privacy Act of 1974. Under "Purposes of this Act" it states that:

2. *(1) The purposes of this Act are to make public bodies more accountable to the public and to protect personal privacy by*
(a) giving the public a right of access to records,
(b) giving individuals a right of access to, and a right to request correction of, personal information about themselves,
(c) specifying limited exceptions to the right of access,
(d) preventing the unauthorized collection, use, or disclosure of personal information by public bodies, and
(e) providing for an independent review of decisions made under this Act.

The Act applies to most records compiled by public agencies in the province, except for court records, records relating to legislative offices, some educational materials, and certain other exceptions. The "head of a public body must make every reasonable effort to assist applicants and to respond without delay to each applicant openly, accurately, and completely." It goes on to specify that the public body must extract a copy of a computerized record provided it is within normal technical expertise and not unduly burdensome.

After providing a mechanism for disclosure, the act discusses circumstances under which the government is not obliged to provide information (or indeed, is required to keep it confidential). It also discusses the need to give notice to third parties who may be harmed by a proposed disclosure (such as that of proprietary business information).

In 2000 Canada enacted the Personal Information Protection and Electronic Documents Act (PIPEDA), which established new privacy standards for government and commercial entities in their handling of personal information. In general the law implements 10 privacy principles, including accountability, statement of purpose, openness, consent, limiting use and collection, disclosure, retention, individual access, safeguards, accuracy, and challenging compliance. Standards for processing of electronic transactions are included.

Other Canadian laws containing information privacy provisions include the Bank Act, Insurance Act, Trust and Loan Companies Act, and the Telecommunications Act.

OTHER COUNTRIES

In general, the EU offers the strongest privacy protection, with countries in the British Commonwealth (such as Canada and Australia) also having high standards. These countries have stricter and more uniform regulation of private enterprise than the United States, but the greater centralization of government and weaker constitutional protection for free speech and the press may make it harder to disclose governmental abuses.

It is hard to compare the United States with other countries because it has both federal and state laws (and courts) that come into play under various circumstances. Regulation of the gathering and use of information by private enterprise is spotty, especially with regard to emerging Internet commerce. Because the United States tends to strike a balance toward freedom of speech and the press and away from government secrecy, governmental abuses can be more easily brought to light.

It is important to note that the right to privacy, like all rights, is dependent on a government not only providing constitutional guarantees, but being willing to abide by them. Dictatorships are unlikely to protect the privacy of their opponents, and parties involved in civil war are unlikely to have a regard for individual rights. China, the world's largest country, has little protection for privacy against the government, and the former U.S.S.R. has not yet replaced its post-Communist chaos with an effective system of legal guarantees.

COURT CASES

There are many cases in the Supreme Court and lower courts that hinge on some aspect of privacy. In keeping with the topic of this book, the selection of cases focuses on those that deal primarily with privacy violations involving the use (or abuse) of information, surveillance, or monitoring.

The following table indexes the cases by the principal topics involved. Within each topic, cases are given in chronological order.

Accountability of Records
Arizona v. Evans
Consumer and Personal Privacy
Ram Avrahami v. U.S. News & World Report
U.S. West v. Federal Communications Commission
In Re Toysmart.com, LLC
Individual Reference Services Group v. Federal Trade Commission
Commonwealth v. Source One Associations
Helen Remsburg v. DocuSearch
Decisional or Intimate Privacy
Griswold v. Connecticut
Driver's License Information
Condon v. Reno

The Law of Privacy

E-mail and Online Postings
Alana Shoars v. Epson America, Inc.
Timothy R. McVeigh v. William Cohen et al.
Encryption
Daniel Bernstein v. U.S. Department of State
Financial Privacy
United States v. Miller
Identification Requirements
Gilmore v. Ashcroft
Hiibel v. Sixth Judicial District Court of Nevada
Medical Privacy
Doe v. Southeastern Pennsylvania Transportation Authority
American Council of Life Insurers v. Vermont Department of Banking, Insurance, Securities, and Healthcare Administration
Privacy Statements
In Re Toysmart.com, LLC
Social Security Numbers
Beacon Journal Publishing v. City of Akron, Ohio
Doe v. Chao
Student Privacy
New Jersey v. T.L.O.
Surveillance and Searches
California v. Ciraolo
Kyllo v. United States
Wiretapping and Data Interception
Olmstead v. U.S.
Katz v. United States
Steve Jackson Games, Inc. v. United States Secret Service
United States v. Nicodemo S. Scarfo et al.
Workplace Privacy
O'Connor v. Ortega
Alana Shoars v. Epson America, Inc.
Workplace Testing
O'Brien v. Papa Gino's of America, Inc.
Soroka v. Dayton Hudson Corp.

OLMSTEAD V. U.S., 277 U.S. 438 (1928)

Background

During the Prohibition era of the 1920s, federal agents waged a relentless war against bootleggers who sold illegal liquor. Agents suspected that Roy Olmstead was a major bootlegger, so they tapped the phone lines in the basement of a building where he had an office, and also tapped phone lines going into his home. The agents did not obtain court warrants before installing the taps.

Using the taps, the agents gained evidence sufficient to convict him. After appeal, the case eventually reached the Supreme Court.

Legal Issues

Olmstead's defense claimed that the use of wiretaps violated Olmstead's constitutional rights under the Fourth Amendment, which states that "The right of the people to be secure in their persons, houses, papers, and effects against unreasonable searches and seizures shall not be violated, and no warrants shall issue but upon probable cause, supported by oath or affirmation and particularly describing the place to be searched and the persons or things to be seized." According to the defense, the wiretap was equivalent to a search and seizure of Olmstead's private office and home, and since it was done without a warrant, it was unconstitutional.

The defense also claimed that the prosecution's use of Olmstead's wiretapped conversations violated the Fifth Amendment, which states (in part) that "No person . . . shall be compelled, in any criminal case, to be a witness against himself." According to the defense, using the wiretapped conversation forced him in effect to become an unwilling witness against himself.

Decision

The majority of the Court upheld Olmstead's conviction and rejected both constitutional challenges. With regard to the Fourth Amendment, the Court noted that "The Amendment itself shows that the search is to be of material things— the person, the house, his papers, or his effects. The description of the warrant necessary to make the proceeding lawful is that it must specify the place to be searched and the person or *things* to be seized." The Court noted that nothing physical had been seized. It also rejected the attempt to make an analogy between phone conversations and mail. While the mail is presumed confidential by the government, "The United States takes no such care of telegraph or telephone messages as of mailed sealed letters. The [Fourth] Amendment does not forbid what was done here. There was no searching. There was no seizure. The evidence was secured by the use of the sense of hearing, and that only."

The Court also insisted that "There was no entry of the houses or offices of the defendants. By the invention of the telephone fifty years ago and its application for the purpose of extending communications, one can talk with another at a far distant place. The language of the [Fourth] Amendment cannot be extended and expanded to include telephone wires reaching to the whole world from the defendant's house or office. The intervening wires are not part of his house or office any more than are the highways along which they are stretched."

The Court also rejected the Fifth Amendment challenge because Olmstead had not been forced or compelled to make the incriminating statements.

Impact

As a result of *Olmstead,* any protection against federal wiretapping would have to come through legislation (until the decision was reversed in *Katz v. United States.*

in 1967). State law, however, could restrict wiretapping by state or local law enforcement agencies.

Perhaps the most important impact of *Olmstead*, however, came from Justice Louis Brandeis's dissenting opinion, which thrust the constitutional issue of privacy into the spotlight. While the Court majority had insisted on a literal interpretation of the Fourth and Fifth Amendments, Brandeis noted that "Since [*McCullough v. Maryland*, 17 U.S. 316, 1819], this Court has repeatedly sustained the exercise of power by Congress, under various clauses of that instrument, over objects of which the Fathers could not have dreamed." Brandeis cited examples of "modern" regulations that would have been considered oppressive or even absurd in earlier times, and insisted that like regulations, protections for rights such as privacy must also be updated when technology or other conditions change.

Brandeis noted that "When the Fourth and Fifth Amendments were adopted, 'the form that evil [of forced self-incrimination] had theretofore taken' had been necessarily simple. Force and violence were then the only means known to man by which a Government could directly effect self-incrimination. It could compel the individual to testify—a compulsion effected, if need be, by torture. It could secure possession of his papers and other articles incident to his private life—a seizure effected, if need be, by breaking and entry."

Brandeis insisted that courts must take changing conditions into account: "Subtler and more far-reaching means of invading privacy have become available to the Government. Discovery and invention have made it possible for the Government, by means far more effective than stretching upon the rack, to obtain disclosure in court of what is whispered in the closet."

The words of Justice Brandeis would prove to be prophetic as even newer technologies (such as video cameras, infrared scopes, and sophisticated "bugs") would become available to both government and private eavesdroppers, and the means of communication (and thus of potential self-incrimination) would come to include the teletype, the fax, and electronic mail.

GRISWOLD V. CONNECTICUT, 381 U.S. 479 (1965)

Background

During the 19th century, "anti-vice" crusaders succeeded in passing laws that made it illegal in most states to provide information about contraception (birth control) methods or to provide devices that could be used to prevent conception. By the 1960s, however, the invention of an effective birth control pill and freer attitudes about sex were leading to pressure to overturn restrictive laws.

Estelle Griswold, the executive director of the Planned Parenthood League of Connecticut, and the organization's medical director were convicted of violating Connecticut's anti-contraception law by providing birth control information and devices to clients. Griswold's attorneys appealed the conviction to the state court of appeals and then to the Connecticut Supreme Court, but both upheld the conviction. The case finally reached the U.S. Supreme Court.

Legal Issues

Griswold's appeal was based on the argument that the state anti-contraception law violated the Fourteenth Amendment to the Constitution. In part, this amendment states: "No State shall make or enforce any law which shall abridge the privileges or immunities of citizens of the United States; nor shall any State deprive any person of life, liberty, or property, without due process of law; nor deny to any person within its jurisdiction the equal protection of the laws."

This amendment had been passed originally just after the Civil War to ensure that the former Confederate states gave their black citizens the same "privileges and immunities" afforded to whites. But the Supreme Court had gradually broadened its interpretation to find that the Fourteenth Amendment "incorporated" many of the rights in the first 10 amendments (the Bill of Rights) and that the states as well as the federal government were required to respect these rights.

Griswold thus argued that the right of a married couple to make decisions about birth control was part of that couple's fundamental privacy: a right just as basic as freedom of speech or freedom of association, and thus incorporated in the Fourteenth Amendment. If the Court agreed, this meant that the state birth control law was unconstitutional and that the conviction would be overturned.

The state of Connecticut argued that the Bill of Rights made no mention of birth control nor indeed, of any "right to privacy." Therefore, no such right was incorporated in the Fourteenth Amendment, and the state was not prevented from outlawing birth control.

Decision

Justice William O. Douglas, writing for the majority, agreed with Griswold's argument. He disposed of the argument that privacy was not mentioned in the Constitution by noting that "The association of people is not mentioned in the Constitution nor in the Bill of Rights. The right to educate a child in a school of the parents' choice—whether public or private or parochial—is also not mentioned. Nor is the right to study any particular subject or any foreign language. Yet the First Amendment has been construed to include certain of those rights."

He then cited a number of cases in which the Court had established that such rights existed even though they are not specifically mentioned in the Constitution. For example, "In *NAACP v. Alabama*, 357 U.S. 449, 462 we protected the 'freedom to associate and privacy in one's associations,' noting that freedom of association was a peripheral First Amendment right. Disclosure of membership lists of a constitutionally valid association, we held, was invalid as entailing the likelihood of a substantial restraint upon the exercise by petitioner's members of their right to freedom of association."

Douglas went on to conclude that

> *The foregoing cases suggest that specific guarantees in the Bill of Rights have penumbras [shadows], formed by emanations from those guarantees that help give them life and substance. . . . Various guarantees create zones of privacy. The right of association contained in the penumbra of the First Amendment is one, as we have seen. The Third Amendment, in its prohibition against the quartering of sol-*

diers "in any house" in time of peace without the consent of the owner, is another facet of that privacy. The Fourth Amendment explicitly affirms the "right of the people to be secure in their persons, houses, papers, and effects, against unreasonable searches and seizures." The Fifth Amendment, in its Self-Incrimination Clause, enables the citizen to create a zone of privacy which government may not force him to surrender to his detriment.

Douglas noted that the Constitution also says, in the Ninth Amendment, that "The enumeration in the Constitution, of certain rights, shall not be construed to deny or disparage others retained by the people." This made it impermissible to argue, as Connecticut had, that the lack of a specific "right of privacy" in the Bill of Rights meant that no such right existed.

Douglas thus replaced narrowly specific guarantees with "zones of privacy" that he believed were implied in the guarantees of the Bill of Rights. He insisted that something as intimate as the marriage relationship must stand at the center of the zone of privacy. The decision to use contraception (and thus the right to obtain information and devices) is thus protected by the Constitution.

Impact

The *Griswold* decision has had a major impact on how courts think about privacy. In effect, it elevates a "right of privacy" to as high a status as freedom of speech, freedom of association, the right against self-incrimination, and other items specifically mentioned in the Bill of Rights. The Court would go on to find a right to obtain an abortion (*Roe v. Wade*, 1973) and to make a decision about life-saving medical care (*Cruzan*, 1990). "Strict constructionists" such as Robert Bork would continue to oppose what they consider to be an illegitimate and subjective "creation" of rights by courts.

It is important to note, however, what *Griswold* did not do. While it created a broad right of privacy regarding personal decisions and intimate relationships, it refused to extend the right to make decisions or obtain information or devices to the marketplace or the public square. Indeed, as Douglas noted, "We do not sit as a super-legislature to determine the wisdom, need, and propriety of laws that touch economic problems, business affairs, or social conditions." In other words, the federal government or the states could still set safety standards for condoms or determine licensing requirements for birth control counselors.

After its brief moment in the sun, the Ninth Amendment has not often been used to argue for the existence of other rights that could limit government power. Instead, it has become part of a political debate over small versus big government.

KATZ V. UNITED STATES, 389 U.S. 347 (1967)

Background

As with Roy Olmstead, federal agents suspected that Charles Katz was engaging in illegal activity (in this case, conducting a multistate gambling operation by phone). The agents placed a "bug" on the outside of a phone booth that Katz was using. They then used the recordings as evidence to convict him for "illegal transmission of wagering information." The conviction was upheld on appeal, with the appeals court citing the *Olmstead* case and noting that the police did not physically enter the area of the phone booth occupied by Katz.

Legal Issues

As noted in the Supreme Court's opinion, the petitioner seeking to overturn the conviction had raised two main issues:

> A. *Whether a public telephone booth is a constitutionally protected area so that evidence obtained by attaching an electronic listening recording device to the top of such a booth is obtained in violation of the right to privacy of the user of the booth.*
> B. *Whether physical penetration of a constitutionally protected area is necessary before a search and seizure can be said to be violative of the Fourth Amendment to the United States Constitution.*

Decision

The Court, however, refused to limit its consideration to the narrow question of just what part of the phone booth might be constitutionally protected. The general legal and social climate had changed considerably since *Olmstead*. During the 1950s and 1960s, the Supreme Court under Chief Justice Earl Warren had become much more willing to interpret broadly constitutional protections in the light of changing social conditions, whether with regard to civil rights (*Brown v. Board of Education*, 1954), privacy (*Griswold v. Connecticut*, 1965), protection against overbroad searches (*Mapp v. Ohio*, 1961), or against compelled self-incrimination (the famous *Miranda v. Arizona*, 1966, which led to the familiar warning heard endlessly on television cop shows). The courts were now heeding Brandeis's call for an explicit and robust constitutional right to personal privacy.

The Court declared that "the Fourth Amendment protects people, not places. What a person knowingly exposes to the public, even in his own home or office, is not a subject of Fourth Amendment protection. . . . But what he seeks to preserve as private, even in an area accessible to the public, may be constitutionally protected."

Looking to a previous Supreme Court decision (*Silverman v. United States*, 365 U.S. 505, 511), the Court noted: ". . . we have expressly held that the Fourth Amendment governs not only the seizure of tangible items, but extends as well to the recording of oral statements, overheard without any technical trespass under . . . local property law. Once this much is acknowledged, and once it is recognized that the Fourth Amendment protects people—and not simply 'areas'—against unreasonable searches and seizures, it becomes clear that the reach of that Amendment cannot turn upon the presence or absence of a physical intrusion into any given enclosure."

The justices had decided that it was not the existence of an enclosed place that created a right of privacy, but a person's engaging in an activity that he or she can reasonably expect to be private:

The Law of Privacy

No less than an individual in a business office, in a friend's apartment, or in a taxicab, a person in a telephone booth may rely upon the protection of the Fourth Amendment. One who occupies [the booth], shuts the door behind him, and pays the toll that permits him to place a call is surely entitled to assume that the words he utters into the mouthpiece will not be broadcast to the world. To read the Constitution more narrowly is to ignore the vital role that the public telephone has come to play in private communication.

The Court therefore concluded that Katz's rights under the Fourth Amendment had been violated. Although the Court acknowledged that the government agents had probable cause to suspect a crime and conducted only enough surveillance to gather relevant evidence, it overturned the conviction because the agents had not obtained a warrant as required under the Fourth Amendment.

Impact

Since *Katz*, law enforcement officials generally have to obtain a warrant before beginning a wiretap or other surveillance of an individual's conversations. (In 1972 this requirement was extended by the courts to include even cases where the government believed there was a threat to "national security.")

There are some exceptions. In *United States v. David Lee Smith* (978 F.2d 171, U.S. App.), 1992, a court of appeals ruled that conversations on cordless telephones (which actually use radio waves to carry conversations) could be tapped by police without obtaining a search warrant. (Congress then passed a law to extend the warrant requirement to cover cordless phones, but not cellular ones.) Changes in technology thus have continued to challenge the boundaries placed around law enforcement activities by the courts. When the Justice Department concluded that the Wiretap Act of 1968 did not require a warrant for intercepting e-mail and other computer communications (because they were not aural or vocal in nature), Congress responded by passing the Electronic Communications Privacy Act of 1986.

There have been a number of cases (ranging from Watergate to the surveillance of left-wing groups and political enemies by the FBI) where the legal system seems to have been ineffective in preventing wiretapping abuses. Some private wiretapping is permissible. Employers generally have the right to monitor employee conversations on company phones if the monitoring is for a legitimate business purpose, such as training or evaluation of employees' performance.

UNITED STATES V. MILLER, 425 U.S. 435 (1976)

Background

In 1970, Congress passed the Bank Secrecy Act, which required banks to report cash transactions over $10,000 and certain other transactions, and to keep copies of bank records such as deposit slips and checks for at least five years. The justification given for the legislation was that it would make it easier for law enforcement agencies to keep track of organized criminal activity such as the "laundering" of drug money.

In *California Bankers Association* (1970), the Supreme Court ruled that the transaction tracking provisions of the Bank Secrecy Act did not violate Fourth Amendment privacy rights. In *Miller* a related issue would be resolved: Were the act's provisions making it easy for the government to obtain copies of a suspected person's bank records also constitutional?

On December 18, 1972, a deputy sheriff in Houston County, Georgia, responding to a tip, stopped a truck that turned out to contain distillery equipment and raw material for making liquor. About a month later, when a warehouse caught fire, firefighters and sheriff's deputies discovered a distillery and illegal liquor. Agents from the Treasury Department's Bureau of Alcohol, Tobacco, and Firearms investigated, and began to suspect a man named Mitch Miller as being leader of the bootlegging ring. They issued a subpoena to obtain Miller's records from two banks where he had accounts. The records showed that Miller had rented the truck, purchased a considerable amount of pipe (useful for distilling), and other materials. The leads and evidence provided by the records helped the government convict Miller of violation of liquor laws.

Legal Issues

Miller's attorneys argued that his bank records required a full-fledged subpoena similar to that used to get permission to search a person's home. (Such a subpoena would be issued by a judge and would specify what is being sought, and show probable cause that a crime had been committed and that the suspected evidence was related to the crime.) The government argued that the Bank Secrecy Act authorized a much simpler subpoena issued by the local U.S. Attorney. The basic issue was whether Miller's bank records were entitled to the full protection of the Fourth Amendment. If so, the Bank Secrecy Act would be unconstitutional and Miller's conviction could be reversed.

Decision

The Fifth District Court of Appeals agreed with Miller and ruled that his rights had been violated by requiring a third party (the bank) to produce Miller's private papers without due process. The government appealed to the U.S. Supreme Court, arguing that Miller had no "Fourth Amendment interest" in his bank records, and that the Bank Secrecy Act did not violate the Constitution.

Justice Lewis F. Powell's majority opinion upheld the government. The Fourth Amendment refers to "the right of the people to be secure in their persons, houses, papers, and effects, against unreasonable searches and seizures . . ." But, Powell writes, ". . . the documents subpoenaed here are not respondent's [Miller's] 'private papers.' . . . respondent can assert neither ownership nor possession. Instead, these are the business records of the banks." Harking back to the earlier decision in *California Bankers Association*, Powell notes that the bank is not "passively" holding records for the depositor, but rather is a party in a business relationship with the depositor, and the bank records are property of the bank used to conduct its business with its customers.

Powell then turned to the possibility that the Bank Secrecy Act nevertheless allowed an impermissible invasion of Miller's privacy by making it too easy for the government to obtain if not papers, the private information contained in them. Powell notes that "Respondent urges that he has a Fourth Amendment interest in the records kept by the banks because they are merely copies of personal records that were made available to the banks for a limited purpose and in which he has a reasonable expectation of privacy." Thus the Fourth Amendment "expectation of privacy" test (from *Katz* and other cases) comes into play.

Powell rejects this challenge as well:

> *Even if we direct our attention to the original checks and deposit slips, rather than to the microfilm copies actually viewed and obtained by means of the subpoena, we perceive no legitimate "expectation of privacy" in their contents. The checks are not confidential communications but negotiable instruments to be used in commercial transactions. All of the documents obtained, including financial statements and deposit slips, contain only information voluntarily conveyed to the banks and exposed to their employees in the ordinary course of business.*

Referring to earlier cases, Powell points out that there is no constitutional protection against information that was voluntarily revealed to a third party in the ordinary course of business being revealed to the government. Nor is their any protection against that third party being subpoenaed. Therefore, the Court ruled, Miller had no Fourth Amendment privacy right, and his conviction was upheld.

Impact

The *Miller* case is an example that shows that the robust privacy right seen emanating from the Constitution in *Griswold* and *Roe v. Wade* apparently does not pass from the bedroom to the checkbook. Further, the principle from *Katz* that changing technology from letters to telephone requires an expansion of privacy rights was not applied in *Miller*, despite the fact that banking might be considered as much of a necessity of modern life as the telephone.

Additionally, *Miller* can also be viewed as part of an ongoing seesaw battle between privacy rights and law enforcement interests. Congress passed the Bank Secrecy Act to help law enforcers fight organized crime. *Miller* upheld the constitutionality of the law. Yet while people have a strong interest in fighting crime, they also have shown a growing interest in protecting privacy. Congress, responding to these conflicting interests, passes some laws that limit privacy in favor of law enforcement and other laws that provide greater protection for privacy. The result of this conflict is that it is far from easy for the average individual to know what personal records or other information is protected, and from whom.

NEW JERSEY V. T.L.O., 469 U.S. 325 (1985)

Background

A teacher in a New Jersey public school noticed that T.L.O. (a 14-year-old girl) and another student were smoking in the school lavatory in violation of school rules. (Since the defendant was a minor, only her initials appear in court documents.) The teacher took her to the assistant vice principal. When confronted by the latter, T.L.O. insisted that she had not been smoking. He demanded to see her purse, which turned out to contain both a pack of cigarettes and a pack of the kind of cigarette papers commonly used by marijuana smokers. Continuing to search the purse, he found a pipe, marijuana, and a list of students and two letters that suggested that T.L.O. was dealing in marijuana.

Legal Issues

In juvenile court, T.L.O.'s attorney argued that the search had violated the Fourth Amendment. The court held that while the Fourth Amendment did apply to searches in schools, the search of T.L.O.'s purse met the standard of being "reasonable." The appeals court upheld the search, but the New Jersey Supreme Court reversed the decision, calling the search unreasonable. The case then went to the Supreme Court.

Decision

The Supreme Court noted that while parents are not bound by the Fourth Amendment, teachers are not just substitutes for parents, but also representatives of the State. As such, they are bound by the restrictions imposed by the Fourth Amendment.

The Court noted, however, that the need for "striking the balance between schoolchildren's legitimate expectations of privacy and the school's equally legitimate need to maintain an environment in which learning can take place requires some easing of the restrictions to which searches by public authorities are ordinarily subject." Thus school officials, unlike police, do not have to obtain a warrant before conducting a search, and do not have to meet the stricter standard of having "probable cause" to believe that there is criminal activity. Instead, they need only have "reasonable grounds for suspecting that the search will turn up evidence that the student has violated or is violating either the law or the rules of the school. And such a search will be permissible in its scope when the measures adopted are reasonably related to the objectives of the search, and not excessively intrusive in light of the student's age and sex and the nature of the infraction."

Impact

New Jersey v. T.L.O. established that on the one hand, students did have some expectation of privacy, but on the other hand, schools could conduct searches that were reasonably related to suspected violations of rules. Such practices as making students walk through a metal detector to prevent them from carrying weapons into the school have similarly been upheld as reasonably related to the school's need to provide a safe educational environment.

CALIFORNIA V. CIRAOLO, 476 U.S. 207 (1986)

Background

After receiving an anonymous tip that respondent Ciraolo was growing marijuana, police in Santa Clara, California, tried to look into his backyard. If they could see the plants, they could get a search warrant. However, the fence around the yard was too high, so they hired a private plane and flew over the house at an altitude of 1,000 feet. Being able to confirm the presence of marijuana plants, they secured a search warrant and then arrested Ciraolo, who pled guilty to cultivation of marijuana. An appeals court, however, ruled that the flyover constituted an illegal search and reversed Ciraolo's conviction. The case eventually reached the U.S. Supreme Court.

Legal Issues

The question posed by the case is whether aerial observation of someone's property without a warrant is allowed by the Fourth Amendment. If so, is there some altitude at which it becomes unacceptable? More broadly, what types of visual surveillance of private property are acceptable?

Decision

The majority decision by Justice Warren Burger ruled that the aerial search was acceptable. He noted that police officers have always been able to look into people's homes from the street. He also noted that the police observations were made "from public navigable airspace" and that "any member of the public flying in this airspace who glanced down could have seen everything that these officers observed."

The dissenting justices, led by Justice Lewis F. Powell, argued that the Court had previously, in *Katz v. United States* (1967), established a standard based on peoples' reasonable expectation of privacy, not on the technology or means used for surveillance. Allowing an observation just because someone else might have seen it seemed to the dissenters to be an unwarranted erosion of Fourth Amendment privacy rights.

Impact

This decision cleared the way for aerial surveillance as a tool in law enforcement. In *Florida v. Riley* (1989), the Court said it was permissible for authorities to search for drugs from planes or helicopters at altitudes as low as 400 feet. Thus far the Supreme Court has not said there is a lower limit of altitude for flyovers. It is also unclear whether searching or surveillance using cameras or instruments that greatly enhance the visual image would be acceptable.

O'BRIEN V. PAPA GINO'S OF AMERICA, INC. 80 F.2D 1067, 1072 (1ST CIR. 1986)

Background

A manager at a Papa Gino's restaurant in New Hampshire confronted an employee, saying that he had been seen using drugs outside of work. The employee took a polygraph test in which he was asked drug-related questions. The examiner said that he believed the employee was lying about his drug use, and the latter was fired. He sued the company.

Legal Issues

O'Brien argued that he had been forced to take the polygraph test or lose his job, and that the test included questions that were not related to his work. Papa Gino's argued that it had a legitimate interest in avoiding the risks caused by an employee who regularly uses drugs, even if the drugs are used only outside of work.

Decision

The jury found that the test and other investigative techniques used by Papa Gino's was "highly offensive to a reasonable person." It awarded $398,200 to O'Brien. The verdict was later upheld by the U.S. Court of Appeals for the First Circuit.

Impact

Public concern about the use of polygraphs and other devices that measure physical stress (such as voice analyzers) led to the passage in 1988 of the Employee Polygraph Protection Act. This law bans employers from using such devices in most cases.

O'CONNOR V. ORTEGA, 480 U.S. 709 (1987)

Background

Dennis O'Connor, director of Napa State Hospital in California, suspected that Dr. Magno Ortega, a psychiatrist and manager of a residency program for doctors, had improperly coerced residents into paying for a computer, and was also concerned that he was involved in sexual harassment. O'Connor instituted a number of searches of Dr. Ortega's office while the doctor was on administrative leave, seizing items that were later used against Ortega in proceedings before the California State Personnel Board.

Legal Issues

Dr. Ortega claimed that the search of his office violated the Fourth Amendment protections against improper search and seizure because he had a "reasonable expectation of privacy" in his office. O'Connor claimed that the search was a routine inventory checkup needed to secure state property and that it did not violate Ortega's privacy.

Decision

The district court upheld O'Connor, agreeing that there was no violation of privacy. The court of appeals, however, reversed that decision, holding that Ortega did have a reasonable expectation of privacy and that the "routine inventory" defense was not applicable because such inventories had previously only been used for dismissed employees, not employees on leave.

O'Connor appealed the decision to the Supreme Court. In a 5-4 decision, the Court found that in keeping with "the realities of the workplace" a supervisor should not be expected to follow the same strict standards as a law enforcement officer. Work-related searches, the Court found, were "merely incident to the primary business of the agency." Requiring that a warrant be obtained for every search would "seriously disrupt the routine conduct of business." The Court held that the employer needed only to meet a standard of "reasonableness" before undertaking a search.

Impact

The *O'Connor* decision served notice to employees that their privacy rights were limited and that employers were not bound by the same rules as government officials or police officers. This did not mean, however, that employees had *no* privacy in the workplace. As the Court noted,

> Not everything that passes through the confines of the business address can be considered part of the workplace context, however. An employee may bring closed luggage to the office prior to leaving on a trip, or a handbag or briefcase each workday. While whatever expectation of privacy the employee has in the existence and the outward appearance of the luggage is affected by its presence in the workplace, the employee's expectation of privacy in the contents of the luggage is not affected in the same way. The appropriate standard for a workplace search does not necessarily apply to a piece of closed personal luggage, a handbag, or a briefcase that happens to be within the employer's business address.

Similarly, the Supreme Court majority agreed with the Appeals Court that Ortega had a "reasonable expectation of privacy" with regard to his locked desk and file cabinet, which he did not share with other employees.

Thus *O'Connor* did not fully resolve the question of what is private in the workplace, but it did provide some principles that could be applied to future cases.

Privacy in the Information Age

ALANA SHOARS V. EPSON AMERICA, INC., NO. B 073234, LOS ANGELES SUPERIOR COURT (1990)

Background

Epson America e-mail administrator Alana Shoars discovered that her supervisor had been retrieving and printing out all the electronic mail sent by employees at the company's Torrance, California, office. When she told the general manager about her discovery and demanded that the practice be stopped, her supervisor fired her. Shoars then sued Epson for wrongful termination. (She also filed a class action suit for invasion of privacy, on behalf of herself and 77 other Epson employees whose e-mail had been intercepted.)

Legal Issues

Shoars's attorney argued that Epson had led her to believe that employee e-mail was considered private, and that the use of secret personal passwords for mail accounts reinforced that sense of privacy. He also argued that the interception of e-mail violated anti-wiretapping provisions in the state penal code.

Epson argued that the monitoring of e-mail was only for making sure the system was working properly. More fundamentally, they also argued that e-mail in a business was a facility provided solely for business purposes, and that Shoars and the other employees had no "expectation of privacy." Finally, they argued that the California anti-wiretapping laws did not apply to the new technology of electronic mail.

Decision

The trial court agreed that e-mail was not covered under California's wiretapping laws, and that any protection for e-mail would have to be provided by new legislation. The court also threw out the class action suit, agreeing with Epson that there was "no sufficient legal or factual basis for extending the right to privacy to cover business-related communications." The appeals court agreed with the decision, but allowed Shoars to go ahead to trial on a separate suit for slander.

Impact

Although this was a state court decision rather than a federal one, the *Shoars* case follows the general pattern in favor of the employer for most workplace and e-mail monitoring cases. Activists who want to strengthen workplace privacy protection must generally direct their efforts not to the courts but to the legislature or to labor negotiations.

The Law of Privacy

SOROKA V. DAYTON HUDSON CORP., 1 CAL. RPTR. 2D 77, 6 IER CASES (BNA) 1491 (APP. 1991)

Background

Sibi Soroka applied for a job as a security supervisor at Target Stores, which is owned by the Dayton Hudson Corporation. As part of his job interview, Soroka was given a "psychological inventory"—a written test that asked him about a variety of beliefs, feelings, and situations. As he worked his way through the test, he encountered questions such as the following:

> 3. *I looked up to my father as an ideal man.*
> 8. *I like* Alice in Wonderland *by Lewis Carroll.*
> 23. *When a person "pads" his income tax report so as to get out of some of his taxes, it is just as bad as stealing money from the government.*
> 73. *Maybe some minorities get rough treatment, but it is no business of mine.*
> 368. *I have no difficulty starting or holding my urine.*
> 466. *My sex life is satisfactory.*
> 492. *I am very strongly attracted by members of my own sex.*
> 506. *I believe in the second coming of Christ.*

Soroka became increasingly disturbed as he read. Some of the questions, such as 23, clearly tested for honesty. Question number 368, however, was clearly looking for health problems. Questions 466 and 492, inquiring into sexual matters, seemed to be none of the store's business, as did questions about social issues (73) or religion (506). Soroka finished the test because he needed a job, but he also made a copy of the test and showed it to an attorney. He decided to sue Target, not for personal damages, but to prevent them from giving anyone else such tests in the future.

Legal Issues

Soroka argued that the test was overly intrusive in seeking personal, intimate information, and thus violated the right to privacy in California's constitution (one of the strongest state privacy codes).

Target argued that shoplifting was a major problem, and that the store was trying to hire effective security personnel. On the other hand, the store was concerned about hiring persons to deal with the public in this sensitive job who were mentally or emotionally unstable or violent. If the store did not take measures to screen out such persons and one of its guards injured someone, the store could be sued for "negligent hiring." The store had adopted the psychological test (called Psychscreen) because it was part of the screening process used by many police departments. Finally, the store insisted that the applicant's privacy was protected because no one at the company ever saw an applicant's actual answer sheet, only a numerical score in each of several categories.

Soroka's lawyer replied that the security job was not all that high level or sensitive, and that there was no proof of the accuracy or reliability of the test. (He pointed out that police departments, unlike the store, conducted a much more extensive background investigation and that test was only a small part of their hiring procedure.)

Decision

Target filed to have the case dismissed, but the California Court of Appeals ruled that Soroka could take his lawsuit to trial. The court found that questions about such matters as sex or religion violated privacy, and that for such questions to be permissible, the store would have to show that it must be justified by a "compelling" interest and must serve a job-related purpose. Target had not met this high standard.

Target appealed to the California Supreme Court. That court agreed to take the case, and combined it with another case, *Hill v. NCAA*, which dealt with drug testing of student athletes. This combination of cases suggested that the court wanted to make a broader application of the right of privacy in the state constitution.

Meanwhile, the Americans with Disabilities Act (ADA) had been passed. Soroka felt that the health-related questions in the test would be illegal under the ADA. Target's attorneys also believed that a jury would be offended by some of the questions on the test. Target therefore agreed to settle the case for the considerable sum of $1,540,000.

Impact

Soroka caused many California employers to revise their employee screening procedures. Target, for example, replaced Psychscreen with detailed personal interviews and more extensive background checks. Meanwhile, the California Supreme Court ruled in the *Hill* case that the NCAA (the collegiate athletic association) was justified in requiring drug tests because it had a compelling interest in promoting the health and safety of athletes, and that the athletes had only a limited expectation of privacy.

In general, the court had determined that someone bringing a claim for invasion of privacy must show that there is a legally recognized privacy interest involved, that the person has a reasonable expectation of privacy in the particular circumstances, and that the invasion of privacy was sufficiently serious. For some kinds of invasion of privacy (such as intrusion on intimate or family relationships), the state must show it has a "compelling interest" justifying its action. In the case of employees and athletes, however, the privacy interest would be balanced against the organization's interests to see if the invasion of privacy is "reasonable."

The Law of Privacy

STEVE JACKSON GAMES, INC. V. UNITED STATES SECRET SERVICE, 816 F. SUPP. 432 (W.D.TEX. 1993)

Background

During the late 1980s, the term "computer hacker" entered popular vocabulary. While the term once referred to exceptionally skillful (if rather obsessed) young programmers, it had come to mean criminals who used their computer skills to break into computer systems for purposes of disruption or theft of valuable information such as credit cards or confidential documents.

In 1990, Secret Service agents organized a wide-ranging investigation of a hacker group called the Legion of Doom. They believed that the group had stolen a confidential document relating to BellSouth telephone company's emergency 911 phone system, which the company valued at almost $80,000. (In reality, the publication, far from being "confidential," was available to the public for only a few dollars.)

The agents learned that a copy of the BellSouth manual was being stored on a computer bulletin board called Phoenix. They downloaded a copy from that board, and then learned that the owner, Lloyd Blankenship, was also an operator of another bulletin board called Illuminati, which was operated by his employer, Steve Jackson Games, a company that published and sold role-playing and board games. Since Blankenship's board had much hacker-related conversation and material, Secret Service agent Tim Foley assumed that Illuminati was also a "hacker board."

On March 1, 1990, the agents raided Steve Jackson Games as part of a massive effort called Operation Sun Devil in which about 150 agents confiscated thousands of computer disks. They seized all of the computer equipment and files used by the company. After examining the contents of the computers, they discovered what they believed was a "how-to" manual for computer criminals. In reality, the document was the rule book for a role-playing game being developed by the company, called "GURPS Cyberpunk," in which players portrayed characters in a futuristic high-tech society.

Jackson asked the Secret Service to return his equipment after copying whatever files they needed, but the agency ignored his pleas. As a result of losing its equipment and having to reconstruct the files for its game, Steve Jackson Games was nearly forced into bankruptcy. Jackson sued the Secret Service for damages.

Legal Issues

The Secret Service argued that its agents had acted in good faith and had reasonable cause to suspect that the Illuminati bulletin board had a copy of the stolen BellSouth document.

Jackson's attorneys argued, however, that the Secret Service had violated the Privacy Protection Act of 1980, which states "Notwithstanding any other law, it shall be unlawful for a government officer or employee, in connection with the investigation . . . of a criminal offense to search for or seize any work product materials possessed by a person reasonably believed to have a purpose to disseminate to the public a newspaper, broadcast, or other similar form of public communication." They argued that the game book was a legitimate publication protected by the Privacy Act. They also accused the Secret Service of violating a law against the "interception" of private e-mail, which the agency had read and destroyed rather than allowing it to reach its intended recipients.

Decision

The court found that the Secret Service had violated Jackson's rights under the Privacy Act:

> *The Court does fault Agent Foley and the Secret Service on the failure to make any investigation of Steve Jackson Games, Inc., prior to March 1, 1990, and to contact Steve Jackson in an attempt to enlist his cooperation and obtain information from him as there was never any basis to suspect Steve Jackson or Steve Jackson Games, Inc., of any criminal activity, and there could be no questions regarding the seizure of computers, disks, and bulletin board and all information thereon, including all back-up materials would have an adverse effect (including completely stopping all activities) on the business of Steve Jackson Games, Inc., and the users of Illuminati bulletin board.*

The judge further noted that "While the content of these publications are not similar to those of daily newspapers, news magazines, or other publications usually thought of by this court as disseminating information to the public, these products come within the literal language of the Privacy Protection Act." The court declined, however, to find that electronic mail had been "intercepted" in the sense meant by the relevant statute.

Jackson was awarded $50,000 in damages plus $1,000 "statutory" damages and attorney's fees. The mail interception issue was appealed by Jackson, but the appeals court found in favor of the Secret Service, stating that the seizing of "stored messages" in a computer fell under the part of the law that had already been dealt with in the preceding case.

Impact

The *Steve Jackson* case had a profound impact on both law enforcement and on the growing online community. Law enforcement was placed on notice that the First Amendment and privacy statutes had to be considered in dealing with computer communications and that although bulletin boards and e-mail don't "look like" traditional newspapers and letter mail, this does not mean they are not constitutionally protected.

For users of bulletin boards and the emerging Internet, the *Steve Jackson* case was a wake-up call about potentially devastating collisions between the seemingly abstract world of cyberspace and the realities of the legal and political system. Some users who were particularly affected included activists John Perry

Barlow and Mitch Kapor, who founded the Electronic Frontier Foundation, a kind of high-tech ACLU, and attorney-activist Mike Godwin, who became immersed in cyberspace issues and would later play an important part in the struggle to prevent censorship on the Internet.

BEACON JOURNAL PUBLISHING V. CITY OF AKRON, 70 OHIO ST. 3D 605 (OHIO 1994)

Background

An editor working on a story for the *Beacon Journal* requested the City of Akron, Ohio, to provide payroll files for city employees under Ohio's public records statute. The city provided the files, which contained information such as employees' names, addresses, phone numbers, education, employment history, and salaries. However, the city deleted the employees' Social Security numbers (SSNs) from the records. The paper then requested the complete records (including the SSNs). The city refused, and the *Journal* filed a complaint saying they were entitled to the complete records under Ohio law.

Legal Issues

The city argued that the SSNs were not "records" as defined by the Ohio statute and that providing them would violate the employees' right to privacy. The appeals court sided with the newspaper, ruling that the SSNs were indeed records and that their disclosure would not impermissibly infringe on privacy. The case then went to the Ohio Supreme Court.

Decision

The supreme court agreed that the SSNs were "records" in that they were part of organized payroll information used by the city. However, the court found that disclosing the SSNs would violate the employees' right of privacy under the federal constitution and therefore cannot be required under the Ohio law. They reasoned that the SSNs were personal information with which the employees had a reasonable expectation of privacy. Further, disclosure of the SSNs could cause serious damage to the persons involved. Quoting a ruling from a similar federal case:

> *Armed with one's SSN, an unscrupulous individual could obtain a person's welfare benefits or Social Security benefits, order new checks at a new address on that person's checking account, obtain credit cards, or even obtain the person's paycheck. . . . Succinctly stated, the harm that can be inflicted from the disclosure of an SSN to an unscrupulous individual is alarming and potentially financially ruinous.*

The court majority found that the high potential for fraud and victimization in releasing the SSNs outweighed any minimal information about government operations that might be gained by the paper and the public. Two dissenting justices, however, complained that the majority had elevated its concern about the effects of disclosure into a legal principle that had no backing in law or precedence.

Impact

This case is a classic conflict between freedom of information and privacy. On the one hand, information about public employees may be necessary for the media to investigate the operation of government. However, the SSN would give investigators a key that could be used to reveal purely personal information and even cause financial ruin.

ARIZONA V. EVANS, 514 U.S. 1 (1995)

Background

Isaac Evans was stopped by Phoenix police because he was driving the wrong way down a one-way street. When asked for his license, Evans told police it had been suspended. The police checked records from their patrol car's computer and discovered an outstanding misdemeanor arrest warrant. Evans was arrested and his car was searched, yielding a bag of marijuana, and he was charged with possession. Later, however, the police discovered that the warrant had been quashed (dismissed) 17 days earlier, but that the computer record had not been updated to reflect the fact.

Legal Issues

Evans's attorney claimed that the bag of marijuana could not be used as evidence because the search had resulted from erroneous computer information. As a general rule, evidence that results from an improper search cannot be used at trial. This is called the "exclusionary rule."

Decision

The trial court agreed with Evans, but the appeals court reinstated the evidence because the mistake had not been made by the police but by a civilian employee. The Arizona Supreme Court then threw the evidence out again, because it concluded that the distinction between police and police employees was not significant, and that one intent of the rule against tainted evidence is to promote careful record keeping.

The case then went to the U.S. Supreme Court. The Court said that regardless of whether the Fourth Amendment might be considered to have been violated, suppressing the evidence was not required when it resulted from a mistake not made by the police itself. The Court did not believe that enforcing the evidence exclusion rule would have any real effect on the accuracy of civilian employees.

Impact

Justice Ruth Bader Ginsburg dissented from the majority opinion, believing that "Widespread reliance on computers to store and convey information generates, along with manifold benefits, new possibilities of error, due to both computer malfunctions and operator mistakes. . . . Computerization greatly amplifies an error's effect, and correspondingly intensifies the need for prompt correction; for inaccurate data can infect not only one agency, but many agencies that share access to the database."

Public concern and pressure for legislation regulating the use of government records (including the ability to correct them promptly) suggests that the public is more in agreement with Ginsburg than with the Court majority.

DOE V. SOUTHEASTERN PENNSYLVANIA TRANSPORTATION AUTHORITY, 72 F.3D 1133 (3D CIR. 1995)

Background

A number of employers provide medical benefits directly rather than through an insurance company. In an effort to combat fraud and drug abuse and contain costs, the Southeastern Pennsylvania Transportation Authority (SEPTA) monitored employees' drug prescriptions. One employee, known in the case under the anonymous name John Doe, had contracted AIDS. Though worried about his condition being disclosed, he was assured by his supervisor that he could fill his prescription for Retrovir, a drug used only for AIDS, without fear of revelation. However, when SEPTA changed pharmacies, it began to receive reports listing employees who had prescriptions costing more than $100, including the name of the drug involved. Doe eventually learned that SEPTA officials had probably become aware of his condition as a result. He sued for violation of privacy. The trial jury awarded Doe $125,000 in damages for his emotional distress. SEPTA appealed.

Legal Issues

The main issue posed in this case is whether a person's medical record is included in the privacy protected by the Constitution. If so, medical privacy must then be balanced against other important interests.

Decision

The appeals court found (referring to the Supreme Court case *Whalen v. Roe*) that persons had a limited right to privacy in their medical records. However, because of Doe's original disclosure of his condition to his supervisor (who was also a doctor), the court held that the fact that Doe's condition was also deduced from the report did not amount to an impermissible violation of privacy. SEPTA had legitimate reasons for monitoring the prescriptions, and they outweighed the relatively minimal infringement on Doe's privacy.

Impact

This case shows a balancing test at work. The fact that SEPTA was a self-insurer gave it a more substantial interest in reviewing the prescription information. However, privacy advocate Daniel Solove argues that the court should have focused on emotional injury Doe suffered because of the fact he could no longer know who was aware of his condition, and the fact that the information was no longer under anyone's control.

RAM AVRAHAMI V. U.S. NEWS & WORLD REPORT, CIRCUIT COURT OF ARLINGTON, VIRGINIA, NO. 95–1318 (1996)

Background

A Virginian named Ram Avrahami was receiving a lot of unwanted junk mail. When he subscribed to *U.S. News & World Report,* he deliberately misspelled his name so he could determine if the magazine would distribute his name without his permission. He then received a mailing from *Smithsonian* magazine using the misspelled name. He sued *U.S. News & World Report* for violation of a Virginia privacy statute (in the modest amount of $1,100).

Legal Issues

Avrahami's attorney argued that the magazine had violated the following language from the Virginia law:

> *Any person whose name, portrait, or picture is used without having first obtained the written consent of such person . . . for advertising purposes or for the purposes of trade, such persons may maintain a suit in equity against the person, firm or corporation so using such person's name, portrait, or picture to prevent and restrain the use thereof; and may also sue and recover damage for any injuries sustained by reason of such use. And if the defendant shall have knowingly used such person's name, portrait or picture in such manner as is forbidden or declared to be unlawful by this chapter, the jury, in its discretion, may award exemplary damages.*

Avrahami's complaint charged that the selling of his name to marketers without consent fit directly into this language, which refers to "name" as well as "portrait or picture."

The magazine disagreed, calling the suit frivolous and arguing that the language of the statute referred to such things as using a name or picture as advertising or in an endorsement, not the routine use of mailing lists by the direct mail industry.

Decision

When the case reached the circuit court the judge ruled against Avrahami, saying that selling a name in a mailing list is not the kind of use "for advertising purposes or for the purposes of trade" that the 1904 statute had in mind. Besides, it was the list itself, not a single name, that had enough value as a commodity for the courts to worry about.

Impact

Direct mailers ridiculed Avrahami's claims as frivolous. Connie F. Heatley, senior vice president of the Direct Mail Marketing Association, also pointed out that "There are 98 million Americans who shop [through mail-order catalogs]. The fact is that people like Mr. Avrahami who don't want their names rented have a way to prevent that." (This can be done by sending one's name to the Direct Mail Preference Service. However, since Avrahami had misspelled his name in order to trace its distribution, the preference service would have been ineffective. Also, such services are not selective, blocking everything or nothing.)

Avrahami lost in the courts, but the argument over junk mail (and its online equivalent, "spam") is far from over. Indeed both Congress and some states have passed anti-spam laws.

DANIEL BERNSTEIN V. U.S. DEPARTMENT OF STATE, 922 F. SUPP. 1426, 1428–1430, N.D. CAL. (1996)

Background

Daniel Bernstein was a mathematician who developed Snuffle, a new encryption algorithm—a method for encoding data by computer so it cannot be read without the code key. He wrote an academic paper describing the algorithm and prepared listings of the source code (the statements in computer language necessary to compile a program that implements the encoding scheme). He wished to present his paper at conferences, including those attended by foreign colleagues.

Encryption technology is regulated under the federal International Traffic in Arms Regulations (ITAR), which regulate the export of "munitions"—weapons or other military hardware. The federal Office of Trade Controls determined that Bernstein's paper was a defense item under ITAR and thus required a license for export. Because the decision seemed vague, Bernstein asked the agency to specify which part—the paper, the encoding system itself, the instruction for use, or the two source code listings—was restricted from export. The agency determined that all five components required a license.

Legal Issues

Bernstein was concerned that the mere act of lecturing about Snuffle or teaching people how to use it might be considered by the government to be illegal "exporting" of a munition. He therefore sued the Department of State, with his main claim being that the application of ITAR to his work violated the First Amendment of the Constitution because it regulated what he could write or speak about on the basis of its content—something the courts have generally forbidden the government to do.

The government lawyers moved that Bernstein's claim be dismissed. They claimed that Bernstein could not appeal the agency's decision in court because under federal law the designation of specific items as non-exportable under ITAR was not "justiciable" (subject to court consideration). Bernstein, however, said that he was not appealing the specific decision, but challenging the constitutionality of the ITAR statute itself.

Decision

Judge Marilyn Hall Patel agreed that the constitutional challenge should be heard. Because the federal agency had removed the paper itself from the restricted export list after Bernstein sued, Patel focused on the remaining issue of the computer source code. Bernstein's lawyer asserted that the source code is, like any other medium of writing, protected under the First Amendment, and that indeed, the fact that computer software can be copyrighted implies that it is a form of creative expression that is constitutionally protected.

The government's defense insisted that software was not a form of speech, because it didn't convey any human-understandable message but rather just carried out actions in the computer. The government therefore argued that software was a form of *conduct* (like flag burning or nude dancing) that shouldn't be protected under the First Amendment—an issue which is itself quite controversial, of course.

The judge noted, however, that in form, source code at least *looks* like writing and that considering it to be "conduct" is an uncomfortable stretch. Once it is decided that source code is a language, the judge believed that

> *the particular language one chooses [does not] change the nature of language for First Amendment purposes. This court can find no meaningful difference between computer language, particularly high-level languages as defined above, and German or French. All participate in a complex system of understood meanings within specific communities. Even object code, which directly instructs the computer, operates as a "language." When the source code is converted into the object code "language," the object program still contains the text of the source program. The expression of ideas, commands, objectives and other contents of the source program are merely translated into machine-readable code.*

The judge also agreed that source code was analogous to other expressions of ideas protected by copyright law.

The judge decided that Bernstein had made "nonfrivolous" constitutional claims that the ITAR statute was overly broad and involved a "prior restraint" (preventing someone from speaking about something rather than simply holding them responsible for any violations of law later).

The government's motion to dismiss Bernstein's claims was denied. And on August 25, 1997, in a final ruling, Judge Patel declared the export restrictions to be unconstitutional and ordered the government not to enforce them. On May 6, 1999, Judge Betty Fletcher of the U.S. Circuit Court of Appeals in San Francisco upheld Patel's decision. In her ruling, she linked access to encryption technology directly to the protection of privacy and the protection of speech given by the First Amendment. However, later in 1999 the court of appeals withdrew its opinion and remanded the case back to the district court. The government then claimed that it would not enforce the cryptography restrictions, making the case against Bernstein moot. However, the original opinion remains influential, and a similar conclusion in favor of speech rights in computer code was eventually reached in *Junger v. Daley* in the 6th Circuit Court of Appeals.

Impact

The *Bernstein* decision gave important protection to the right of free expression for computer scientists developing encryption algorithms or other programs that the government might want to suppress for national security reasons. Thus far, however, the export of actual products that contain only compiled programs, not source code, remains a major issue.

Seeing cryptography as an essential tool for privacy and liberty in the information age, privacy activists continue to challenge government restrictions on the distribution and use of powerful encryption programs. Meanwhile, the government attempted a final run around the issue by offering to provide an officially approved encryption device (the Clipper Chip) that included the capability for the government to read encrypted messages after obtaining a court order.

TIMOTHY R. MCVEIGH V. WILLIAM COHEN ET AL., CIVIL ACTION 98–116, UNITED STATES DISTRICT COURT FOR THE DISTRICT OF COLUMBIA (1998)

Background

The Timothy McVeigh in this case is no relation to the convicted Oklahoma City bomber who shares the same name. He was a highly decorated navy chief petty officer, and the highest-ranking enlisted person aboard the nuclear submarine USS *Chicago*. On September 2, 1997, however, a civilian naval volunteer received an America Online e-mail in connection with a toy drive for the sub crew's children. She noticed that the message sender's online "handle" (a nickname used by users of many online systems) was "boysrch," presumably meaning "boy search." She looked the handle up in the AOL member directory and discovered that the owner of the account was named "Tim." Reading his "member profile," she noticed that he had listed favorite activities such as "collecting pics of other young studs" and "boy watching" and that he had listed his marital status as "gay."

At this point the volunteer only knew that someone who had some connection with the submarine was named Tim and had said that he was gay. She forwarded the mail to her husband, who was also a noncommissioned officer aboard the *Chicago*. The mail found its way to the boat's captain, Commander John Mickey, and a formal investigation began. The investigators suspected that "boysrch" was Timothy McVeigh, and they instructed a paralegal assistant to contact AOL to get information about the identity of that account. An AOL representative identified the customer as Timothy McVeigh.

McVeigh was then informed that the navy had obtained "some indication that he made a statement of homosexuality," which was a violation of the military's new "Don't Ask, Don't Tell, Don't Pursue" policy. This policy was the result of a political compromise that allowed gay people to serve in the military as long as they did not tell people about their sexual preference. In return, the military was not supposed to go out of its way to find and discharge gay personnel.

The navy conducted an administrative discharge hearing where the e-mail was the major item of evidence, and ordered that McVeigh be discharged from the navy on January 16, 1998. But the day before his discharge, McVeigh filed suit to win an injunction, or order from the court, blocking the discharge.

Legal Issues

In seeking the injunction, McVeigh argued that the order should be granted because discharge would cause him great harm by ending his naval career and losing his pension, and that he had a case that was likely to win in a later lawsuit. He said that the U.S. Navy had violated its own "Don't Ask, Don't Tell, Don't Pursue" policy because McVeigh had not "told" anyone about his sexual preference, that the navy should not have launched an investigation on the basis of a "handle" on an otherwise unidentified AOL account, and that in doing so, it had violated McVeigh's privacy.

Decision

Judge Stanley Sporkin agreed that McVeigh's anonymous e-mail was not the kind of revelation that should have triggered an investigation under "Don't Ask, Don't Tell, Don't Pursue." Further, he said, the navy had probably violated the Electronic Communications Privacy Act of 1986. As the judge explained, the ECPA says that the government can obtain information from an online service provider such as AOL "only if (a) it obtains a warrant issued under the Federal Rules of Criminal Procedure or state equivalent; or (b) it gives prior notice to the online subscriber and then issues a subpoena or receives a court order authorizing disclosure of the information in question." The U.S. Navy had not complied with either of these procedures.

Judge Sporkin therefore issued the injunction, blocking McVeigh's discharge. The navy, while not discharging McVeigh, relegated him to clerical duties and refused to allow him to return to his post on the *Chicago*. Judge Sporkin then told the navy that it had to restore McVeigh to his prior position (or an equivalent). The navy at first announced it would appeal the decision, but it then reached a settlement with McVeigh. In May 1998, McVeigh was promoted to master chief petty officer, gaining increased pension benefits as well as payment of his legal fees, and then was honorably discharged.

Impact

The *McVeigh* case did not address the issue of whether the "Don't Ask, Don't Tell, Don't Pursue" policy is itself constitutional, though it has probably discouraged aggressive pursuit of suspected gays by the military. As a privacy issue, however, *McVeigh* affirmed an important privacy right for users of all online systems under the Electronic Communications Privacy Act.

U.S. West v. Federal Communications Commission (U.S. Court of Appeals, 10th District, No. 98-9518 [1999])

Background

This case involves a dispute over regulations developed by the Federal Communications Commission (FCC) to implement privacy provisions of the Telecommunications Act of 1996. Specifically, the provisions required telecommunications providers to "protect the confidentiality of proprietary information of, and relating to . . . customers." This information includes the phone numbers called by a user, the time a call was placed, and the duration of the call. According to the regulation, such information was generally to be used only when necessary for providing the phone service itself—such as for billing, or for purposes such as system testing or security.

A provider could use the information for marketing to its existing customers, as long as the customer already subscribed to the category of service being marketed. (For example: local telephone service, long-distance service, or wireless/cellular service.) However, the permissible marketing was narrowly defined: Phone companies could not use the customer information to market additional services such as voice mail or Internet access, or to attempt to regain a customer who had switched to a competing company. Finally, customers had to "opt in," or agree to the use of their information for marketing.

The telecommunications company U.S. West challenged these regulations in court, seeking to be able to use customer information for a much wider array of marketing efforts and without having to obtain permission first.

Legal Issues

U.S. West and other telecommunications providers argued that the FCC regulations violated the First Amendment by restricting its ability to use "commercial speech" in communicating with customers. The providers also argued that the regulations violated the Fifth Amendment by, in effect, taking away its right to use its property—the proprietary information it had gathered in the course of doing business. The government argued that the regulations did not violate any constitutionally protected right. The regulations did not say that U.S. West could not communicate with its customers; rather, they restricted the use of information that customers might well consider to be private.

Decision

In its decision, the federal appeals court determined that the marketing efforts by phone companies are indeed a form of commercial speech entitled to some protection under the First Amendment if it is not deceptive or misleading. The court then balanced the right to commercial speech against the government's contention that its restrictions on use of telephone customer information were necessary to protect privacy—another important constitutional value. However, the court set a high standard for the government to meet:

> *In the context of a speech restriction imposed to protect privacy by keeping certain information confidential, the government must show that the dissemination of the information desired to be kept private would inflict specific and significant harm on individuals, such as undue embarrassment or ridicule, intimidation or harassment, or misappropriation of sensitive personal information for the purposes of assuming another's identity. Although we may feel uncomfortable knowing that our personal information is circulating in the world, we live in an open society where information may usually pass freely. A general level of discomfort from knowing that people can readily access information about us does not necessarily rise to the level of a substantial state interest . . . for it is not based on an identified harm.*

The court concluded that the government had not shown that the use of telephone customer information in marketing created "substantial harm" in the ways described above, nor did it put customers at any special risk of fraud or other direct harm. Further, regulations like these must be "narrowly tailored" to accomplish their goals without unnecessarily infringing on protected speech. The court believed the government had not shown that an "opt out" system (where customers could say they did not want their information to be used for marketing services to them) would not adequately protect those customers who were concerned about their privacy.

Accordingly, the court overturned the FCC regulations for violation of the First Amendment (the Fifth Amendment "takings" issue, which was pretty weak, was not discussed). The U.S. Supreme Court declined to hear the case on appeal.

Impact

This decision suggests that there is a difference between being offered further products or services from a company with which one has an existing business relationship and being solicited by third parties. Regulations may assume that a customer does not mind solicitations within an existing relationship, or at least, that the company can assume they are acceptable unless the customer opts out. A complication arises, however, when a company includes many unrelated businesses or has developed affiliations with other companies and wants to provide customer information to these other businesses.

CONDON V. RENO, 528 U.S. 141 (2000)

Background

In the 1980s and early 1990s, privacy advocates became increasingly alarmed about the fact that a number of states sold the information on their drivers' licenses to any business that wanted it. Such information included names, addresses, phone numbers, a photograph, certain information about medical conditions, and even Social Security numbers. In response, Congress passed the Driver's Privacy Protection Act. This law prohibited states (or private parties) from selling this type of information without the subject's consent.

The states that had been selling DMV information faced a loss of millions of dollars in annual revenue. One state, South Carolina, sued to overturn the law.

Legal Issues

South Carolina argued that the Driver's Privacy Protection Act violated the Tenth and Eleventh amendments to the U.S. Constitution. The state's argument was based on federalism, or the sharing of power between the federal government and the states. In this view the Congress had no right to tell states what they could do with their own records. The U.S. Attorney General in turn defended the law by saying that the selling of state motor vehicle records necessarily involved interstate commerce (the records could be bought by anyone and were generally used for marketing goods). Thus the DPPA was a proper exercise of the power of Congress to regulate interstate commerce.

Decision

The federal district court agreed with the state and blocked enforcement of the DPPA against the state and its agencies. The Court of Appeals for the Fourth Circuit also agreed with the state's position. The Justice Department then appealed to the U.S. Supreme Court.

The Court's opinion, written by Chief Justice William Rehnquist, squarely concluded that state motor vehicle records fell within the power of Congress to regulate interstate commerce:

> *The motor vehicle information which the States have historically sold is used by insurers, manufacturers, direct marketers, and others engaged in interstate commerce to contact drivers with customized solicitations. The information is also used in the stream of interstate commerce by various public and private entities for matters related to interstate motoring. Because drivers' information is, in this*

context, an article of commerce, its sale or release into the interstate stream of business is sufficient to support congressional regulation.

The Court also rejected the Tenth Amendment challenge, noting that the law does not require that states enforce the regulations against their citizens. Rather, it is the states themselves, as owners of the records, that are regulated.

Impact

By upholding the Drivers Privacy Protection Act, the Supreme Court left in place protections against a person's motor vehicle or driving information being sold by states to marketers or others who might use them for solicitation or even criminal harassment.

In Re Toysmart.com, LLC (Case No. 00-13995-CJK [Bankr. E.D. Mass. July 20, 2000])

Background

Toysmart.com, an Internet toy store, was one of many "dot-coms" that went bankrupt in the 2000–01 period. The bankruptcy court had to decide what to do with one of Toysmart's most potentially valuable assets, its list of more than 200,000 customers. The customer information included names, addresses, ages of children, records of purchases, and a toy wish list.

What complicated matters was that Toysmart had posted a privacy policy that pledged that any information submitted by customers would only be used to "personalize" the Web shopping experience. The information would never be shared with a third party. This privacy policy also allowed Toysmart to display the TRUSTe seal, a certification of privacy practices relied upon by many online consumers.

Nevertheless, when it entered bankruptcy, Toysmart attempted to sell its customer list in order to help pay back creditors. The Federal Trade Commission (FTC) filed a complaint to try to stop the sale.

Legal Issues

The FTC argued that by promising never to disclose customer information and then doing so, Toysmart was engaging in a "deceptive practice" in violation of the FTC Act. Further, Toysmart had, during a "dinosaur trivia" contest, collected information from children under 13 years of age, without providing notice to parents and obtaining their consent. This was a violation of the Children's Online Privacy Protection Act.

Decision

Toysmart and FTC settled the case. Toysmart agreed that it would sell the customer list only to a "qualified buyer" approved by the bankruptcy court who would agree to be bound by the original privacy agreement and be liable for any subsequent violations. If the buyer wants to change the privacy policy, it must give notice, and the changes can apply only to customer information provided after the change in policy, unless the consumer opts in (or affirmatively consents).

One FTC commissioner dissented from the settlement. While he agreed that binding any new buyer to the privacy agreement was much better than an unrestricted sale, consumers were entitled to rely on the original promise that their information would "never" be disclosed to a third party.

Impact

This case puts some enforceable teeth in privacy agreements as contracts between consumers and retailers. However, one of the biggest online retailers, Amazon.com, subsequently changed its privacy agreement to allow transfer of customer information as an "asset" to any company that acquires them in the future.

INDIVIDUAL REFERENCE SERVICES GROUP V. FEDERAL TRADE COMMISSION (U.S. DISTRICT COURT DC, CIVIL ACTION NO.: 00-1828 [ESH], 2001)

Background

TransUnion is a major credit bureau that is also considered to be a "credit reporting agency" under the Fair Credit Reporting Act. The company collects transaction information from financial institutions, storing the information in a massive database called CRONUS. The database is used to generate credit reports that include identifying information (the consumer's name, address, Social Security number, and so on) and "tradeline" data containing account details and payment history for credit cards, car loans, mortgages, and other forms of credit. (Although details differ, other credit reporting agencies have similar procedures.)

Credit reporting agencies make the "credit headers" containing identifying information available to businesses and government agencies that use them for marketing (targeted mailings or phone calls) and for fraud prevention, and for such services as searching for potential organ donors. TransUnion and other companies also offer targeted marketing programs in which they use the header and credit information to identify persons who might be likely to be interested in a particular product or service, as well as providing aggregate data for consumer and market research.

A provision of the Gramm-Leach-Bliley Act (GLBA) of 1999 specifies that financial institutions protect certain aspects of the privacy of customer's personal information. Individual References Services Group is an industry coalition consisting of the major credit bureaus (TransUnion, Experian, and Equifax) plus database companies such as LEXIS-NEXIS. This group went to court to overturn the privacy regulations, which threatened their ability to create and sell reports on consumers.

Legal Issues

The Individual Reference Services Group made several arguments against the regulations the FTC had designed to implement the GLBA. First, the industry group argued that the regulations covered "nonpublic personal" information that was not financial in nature, even though the GLBA statute said that it was restricted to financial information. They also argued that the regulations should not have extended to nonfinancial institutions and that the GLBA (but not the regulations) allowed consumer reporting agencies to use account numbers for marketing purposes.

The industry group also made several constitutional arguments: that the regulation was overbroad and restricted commercial speech protected by the First Amendment, and that the lack of due process in adopting the regulations and their differing treatment of consumer reporting agencies and other types of companies violated the Fifth Amendment.

Decision

The court noted that in a previous decision, *TransUnion v. FTC* (2001), it had ruled that lists of names and addresses of consumers whose tradeline information (such as credit limits or types of loans) were selected for marketing purposes qualified as consumer reports under the Fair Credit Reporting Act. Meanwhile, the GLBA had been passed and implemented. It was designed primarily to make the financial services industry more competitive. However, the act's authors, knowing that competitive pressure might also lead to practices that intrude on consumer privacy, also included provisions requiring that institutions protect that privacy. The law broadly defined information relating to financial transactions.

The court disposed of the argument that the records sold to marketers were not covered by the GLBA, as well as the argument that credit reporting companies (such as TransUnion) were not "financial institutions" subject to the regulations. The industry's constitutional arguments were also disposed of as similar to those rejected in the earlier *TransUnion* decision. The kind of information involved in credit reporting has little to do with speech about public issues envisaged by the First Amendment: It is "commercial speech" that receives a lesser degree of First Amendment protection.

Because the GLBA specifies its privacy concerns and is narrowly tailored to protecting them, the provisions restricting selling credit information to marketers are constitutional. (The court observed that TransUnion and other credit reporting agencies can still distribute information if they obtain the permission of the affected consumers.) The regulations are not "arbitrary and capricious" and do not single out credit reporting agencies, since they apply to any company that obtains and seeks to use consumer credit information.

Impact

This and other decisions such as *TransUnion Corp. v. Federal Trade Commission* (2001) establish that credit reporting companies have no inherent right to repackage and sell the information they gather in the course of the billions of transactions that take place every year in the marketplace. Whether consumers must "opt out" or companies are required to ask for explicit permission to use data is a matter for Congress and the political process.

KYLLO V. UNITED STATES, NO. 99-8508 (2001)

Background

When an agent of the U.S. Department of the Interior suspected that Danny Kyllo was growing marijuana in his home in Florence, Oregon, he and a colleague used a thermal imager to scan Kyllo's home at night. The imager detects infrared (heat) radiation, giving outlines of areas or sources that are relatively warmer than their surroundings. The scan showed that the roof over Kyllo's garage and one wall of his house were hotter than the rest of the home or neighboring homes. The agent concluded that Kyllo was using halide lights ("grow lights") to grow marijuana. Based on the imagery and other evidence, such as excessive utility bills, the agent obtained a warrant, entered Kyllo's home, and discovered more than 100 growing marijuana plants. When Kyllo was indicted for growing marijuana, he moved to have the evidence seized from his home suppressed on grounds that it was based on an unlawful search.

The Court of Appeals for the Ninth Circuit ordered the district court to determine whether the device used was "intrusive." The district court concluded that because the device showed only a crude image of heat sources and "did not show any people or activity within the walls of the structure," use of the device was not intrusive. The court of appeals eventually affirmed the district court's opinion, and Kyllo appealed to the U.S. Supreme Court.

Legal Issues

The issue here is whether use of a "passive" surveillance technology (a thermal imager in this case) is intrusive enough to amount to a "search" under the Fourth Amendment. The district court had concluded that the crude and limited nature of the imagery obtained meant that it did not show the kind of activities for which Kyllo had a legitimate expectation of privacy.

Decision

The Supreme Court disagreed with the district court. In an opinion written by Justice Antonin Scalia, the Court noted that it had previously declared that a mere visual inspection from outside is not a "search" in the meaning of the Fourth Amendment. However, in *Katz v. United States* (1967), the Court ruled that use of a listening device attached to the outside of a phone booth did violate the Fourth Amendment because the user of the booth has a reasonable expectation of privacy. Similarly, aerial surveillance of a house was not considered a "search" because a resident has no reasonable expectation that the outside and surroundings of a house won't be seen from the air.

Next, the Court considered how much "technological enhancement" of a search from the outside of a house might be permissible. For example, the Court reserved the question of whether "enhanced aerial photography" might be too intrusive, especially when the area searched is directly outside or adjacent to a house (such as a backyard).

The Court concluded that

> *obtaining by sense-enhancing technology any information regarding the interior of the home that could not otherwise have been obtained without physical "intrusion into a constitutionally protected area" . . . constitutes a search—at least where the technology in question is not in general public use. This assures preservation of that degree of privacy against government that existed when the Fourth Amendment was adopted. On the basis of this criterion the information obtained by the thermal imager in this case was the product of a search.*

The majority opinion rejected claims by the government that use of the imager was permissible because it only detected heat from "off the wall" and did not penetrate "through the wall." It also rejected the idea that the limited amount of information obtained should be a criterion for whether a search violates the Fourth Amendment. The case was therefore returned to the Circuit Court of Appeals to determine if evidence other than that obtained from imagery was sufficient to have obtained a warrant.

Impact

With the ever-growing capability of surveillance technology and the impetus of the war on drugs (and today, the war on terrorism), the Supreme Court seems in recent years to be trying to draw some sort of line to protect the privacy in and around a home that people expect and need. Such an effort would seem necessary if the Fourth Amendment is to continue to have meaning in the 21st century.

UNITED STATES V. NICODEMO S. SCARFO ET AL. CRIMINAL ACTION NO. 00-404 (NHP) (2001)

Background

The issue of interest in this case arose during pretrial discovery motions in the case of Nicodemo S. Scarfo and codefendant Frank Paolercio, who were accused of conducting illegal gambling and loansharking operations. After an initial search of their premises, FBI agents discovered a personal computer that contained an encrypted file titled "Factors." The agents believed that this file contained evidence of illegal activity.

Because they were unable to determine the passphrase needed to open the file, the agents obtained a warrant to install a "keylogger" on the computer. This software surreptitiously intercepts and records the user's keystrokes. It enabled the agents to capture and use the passphrase to open the Factors file.

Legal Issues

Scarfo's attorneys argued that the evidence from the Factors file should be suppressed because use of the keylogger violated federal wiretapping statutes. This is because the computer in question had a modem connection and the user had an America Online account. If the keylogger captured keystrokes while the computer was online, its use might amount to an illegal interception of wire communications.

The federal district judge asked the government to provide details on how the keylogger operated, in order to determine whether use of the device violated federal law. The government refused to provide these details to the defendant but offered them to the judge, requesting that they be treated as classified. After viewing the classified material, the judge agreed with the government that the details of the keylogger could be kept secret. Scarfo's attorneys were provided with an unclassified summary.

Scarfo's attorneys claimed that the unclassified summary was inadequate and did not enable them to effectively challenge the warrant. In addition to claiming that the keylogging amounted to an illegal wiretap, the defense also argued that by capturing keystrokes other than the needed passphrase, the warrant authorizing the keylogging was an overbroad "general warrant" that violated the Fourth Amendment.

Decision

The district judge ruled that the search warrant was specific (in describing the passphrase) and was supported by probable cause. The fact that additional keystrokes must necessarily be captured does not turn the search into a general "fishing expedition" any more than having to go through irrelevant folders in a filing cabinet would invalidate a more traditional form of search.

The judge ruled that the unclassified summary provided by the government was sufficient to allow for an effective defense. Finally, the judge concluded that a keyboard logging system did not intercept any wire communications—and in fact, had been configured by the agents to avoid intercepting keystrokes while data was being sent through the modem. Scarfo later entered into a plea bargain, and thus the judge's decision was not appealed.

Impact

The real interest in this case arose from the use of secret surveillance technology by the government. The government's insistence that details of the keylogging system be classified conflicted with the defendant's ability to challenge the warrant and, more broadly, the ability of citizens to decide what forms of government surveillance are appropriate. This conflict has been heightened during the "war on terrorism" period and is likely to remain vigorous.

COMMONWEALTH V. SOURCE ONE ASSOCIATES, 436 MASS. 118 (2002)

Background

An investigation company called Source One Associates offered to obtain (for a fee) financial information relating to persons of interest for financial institutions, investigators, or other third parties. Source One's investigators frequently obtained this information by first using credit reports to find a person's bank accounts, and then calling the bank while posing as a bank security official or as the account holder. This enabled them to obtain the desired information (such as the amount of the bank balance).

Legal Issues

The state of Massachusetts sued Source One in Superior Court, claiming that the company obtained information about persons without their consent and used deceptive practices in violation of state consumer protection laws. Source One claimed that its use of credit reports was legitimate and that the state had not proved otherwise.

Decision

The Superior Court judge noted that under the federal Fair Credit Reporting Act, credit reports could only be obtained with the permission of the person being reported on, or in connection with certain legitimate transactions such as credit requests or employment or insurance applications. Source One had not obtained the reports in order to process a legitimate transaction by the reported person. Rather, they used the reports in order to obtain information that could be used for further investigation and creation of a report to sell to a third party. Further, the judge agreed that Source One must have used deception in order to obtain financial information from banks in violation of state law.

The court ordered Source One to pay $500,000 in damages (plus court fees and costs) for an estimated 1,000 instances of violating state law. Source One was also ordered no longer to obtain information without the subject's permission and not to use deceptive practices in obtaining information from banks or other third parties. Source One appealed to the Massachusetts Supreme Court, but that court affirmed the lower court's decision.

Impact

The illegitimate use of credit reports by private investigators and data brokers is a significant threat to privacy. Further, impersonation or "pretexting" can often be used to obtain information despite whatever privacy safeguards banks or other institutions might have in place. Decisions like this one give victims some recourse and may enable states to more effectively prevent such abuses.

HELEN REMSBURG V. DOCUSEARCH, No. 2002-55, NEW HAMPSHIRE SUPREME COURT (2003)

Background

On October 15, 1999, cyberstalker Liam Youens fatally shot Amy Boyer outside her workplace. Youens had learned of Boyer's place of employment after obtaining her Social Security number and other personal information by hiring DocuSearch, an online "information broker" that had in turn obtained access to Boyer's credit records by pretending to be doing a legitimate credit check.

Legal Issues

Boyer's estate sued DocuSearch, arguing that the agency was liable for subjecting Boyer to "an unreasonable risk of harm" in providing information about her to Youens. Among others, there was also the question of whether DocuSearch committed an "intrusion against seclusion" against Boyer and whether she had a reasonable expectation of privacy that was violated by the firm's actions.

Decision

The court ruled that an information broker does have a legal duty toward someone whose information is being obtained without their consent. A Social Security number is something that persons have an expectation will be private, and an information broker is liable for damages that might be caused by revealing it without permission.

Impact

Information brokers are largely unregulated and have provided information useful to cyberstalkers and identity thieves. Holding them legally liable for releasing certain personal information may at least deter legitimate information brokers and allow for recovery of damages against illegitimate ones.

AMERICAN COUNCIL OF LIFE INSURERS V. VERMONT DEPARTMENT OF BANKING, INSURANCE, SECURITIES, AND HEALTHCARE ADMINISTRATION, DOCKET No. 56-1-02 (WASHINGTON SUPERIOR COURT, FEB. 12, 2004)

Background

The Vermont Department of Banking, Insurance, Securities, and Healthcare Administration (BISHCA) issued a regulation that required that insurance companies obtain policyholders' permission before disclosing nonpublic financial and health information to unaffiliated companies. This is called an "opt-in" system, as opposed to "opt-out," where the company can reveal information unless explicitly asked not to. The life insurance association sued, seeking to overturn the regulation.

Legal Issues

The insurers argued that opt-in was too strict a standard and that most states, following the lead of the federal Gramm-Leach-Bliley Act (GLBA), had adopted an opt-out standard. They argued that the state legislature had not delegated to the BISHCA the power to adopt such regulations. Further, they argued that the opt-in requirement violated the insurers' commercial speech rights under the First Amendment because it went beyond what was necessary to further the state's legitimate interest in protecting privacy.

Decision

The court found that the legislature's statutory language had delegated sufficient power to the BISHCA. Further, it found that the state's "substantial interest" in privacy would be equally served by an opt-in or opt-out requirement. While acknowledging that opt-in is likely to make it harder for the insurance companies to disclose information, opt-out would leave more consumers not having consented to have their information shared. Therefore, requiring opt-in is a "reasonable fit" between the regulation and the state's interest in protecting privacy. The regulation was upheld.

Impact

This state court decision obviously does not set a national precedent. However, the relatively light weight courts often give to commercial speech as against substantial state interests (such as privacy) may suggest that First Amendment arguments against opt-in requirements will not generally succeed. Business interests are likely to focus their efforts on enshrining opt-out in federal laws and then having those laws preempt state legislation.

DOE V. CHAO, U.S. SUPREME COURT, NO. 02-1377 (2004)

Background

A group of coal miners filed claims with the Department of Labor for benefits for "black lung" disease. In the process of investigating the claims, the government disclosed the miners' Social Security numbers (which were used as identification numbers) to a variety of interested parties. The numbers also found their way into legal decisions and research databases. Several miners sued the

Department of Labor, alleging that disclosure of the SSNs violated the federal Privacy Act and that they were entitled to statutory damages. Although the lower court rejected most of the claims, it granted $1,000 damages to complainant Doe (an anonymously named miner), saying he had shown sufficiently that he had suffered "actual damages" as a result of the disclosure of his SSN.

Legal Issues

The other miners appealed, arguing that it is not necessary to prove actual damages to prevail under the Privacy Act, or at least that emotional damages were sufficient. The government argued that actual damages means monetary loss, not emotional harm. The Appeals Court for the Fourth Circuit sided with the government. The U.S. Supreme Court then agreed to hear the case.

Decision

By a 6-3 majority, the Supreme Court ruled that the plain language of the Privacy Act requires that actual monetary harm must be suffered before a person can recover under the Privacy Act for disclosure of a Social Security number.

Impact

Privacy advocates were naturally disappointed by this ruling and have pointed out that any disclosure of a person's Social Security number has potentially serious consequences that at minimum are likely to cause emotional distress. However, they will have to seek a legislative remedy.

GILMORE V. ASHCROFT (DISTRICT COURT FOR NORTHERN DISTRICT OF CALIFORNIA, NO. C 02-3444 SI [2004])

Background

In recent years passengers wishing to board airlines within the United States have generally been required to present an official picture ID such as a driver's license or to submit to a physical search. However, it has not always been clear whether this requirement is a matter of federal directive or airline policy. Civil liberties activist John Gilmore decided to challenge this requirement, believing that it violated privacy and the right to travel and did not contribute to security against terrorism. When Gilmore was refused boarding at the airport on July 4, 2002, he sued the U.S. government and Southwest Airlines.

Legal Issues

Gilmore alleged that the policy violated the U.S. Constitution in several ways. The requirements (and the authority for them) were not clearly stated, and this vagueness violated due process rights under the Fourteenth Amendment. The requirement amounted to an unreasonable search and seizure under the Fourth Amendment (since there was no probable cause), and finally, by preventing Gilmore from traveling by air, the policy violated the First Amendment's guarantees of freedom of association and the right to petition the government for redress of grievances. Further, in his brief Gilmore argued that the government was using the identification requirement in connection with credit records and other databases "in order to create dossiers on every traveling citizen."

The federal government argued that such claims about government surveillance programs were essentially irrelevant and that Gilmore only had standing to challenge the requirement for identification. Further, Gilmore had not suffered any legally recognizable injury.

Decision

The court began by agreeing with the government's argument about standing, dismissing all Gilmore's claims except the challenge to the identification requirement itself. The court then said that, assuming identification was actually being required by the government, such an order would have to have come from the Federal Aviation Administration (FAA) or Transportation Security Administration (TSA). By statute, any question about the requirement's vagueness could be reviewed only by an appeals court, not the district court.

The court dismissed Gilmore's complaint about unreasonable search and seizure by noting that this Fourth Amendment requirement applies only to a situation where someone faces arrest, detention, or some other sanction by the government. Gilmore faced only the loss of the ability to fly. While significant, this does not create a Fourth Amendment issue.

The court also dismissed Gilmore's argument about being denied the right to travel without being given due process. The court explained that the Constitution did not guarantee the right to travel by any particular means of transportation.

Finally, the court rejected the argument that barring Gilmore from the plane violated his right to free association and to petition the government for redress of grievances. The judge pointed out that Gilmore had other ways to travel and that any effect of the identification requirement was thus too indirect to amount to a constitutional violation.

Impact

Even most privacy advocates would probably agree that Gilmore's challenge to the identification requirement was quixotic and unlikely to succeed. Gilmore and others have made plausible arguments that identification requirements are not likely to prevent terrorists from getting onto a plane, at least until the ID cards are backed up by biometrics and the kind of database Gilmore seems to be objecting to.

The judge's noting that the right to travel does not imply a right to travel by a particular means echoes the ruling of the Supreme Court in *U.S. v. Miller* in refusing to acknowledge that certain institutions (such as airlines and banks) are not really optional for participation in modern life. Privacy advocates consider such reasoning to be narrow and unrealistic.

HIIBEL V. SIXTH JUDICIAL DISTRICT COURT OF NEVADA, NO. 03-5554 (2004)

Background

Nevada and a number of other states have laws requiring that a person stopped by police give them his or her name. (The person need not respond to any other inquiry nor provide an ID card.) Larry Dudley Hiibel was stopped by Deputy Lee Dove, who was investigating a tip that a man was punching a woman in his pickup truck. Hiibel was standing next to a pickup truck; his teenaged daughter was in the cab. In the stop, which was filmed by a camera mounted on the police car, Hiibel, possibly intoxicated, repeatedly refused to tell Dove his name. Dove arrested Hiibel for that refusal. He was convicted and fined $250. The case was then appealed and eventually reached the U.S. Supreme Court.

Legal Issues

Hiibel's attorneys, supported by the ACLU and other civil liberties groups, argued that the Nevada law violated the Fifth Amendment by effectively making it a crime to remain silent when questioned by a police officer. They were joined by homeless advocates who feared that police might harass the homeless (many of whom may be mentally ill) by demanding they identify themselves.

Decision

The Supreme Court upheld the Nevada law by a narrow 5-4 majority. Justice Anthony Kennedy said that asking a person only for a name was not a significant intrusion on privacy and did not provide information that could be legally used against the person. This minimal intrusion did not weigh heavily against the state's need to investigate crime and for police officers to identify possibly dangerous persons.

In dissent, Justice John Paul Stevens said that Hiibel's name could be used to learn incriminating information about him. Thus, compelling him to give his name was compelling him to aid in his own incrimination. Several other dissenters agreed with a concurring opinion in *Terry v. Ohio* (1968), which suggested that while police have the right to stop persons when they have a reasonable suspicion of illegal activity, the person stopped has no obligation to talk to the police.

Impact

Most people would not consider it unreasonable for the police to merely ask their name. However, the existence of interlinked computer records and a possibly emerging national database means that a name can potentially give the police access to a vast amount of information, incriminatory or otherwise. (It should be noted, however, that the Nevada law did not require that a person show any form of identification. It is unclear whether such a requirement would be upheld.)

CHAPTER 3

CHRONOLOGY

This chapter presents a chronology of important events involving privacy issues, particularly issues related to information privacy.

1690

■ John Locke writes *Two Treatises on Government*, in which he lays the basis that the government is accountable for protecting the rights of the individual.

1791

■ The Bill of Rights to the U.S. Constitution is ratified, including the Fourth and Fifth Amendments, which protect citizens against unwarranted violation of privacy by the government.

1800s

■ The Industrial Revolution and urbanization lead to new social rules defining places and activities that should be considered private.

1861

■ The American Civil War begins, and new communications technology plays a vital role. The Union and Confederacy tap each other's telegraph lines.

1876

■ Alexander Graham Bell introduces the telephone. The invention changes the nature of conversation and raises the question of whether phone conversations are presumed to be private.

1890

■ Samuel D. Warren and future Supreme Court justice Louis Brandeis write a groundbreaking legal article titled "The Right of Privacy." They also warn that the telephone and other inventions may be threatening that right.

■ The use of electromechanical punch card machines by the U.S. Census foreshadows the later development of computerized databases.

1928

■ In *Olmstead v. U.S.*, the Supreme Court refuses to apply the Fourth Amendment to prohibit wiretapping without a warrant.

1939

■ World War II begins. Allies use primitive electronic computers to break codes from Axis cipher machines.

1948

■ Claude Shannon of MIT writes a seminal paper on cryptographic theory, which ties into the growing interest in the field by government security agencies.

1952

■ As the Cold War deepens, secret government cryptography efforts are assigned to the new National Security Agency (NSA).

1965

■ In the *Griswold* case, the Supreme Court declares that the Constitution implies a right of privacy with regard to contraception.
■ A proposed central government data bank arouses the concern of privacy advocates.

1966

■ Congress passes the Freedom of Information Act, which provides a way for citizens to request many kinds of information about the operation of government.

1967

■ Journalist David Kahn publishes *The Codebreakers*, arousing public interest in cryptography.
■ The Supreme Court reverses the *Olmstead* decision, declaring that the government must get a warrant to wiretap a suspect *(Katz v. United States)*.

1968

■ Congress passes the Wiretap Act of 1968, codifying the previous year's Supreme Court decision in *Katz v. United States*.

Chronology

1969

- The ARPANET, funded by the Defense Department, comes online. At first restricted to government agencies and universities, it would eventually evolve into the Internet.

1970s

- Credit cards begin to come into widespread use. While hailed as a convenience, their use requires the compilation of large databases of information about cardholders, leading to privacy concerns.

1970

- Congress passes the Fair Credit Reporting Act, giving consumers the right to request and correct information kept by credit bureaus.

1972

- The Advisory Committee on Automated Personal Data Systems to the Secretary of the Department of Health, Education, and Welfare states basic principles for protecting privacy in the Information Age. These include disclosure of information-gathering activities, the right of individuals to correct information about them, and guarantees for accuracy and control of disclosure of information.
- The Watergate break-in and cover-up leads to greater public concern about the misuse of surveillance by the government.

1973

- In *Roe v. Wade*, the Supreme Court limits the ability of the government to regulate abortion, seeing an expanded area of "decisional" privacy in intimate and family matters.

1974

- Congress passes the Privacy Act of 1974, implementing fundamental principles of privacy and access to government records.
- Congress passes the Family Education Rights and Privacy Act of 1974, which gives parents or adult students the right to access and correct their school records, as well as limiting disclosure to third parties.
- The Supreme Court upholds the Bank Secrecy Act, which requires that banks track many details of transactions in order to fight drugs and money laundering *(California Bankers' Association v. Schulz)*.

1976

- Whitfield Diffie and Martin Hellman publish "New Directions in Cryptography," a paper that creates the basis for public-key cryptography.

- The Supreme Court declares that individuals have no "expectation of privacy" in their banking or other financial transactions *(United States v. Miller)*.
- Congress passes tax reform legislation that authorizes state agencies to use Social Security numbers for identification purposes. As this practice is taken up by private companies for identifying financial accounts, the numbers will make people vulnerable to invasion of privacy or identity theft.

1977

- The U.S. Privacy Protection Study Commission warns of the growing threat to privacy caused by large, increasingly interlinked computer databases.
- Congress passes the Fair Debt Collection Practices Act, which prohibits a variety of abusive activities by bill collectors.

1978

- Congress passes two laws to strengthen financial privacy: the Electronic Funds Transfer Act of 1978 and the Right to Financial Privacy Act of 1978.
- Ron Rivest, Adi Shamir, and Len Adelman at MIT fill in the gaps in the theory of public-key cryptography and create a cryptosystem that will be called RSA.

1985

- The Supreme Court rules that students are protected by the Fourth Amendment, but that schools can conduct "reasonable" searches without obtaining a warrant *(New Jersey v. T.L.O.)*.

1986

- Congress passes the Electronic Communications Privacy Act of 1986, which extends the protections of the Wiretap Act of 1968 to include computer data transmissions and e-mail.
- Congress passes the Electronic Freedom of Information Act (EFOIA), which applies freedom of information principles to requests for computerzied government records.

1987

- The Supreme Court rules that employers can conduct "reasonable" searches in the workplace, but that employees do have an "expectation of privacy" in some areas *(O'Connor v. Ortega)*.
- During the failed nomination of Robert Bork to the Supreme Court, the judge's video rental records are revealed by the press. This leads to the passage of the Video Privacy Protection Act of 1988.

1988

- Congress passes the Employee Polygraph Protection Act of 1988, which bans the use of lie detectors and similar devices by employers in most cases.

■ Congress passes the Computer Matching and Privacy Protection Act of 1988, which provides appeals procedures and other protections for individuals threatened with loss of benefits based on computer matching of government databases (such as comparing tax records with welfare rolls).

1990

■ A massive anti-hacker sweep by the Secret Service leads to the seizure of computers belonging to Steve Jackson, a game publisher. In 1993, a court rules the seizure violates protection for publishers under the Privacy Act of 1980 and awards Jackson modest damages.
■ A California court rules that employers have the right to monitor workplace e-mail *(Alana Shoars v. Epson America, Inc.).*

1991

■ In two cases the California Supreme Court balances the "reasonable" interests of the organization against the individual's right to privacy *(Soroka v. Dayton Hudson Corp., Hill v. NCAA).*
■ Lotus and Equifax plan to offer a CD-ROM database of information on 120 million consumers, but withdraw the plan after public and privacy advocates object.
■ Programmer-activist Philip Zimmermann releases Pretty Good Privacy, an easy-to-use encryption program. Government security agencies are not amused.
■ The federal government proposes the Clipper Chip, a device that would provide data encryption but would also allow the government to read encrypted data. Privacy advocates and industry groups strongly oppose the proposal.
■ Congress passes the Telephone Consumer Protection Act, which requires that telemarketers maintain a list of people who do not wish to be called.

1992

■ The Justice Department promotes legislation that would force phone companies to add built-in wiretapping facilities to phone systems in order to facilitate government surveillance efforts. (The legislation failed, but was revived in 1994 as the Digital Telephony Act.)
■ Congress passes the Fair Credit Reporting Act, strengthening protections for consumers in dealing with credit bureaus and users of credit information.

1993

■ The first graphical web-browsing software is released. Use of the Internet by the general public starts to grow rapidly.
■ A report by the federal Office of Technology Assessment criticizes the lack of safeguards for patients' medical information.

1994

- Congress passes the Telemarketing and Consumer Fraud and Abuse Prevention Act, which regulates deceptive or annoying practices by telemarketers.
- The Clinton administration proposes that telephone companies be required to build into their systems the capability for the FBI and other law enforcement agencies to tap phone lines automatically. Privacy advocates view the proposal as an invitation to widespread abuse.

1995

- The Supreme Court rules that computer mistakes made by a civilian employee do not taint evidence gathered by police relying on that record *(Arizona v. Evans)*.
- The European Union's Data Protection Directive provides for strong privacy protection.
- The U.S. Secret Service and the Drug Enforcement Agency (DEA) obtain the first Internet wiretap to gather evidence on illegal "cloning" of cell phone service.
- The federal Privacy Working Group issues its *Principles for Providing and Using Personal Information*. The principles would influence many subsequent privacy regulations and policies.

1996

- "Electronic commerce" (e-commerce) grows, but identity theft becomes a bigger problem, with cases more than doubling since 1992.
- Ram Avrahami fails in his attempt to sue *U.S. News & World Report* for selling his name to marketers without his permission.

1997

- *July:* The Federal Trade Commission warns marketers not to collect information from children online without disclosure and parental permission.
- *August 25:* A California district court rules that the source code (computer language) of Daniel Bernstein's cryptography program is protected by the First Amendment *(Daniel Bernstein v. U.S. Department of State)*.
- *September:* An AOL user profile with gay-related sentiments triggers the investigation of U.S. Navy Chief Petty Officer Timothy McVeigh.

1998

- *January:* McVeigh wins a court order blocking the navy from discharging him. The order is based in part on the navy's probable violation of the Electronic Communications Privacy Act.
- *August:* The Federal Trade Commission settles a complaint against GeoCities, a major online service provider. The company agrees to explain its pri-

vacy policies and agrees not to collect information from children without parental consent.

- *Fall:* American online businesses face being excluded from Europe because American privacy standards are much weaker than those of Europe. Negotiations continue in an attempt to resolve the issue.
- *December:* The Federal Deposit Insurance Corporation announces "Know Your Customer" regulations. The regulations, strongly opposed by bankers and privacy advocates, would require banks to create "profiles" of a customer's typical activity and to watch closely for "unusual" transactions. After the Libertarian Party and other opponents organized a campaign that flooded the FDIC with e-mail, the proposed regulations were withdrawn March 1999.

1999

- *January:* The giant computer chip maker Intel arouses the concern of privacy activists when plans are revealed to include serial numbers in forthcoming Pentium III chips that could be used to track the location of computers.
- *February:* Faced by strong criticism from privacy groups, the states of Florida, South Carolina, and Colorado back down from their plans to sell driver's license photos to a private company for use in preventing check fraud.
- *February 2:* A federal jury brought in a verdict of more than $107 million against the operators of an anti-abortion web site that had listed the names and home addresses of abortion providers. The jury concluded the listings constituted threats that were not protected by freedom of speech. The verdict is eventually affirmed by the U.S. Supreme Court.
- *April:* Microsoft Corporation and the Electronic Frontier Foundation Jointly propose new guidelines for the Privacy Preferences Project, which would assure online consumers that businesses were adhering to industry privacy standards.
- The Federal Trade Commission issues regulations implementing legislation that in most cases requires parental consent for online gathering and distribution of information from children under 13.
- In response to privacy concerns, the federal Health Care Financing Administration scales back its plans to collect personal information from patients receiving home health care.
- The Federal Aviation Administration (FAA) proposes the use of computer-assisted screening procedures to select passengers for additional searches both randomly and on those who fit the profile of suspected terrorists. Privacy advocates argue that such searches are unreasonable and lack probable cause, thereby violating the Fourth Amendment.
- *May:* The U.S. Ninth District Court of Appeals affirms an earlier district court ruling declaring that export restrictions on cryptographic "software and related devices and technology are in violation of the First Amendment on the grounds of prior restraint." The government files an appeal to the Supreme Court.

- *May:* An e-commerce industry survey reveals that 90 percent of web sites still do not have comprehensive privacy policies that give customers control over the use of their information.
- *August:* The 10th U.S. Circuit Court of Appeals rules that telephone companies can share information about subscribers' calling habits with marketers without getting permission.
- *October:* Amy Boyer, a 20-year-old college student, is murdered in a parking lot. Investigation reveals that she had been stalked online for several years by Liam Youens, a fellow student. Youens had used the Internet to obtain Boyer's personal information and had recounted his obsession with her in an online diary. It is the first known cyberstalking murder.
- *November 11:* President Clinton signs the Gramm-Leach-Bliley Act. While making it easier for financial institutions to merge into conglomerates, the law also imposes some restrictions on sharing of information and allows consumers to deny permission for sharing data with unaffiliated companies.

2000

- The FBI begins secretly to use a program called Carnivore to sift through e-mail and other communications. The program is used only in a handful of investigations.
- In this census year a number of privacy advocates object to questions in the "long form" version of the census, which includes questions about physical and mental disabilities and details about housing.
- *January:* The FTC reaches a settlement with ReverseAuctions.com. The company had "harvested" information about eBay users without their permission and then sent them deceptive spam soliciting their business. ReverseAuctions.com agrees to no longer continue these practices and to destroy information for which it does not have informed consent.
- *January 12:* The Supreme Court rejects state challenges to a federal law requiring privacy safeguards for motor vehicle records.
- *February 8:* President Clinton issues an executive order prohibiting the use of any genetic information in the hiring or promoting of government personnel. Legislation is also introduced in Congress to extend this prohibition to the private sector.
- *April:* Investigators with the European Parliament charge that the United States may be using its Echelon electronic communications monitoring system to aid U.S. companies in industrial espionage against European competitors.
- *April 4:* In *Junger v. Daley* the Sixth U.S. Circuit Court rules that computer code used for encryption is "speech" protected by the First Amendment.
- *July 5:* The European Parliament and the United States agree on "Safe Harbor principles" that allow U.S. companies to share data in a way that meets Europe's strict privacy requirements.
- *July 10:* The Federal Trade Commission tries to stop Toysmart, a failed "dotcom," from selling its customer lists. The company had previously promised consumers that their information would not be disclosed to third parties.

- *August:* A poll by the Pew Internet & American Life Project finds that most online users want their privacy protected but don't know how to protect their information from abuse. Eighty-six percent of Internet users want information not to be shared unless they "opt in."
- *September:* A survey by the General Accounting Office finds that 97 percent of government web sites do not fully comply with the Federal Trade Commission's "fair information practices," which require notice, choice, access, and security.

2001

- *January:* Canada's Personal Information Protection and Electronic Documents Act goes into effect. The comprehensive regulations for the collection, use, and disclosure of personal data will at first only apply to federally regulated industries but will later be extended to cover provincial ones as well.
- *January 22:* The Federal Trade Commission concludes its investigation of the Internet advertising company DoubleClick by determining that the firm had not used or disclosed personally identifying information in violation of its privacy policy. Under pressure from state attorneys general and private citizens, DoubleClick had abandoned its plan (announced in 2000) to create consumer profiles by combining web-browsing records with identifying information.
- *April:* A study by the American Society of Newspaper Editors and the Freedom Forum suggests that Americans are conflicted about privacy: a majority believes that access to government information is vital for good government, but they are also concerned that governments and private companies not release information that infringes on individual privacy.
- *April:* A survey of children's web sites released by the Federal Trade Commission showed that while most of the sites offered some form of privacy notice, most do not comply with all the provisions of the Children's Online Privacy Protection Act (COPPA). The Electronic Privacy Information Center and 11 consumer organizations file suit against Amazon.com and eBay alleging COPPA violations.
- *May:* A report released by the Administrative Office of the U.S. federal courts reveals that 60 percent of "wiretaps" are actually "wireless taps" on cell phones and pagers. Where encryption was encountered, authorities were able to obtain the plaintext.
- *May:* The U.S. Supreme Court in *Bartnicki v. Vopper* rules that the media cannot be held liable for revealing illegally intercepted communications received from a third party.
- *May:* The Federal Trade Commission concludes that Amazon.com did not engage in deceptive behavior by changing its privacy policy to allow it to sell customer information as an asset in any merger or acquisition.
- *May:* A Gallup poll reports that two thirds of Internet users want new federal legislation to protect privacy online. Support for privacy legislation is highest among the most frequent users of the Internet.

- ■ *June:* In *Kyllo v. United States* the Supreme Court rules that use of an infrared thermal imaging device to detect heat coming from a person's home in a search for marijuana-growing facilities is a violation of the Fourth Amendment.
- ■ *September 7:* Groups of activists conduct skits in front of public cameras to protest video surveillance.
- ■ *September 11:* The devastating terrorist attacks on the World Trade Center and Pentagon create a political earthquake that shifts the balance for many Americans from privacy to the need to identify potential terrorists.
- ■ *October 25:* President George W. Bush signs the USA PATRIOT Act. The law expands the kinds of personal information that government agencies can examine and eases restrictions on some forms of wiretapping and data interception. The law also makes it easier to conduct secret searches.

2002

- ■ *January:* The Electronic Privacy Information Center files a suit asking for disclosure of records relating to the sale of personal information to law enforcement agencies. Experian and ChoicePoint have sold information in the past, but agencies had not responded to requests under the Freedom of Information Act.
- ■ *February:* A large coalition of civil liberties and privacy groups urges the rejection of a plan to create a de facto national ID card through the standardization of driver's license information.
- ■ *February:* Cable and Internet provider Comcast agrees to stop tracking the web-browsing activities of its 1 million broadband Internet subscribers.
- ■ *February 21:* The Massachusetts Supreme Court rules that an investigation company called Source One cannot impersonate bank officers or account holders in order to learn the amount of their bank balance.
- ■ *April:* The Colorado Supreme Court rules that records of book purchases can be turned over to police only if there is a "compelling interest" that outweighs customers' First Amendment rights.
- ■ *April:* The Platform for Privacy Preferences (P3P) specifications are released. The system seeks to match web site privacy policies with users' privacy settings.
- ■ *July:* The Federal Communications Commission issues new regulations that will allow telephone companies to share information about customers' phone habits with other companies that sell phone-related services. Companies will only need to seek permission from customers if the data is going to an unrelated company.
- ■ *July 4:* Activist John Gilmore is turned away at Oakland International Airport when he tries to board a plane without showing ID. He files suit, claiming that the ID requirement for travel is unconstitutional and does not contribute in any real way to the fight against terrorism.
- ■ *October:* The Transportation Security Agency finally acknowledges that it has been maintaining a secret "No Fly" watch list of individuals considered to be potential threats. Persons on the list can be prevented from boarding aircraft or will be subject to intensive scrutiny. Privacy advocates decry the secrecy of

the criteria used and the inability of innocent persons to get themselves removed from the list.

2003

- *January:* According to an annual report by the Federal Trade Commission, consumer fraud has continued to increase rapidly. The leading fraud category is identity theft, making up 43 percent of complaints. The number of reported identity theft cases has risen sharply from 31,117 in 2000 to 161,819 in 2002.
- *January:* Gillette Co. and Wal-Mart jointly test "smart shelf" technology using radio frequency identification chips to track the disposition of products. Privacy advocates are concerned that they may someday be used to track consumers.
- *February 18:* The New Hampshire Supreme Court rules in *Remsberg v. DocuSearch* that information brokers and private investigators can be held liable for the "foreseeable harms" involved in selling someone's personal information.
- *February 23:* The Federal Trade Commission fines Mrs. Fields Cookies $100,000 and Hershey Foods $85,000. The two companies had been charged with violating the federal Children's Online Privacy Protection Act by collecting information from children under 13 years old without ensuring that parents had consented.
- *March 5:* The U.S. Supreme Court upholds state sex offender registration laws, commonly called "Megan's Law," saying that they are not punitive in nature and can be applied retroactively. Privacy advocates believe that such laws are often overbroad and can undo the goal of rehabilitation.
- *April 14:* The federal Health Insurance Portability and Accountability Act (HIPAA) goes into effect. For most patients the main effect is having to sign a new disclosure form at the doctor's office. Smaller health plans are allowed an additional year before they have to comply with the new rules.
- *May:* An annual report reveals that secret FISA (Foreign Intelligence Surveillance Act) wiretaps were at an all-time high in 2002. All 1,228 wiretaps applied for were granted.
- *June:* The FCC and FTC begin to operate jointly a national telemarketing "do not call" registry.
- *July:* Wal-Mart announces that it will begin to use wireless identification (RFID) tags in its warehouses but will not attach the tags to merchandise being sold in its stores.
- *August:* Retired Admiral John M. Poindexter resigns as head of the Defense Advanced Research Projects Agency's Information Awareness Office. The Terrorist Information Awareness program has its funding sharply curtailed.
- *August:* The U.S. Department of Housing and Urban Development (HUD) announces guidelines for the gathering of information about homeless people. Although no national database on homelessness exists, privacy advocates are concerned that the standardized information could easily be used for such a project and readily shared with law enforcement agencies.

- *September:* A coalition including EPIC, the Health Privacy Project, and 28 health care provider and labor rights advocates urges that the federal government issue an explicit requirement that personal health information sent through the banking network be accessible only to the providers or health plans for whom it is intended.
- *September:* Congress kills funding for the controversial Terrorist Information Awareness project.
- *December:* President Bush signs the Fair and Accurate Credit Transactions Act of 2003 into law. It strengthens federal privacy protections and provides for consumers to obtain free annual credit reports. However, the law may preempt and thus weaken some state privacy laws.

2004

- *January:* The U.S. Visitor and Immigrant Status Indicator Technology (US-VISIT) program is launched. Beginning with 115 airports and 14 seaports, the program uses fingerprints, biometric data, background data, and itineraries to determine whether persons should be admitted into the United States.
- *February:* The U.S. Court of Appeals for the Tenth Circuit upholds the Federal Trade Commission's Do-Not-Call list, including fees charged to telemarketers to operate it.
- *February:* A group of physicians and hospitals tries to block the Justice Department from obtaining medical records relating to late-term abortions. The government says it needs the records for its legal defense of Partial Birth Abortion Act of 2003.
- *February:* A Vermont state court rules that an opt-in requirement for insurers sharing personal information does not violate First Amendment commercial speech rights.
- *February:* The Privacy Office of the Office of Homeland Security criticizes the Transportation Security Agency for its role in the inappropriate transfer of passenger data from JetBlue airlines to the Department of Defense for use by data mining contractors. A number of other airlines will eventually reveal that they, too, secretly shared passenger records with government agencies.
- *March:* A Barcelona nightclub becomes one of the first businesses to verify customers using "VeriChip," a tiny identification device implanted under the skin of patrons' arms.
- *May:* A report by the General Accounting Office reveals that the federal government has nearly 200 data-mining projects either in operation or in the planning stage.
- *May:* A federal court frees Brandon Mayfield, a lawyer and convert to Islam who had been mistakenly identified through fingerprints as being involved in train bombings in Madrid. The mistake may have arisen from a combination of poor imaging and human error by analysts.
- *June 21:* The U.S. Supreme Court rules (5-4) that a state can require persons stopped by the police to tell them their names.

Chronology

- *July:* Department of Homeland Security head Tom Ridge announces that CAPPS II, the latest airline-passenger profiling system, has been scrapped. Privacy concerns are credited as a consideration in the decision.
- *July:* California begins enforcing the toughest state financial privacy law in the United States. It allows consumers to opt out of sharing information with affiliated companies and requires companies to get permission before sharing data with unrelated companies. Banking groups had challenged the law, but the court ruled that federal law did not preempt the state provisions.
- *July:* President George W. Bush signs the Identity Theft Penalty Enhancement Act. The law adds two years to prison sentences for persons convicted of using a stolen credit card or Social Security numbers to commit crimes.
- *November:* The Transportation Security Agency requires that 72 airlines turn over one month's worth of passenger data for use in developing a new passenger screening program. Privacy advocates strongly protest as airlines continue to come under pressure to explain previous sharing of data with the TSA.

2005

- *January:* Police in Truro, Massachusetts, ask 800 male residents to provide samples to be matched against DNA found in the body of a woman who had been murdered three years earlier. Although authorities insist that giving a sample is voluntary, they have also said that persons who do not cooperate would have to be "looked at."
- *January:* Britain's new freedom of information act goes into effect. An information commissioner is now empowered to go to court on behalf of citizens seeking information about government operations.
- *January 4:* The Securely Protect Yourself Against Cyber Trespass Act (SPY Act) is reintroduced in the Senate. The House had passed the law the previous year. It would allow for fines of up to $3 million for makers of software that obtains personal information from users' PCs without permission.
- *February:* ChoicePoint, the nation's largest data broker, reveals it had sold personal information on about 145,000 consumers to identity thieves who had posed as a legitimate business. The company offers to help potential victims but state and federal legislators soon demand tough new regulations on selling such information.
- *February:* A California public elementary school drops plans to require students to wear radio frequency ID badges. Privacy advocates had strongly objected, saying the experimental program would treat students like "inventory items."
- *February:* It is revealed that the attorney general of Kansas has issued subpoenas for the complete medical records of women who sought late-term abortions at two clinics. The records were said to be needed for investigation of child sexual abuse laws and of laws limiting late-term abortions. The two clinics have gone to court to try to block the subpoenas.
- *February 18:* The Senate unanimously passes the Genetic Information Nondiscrimination Act of 2005. Similar legislation died in the House the

129

previous year. The bill would prohibit the use of genetic information in employment decisions and would also prevent health insurance companies from denying coverage based on genetic information.

- *March 24:* The Federal Reserve Board tells banks that they should notify customers "as soon as possible" if their financial information has been stolen or improperly accessed. Such notification may help deal with a growing epidemic of identity theft.
- *March 25:* A report from the inspector's office of the Department of Homeland Security says that the Transportation Security Administration misled the public about the use of passenger data in developing its computerized passenger screening system. At least 12 million passenger records were transferred in 2002 and 2003 without passenger knowledge or permission.
- *April:* The House begins hearings on the renewal or modification of a number of provisions of the USA PATRIOT Act, including one allowing the searching of library and bookstore records and another providing for secret "sneak and peek" warrants.
- *April:* The Senate Judiciary Committee grills representatives of ChoicePoint and Lexis/Nexis, data services that have inadvertently sold thousands of consumer data records to cybercriminals.
- *July 12:* British police announce that they had used footage from ubiquitous closed-circuit TV public surveillance cameras to identify four suspected bombers who killed more than 50 people in London on July 7. Suspects from the unsuccessful July 21 attacks will also be quickly identified from camera images.
- *November:* House and Senate negotiators agree to make most provisions of the USA PATRIOT Act permanent. However, provisions associated with searching of library and bookstore records, as well as "sneak and peek" searches would be renewed for only seven years.
- *November 2:* The U.S. Circuit Court of Appeals for the Ninth Circuit rules that parents have no right to prevent public schools from asking students "intrusive" questions about sex in a classroom survey.
- *December:* Revelations of secret wiretaps without court authorization provoke widespread controversy. President Bush argues that eavesdroppng on domestic conversations with suspected foreign terrorists is within his constitutional power and was also authorized by Congress. Many civil libertarians disagee.
- *December 30:* Unable to agree on renewing a number of controversial provisions, Congress passes a one-month extension of the USA Patriot Act.

CHAPTER 4

BIOGRAPHICAL LISTING

This chapter offers brief biographical entries for a variety of persons who have played an important role in the development of privacy issues, from the technical side, through their fiction or nonfiction writing, or in litigation and activism. Note that these entries include only material relevant to privacy issues; they are not intended to be complete biographical sketches. See Chapter 7, Annotated Bibliography, for more information on book titles cited.

John Ashcroft, attorney general of the United States, 2000–04. A former governor of Missouri and then senator, Ashcroft's nomination as attorney general proved to be the most contentious of George W. Bush's cabinet picks. After the attacks of September 11, 2001, Ashcroft, as the nation's chief law enforcer, did pledge to uphold civil liberties but also suggested that critics who raised constitutional issues were aiding terrorism. He espoused stronger powers for law enforcement (such as those in the USA PATRIOT Act of 2001) with its expanded surveillance powers and resisted attempts to get information about the treatment of terrorism suspects and the details of proposed new surveillance programs.

David Banisar, prominent information privacy expert. He is currently a Policy Fellow in the Open Society Institute and Visiting Research Fellow at the University of Leeds, England. Previously he was a Research Fellow at the Kennedy School of Government at Harvard University, where he worked with the Harvard Information Infrastructure Project. Banisar is also Deputy Director of Privacy International, a U.K.-based privacy advocacy group. Earlier, Banisar was a founder and privacy director of the Electronic Privacy Information Center and has contributed to various EPIC publications, as well as serving as contributing editor to *Privacy Times.*

John Perry Barlow, a retired Wyoming cattle rancher and Grateful Dead lyricist. Barlow found himself in the unlikely position of Internet activist and visionary of virtual communities. In response to the Operation Sundevil Secret Service raids and the seizing of Steve Jackson's computers, Barlow cofounded the Electronic Frontier Foundation, often described as an "ACLU for cyberspace."

Daniel Bernstein, mathematician and cryptographer. Bernstein wrote a cryptography-related paper and computer program and was told by the federal government that it was classified as a "munition" and could not be exported. Aided by John Gilmore and the Electronic Freedom Foundation, Bernstein sued and won a decision that declared that computer source code was a form of speech protected by the First Amendment.

Robert Bork, law professor and former solicitor general and acting attorney general of the United States during the Nixon administration. As acting attorney general he played a controversial role in the Watergate affair. He then became a judge in the U.S. Court of Appeals. Bork's nomination to the Supreme Court was embroiled in controversy, in part because he believed in a stricter, more literal construction of the Constitution and opposed the finding of a broad right of privacy (as had been done in *Roe v. Wade*). Ironically, Bork's own privacy was violated by the publication of his video rental records, which led to the passage of the Video Privacy Protection Act of 1988.

Louis Brandeis, chief justice of the U.S. Supreme Court, 1916–39. Brandeis took a liberal position on antitrust issues and the right of the government to impose regulations such as minimum wage and maximum working hours. While supporting expanding government powers to control commerce, he took a libertarian position in favor of the individual in dealing with government power. In 1928, Brandeis wrote a dissent to the *Olmstead* decision in which he said that the Court must reinterpret the constitutional protection for privacy to take account of new technologies that threatened it.

David Brin, science-fiction author and writer on cyberspace and virtual communities. His book *The Transparent Society* (1998) promotes an unusual approach to the privacy issue. Brin argues that creating effective privacy protections is impossible due to the pervasiveness of new information and communications technology. Instead, activists should concentrate on putting individuals, the government, and corporations on a more equal footing by making sure that the watchers can be watched in turn.

Fred Cate, expert on privacy and information law, including international privacy. From 1994 to 1996 he chaired the Annenberg Washington Program's project on Global Information Privacy. He is the author of the handbook *Privacy in the Information Age*.

Simon Gordon Davies, pioneer privacy activist, founder of Privacy International, a London-based worldwide privacy watchdog group. The group highlights privacy concerns and campaigns for stronger privacy protections. Davies is also Visiting Research Fellow at the London School of Economics and Political Science. Davies received a 1999 Electronic Frontier Foundation Pioneer Award for his work. He also created the Big Brother Award, a "prize" granted to organizations that commit particularly flagrant violations of privacy.

Dorothy Denning, professor of computer science at Georgetown University. Denning is a widely recognized expert on data security and "information warfare." She was involved in the Clipper Chip debate with cryptography activists. Denning is director of the Georgetown Institute for Information Assurance. She has written numerous publications on data protection, information security, computer crime, and cyberterrorism. She has been honored with a fellowship by the Association for Computing Machinery and is a recipient of the organization's Augusta Ada Lovelace Award.

Whitfield Diffie, cryptographer and developer of public key cryptography (with Martin Hellman and Ralph Merkle) in 1975. Diffie has become an activist for widespread use of cryptography to protect privacy, as well as a kind of elder statesman for the activists known as "cypherpunks." Diffie has been with Sun Microsystems since 1991 and today is the corporation's chief security officer. He is coauthor (with Susan Landau) of *Privacy on the Line: The Politics of Wiretapping and Encryption (1998).*

Amitai Etzioni, sociologist and founder of a movement called communitarianism that combines liberal social activism with conservative values of personal responsibility. In his book *The Limits of Privacy*, Etzioni criticizes what he sees as an overemphasis on individual privacy that can prevent society from dealing with problems such as terrorism, crime, and the spread of AIDS. He believes that government can use databases of personal information responsibly in carrying out social programs.

Louis J. Freeh, director of the FBI, 1993–2001. Freeh found himself in the center of major cases such as the Oklahoma City bombing and the 1996 Atlanta Olympics bombing. Freeh expressed the FBI's concern that it be given sufficient means to conduct surveillance and carry out search warrants in the computer age. This was translated into such proposals as the Clipper Chip and the key escrow proposals, both vigorously opposed by privacy advocates.

Simson Garfinkel, computer security expert, journalist, and author. Garfinkel has written articles on computer-related issues for *The Boston Globe*, *The San Jose Mercury News*, and other publications. He was a founding contributor to *Wired* magazine and continues to be a regular contributor. Garfinkel has also written many books on computer security and other technical issues, but he is best known for his 2000 book *Database Nation*. In it Garfinkel sounded an alarm about the pervasiveness of information gathering and surveillance technology at the turn of the millennium. (Consumer advocate and political maverick Ralph Nader praised this book as "a graphic and blistering indictment.")

William Gibson, science-fiction writer. His novel *Neuromancer* (1984) described a future in which people directly experienced a computer-generated world called cyberspace. Gibson and other science-fiction writers have explored the implications of such a world for privacy, anonymity, and even identity.

John Gilmore, cryptographer, activist, and cofounder of the Electronic Frontier Foundation. Gilmore is passionately involved in the development of free software and the promotion of cryptography to protect ordinary people's data from government surveillance. Among his attributed sayings is "the Net treats censorship as damage and routes around it." Recently Gilmore undertook what many view as a quixotic challenge to post–September 11 airport regulations by trying to fly without showing identification. Gilmore argues that current identification systems provide no real security since they can be easily fooled by terrorists.

Beth Givens, founder and director of the Privacy Rights Clearinghouse in San Diego and author of the *Privacy Rights Handbook.* Her background includes library and information science, telecommunications policy, and consumer activism (particularly with regard to utilities).

Mike Godwin, counsel to the Electronic Frontier Foundation. Godwin has been involved in numerous high-profile online issues including libel, intellectual property, privacy, and freedom of expression. He is best known for playing a major role in the successful court fight against the Computer Decency Act of 1996. He recounts his battles in *Cyber Rights: Defending Free Speech in the Digital Age.*

Emmanuel Goldstein, editor of *2600,* the "Hacker quarterly." His name is a pseudonym taken from the character in George Orwell's *1984.* He has become a visible spokesperson for the virtues of hacking (in the original sense of creative exploration of computing) and an advocate for free access to information.

Al Gore, former representative and senator; vice president of the United States (1993–2000). Gore took a leading role as the Clinton administration's spokesperson and advocate for developing the "information superhighway" and providing widespread access to the Internet. He also promoted the administration's "bill of rights for the Information Age" proposals, including expanded consumer and patient privacy protections.

Johan Helsingus, developer of a controversial anonymous remailing service. The service, called anon.penet.fi, allowed users to strip the original address headers from e-mail and send it anonymously. In August 1996, Helsingus shut down the service rather than comply with a court order to reveal the identity of a user. Helsingus continued to advocate for the protection of privacy and anonymity on the Internet.

Chris Jay Hoofnagel, director of the West Coast office of the Electronic Privacy Information Center. In his congressional testimony and writings, Hoofnagel has specialized in financial services privacy and related issues such as the misuse of Social Security numbers, identity theft, and abuses by commercial data brokers.

J. Edgar Hoover, director of the FBI, 1924–72. He largely shaped the practices of the FBI, taking it from Prohibition to the radical tumult of the 1960s. Along the way, he organized high-profile efforts against gangsters and Communists, expanded the use of wiretapping, surveillance, and infiltration, which he often turned against political enemies, arousing civil liberties concerns.

Steve Jackson, designer and publisher of role-playing and board games. In 1990, his company's computers were seized by the Secret Service because of vague connections to a stolen phone-company document. Jackson sued the government and eventually collected damages.

Mitch Kapor, entrepreneur and founder of Lotus Corporation, which was one of the early success stories in the personal computer revolution. He has a wide background in psychological and spiritual studies as well as computer science. In 1990, he joined with John Perry Barlow to found the Electronic Frontier Foundation to defend civil liberties in the Information Age.

John Locke, English philosopher and political scientist, 1643–1704; author of *Two Treatises on Government* (1690). Locke's writings were very influential in establishing constitutional government and the protection of individual rights. Locke believed that government held its power only so long as it fulfilled the people's need for security, and that individuals had inherent rights (such as the right to property). This creates fertile ground for the development of privacy rights.

Timothy McVeigh, chief petty officer in the U.S. Navy (not the same man as the Oklahoma City bomber). His 17-year distinguished naval career was threatened in September 1997 when the navy obtained information from America Online that revealed that he was a user who had described gay-related interests in his user profile. McVeigh sued in 1998, arguing that the navy had violated the Electronic Communications Privacy Act. He won a court order blocking the navy from discharging him and eventually retired with a promotion.

Norman Y. Mineta, former U.S. Secretary of Transportation and current head of the Transportation Security Agency (2001–). After the attacks of September 11, 2001, President George W. Bush created the Transportation Security Agency (TSA) to overhaul airport security in the face of the terrorist threat. In this challenging post Mineta faced great pressure to install new screening equipment, train the now federalized airport security personnel, and to provide additional security for the nation's seaports, highways, pipelines, and other connecting infrastructure. However, a number of related initiatives such as the Computer-Assisted Passenger Pre-Screening System (CAPPS I and CAPPS II) and the later "Secure Flight" program would raise objections from privacy advocates.

Kevin Mitnick, convicted hacker turned computer security expert. Mitnick served nearly five years in prison for unauthorized computer access, stealing credit card numbers, and fraud. After his release in 2000, Mitnick began to speak and write about computer security: His 2002 book, *The Art of Deception,* provides a sobering portrait of how hackers routinely trick people into revealing information and providing access to sensitive computer systems. (Mitnick covered other hacking techniques in a companion book, *The Art of Intrusion,* published in 2005.)

Robert S. Mueller, head of the Federal Bureau of Investigation (2001–). In the first half of the year 2001, Mueller served as U.S. deputy attorney general and was then nominated and confirmed as Director of the FBI, taking office only a week before the September 11 terrorist attacks. Mueller, who already faced the challenge of reforming an agency that suffered considerable embarrassment, such as quality control problems in the FBI labs, had to change the priorities of the organization to deal with the terrorist threat while building coordination with the CIA and later, with the newly organized Department of Homeland Security. As head of the FBI, Mueller continues to deal with both the perceived shortcomings of the agency in detecting terrorists and accusations that investigative methods are unfair or poorly targeted, threatening freedom of association and privacy, particularly of Muslim Americans.

George Orwell (pseudonym of Eric Arthur Blair) early 20th-century British writer. His novel *1984*, published in 1948, describes a world in which television and other technology is used by a totalitarian government for complete surveillance and control that extends to the use of language and thinking itself. Government thus acts as, what Orwell termed, a "Big Brother" who constantly watches over his younger siblings (the nation's citizens) making sure they don't "misbehave." Privacy advocates have noted that while a centralized Big Brother has not emerged (at least in the Western democracies), the abuse of technology to spy on and control the individual is a very real threat, although decentralized technology, such as the personal computer and the Internet, can also be used to resist totalitarian projects and to create alternative forms of community and governance.

John M. Poindexter, an admiral who authorized illicit arms-for-hostages deals in the Iran-contra scandal of the 1980s and who reemerged after 2001 with controversial ideas for fighting terrorism. He first proposed a "terrorism futures" project in which successful predictions of attacks could be rewarded using a sort of market mechanism. After quickly backing away under a storm of criticism, Poindexter then headed the Total Information Awareness (later Terrorism Information Awareness) research project for the Department of Defense. This project, which proposed to use massive integration and data-mining facilities, was strongly criticized by privacy advocates; funding was stopped by Congress in February 2003.

John Postel, distinguished computer scientist and a major architect of the Internet. His interests ranged from the highly technical (data protocols and switching systems) to the realm of social communications (e-mail and multimedia conferencing services). Postel established the Internet Assigned Numbers Authority (IANA), which devised the system of address numbers on which the Internet relies for making connections. As a trustee of the Internet Society, Postel was involved with privacy concerns and received a posthumous 1999 Electronic Frontier Foundation Pioneer Award.

Marc Rotenberg, director of the Electronic Privacy Information Center and former head of the Washington office of the Computer Professionals for Social Responsibility. Rotenberg teaches information privacy law at Georgetown University Law Center. Rotenberg has served on numerous important panels relating to privacy issues and testified before the 9-11 Committee on "Security and Liberty: Protecting Privacy, Preventing Terrorism." He is chair of the American Bar Association Committee on Privacy and Information Protection and has edited *The Privacy Law Sourcebook* and is coeditor of *Information Privacy Law.*

Susan Scott, technology analyst and publisher; former CEO of Upside Publishing. From 1996 to 1999 Scott was executive director of TRUSTe, an organization that verifies and guarantees the privacy policies of online businesses.

Robert Ellis Smith, prolific writer on the legal and cultural aspects of privacy. His latest publication, *Ben Franklin's Web Site*, describes the interplay of "privacy and curiosity from Plymouth Rock to the Internet." Smith has also been publisher of *Privacy Journal* since 1974 and has written compilations of privacy laws and incidents of invasion of privacy.

Richard Stallman, founder of the Free Software Foundation, which promotes the cooperative creation and distribution of noncommercial software. This movement has been influential in providing alternative operating systems, promoting free access to technical information, and creating freely distributable software that is free from corporate or governmental control.

Lawrence Tribe, noted constitutional expert and civil libertarian. In his address to the First Conference on Computers, Freedom, and Privacy (March 6, 1991) entitled "The Constitution in Cyberspace: Law and Liberty Beyond the Electronic Frontier," Tribe suggested that a new constitutional amendment might make it clear that the fundamental rights of free expression and privacy will be guaranteed regardless of the type of technology involved.

Earl Warren, chief justice of the U.S. Supreme Court, 1953–69. Warren played a major role in the expansion of civil rights and civil liberties, including the *Griswold* case, which established a right of personal privacy as implied in the language of the Constitution.

Liam Youens, the first known cyberstalker-murderer. Youens became obsessed with Amy Boyer, a 20-year-old dental-hygiene student. Besides physically following her, Youens used the Internet to find Boyer's Social Security number and work address. He also posted a web diary in which he chronicled his growing obsession, details of the stalking, and eventually his plans to murder Boyer. Despite the web site being online for at least two years, no one reported it to the police. Boyer eventually carried out his plan, shooting Boyer as she drove home from work. The murder publicized the growing problem of cyberstalking and the ease with which stalkers could obtain information via the Internet.

Philip Zimmermann, software engineer and cryptographer. Zimmermann developed the Pretty Good Privacy (PGP) program in 1991 and became embroiled in legal skirmishes with government agencies that tried to restrict its export. When the government dropped its legal efforts in 1996, Zimmermann founded a company to develop and market his encryption software.

CHAPTER 5

GLOSSARY

affiliated company   A company that is owned or controlled by a parent company. Privacy policies and regulations often treat a company's affiliates and unrelated companies differently.

American Civil Liberties Union (ACLU)   An organization founded in 1915 to protect the civil liberties asserted in the Bill of Rights. This mission has involved the ACLU in many privacy issues.

anonymity   The online world allows opportunities to interact with people without identifying oneself. Anonymity is related to privacy in that it protects personal identity, and it can be a liberating experience. But anonymity creates the problem of lack of accountability for harmful actions.

Big Brother   A pervasive, all-seeing government surveillance and control system; named after a character in George Orwell's *1984.*

Bill of Rights   The first 10 amendments to the U.S. Constitution. Of these, the Fourth, Fifth, and Ninth amendments have particular relevance to the protection of privacy.

biometrics   Automatic identification or matching of persons based upon physical characteristics such as facial geometry, fingerprints, or retinal patterns.

bulletin board systems (BBS)   Dial-up computers where users can leave messages or download or upload files. They became popular in the mid-1980s but have been largely superseded by the Internet.

Caller ID   Telephone service that allows callers to know the phone number from which incoming calls originate. Caller ID raises privacy concerns when callers wish to remain anonymous.

CAPPS (Computer Assisted Passenger Pre-screening System)   A system in development starting in 2002 to profile or identify potential terrorist threats by analyzing data gathered by airlines as part of the passenger booking process. CAPPS-2 is an enhanced and expanded version.

Carnivore   A software program used by federal law enforcement agencies in 2000 and 2001. It could identify the sources and destinations of electronic communications. It was replaced by the use of commercial software.

CCTV   Closed circuit television used for monitoring or surveillance.

ciphertext   In cryptography, text that has been made unreadable by applying a code key and an encryption method.

Glossary

Clipper Chip   A proposed device that would provide encryption services but also allow the government to read encrypted messages.

COINTELPRO (Counterintelligence Program)   Widespread FBI surveillance and infiltration of dissident groups (such as civil rights and antiwar activists) from the 1960s into the 1980s. When revealed, it fueled privacy concerns.

compelling state interest   The strictest test applied by courts to see whether an invasion of privacy by the government is justified. It is applied, for example, to matters of contraception or abortion.

computer matching   The comparison of two or more databases to find individuals who should be investigated: for example, matching a database of persons who are delinquent in paying child support with a database of tax refunds.

cookie   A small file that some web sites write onto the user's hard drive. It can be used to recognize that user in subsequent sessions, customize the user interface, or to create a profile of that user that can be sold to marketers. It is this third use that raises privacy concerns.

credit reporting agency (CRA)   A central clearinghouse for information about credit purchases and payments; the three major credit bureaus are TRW, Equifax, and TransUnion.

cryptography   The science of code making (and code breaking).

cryptosystem   A system for encoding text so that it can be read only by someone who has the key.

customer proprietary network information   Industry term for records kept by a telecommunications company that show the time, destination, duration, and other information about customers' calls. Recent regulatory decisions have allowed this information to be shared with related companies without requiring the customer's permission.

cyberspace   The imaginary world experienced by online users. It can include many places such as schools, libraries, stores, game arenas, and private "chat" rooms that are analogous to their "real-life" counterparts.

cypherpunks   Self-designation of a group of activists who promote the widespread use of cryptography to protect privacy, and who oppose government controls on the technology.

database   An organized collection of information maintained on a computer system. It usually consists of a number of related files containing records that are further broken down into fields such as name, address, and Social Security number.

data broker (or information broker)   A person or company that collects, packages, and sells computerized information (such as mailing lists or individual profiles). Data brokers have little specific regulation.

data mining   The extraction of data (such as from consumer purchase records) that can be used or sold to marketers.

Data Protection Directive   The European Union's comprehensive regulations (announced in 1995) governing the collection, disclosure, distribution, and access to computerized information.

decisional privacy   The right to make decisions in certain matters (such as reproduction or sexual relations) without being subjected to government scrutiny.

DES   A government-approved system for encoding text; comes in different strengths measured by the number of bits in the code key. First introduced in 1977, DES came under attack as being too weak; the 56-bit DES has already been "cracked" by teams of programmers.

digital signature   One of various methods of combining an individual's private encryption key with a message. Readers can use the individual's public key to verify that the message was created by that individual.

direct mailer   An organization that gathers or obtains mailing lists and sends advertising to everyone on the list.

disclosure   In privacy policies, the requirement that an organization reveal to affected persons what it intends to do with the information it collects. Also, the revealing of information collected from an individual to a third party.

"Don't Ask, Don't Tell, Don't Pursue"   A controversial policy that allows gays to serve in the military if they don't reveal their sexual orientation. Authorities are not supposed to initiate investigations unless there is such a revelation. The policy has aroused privacy concerns, such as in the case of Chief Petty Officer Timothy McVeigh.

eavesdropping   Listening to a conversation without the knowledge or consent of the participants. Wiretapping is eavesdropping on telecommunications; surveillance is the systematic surreptitious observation of someone or someplace.

Echelon   A shadowy international communications-monitoring network led by the United States and believed to be able to scan millions of e-mails, faxes, phone calls, and other messages for items of interest.

electronic commerce (e-commerce)   The buying and selling of goods and services online, usually through web sites. It has been rapidly growing since the mid-1990s.

Electronic Communications Privacy Act of 1986   Federal legislation that extended the Privacy Act of 1974 to include most forms of telecommunications and data networks.

Electronic Freedom of Information Act of 1986   The Electronic Freedom of Information Act of 1986 extended the principles of the 1966 Freedom of Information Act to computerized records.

Electronic Frontier Foundation (EFF)   A civil liberties organization founded by John Perry Barlow and Mitch Kapor in 1990 in response to government seizure of computers in the Operation Sundevil hacker sweep. It quickly became involved in other issues, such as privacy and free speech.

Electronic Privacy Information Center (EPIC)   A public interest research group founded in 1994, EPIC is concerned with issues of privacy and free speech in the online world, and includes a legal team as well as educational outreach.

e-mail (electronic mail)   Messages sent to one or more individuals over a computer network.

Glossary

encryption   The process of applying a code key to text in order to create a message that cannot be read without the proper key.

Event Data Recorder (EDR)   A "black box" device that records data about the operation of a vehicle, similar to flight data recorders used in aircraft. Data from an EDR can indicate unsafe driving but raises privacy concerns.

Fair Credit Reporting Act of 1992   Federal legislation that sets basic requirements for the preparation and distribution of credit reports; regulates purposes for which reports can be disclosed and gives individuals the right to see and correct their reports.

Fair Information Principles   Basic protections for privacy suggested by experts and advocates starting in the 1970s. They include disclosure of information-gathering activities and the right of an individual to view and correct records pertaining to him or her. The Privacy Act of 1974 attempted to implement these principles.

Federal Trade Commission (FTC)   Government agency that sets many rules for how goods and services are bought or sold in the marketplace. It has proposed stronger privacy regulations, particularly where children are involved.

Fifth Amendment   Part of the Bill of Rights of the U.S. Constitution. One clause prevents the government from forcing an accused individual to confess guilt; it has thus been interpreted as a protection of privacy.

firewall   A program and/or hardware device that inspects Internet packets and can block and alert users to possible attacks involving viruses, worms, and Trojan horse programs. More sophisticated firewalls also examine outgoing packets that might contain sensitive information.

Fourth Amendment   Part of the Bill of Rights of the U.S. Constitution. It protects against law enforcement officers searching property or seizing evidence without a warrant.

Freedom of Information Act of 1966   Federal legislation that implements the principle that citizens have the right to know about government activities and see government records pertaining to them.

genetic information   Information from tests that reveal genetic (hereditary) characteristics such as susceptibility to a particular disease.

Geographical Information System (GIS)   A system that draws maps from computer databases that can include physical data, census data, or other information. Such systems have the potential for being used to aid intrusive surveillance or marketing.

GPS (Global Positioning System)   A system in which signals from several satellites are timed in order to determine the precise location of the receiver on the Earth's surface. It can be used to track the location of vehicles, cell phones, and so on.

hacker   Originally, this term referred to an unusually skilled and often obsessed programmer; in recent years it has come to mean someone who illegally breaks into computer systems to destroy them or to steal information.

health maintenance organizations (HMOs)   Health care providers that offer a package of health benefits through employers or directly to individuals.

141

Their attempt to reduce high medical costs has led to a number of issues including privacy concerns.

Hippocratic Oath   An ancient physician's oath that, among other things, promises that a doctor will not divulge information about a patient's medical condition to a third party.

home is your castle   The idea enshrined in English law that any person's home should be protected against intrusion by the government except through proper legal process.

honesty test   A psychological test designed to identify persons who have a tendency to lie, steal, or engage in other dishonest behavior. The tests have aroused concerns about both their validity and their abuse of privacy.

identity theft   The use of stolen credit information (such as name, Social Security number, and bank account numbers) to assume another person's identity in order to make credit purchases or cash withdrawals.

incorporation doctrine   Developed gradually during the mid-20th century, the principle that the Fourteenth Amendment guarantees of due process and equal treatment require the states as well as the federal government to enforce the guarantees in the Bill of Rights.

information privacy   The aspect of privacy that focuses on the right of the individual to control how personal information is obtained or used.

International Traffic in Arms Regulations (ITAR)   A regulation that has been used to restrict the export of encryption software; challenged in *U.S. Department of State v. Bernstein.*

Internet   The rapidly growing worldwide interconnection of computers and networks that communicate using a standard protocol called TCP/IP.

Internet service provider (ISP)   A company that offers connections to the Internet, usually for a monthly fee.

key   A string of text (or piece of data) that when input into a coding system with the coded ciphertext, reveals the original message (plaintext).

key escrow   The placing of a copy of a user's encryption key with a third party so it can be retrieved by law enforcement officials who have obtained a court order.

keylogger   A program that surreptitiously intercepts information being typed at the keyboard, such as passwords.

loyalty card   A card used to provide discounts and targeted offers to customers (such as in supermarkets). Use of the card allows the store to track the customer's buying habits.

Medical Information Bureau   A private database used by life and medical insurance companies to share medical information about applicants and to determine whether to offer coverage.

Ninth Amendment   Part of the Bill of Rights. It states that "The enumeration in the Constitution, of certain rights, shall not be construed to deny or disparage others retained by the people." During the 1960s and 1970s, a majority of Supreme Court justices used the idea of unspecified rights to find that the Constitution implied a broader individual right of privacy regarding matters such as contraception, abortion, and reproduction.

online services   Companies that set up computers with services such as message forums, chat rooms, and file libraries. Examples include America Online and CompuServe. These services were originally stand-alone, but during the 1990s they connected to the Internet and became value-added Internet service providers.

opt-in   Requirement that persons specifically authorize use or sharing of personal information by a company or institution.

opt-out   System under which a company can share personal information or market to a consumer unless the consumer specifically tells them not to do so.

pen register   A device used at the telephone company office to record the numbers dialed from a person's phone. Pen registers can be installed by law enforcement agencies after obtaining a court order, or may be used by phone companies to investigate both fraudulent use of the service and harassing calls.

plaintext   The result of decoding an encrypted message into readable text.

Platform for Privacy Preferences (P3P)   A software standard developed by the World Wide Web Consortium allowing users to match their privacy requirements to the privacy policies of web sites.

polygraph   A device used to assess the truthfulness of statements by measuring symptoms of physical stress; commonly called a "lie detector."

pretexting   The use of impersonation or other forms of deception to obtain private information without the subject's consent.

Pretty Good Privacy (PGP)   A popular software package that lets users encrypt their e-mail and other data files.

Principles for Providing and Using Personal Information   Principles for information use originating from a committee of U.S. government agencies and published in 1995. Subjects covered include respect for individual privacy in collecting and disclosing information, informing affected persons about their rights and responsibilities, and offering the opportunity to correct incorrect information.

privacy   The ability of an individual to prevent intrusion or to control the gathering or use of personal information.

Privacy Act of 1974   Basic federal law that regulates the distribution of information by federal agencies and the right of an individual to obtain (and possibly correct) records pertaining to him or her.

profile   A description of characteristics of a suspect or person of interest that can be matched against databases.

public-key certificate   A digital record created by a certification agency using an individual's private key and other information, and containing the public key. An individual can verify the certificate's integrity and be assured that the public key belongs to the individual identified.

public-key cryptography   A system where each user has two related code keys, one public and one private. The public key can be used by anyone to send a message, which can be read only by the user with the corresponding private key. The private key in turn can authenticate the user by creating a message that can be read by anyone with the public key.

reasonable expectation of privacy   A test used by courts in deciding privacy cases. It describes circumstances (such as making a call in a phone booth) where a person should be allowed to assume that he or she is engaging in private conduct.

reasonable relationship   A less rigorous test applied by courts to determine whether an invasion of privacy is justified. Applied, for example, to businesses monitoring employee performance, to determine if the monitoring has a reasonable relationship to business objectives.

reverse directory   A telephone directory that can be used to look up the address corresponding to a phone number. It can be used by telemarketers to create mailing lists.

RFID (Radio Frequency Identification Device)   A small tag attached to merchandise that transmits an identifier for inventory management purposes. Critics suggest that the tags could also be used to track the owners of the merchandise or compile information about their purchases.

RSA   An algorithm (method) for encoding text by means of public-key cryptography. Named for the last names of its developers at MIT (Rivest, Shamir, and Adelman). See **public-key cryptography.**

Secure Server   A web program that can be used by online consumers to place orders safely. Credit card information is encrypted so it cannot be read by hackers.

security-industrial complex   The idea that in the post–September 11 environment, law enforcement and intelligence agencies are working closely with private companies to obtain and use large databases of personal information in ways that could compromise freedom and privacy.

Smart Card   A small card equipped with a computer processor and memory. Smart cards can be used for simple identification but also for carrying data such as the level of access, credit balance, or health information.

sneak and peek   A warrant that allows a search without prior notification; contained in a controversial provision of the USA PATRIOT Act.

spam   Unsolicited e-mail sent to a large number of recipients.

spyware   Software that transfers information from a user's PC without their knowledge; it is often concealed within attractive downloadable software packages.

Super Bureau   A company that offers (for a fee) the ability to obtain just about any sort of information about a person using government, credit, or other databases. A "bureau" sometimes obtains information under false pretenses.

surveillance technology   General term for devices that allow a person's activities or conversations to be observed from a distance, such as through microphones, cameras, or infrared sensors.

telecommunications   General term for electronic transmission of information, whether voice (phone), fax, or computer data.

telemarketer   A salesperson who contacts consumers by telephone; often accused of deceptive or high-pressure tactics.

trap and trace   A device that records the number from which an incoming call originates. A court order is required except in cases involving harassing calls or fraudulent use of the telephone service.

TRUSTe   An organization that certifies the privacy practices of online businesses that follow its guidelines.

Universal ID   Proposed single number that would uniquely identify an individual in all government databases. To some extent Social Security numbers have been used for this purpose. Its proposal arouses concerns because it in effect puts all a person's private information in one basket.

US-VISIT (U.S. Visitor and Immigrant Status Indicator Technology)   A program begun in 2004 that uses identification, background, and travel data to attempt to detect persons with criminal or terrorist records before they enter the country.

USA PATRIOT Act   Post–September 11, 2001, law that contains several provisions expanding government search and surveillance powers.

web browser   A program that lets users find and navigate through pages of information, graphics, etc., on the World Wide Web.

webcam   A camera set up by a person to continually broadcast his or her activities to the Internet. The opposite of privacy; a form of electronic exhibitionism and perhaps a cultural artifact.

Wiretap Act of 1968   Federal law that extended Fourth Amendment privacy protections to telecommunications.

wiretapping   The interception of telephone voice or data transmission by someone other than its intended recipient.

World Wide Web   A system that links pages of text, graphics, sound, and other resources on the Internet to one another, giving each a unique address. A web browser can be used to display and navigate the pages.

PART II

GUIDE TO FURTHER RESEARCH

CHAPTER 6

HOW TO RESEARCH
PRIVACY ISSUES

The tremendous growth in the amount of resources and services available through the Internet (and particularly, the World Wide Web) is providing powerful new tools for researchers. Mastery of a few basic online techniques enables today's researcher to accomplish in a few minutes what used to require hours in the library poring through card catalogs, bound indexes, and printed or microfilmed periodicals.

Not everything is to be found on the Internet, of course. While a few books are available in electronic versions, most must still be obtained as printed text. Some periodical articles, particularly those more than 15 years old, must still be obtained in "hard copy" form from libraries. Nevertheless, the Internet has now reached "critical mass" in the scope, variety, and quality of material available. Thus, it makes sense to make the Net the starting point for most research projects. This is particularly true regarding privacy issues. Since so many privacy concerns have arisen in connection with the Internet and other computerized information systems, many advocates of privacy rights have made the Internet their home base for organizing and education.

STARTING PLACES ON THE WEB

One basic principle of research is to take advantage of the fact that other people may have already found and organized much of the most useful information about a particular topic. For privacy issues, there are three web sites that can serve as excellent starting points for research.

The Electronic Privacy Information Center (EPIC) at http://www.epic. org is, according to its web site, "a public interest research center in Washington, D.C. It was established in 1994 to focus public attention on emerging civil liberties issues and to protect privacy, the First Amendment, and constitutional values." EPIC provides news of current developments (including court cases and pending legislation), as well as an extensive collection of guides and resources:

- *EPIC Alert*, an online newsletter, which can also be subscribed to by e-mail from the web page.
- A bookstore, where EPIC publications and other recommended books can be ordered.
- An online guide to "practical privacy tools," including aids for encryption and anonymity.
- An extensive collection of links to resources, including organizations, publications, and other web sites.
- A policy archives section, with pages of links for each topic.

Another privacy-related "megasite" is that of the Electronic Frontier Foundation (EFF) at http://www.eff.org. It is described as "a non-profit, non-partisan organization working in the public interest to protect fundamental civil liberties, including privacy and freedom of expression, in the arena of computers and the Internet." The EFF's home page provides links to the latest privacy-related news developments. Its information tends to be organized for easy use by activists. For example, a story about a privacy abuse or free speech case is often accompanied by links that can be used to respond to the situation, such as by participating in protests or contacting legislators.

Like EPIC, the EFF has extensive archives. (Indeed, the archives on the two sites are different enough that exploring both is a good way to get a very comprehensive survey of privacy-related resources on the Net.) The EFF archive categories most related to privacy are: anonymity, biometrics, CAPPS II, public records/FOIA, surveillance, USA PATRIOT Act, and, of course, privacy.

The Privacy Rights Clearinghouse is a third major advocacy resource site. It provides news links, legislative updates, and reports. Relevant topical links include Identity Theft, Background Checks & Workplace, Financial Privacy, Internet Privacy, Medical Records, Telephone & Telecommunications, and Public & Government Records.

Since these sites are oriented toward activism, the researcher should take into account possible bias in the selection or presentation of materials. For example, in legal cases or legislative debates, the arguments opposed to the expansion of privacy rights may not be presented, although they may be available through some of the many links to other sites.

After delving into the resources offered by EPIC, EFF, and the Privacy Rights Clearinghouse (either directly or through links), the researcher should note that many other privacy-related organizations and government agencies have web sites.

OTHER GENERAL INFORMATION RESOURCE SITES

In addition to these major advocacy sites, there are a number of other useful resource sites on various aspects of privacy and related issues. One of these is the

Center for Democracy and Technology's Headlines at http://www.cdt.org/headlines/, which includes topical links for data privacy, government surveillance, cryptography, security, authentication, and the right to know. The Legal Information Institute offers a resource page and links under "Right of Privacy" at http://www.law.cornell.edu/topics/privacy.html. The topic is further divided into access to personal information, personal autonomy, and the right of publicity.

A number of sites are directed toward consumer protection. Examples include Consumer Privacy Guide at http://www.consumerprivacyguide.org. One should also not overlook government sites such as that of the Federal Trade Commission. Its "Privacy Initiatives" pages at http://www.ftc.gov/privacy/ index.html include sections on financial privacy, credit reporting, and children's privacy.

The Health Privacy Project web site at http://www.healthprivacy.org provides links to laws (including HIPAA) as well as an overview of issues and links to other resources relating to medical privacy. As the name suggests, while Privacy International at http://www.privacyinternational.org covers all the usual privacy topics, the site emphasizes news, reports, and links relating to issues in many different countries.

TECHNICAL RESOURCES

Many issues related to online privacy involve technical matters such as security and encryption software. General-interest computer magazines and web sites may prove useful, especially for practical discussions of privacy protection from a user's perspective, reviewing the latest products and industry initiatives. Some examples of these sites include

- ComputerWorld (http://www. computerworld.com)
- InformationWeek (http://www.informationweek.com)
- InfoWorld (http://www.infoworld.com)
- PC Magazine (http://www.pcmag.com)

There are also portals that offer extensive product reviews, free software, or low-cost shareware. They are a good place to compare and shop for security products such as spam filters and antivirus programs. Some examples are

- CNet (http://www.cnet.com)
- Shareware.com (http://www.shareware.com)
- Tucows.com (http://www.tucows.com)
- ZDNet (http://www.zdnet.com)

If one has the technical background to pursue computer science resources, two very extensive portals can provide access to journals, abstracts, and other resources. These are Association for Computing Machinery (http://www.acm.org) and Institute of Electrical and Electronics Engineers (http://www.ieee.org). Note that membership is required for some of these technical resources.

PERIODICALS

Not surprisingly, a number of journals and newsletters (both print and electronic) discuss privacy or related issues. These include technical, legal, and general news coverage. Some examples are included in the following list, along with web addresses that link either to the publication's homepage or to a page further describing the publication.

- *2600 Magazine* (http://www.2600.com)
- *Canadian Privacy Law Review* (http://www.grantthornton.ca/fais/articles/Lawyers_Weekly_01-09-04.pdf)
- *IEEE Security & Privacy Magazine* (http://ieeexplore.ieee.org/xpl/periodicals.jsp; click on link)
- *Information & Technology Law* (http://www.carswell.com/law/product_samples/information_tech_law_1.asp)
- *International Privacy Bulletin* (http://www.privacy.org/pi)
- *Journal of Online Law* (http://warthog.cc.wm.edu/law/publications/jol)
- *Mealey's Privacy Report* (http://bookstore.lexis.com/bookstore/catalog; by search engine)
- *Privacy & American Business Newsletter* (http://www.pandab.org/; contains many links)
- *Privacy Journal* (http://www.privacyjournal.net)
- *Privacy Watch* (http://www.cotse.net/privacy/)
- *Privacy Times* (http://www.privacytimes.com)
- *Surveillance & Society* (http://www.surveillance-and-society.org)

BIBLIOGRAPHIC RESOURCES

Bibliographic resources is a general term for catalogs, indexes, bibliographies, and other guides that identify books, periodical articles, and other printed resources that deal with a particular subject. They are essential tools for the researcher.

LIBRARY CATALOGS

Most public and academic libraries have replaced their card catalogs with online catalogs, and many institutions now offer remote access to their catalog, either through dialing a phone number with terminal software or connecting via the Internet.

Access to the largest library catalog, that of the Library of Congress, is available at http://catalog.loc.gov. This page explains the different kinds of catalogs and searching techniques available.

Yahoo! offers a categorized listing of libraries at http://dir.yahoo.com/ Reference/ Libraries/. Of course one's local public library (and for students, the high school or college library) is also a good source for help in using on-line catalogs.

With traditional catalogs, lack of knowledge of appropriate subject headings can make it difficult to make sure the researcher finds all relevant materials. On-line catalogs, however, can be searched not only by author, title, and subject, but also by matching keywords in the title. Thus a title search for "privacy" will re-trieve all books that have that word somewhere in their title. (Of course a book about privacy may not have the word "privacy" in the title, so it is still necessary to use subject headings to get the most comprehensive results.)

The basic subject heading for privacy is "privacy, right of." The LC Subject headings file breaks this heading down into the following subdivisions and cross-references (some less relevant ones have been omitted):

Privacy, Right of
(TERM MAY BE SUBDIVIDED GEOGRAPHICALLY)*
Used for:
    Invasion of privacy
    Right of privacy
Narrower terms:
    Archives—Access control
    Confidential communications—Third parties
    Personnel records—Access control
    Public health—Statistical services—Access control
    Public records—Access control
    Records—Access control
Related terms:
    Computer crimes
    Confidential communications
Data protection—Law and legislation
    Secrecy—Law and legislation
Broader terms:
    Civil rights
    Libel and slander
    Personality (Law)
    Press Law
Call Number Ranges:
    JC596—JC596.2: Political theory

Once the record for a book or other item is found, it is a good idea to see what additional subject headings and name headings have been assigned. These in turn can be used for further searching.

---

* [That is, it can be specified by place, as in "Privacy, Right of—United States."]

BIBLIOGRAPHIES

Bibliographies in various forms provide a convenient way to find books, periodical articles, and other materials. Much of the material related to information privacy issues is quite recent, however, and the few book-length bibliographies still in print are pretty much out of date. However, many of the recent books described in Chapter 7 include extensive bibliographies (some annotated). EPIC, the EFF, and other web sites also include bibliographies.

BOOKSTORE CATALOGS

Many people have discovered that online bookstores such as Amazon.com (http://www.amazon.com) and Barnes & Noble (http://www.barnesandnoble. com) are convenient ways to shop for books. A lesser-known benefit of online bookstore catalogs is that they often include publisher's information, book reviews, and readers' comments about a given title. They can thus serve as a form of annotated bibliography.

On the other hand, a visit to one's local bookstore also has its benefits. While the selection of titles available is likely to be smaller than that of an online bookstore, the ability to physically browse through books before buying them can be very useful.

PERIODICAL DATABASES

Most public libraries subscribe to database services such as InfoTrac that index articles from hundreds of general-interest periodicals (and some moderately specialized ones). The database can be searched by author or by words in the title, subject headings, and sometimes words found anywhere in the article text. Depending on the database used, "hits" in the database can result in just a bibliographical description (author, title, pages, periodical name, issue date, etc.), a description plus an abstract (a paragraph summarizing the contents of the article), or the full text of the article itself.

Many libraries provide dial-in, Internet, or telnet access to their periodical databases as an option in their catalog menu. However, licensing restrictions usually mean that only researchers who have a library card for that particular library can access the database (by typing in their name and card number). Check with local public or school libraries to see what databases are available.

A somewhat more time-consuming alternative is to find the web sites for magazines likely to cover a topic of interest. Some scholarly publications are putting all or most of their articles online. Popular publications tend to offer only a limited selection. Some publications of both types offer archives of several years' back issues that can be searched by author or keyword.

NEWS RESOURCES

Turning from Web resource sites to other types of resources, news, both online and offline, is always important to researchers. While the more specialized or technically oriented sources (such as computer industry magazines and portals) are more likely to have detailed, accurate information about computer crimes, general news services offer immediate "breaking" news.

The major broadcast and cable networks, news (wire) services, most newspapers, and many magazines have web sites that include news stories and links to additional information. For breaking news the following sites are also useful:

- Associated Press (AP) wire: http://wire.ap.org/public_pages/WirePortalpcgi/us_portal.html
- Cable News Network (CNN): http://www.cnn.com
- *New York Times:* http://www.nytimes.com
- Reuters: http://www.reuters.com
- *Time* magazine: http://www.time.com
- *Wall Street Journal:* http://online.wsj.com/public/us
- *Washington Post:* http://www.washingtonpost.com/

Also, Yahoo! maintains a large set of links to many newspapers that have web sites or online editions at http://dir.yahoo.com/News_and_Media/Newspapers/Web_Directories/.

Another useful site for tracking down recent news stories is Google News at http://news.google.com. The site assembles news automatically into headlines and sections.

NETNEWS

Netnews is a decentralized system of thousands of "newsgroups," or forums organized by topic. Most web browsers have an option for subscribing to, reading, and posting messages in newsgroups. The Google Groups site (http://groups.google.com) also provides free access and an easy-to-use interface to newsgroups. Some examples of privacy-related newsgroups include:

- **alt.privacy**   General discussion on privacy issues
- **alt.privacy.anon-server**   Setups for anonymous Internet use
- **alt.privacy.pgp**   Pretty Good Privacy (encryption)
- **alt.privacy.spyware**   Discussion of spyware and other malicious software
- **comp.org.eff.talk**   Discussion relating to activities of the Electronic Frontier Foundation
- **comp.privacy**   General privacy discussions
- **comp.risks**   Discusses computer risks including loss of privacy
- **sci.crypt**   Focuses on technical aspects of encryption

MAIL LISTS

Mail lists offer another way to keep up with (and discuss) recent developments. Many organizations such as the Electronic Frontier Foundation maintain such lists, which you can subscribe to through the web site or by sending a specially formatted e-mail message using the instructions provided. The mailing list software automatically collates and distributes the e-mail messages.

Netnews and mail lists are generally most valuable when they have a moderator who keeps discussions focused and discourages "flaming" (the writing of heated or personally insulting statements).

SEARCHING THE WEB

A researcher can explore an ever-expanding web of information by starting with a few web sites and following the links they offer to other sites, which in turn have links to still other sites. But since this is something of a hit-and-miss proposition, some important sites may be missed if the researcher only "Web surfs" in this fashion. There are two more focused techniques that can fill in the information gaps.

WEB INDEXES

A web index is a site that offers a structured, hierarchical outline of different subject areas. This enables the researcher to zero in on a particular aspect of a subject and find links to web sites for further exploration.

Yahoo!'s directory is perhaps the best-known web index. The main Yahoo! directory page can be found at http://dir.yahoo.com. From this top level, one can click on Computers and Internet, then Issues, then Internet Issues, and finally, Privacy. There one will see a page with further topics, such as Children's Internet Privacy, Privacy Organizations, Security and Encryption, Privacy Software, and Spyware and Adware. Moving back up to Internet Issues, one can also explore such topics as Abuse, Computer and Internet Crimes, Cyberstalking, Encryption, and Law.

In addition to following Yahoo!'s outlinelike structure, there is also a search box into which the researcher can type one or more keywords and receive a list of matching categories and sites.

Web indexes such as Yahoo! have two major advantages over undirected surfing. First, the structured hierarchy of topics makes it easy to find a particular topic or subtopic and then explore its links. Second, Yahoo! does not make an attempt to compile every possible link on the Internet (a task that is virtually impossible, given the size of the Web). Rather, sites are evaluated for usefulness and quality by Yahoo!'s indexers. This means that the researcher has a better chance of finding more substantial and accurate information. (This advantage is also provided by sites like EFF and EPIC, of course.) The disadvantage of web indexes is the flip side of their selectivity: The researcher is dependent on the indexer's judgment for determining what sites are worth exploring.

Two other web indexes are LookSmart (http://www.looksmart.com) and About.com (http://www.about.com).

How to Research Privacy Issues

SEARCH ENGINES

Search engines take a very different approach to finding materials on the Web. Instead of organizing topically in a "top down" fashion, search engines work their way "from the bottom up." Basically, a search engine consists of two pieces of software. The first is a "web crawler" that systematically and automatically surfs the Net, following links and compiling them into an index with keywords (drawn either from the text of the sites themselves or from lists of words that have been flagged in a special way by the site's creators). The second program is the search engine's "front end": It provides a way to match user-specified keywords or phrases with the index and display a list of matching sites. Google (http://www.google.com) is the largest and best-known search engine, but there are a number of others, including

- Alta Vista (http://www.altavista.com)
- Excite (http://www.excite.com)
- Hotbot (http://www.hotbot.com)
- Lycos (http://www.lycos.com)
- WebCrawler (http://www.WebCrawler.com)

Search engines are generally easy to use by employing the same sorts of keywords that work in library catalogs. There are a variety of web-search tutorials available online (try "web search tutorial" in a search engine). One good one is published by The Web Tools Company at http://thewebtools.com/tutorial/tutorial.htm.

Here are a few basic rules for using search engines:

- When looking for something specific, use the most specific term or phrase. For example, when looking for information about the PGP encryption program, use "PGP," not "encryption."
- When looking for a more general topic, use several descriptive words (nouns are more reliable than verbs). For example, "privacy medical records." (Most engines will automatically put pages that match all three terms first on the results list.)
- Use "wildcards" when a desired word may have more than one ending. For example, "crypto" matches cryptography, cryptographic, or the slang term "crypto" used by some people in the field.
- If applicable, try to use a commonly accepted phrase that is likely to be associated with that topic. For example, if researching the use of the legal principle of "expectation of privacy," use that phrase (use quotes, so it will be matched as a phrase).
- Most search engines support Boolean (*and, or, not*) operators that can be used to broaden or narrow a search.

157

- Use AND to narrow a search. For example, "internet AND privacy" will match only pages that have *both* terms.

- Use OR to broaden a search: "encryption OR cryptography" will match any page that has *either* term.

- Use NOT to exclude unwanted results: "cryptography NOT pgp" finds articles about cryptography that do not discuss PGP.

Since each search engine indexes somewhat differently and offers somewhat different ways of searching, it is a good idea to use several different search engines, especially for a general query. Several "metasearch" programs automate the process of submitting a query to multiple search engines. These include Metacrawler at http://www.metacrawler.com and SurfWax at http://www.surfwax.com.

There are also search utilities that can be run from the researcher's own PC rather than through a web site. A good example is Copernic, available at http://www.copernic.com.

FINDING ORGANIZATIONS AND PEOPLE

Lists of privacy-related organizations can be found on archive sites such as EPIC and EFF and index sites such as Yahoo! If such sites do not yield the name of a specific organization, the name can be given to a search engine. Generally the best approach is to put the name of the organization in quote marks, such as "Americans for Computer Privacy."

Another approach is to take a guess at the organization's likely web address. For example, the American Civil Liberties Union is commonly known by the acronym ACLU, so it is not a surprise that the organization's web site is at http://www.aclu.org. (Note that noncommercial organization sites normally use the .org suffix, government agencies use .gov, educational institutions have .edu, and businesses use .com.) This technique can save time, but doesn't always work.

There are several ways to find a person on the Internet:

- Put the person's name (in quotes) in a search engine and possibly find that person's homepage on the Internet.

- Contact the person's employer (such as a university for an academic, or a corporation for a technical professional). Most such organizations have web pages that include a searchable faculty or employee directory.

- Try one of the people-finder services such as Yahoo! People Search (http://people.yahoo.com) or BigFoot (http://www.bigfoot.com). This may yield contact information such as e-mail address, regular address, and/or phone number.

LEGAL RESEARCH

As information privacy issues continue to capture the attention of legislators and the public, a growing body of legislation and court cases has emerged.

How to Research Privacy Issues

Because of the specialized terminology of the law, legal research can be more difficult to master than bibliographical or general research tools. Fortunately, the Internet has also come to the rescue in this area, offering a variety of ways to look up laws and court cases without having to pore through huge bound volumes in law libraries (which may not be accessible to the general public, anyway).

FINDING LAWS

When federal legislation passes, it becomes part of the United States Code, a massive legal compendium. Laws can be referred to either by their popular name or by a formal citation. For example, the Fair Credit Reporting Act is cited as 15 U.S.C. §1681, meaning title 15 of the U.S. code, section 1681.

The U.S. Code can be searched online in several locations, but the easiest site to use is Cornell Law School's site (a major provider of free online legal reference material) at http://www4.law.cornell.edu/uscode/.

The fastest way to retrieve a law is by its title and section citation, but phrases and keywords can also be used.

Federal laws are generally implemented by a designated agency that writes detailed rules, which become part of the Code of Federal Regulations (C.F.R.). A regulatory citation looks like a U.S. Code citation and takes the form *vol.* C.F.R. sec. *number*, where *vol.* is the volume number and *number* is the section number.

Regulations can be found at the web site for the relevant government agency (such as the Federal Trade Commission or Federal Communications Commission).

Many states also have their codes of laws online. FindLaw has a page of links to state laws at http://www.findlaw.com/library/state_laws.html.

KEEPING UP WITH LEGISLATIVE DEVELOPMENTS

The Library of Congress Thomas web site (http://thomas.loc.gov) includes files summarizing legislation by the number of the Congress. Each two-year session of Congress has a consecutive number: For example, the 109th Congress will be in session in 2005 and 2006. Legislation can be searched for by the name of its sponsor(s), the bill number, or by topical keywords. Laws that have been passed can be looked up under their Public Law number.

For example, selecting the 109th Congress and typing in the phrase "financial privacy" into the search box will retrieve a number of bills pertaining to that subject. Clicking on the highlighted bill number brings up a display that includes the bill's status and text, as well as further details, including sponsors, committee action, and amendments.

Privacy advocacy and industry-related sites also keep track of bills that affect them. For example, EPIC maintains a "Bill-Track" showing pending legislation (http://www.epic.org/privacy/bill_track.html).

FINDING COURT DECISIONS

Like laws, legal decisions are organized using a system of citations. The general form is: *Party 1 v. Party 2, volume reporter,* [optional *start page*] *court (year).*
Here are some examples from Chapter 2:

Katz v. United States, 389 U.S. 347 (1967)

Here the parties are Katz and the United States government, the case is in volume 389 of the U.S. *Supreme Court Reports,* and the case was decided in 1967. (For the Supreme Court, the name of the court is omitted).

Daniel Bernstein v. U.S. Department of State, 922 F. Supp. 1426, 1428–1430, N.D. Cal. (1996)

Here the parties are Daniel Bernstein and the U.S. Department of State. The decision is in volume 922 of the *Federal Supplement* (which reports on cases in district courts). The court is the North California District Federal Court, and the case was decided in 1996.
To find a federal court decision, first ascertain the level of court involved: district (the lowest level, where trials are normally held), circuit (the main court of appeals), or the Supreme Court. The researcher can then go to a number of places on the Internet to find cases by citation and, often, the names of the parties. Some of the most useful sites are:

- The Legal Information Institute (http://supct.law.cornell.edu/supct/) has all Supreme Court decisions since 1990 plus 610 of "the most important historic" decisions.
- Washlaw Web (http://www.washlaw.edu/) has a variety of courts (including states) and legal topics listed, making it a good jumping-off place for many sorts of legal research.
- EPIC maintains a "Litigation docket" of pending court cases (http://www.epic.org/privacy/litigation/).

LEXIS AND WESTLAW

Lexis and Westlaw are commercial legal databases that have extensive information including an elaborate system of notes, legal subject headings, and ways to show relationships between cases. Unfortunately, these services are too expensive for use by most individual researchers unless they are available through a university or corporate library.

MORE HELP ON LEGAL RESEARCH

For more information on conducting legal research, see the "Legal Research FAQ" at http://www.eff.org/legal/?=law_research.faq.txt. This also explains more advanced techniques such as "Shepardizing" (referring to *Shepard's Case Citations*), which is used to find how a decision has been cited in subsequent cases and whether the decision was later overturned.

EVALUATING WEB SOURCES

Thanks to the Web there is more information from more sources available than ever before. There is also a greater diversity of voices, since any person or group with a PC and Internet service can put up a web site—in some cases a site that looks as polished and professional as that of an established group. One benefit is that dissenting views can be found in abundance. However, as can be seen in the reports of Internet hoaxes and scams, the Web is also inundated with deliberate misinformation and deception as well as hoaxes and urban legends.

Thus the student or researcher must not let the attractions of the Web override the need for the same kind of critical thinking that would be applied to printed materials. Further, the nature of the Web means that the researcher should take extra care to try to verify facts and to understand the possible biases of each source. Some good questions to ask include

- Who is responsible for this web site?
- What is the background or reputation of the person or group?
- Does the person or group have a stated objective or agenda?
- What biases might this person or group have?
- Do a number of high-quality sites link to this one?
- What is the source given for a particular fact? Does that source actually say what is quoted? Where did *they* get that information?

If one uses a good variety of the tools and resources that have been highlighted here, that will help ensure that the results of research are balanced and comprehensive.

CHAPTER 7

ANNOTATED BIBLIOGRAPHY

This chapter provides an extensive annotated bibliography on information privacy issues. Materials have been selected with a view to providing a diversity of views and range from popular accounts to legal and technical works. The listings are divided into the following 14 categories:

Reference and Background
Reference Works
General Introductions and Overviews
Perspectives on Privacy

Areas of Privacy
Personal and Consumer Privacy
Privacy and Health Care
Corporate and Workplace Privacy
Privacy and Young People
The Surveillance Society

Privacy Issues
General and International Privacy Law
Privacy, Law Enforcement, and National Security
Identification Systems and Biometrics
Surveillance, Screening, and Tracking Systems
Government Accountability and Freedom of Information
Tools and Standards for Privacy and Anonymity

Within each category the listings are divided as applicable into books, articles and papers, and web documents. Note that although all web addresses (URLs) have been checked, web pages are often moved or removed. If an address is not found, a keyword search using a search engine is recommended. Note that many newspaper and magazine articles may be available online, either through online databases or directly from the publication's web site. See chapter 6 for more information about Internet research and resources.

Annotated Bibliography

REFERENCE AND BACKGROUND

REFERENCE WORKS

This section includes general and specialized encyclopedias, handbooks, and bibliographies.

Books

Allen, Anita L., and Richard Turkington. *Privacy Law: Cases and Materials.* St. Paul, Minn.: West Group, 2002. An extensive casebook including overviews and case excerpts. It includes an introduction to the concept of privacy (including informational privacy) as well as relevant sections on federal and state privacy statutes, e-mail and Internet privacy, and privacy torts.

Bloom, Robert M. *Searches, Seizures, and Warrants: A Reference Guide to the United States Constitution.* Westport, Conn.: Praeger, 2003. Describes the mechanisms by which law enforcement seeks to gain access to private property and possessions in order to investigate crime. Bloom explains how the courts have sought to balance privacy rights as guaranteed by the Fourth Amendment with the need to protect society from criminal behavior.

Electronic Privacy Information Center. *Consumer Law Sourcebook 2000.* Washington, D.C.: Electronic Privacy Information Center, 2000. A useful collection of legislation and other documents relating to consumer rights (including privacy) and the responsibility of businesses in electronic commerce.

———. *Privacy & Human Rights: An International Survey of Privacy Laws and Developments.* Washington, D.C.: Electronic Privacy Information Center and London: Privacy International, 2004. An annual compilation that includes background to privacy issues and significant developments throughout the world. The book also includes useful summaries of the privacy laws in force in each nation and an international list of privacy resources. Updates are available at http://www.epic.org and http://www.privacyinternational.org.

Isenberg, Doug. *Gigalaw Guide to Internet Law.* New York: Random House, 2002. A comprehensive guide to laws and legal issues affecting Internet use, with an emphasis on e-commerce. The book includes discussions of privacy considerations, including European and Canadian regulations. It can be supplemented by browsing the companion web site http://www.gigalaw.com.

Plunkett, Jack W. *Plunkett's Banking, Mortgages and Credit Industry Almanac 2005: The Only Complete Guide to the Business of Banking, Lending, Mortgages, and Credit Cards.* Houston, Tex.: Plunkett Research, 2004. Provides detailed background to the corporate players involved in much of the controversy over the use (or misuse) of consumer data. The almanac includes overviews and discussion of significant industry trends.

Rotenberg, Marc. *The Privacy Law Sourcebook 2003: United States Law, International Law, and Recent Developments.* Washington, D.C.: Electronic Privacy Information Center, 2003. A comprehensive compendium of United States and international privacy law. The book includes excerpts from laws, resolutions, and policies and concludes with a bibliography and list of resources. Readers should check for the most recent edition.

Smith, Robert Ellis. *Compilation of State and Federal Privacy Laws.* Updated 2002 edition with 2004 Supplement. Providence, R.I.: Privacy Journal, 2004. This concise reference organizes state and federal privacy laws by what they regulate, from bank and financial records and cable television to polygraphs and Social Security numbers. Legal citations are given for each law.

GENERAL INTRODUCTIONS AND OVERVIEWS

Works in this section provide a general introduction or overview on privacy issues.

Books

Agre, Philip, and Marc Rotenberg, eds. *Technology and Privacy: The New Landscape.* Cambridge: MIT Press, 1997. Experts in computer science, law, politics, and sociology trace the roots and implications of privacy issues.

Alderman, Ellen, and Caroline Kennedy. *The Right to Privacy.* New York: Knopf, 1995. Uses a wealth of cases and anecdotes to illustrate privacy issues, including law enforcement abuses, privacy for intimate life, and privacy in the workplace.

Bennett, Colin J., and Rebecca Grant, eds. *Visions of Privacy: Policy Choices for the Digital Age.* Toronto: University of Toronto Press, 2000. Provides a variety of perspectives and ways to view privacy in the light of a business and social environment that features pervasive technologies of surveillance and data gathering. Many authors focus on practical solutions for safeguarding privacy from various threats.

Bennett, John, Jr. *The Digital Umbrella: Technology's Attack on Personal Privacy in America.* Boca Raton, Fla.: BrownWalker Press, 2004. Gives real-world examples of the policies and technologies by which the federal government, corporations, employers, and others are obtaining and often misusing information that most people would consider to be personal and private.

Bridegam, Martha. *The Right to Privacy.* Langhorne, Penn.: Chelsea House, 2003. This overview for high school or older students provides pro and con arguments on privacy issues, particularly the conflict between privacy and law enforcement or security in the post–September 11 United States.

Cate, Fred H. *Privacy in Perspective,* Washington, D.C.: AEI Press, 2001. An overview of privacy issues, privacy law, and the various tools available for strengthening privacy. The benefits and costs of privacy legislation are considered.

Fridell, Ron. *Privacy vs. Security: Your Rights in Conflict.* Berkeley Heights, N.J.: Enslow Publishers, 2004. Provides a good overview of privacy issues for junior high and older students. Fridell discusses the development of the concept of privacy, legal issues, and the modern technologies of surveillance.

There is particular emphasis on issues potentially affecting young people, such as student records, school drug testing, and searches. The concluding chapter covers privacy threats related to the war on terrorism and government programs such as the now discontinued Terrorist Information and Prevention System (TIPS) and Total (or Terrorist) Information Awareness (TIA).

Garrett, Brandon. *Right to Privacy.* New York: Rosen Publishing Group, 2001. A well-organized basic introduction to privacy issues for high school students. The book includes discussion of constitutional protections, privacy, search and seizure, and the rights of students.

Gottfried, Ted. *Privacy: Individual Right vs. Social Needs.* Brookfield, Conn.: Millbrook Press, 1994. Introduces the privacy debate to high school–age readers by discussing court cases and issues involving law enforcement, abortion, birth control, medical privacy, and misuse of databases.

Ojeda, Auriana, ed. *Civil Liberties: Opposing Viewpoints.* Farmington Hills, Mich.: Greenhaven Press, 2004. Presents pro and con articles on a variety of civil liberties issues, including technological threats to privacy and the effect of the war on terrorism on civil liberties. The book includes bibliographies.

Smith, Robert Ellis. *Ben Franklin's Web Site: Privacy and Curiosity from Plymouth Rock to the Internet.* Providence, R.I.: Privacy Journal 2000. A marvelous tapestry of observations and quotes on privacy, including the busy-body Puritans, the lack of privacy in 19th-century living, the establishment of privacy of the mails, technologies from the telegraph and phonograph to miniature wiretaps, and the development of modern legal doctrines of privacy (including behind-the-scenes looks at the Supreme Court).

Spinello, Richard A., and Herman T. Tavani, eds. *Readings in CyberEthics.* Sudbury, Mass.: Jones and Bartlett, 2001 An anthology of essays on the ethics and governance of cyberspace. Topics include free speech, responsibility for content, intellectual property, privacy, security, and codes of ethical conduct.

Strum, Philippa. *Privacy: The Debate in the United States Since 1945.* Fort Worth, Tex.: Harcourt College Publishers, 1998. Discusses the major aspects of the privacy issue, including the use of genetic information and Social Security numbers, access to public records, intrusions by law enforcement, the growing use of surveillance, and privacy in the workplace.

Wacks, Raymond, ed. *Privacy.* New York: New York University Press, 1993. Consists of two volumes of essays, the first dealing with the development of the concept of privacy, and the second discussing legal aspects of privacy.

Articles and Papers

Colin, Thomas J., ed. "Is Privacy Under Attack." *CQ Researcher,* vol. 11, June 15, 2001, pp. 507–526. An issue on the theme of privacy where *Congressional Quarterly* staff writers provide background on privacy issues, laws, and legislation. The article includes a chronology and recommended readings.

Glancy, Dorothy J. "The Invention of the Right to Privacy." *Arizona Law Review,* vol. 21, 1979, pp. 1–39. Discusses the early development of legal concepts of privacy in America, particularly the opinions of Justice Louis Brandeis.

Privacy in the Information Age

Gormley, Ken. "One Hundred Years of Privacy." *Wisconsin Law Review*, 1992, p. 1,335ff. Also available online. URL: http://cyber.law.harvard.edu/privacy/Gormley—100%20Years%20of%20Privacy.htm. Examines the evolution of privacy law in the United States in the century following the publication of a seminal *Harvard Law Review* article by Samuel Warren and Louis Brandeis. Aspects discussed include tort privacy, Fourth Amendment privacy, First Amendment privacy, "fundamental-decision privacy," and state constitutional privacy.

Karaim, Reed. "The Invasion of Privacy." *Civilization*, October/November 1996, n.p. [also reprinted in Winters, Paul A., ed. *the Information Revolution: Opposing Viewpoints.* San Diego, Calif.: Greenhaven Press, 1998, pp. 151–158]. An overview of the history and development of the idea of privacy with examples of how the right to privacy is becoming threatened in the information age.

Web Documents

"EPIC Online Guide to Privacy Resources." Electronic Privacy Information Center. Available online. URL: http://epic.org/privacy/privacy_resources_faq.html. Updated on May 6, 2002. A basic listing of privacy-related organizations, printed publications, resource web sites, mailing lists, newsletters, and privacy tools.

Fallows, Deborah. "The Internet and Daily Life: Many Americans Use the Internet in Everyday Activities, but Traditional Offline Habits Still Dominate." Pew Internet & American Life Project. Available online. URL: http://www.pewinternet.org/PPF/r/131/report_display.asp. Posted on August 11, 2004. Because Internet use exposes consumers to a variety of threats to their privacy, this survey of the extent and nature of online activity provides useful background for assessing privacy issues.

Fox, Susannah. "Trust and Privacy Online: Why Americans Want to Rewrite the Rules." Pew Internet and American Life Project. Available online. URL: http://www.pewinternet.org/pdfs/PIP_Trust_Privacy_Report.pdf. Posted on August 20, 2000. A report on Internet use at the start of the millennium found that a growing number of Americans were concerned about online privacy but had little knowledge of specific threats and did little to counter them.

"Privacy in Cyberspace: Rules of the Road for the Information Superhighway." Privacy Rights Clearinghouse. Available online. URL: http://www.privacyrights.org/fs/fs18-cyb.htm. Updated in August 2003. A useful primer on the privacy implications of various online activities. Most forms of online communication have little expectation of privacy except for e-mail (outside of a work setting). The site also explains how one's online activities can be monitored by web sites using cookies or other means. It concludes with tips on how to determine the level of privacy in various online venues.

"Privacy Survival Guide: How to Take Control of Your Personal Information." Privacy Rights Clearinghouse. Available online. URL: http://www.privacyrights.org/fs/fs1-surv.htm. Updated in January 2005. Includes discussions of credit reports (and how to obtain them for free), opting out of telemarketing and junk mail, checking medical records, and limiting disclosure of Social Security numbers and other sensitive information. The site urges readers to "Be Aware. Be Assertive. Be an Advocate."

"Public Opinion on Privacy." Electronic Privacy Information Center. Available online. URL: http://www.epic.org/privacy/survey/default.html. Updated on July 15, 2004. Cites recent polls showing strong public support for privacy rights and demands for control of personal information and the desire for accountability by providers. Includes a critique of Alan Westin's characterization of privacy "fundamentalists" vs. "pragmatists."

PERSPECTIVES ON PRIVACY

This section includes works that provide a variety of sociological, cultural, or philosophical perspectives on privacy issues.

Books

Bailey, Dennis. *The Open Society Paradox: Why the 21st Century Calls for More Openness—Not Less.* Washington, D.C.: Brassey's, 2004. The author takes the paradoxical—and controversial—position that the security benefits of universal IDs and pervasive surveillance can be safely secured as long as the institutions of government are themselves open and accountable to the public. He also suggests that privacy advocates have been too extreme in demanding a level of privacy that has not been historically sustainable.

Boling, Patricia. *Privacy and the Politics of Intimate Life.* Ithaca, N.Y.: Cornell University Press, 1996. Analyzes privacy issues from a feminist and legal theory perspective, exploring the characterization of intimate and public life and drawing upon the work of Hannah Arendt. One prominent example used is the process of "outing" of lesbians and gay men and its turning of the private into the political. The author argues that while the right of privacy can protect vulnerable people, concepts of privacy can also hide the results of oppression and disparities in power.

Branscomb, Ann Wells. *Who Owns Information?: From Privacy to Public Access.* New York: Basic Books, 1995. A wide-ranging account that explores the background and issues of today's controversies about the misuse of information. The author suggests that a question that starts with Social Security numbers and health records has far-reaching legal and philosophical implications.

Brin, David. *The Transparent Society: Will Technology Force Us to Choose Between Privacy and Freedom?* Reading, Mass.: Addison-Wesley, 1998. The author, a noted science fiction writer and futurist, offers a controversial solution to the problem of privacy. Surveying a variety of viewpoints, Brin suggests that the only viable option is to promote transparency, where the playing field is leveled because everyone has access to the same information.

DeCew, Judith W. *In Pursuit of Privacy: Law, Ethics, and the Rise of Technology.* Ithaca, N.Y.: Cornell University Press, 1997. The author reviews the legal history of the right of privacy and then describes a number of perspectives on privacy from the point of view of control of information, personal autonomy, property rights, intimacy, and feminist interpretations. Ultimately these claims can be seen as aspects of how privacy empowers the self-creation of individuals by providing a protective sphere against the forces of conformity. The author concludes with discussion of the balance between privacy and public safety and of the impact of new technologies.

Ermann, David M., and Michele S. Shauf, eds. *Computers, Ethics, and Society.* 3d ed. New York: Oxford University Press, 2002. An undergraduate-level introduction to computer-related ethical problems, including privacy issues.

Etzioni, Amitai. *The Limits of Privacy.* New York: Basic Books, 1999. Communitarian philosopher Amitai Etzioni argues for social needs trumping privacy rights when a clear benefit can be seen. For example, he believes the FBI's need to crack messages from terrorists justifies some compromise of e-mail privacy, and he supports a national ID card. Similarly Etzioni supports medical testing of infants for HIV without parental consent and also supports Megan's law to protect society against sex offenders. As a communitarian he believes in creating a responsible government and giving it broad powers, but he is much less sanguine about abuses of privacy by commercial interests. This articulate but controversial book provides a good counterpoint to the much larger number of writers who advocate increased privacy protections.

Gandy, Oscar H. *The Panoptic Sort: A Political Economy of Personal Information.* Boulder, Colo.: Westview Press, 1993. Describes the pervasive effects of information as power in both the political and economic realms. Bentham and Foucault had envisioned the "panoptic prison" of total surveillance, but Gandy suggests that in the modern world it is the "panoptic sort" of information technology that enables the sophisticated classification and management of individuals.

Garrow, David G. *Liberty and Sexuality: The Right to Privacy and the Making of* Roe v. Wade. Berkeley: University of California Press, 1998. Exhaustively analyzes the legal reasoning that led to the *Roe v. Wade* abortion rights decision. *Roe* represented an expansion of an assertion of privacy as a constitutional right in *Griswold v. Connecticut* and has had an impact on expanding rights to information privacy.

Gerstein, Robert S., ed. *Philosophical Dimensions of Privacy.* New York: Cambridge University Press, 1984. Published in a symbolically significant year, this anthology presents a larger variety of perspectives than the title might suggest. It includes classic legal papers, plus perspectives from anthropology, economics, and of course philosophy.

Gilliom, John. *Overseers of the Poor: Surveillance, Resistance, and the Limits of Privacy.* Chicago: University of Chicago Press, 2001. Argues that discussions about privacy have focused too much on issues faced by middle-class persons. Welfare clients and other low-income persons are interviewed by the author for insights into their experience of surveillance and social control. They are stripped bare of privacy to a considerable extent, but they also devise ways to resist the intrusion.

———. *Surveillance, Privacy, and the Law.* Ann Arbor: University of Michigan Press, 1994. From a perspective of political theory, the author sees the establishment of drug testing in many places of employment as the harbinger of a broader surveillance society and more pervasive social control. Ideologically, these developments are seen in the context of a triumph of conservatism in the courts and Congress in the 1990s.

Gurak, Laura J. *Persuasion and Privacy in Cyberspace: The Online Protests Over Lotus Marketplace and the Clipper Chip.* New Haven: Yale University Press, 1997. Discusses two defining privacy controversies of the mid-1990s: the reaction to a Lotus Corporation database marketing proposal, which would have distributed personal consumer information without consent, and a government proposal for the Clipper Chip, which offered data protection in exchange for government access.

Gutwirth, Serge. *Privacy and the Information Age.* Lanham, Md.: Rowman & Littlefield Publishers, 2002. An interesting perspective on privacy that sees it as bound up with another fundamental right—liberty. Privacy is required if a person is to be able to decide who he or she is or does. Yet modern technologies threaten privacy and liberty in new ways.

Inness, Julie C. *Privacy, Intimacy, and Isolation.* New York: Oxford University Press, 1992. Explores the roots of privacy in the need to protect the intimate, personal sphere of human life.

Jensen, Derrick, and George Draffan. *Welcome to the Machine: Science, Surveillance, and the Culture of Control.* White River, Vt.: Chelsea Green Publishing, 2004. The authors take a radical approach to understanding the mechanisms of surveillance and social control. Using the image of the panopticon (the all-seeing central "eye"), they argue that modern information technology is being used to dehumanize citizens and consumers in an increasingly dysfunctional capitalist system. At the same time, however, they see hope in the way hackers, independent developers, and others are using the same technology to empower individuals.

Kizza, Joseph Migga. *Ethical and Social Issues in the Information Age.* New York: Springer Verlag, 2002. The author suggests that rapid technological change has thrown legal and ethical systems into confusion. Researchers and policymakers must find new paradigms for looking at issues such as workplace surveillance, harassment, encryption, and other privacy and civil liberties issues.

Levin, Thomas Y., Ursula Frohne, and Peter Weibel, eds. *CTRL [SPACE]: Rhetorics of Surveillance from Bentham to Big Brother.* Cambridge, Mass.: MIT Press, 2002. Describes the development of visual art and photography reflecting the perception of the "surveillance society," from Bentham's panopticon prison in the 19th century to today's electronics. The book includes writings by postmodern essayists Jean Baudrillard and Michel Foucault as well as the works of artists including Yoko Ono and Andy Warhol. It was published in conjunction with an exhibition at the ZKM Center for Art and Media in Karls-ruhe, Germany.

Lyon, David, ed. *Surveillance as Social Sorting: Privacy, Risk and Automated Discrimination.* New York: Routledge, 2002. Describes how geographical information systems (GIS), "intelligent" transportation systems, biometrics, and use of genetic data are having the effect of categorizing people into different social groups. This threatens to reinforce existing social divisions, racism, and other problems.

Marlin-Bennett, Renée. *Knowledge Power: Intellectual Property, Information, and Privacy.* Boulder, Colo.: Lyne Rienner Publishers, 2004. Discusses the shifting boundaries of personal and information privacy for adults, teens, and children. Marlin-Bennett emphasizes the need to become aware of how one is sharing information in business, government, and social transactions and how the flow of information reflects power relationships.

Neill, Elizabeth. *Rites of Privacy and the Privacy Trade.: On the Limits of Protection for the* Self. Ithaca, N.Y.: McGill-Queen's University Press, 2001. Focuses on the need to determine what a right to privacy does or should mean in the context of modern society and changing technology. The author draws on history, sociology, law, literature, and other fields to create a contemporary privacy concept based on natural or inherent rights. However, rather than proceeding to an expansive application of privacy, she suggests that other considerations require that it be limited in a number of significant ways, such as with regard to health care.

Peacock, Margaret, ed. *The Private I: Privacy in a Public World.* St. Paul, Minn.: Graywolf Press, 2001. A collection of essays exploring the experience of privacy (and of its violation) and the relationship of privacy to creativity. Venues range from cyberspace to literature and the media.

Rosen, Jeffrey. *The Unwanted Gaze: The Destruction of Privacy in America.* New York: Random House, 2000. According to the author, the Internet and other technologies have created a society where people are awash in information that they are largely unable to use effectively and at the same time are unable to control their self-disclosure through the tracks left by every communication or transaction. Privacy has thus become crucially important for reclaiming the self.

Rossler, Beate, Mieke Bal, and Hent de Vries, eds. *Privacies: Philosophical Evaluations.* Stanford, Calif.: Stanford University Press, 2003. A collection of papers (mainly from a May 1999 conference in Amsterdam) discussing philosophical and sociological aspects of privacy. Contributors agree that privacy remains a vital value in modern democratic societies but find it difficult to draw reliable lines between private and public spaces.

Wacks, Raymond. *Law, Morality and the Private Domain.* Hong Kong: Hong Kong University Press, 2001. Develops the relationship between the concept of privacy and its ethical dimensions and the need for the law to define and protect a sphere of personal privacy.

Weintraub, Jeff, and Krishan Kumar, eds. *Public and Private in Thought and Practice: Perspectives on a Grand Dichotomy.* Chicago: Chicago University Press,

1997. Contributors provide philosophical analysis of the distinctions between private and public that underlie much of the current privacy debates. Proper understanding of the relationship between public and private spheres is shown to be necessary for dealing with many "hot button" social issues such as abortion rights and affirmative action.

Articles and Papers

Etzioni, Amitai, and Nadine Strossen. "Should Americans Be Willing to Give Up Some of Their Privacy to Advance Policies that Are Generally Perceived to Be in Society's Best Interest? *CQ Researcher*, vol. 7, March 21, 1997, p. 257. Debate between Etzioni, a communitarian philosopher and Strossen, director of the ACLU, that pits collective good against the individual rights of privacy.

Flood, Barbara. "The Emotionality of Privacy." *Bulletin of the American Society for Information Science*, vol. 123, February–March 1997, p. 7ff. Explores the importance of privacy to self-image and to the sense of control people have over their own lives.

Rust, Michael, and Susan Crabtree. "Access, Privacy and Power." *Insight on the News*, vol. 12, August 19, 1996, p. 8ff. Explores the trade-off between the power and convenience of computer technology and the ability it gives people to invade other peoples' privacy.

Walker, Kent. "The Costs of Privacy." *Harvard Journal of Law & Public Policy*, vol. 25, Fall 2001, p. 87ff. Privacy is both an individual and a social good, but it comes with costs: more paperwork to deal with, higher prices, fewer free services, less convenience, and (paradoxically) less security. Greater efforts to protect privacy can also impinge on the right of free expression. Therefore the benefits and costs of each proposed privacy measure must be carefully evaluated.

Web Documents

Charbeneau, Travis. "The Future of Privacy: Moot?" ItmWeb.com. Available online. URL: http://www.itmweb.com/f010501.htm. Posted on January 5, 2001. The author, a futurist, argues that as society becomes more enlightened and tolerant about sexual and other personal matters, the need to protect personal privacy will diminish. At the same time, stronger legislation and tools such as encryption may provide better protection for those matters that still need to remain private.

Godwin, Mike. "Privacy Please." Salon.com. Available online. URL: http://archive.salon.com/tech/books/1999/04/26/privacy/. Posted on April 26, 1999. Godwin, a civil liberties attorney, reviews *The Limits of Privacy* by Amitai Etzioni, whom he argues uses extreme examples (Megan's law and HIV testing of infants) to attack privacy advocates and is generally too supportive and uncritical of government social goals even when they infringe on privacy.

Johnson, David R. "Barbed Wire Fences in Cyberspace: The Threat Posed by Calls for Ownership of Transactional Information." Electronic Frontier

Foundation. Available online. URL: http://www.eff.org/Misc/Publications/
David_Johnson/cyber_barbwire_johnson.article. Posted on April 4, 1994.
Argues that giving individuals property rights in their data may not be an effective way to protect privacy because people might just trade away their
rights for convenience or other incentives. Johnson suggests strong, fully disclosed privacy policies as an alternative.

Obser, Jeffrey. "Privacy Is the Problem, Not the Solution." Salon.com. Available
online. URL: http://archive.salon.com/june97/21st/privacy970626.html.
Posted on June 26, 1997. Argues that the demand for privacy may be excessive and reflect "a fearful reaction to the collapse of trust in our culture" and
that privacy laws may have a downside in protecting the criminal and corrupt
from scrutiny.

Taylor, Humphrey. "Most People Are 'Privacy Pragmatists' Who, While Concerned About Privacy, Will Sometimes Trade It Off for Other Benefits." Harris Poll. Available online. URL: http://www.harrisinteractive.com/harris_
poll/index.asp?PID=365. Posted on March 19, 2003. A survey of attitudes
about privacy threats finds that about a quarter of the adult population are
"privacy fundamentalists" who believe they have lost much of their privacy
and are highly resistant to further encroachments. About a tenth of the population are basically unconcerned about privacy issues. However, the largest
group, about two thirds of the population, are "privacy pragmatists" who
have strong concerns about privacy but are willing to allow access to their information when they can see tangible benefits.

AREAS OF PRIVACY

PERSONAL AND CONSUMER PRIVACY

Works in this section focus on the privacy rights and issues arising from modern commerce, as well as other issues involving the collection and use of personal identification information.

Books

Bahadur, Gary. *Privacy Defended: Protecting Yourself Online.* Indianapolis, Ind.:
Que, 2002. Gives detailed how-to information for PC users who want to protect themselves from potential invasions of privacy or other attacks. The book
includes discussions of software (such as antivirus and encryption programs),
privacy laws and legal protections, and online payment systems.

Cady, Glee Harroh, and Pat McGregor. *Protect Your Digital Privacy! Survival Skills
for the Information Age.* New York: Que, 2001. A guide to online privacy threats
that explains how users can protect their personal information and prevent intrusive companies or individuals from learning about one's online activities.

Cate, Fred H., et al. *Financial Privacy, Consumer Privacy, and the Public Good.*
Washington, D.C.: American Enterprise Institute Press, 2003. Describes the
emerging issues involving regulation of credit bureaus as parts of the federal

Annotated Bibliography

Fair Credit Reporting Act expire and many states seek tougher restrictions on dissemination of credit information. The authors argue that a federal standard is required because conflicting state laws would disrupt the system that now provides consumers with instant credit.

Cavoukian, Ann, and Tyler Hamilton. *The Privacy Payoff: How Successful Businesses Build Customer Trust.* New York: McGraw Hill, 2002. Convincingly argues that privacy policies should not be regarded by business leaders as an expensive nuisance but as an opportunity to build advantageous relationships with customers. To do so, companies need to create a culture that fosters privacy in marketing and in the workplace.

Chesbro, Michael. *Privacy Handbook: Proven Countermeasures for Combating Threats to Privacy, Security, and Personal Freedom.* Boulder, Colo.: Paladin Press, 2002. An uncompromising libertarian takes an "edgy" approach to protecting privacy. He argues that both government and big corporations have run amok in their disregard for personal privacy, and he suggests dozens of privacy-protecting and personal security measures with varying degrees of practicality.

Frye, Curtis D. *Privacy-Enhanced Business: Adapting to the Online Environment.* Westport, Conn.: Quorum Books, 2001. Analyzes the privacy concerns of online users that are leading to a growing regulatory movement in Europe and the United States. Frye describes a variety of scenarios that show how corporations can address privacy concerns, particularly in marketing and sales.

Gertler, Eric J. *Prying Eyes: Protect Your Privacy from People Who Sell to You, Snoop on You, and Steal from You.* New York: Random House, 2004. The author, former CEO of a credit protection company, has created a well-organized handbook that explains the issues involved with every aspect of personal privacy. It also provides a variety of steps and tips for securing one's information and detecting and responding to its misuse.

Givens, Beth. *Privacy Rights Handbook: How to Take Control of Your Personal Information.* New York: Morrow, 1997. A classic and still useful discussion of the major threats to personal and consumer privacy and the steps one can take to protect information and minimize risk.

Ham, Shane, and Robert D. Atkinson. *Online Privacy and a Free Internet: Striking a Balance.* Washington, D.C.: Progressive Policy Institute, 2001. Also available online. URL: http://www.bbbonline.org/UnderstandingPrivacy/library/whitepapers/E-Privacy2.pdf. Takes a generally pro-industry approach to privacy, emphasizing the use of clear privacy policies, plus opt-out rather than opt-in for consumers. The authors believe that particular technologies should not be mandated because that would impair the flexibility and innovation of the Internet.

Hendricks, Evan. *Credit Scores & Credit Reports: How the System Works: What You Can Do.* Cabin John, Md.: Privacy Times, 2004. The information in consumer credit reports can have a decisive effect on many aspects of daily life, but the mechanism used for gathering information and assigning credit scores is obscure. The author (and editor of the newsletter *Privacy Times*) explains how the system works and how to deal with problems such as identity theft, credit repair services, and discriminatory practices in insurance and other areas.

Jennings, Charles, and Lori Fena. *The Hundredth Window: Protecting Your Privacy and Security in the Age of the Internet.* New York: Free Press, 2000. The metaphor used by the authors is that one open window in a hundred can compromise the security of the castle. As people can now look out into the wide world of the Internet, they are equally vulnerable to people peering in. The authors (founders of the TRUSTe privacy certification service) describe how many sorts of web sites use various techniques to track users and obtain information about them.

Kasanoff, Bruce. *Making It Personal: How to Profit from Personalization Without Invading Privacy.* Cambridge, Mass.: Perseus, 2001. Gathering knowledge from the stream of transactions and communications with suppliers, employees, and customers makes it possible for businesses to be more efficient and effective. For example analysis of work patterns can improve efficiency, while buying patterns can be analyzed in order to target customers with special offers. However, technologies such as data mining, monitoring, and even biometrics can have many implications in terms of legality, labor relations, and public attitudes. The author uses many contemporary examples to illustrate these issues.

Lane, Carole A. *Naked in Cyberspace: How to Find Personal Information Online.* 2d ed. Medford, N.J.: CyberAge Publications, 2002. Presents eye-opening "how-tos" for finding information about people from online sources—and for protecting oneself from other peoples' snooping. The book includes a detailed listing of sources of public records.

Levine, J., R. Everett-Church, and G. Stebben. *Internet Privacy for Dummies.* New York: Hungry Minds, 2002. Using the familiar and accessible "for Dummies" format, the authors provide common sense guidance and techniques for protecting personal information online while using the Internet as an effective information tool.

Luna, J. J. *How to Be Invisible: The Essential Guide to Protecting Your Personal Privacy, Your Assets, and Your Life.* Revised and updated edition. New York: Thomas Dunne Books, 2004. The author, an experienced security consultant, has revised this handbook to account for the recent growth in privacy intrusion both by the government (post September 11) and through corporate databases and online predators. Sections describe how to secure personal and financial information, maintain a low profile to avoid snoopers, and obtain anonymity in transactions and ownership.

Murphy, M. Maureen. "Privacy Protection for Customer Financial Information." Washington, D.C.: Congressional Research Service, 2003. Also available online. URL: http://www.epic.org/privacy/glba/RS20185.pdf. Gives background on financial privacy issues, explains privacy provisions of the Gramm-Leach-Bliley Act, and summarizes industry concerns.

Nott, Loretta. *The Role of Information in Lending: The Cost of Privacy Restrictions.* Washington, D.C.: Congressional Research Service, 2003. Also available online. URL: http://www.law.umaryland.edu/marshall/crsreports/ crsdocuments/RL31847_05192003.pdf. Argues that overly restrictive regulations on access to data on consumer borrowing behavior would make the credit market inefficient. Some results could be higher interest rates, less accessible credit, and lending to persons who are unlikely to manage their debt.

Privacy Online: Fair Information Practices in the Electronic Marketplace. Washington, D.C.: Federal Trade Commission, 2000. Also available online. URL: http://www.ftc.gov/reports/privacy2000/privacy2000.pdf. A key survey of information-handling practices by commercial web sites. The results showed that most sites now had privacy policies, but only 20 percent implemented, at least partially, the four basic fair information practices: notice, choice, access, and security.

Rubin, Paul H., and Thomas M. Lenard. *Privacy and the Commercial Use of Personal Information.* Boston: Kluwer Academic Publishers, 2002. Also available online. URL: http://www.pff.org/issues-pubs/books/010701privacyandpersonalinfo. pdf. This report from the pro-business Progress and Freedom Foundation argues that the costs and other negative effects of increased regulation of the sale of personal information outweigh any benefits in enhanced privacy protection. In effect, such policies would make information more expensive, marketing less efficient, and the consumer experience less satisfying. Besides, the market is capable of responding to consumer demands for greater privacy protection.

Shaw, Paul. *E-Business Privacy and Trust: Planning and Management Strategies.* New York: Wiley, 2001. The author stresses the need for a secure e-commerce environment and a well-written privacy policy. Failure to address privacy concerns can lead to serious lawsuits, bad publicity, and loss of customer loyalty. Special legal concerns involving financial information, health data, and data involving children are also covered.

Staten, Michael E., and Fred E. Cate. *The Adverse Impact of Opt-In Privacy Rules on Consumers: A Case Study of Retail Credit.* Washington, D.C.: Privacy Leadership Initiative, 2002. This case study based on the operations of MBNA Corporation concludes that requiring opt-in (explicit consumer consent) for the collection, transfer, or use of personal information would be costly to both businesses and consumers. It would also impair access to information needed for fighting fraud and identity theft.

Turow, Joseph. *Americans & Online Privacy: The System is Broken.* Philadelphia: University of Pennsylvania Annenberg Public Policy Center, 2003. Also available online. URL: http://www.asc.upenn.edu/usr/jturow/internet-privacy-report/36-page-turow-version-9.pdf. This survey has discouraging news for privacy advocates: It finds that most adults who go online do not understand the purpose of privacy statements or the implications of their sharing information with e-commerce companies. Most users also do not understand how their clicking on web pages can be combined with "cookies" to create profiles.

Privacy in the Information Age

Articles and Papers

Ambrose, Stephen F., Jr., and Joseph W. Gelb. "Consumer Privacy Regulation and Litigation in the United States." *Business Lawyer*, vol. 59, May 2004, p. 1,251ff. Summarizes recent court decisions and regulatory rulings relating to financial privacy under the Gramm-Leach-Bliley Act and data security issues under the Children's Online Privacy Act.

Arrison, Sonia. "How You Can Protect Your Privacy." *Consumers' Research Magazine*, vol. 85, February 2002, p. 10ff. Succinctly summarizes privacy-protection services, privacy policies and "seals," and tools to protect online privacy. Such tools include the "Anonymizer," systems that allow for purchases without giving credit card numbers to stores, ways to control "cookies," e-mail protection, and encryption tools.

Bayne, Kim M. "Privacy Still Burning Web Issue: Marketers Scramble to Come Up with Self-Regulation Methods." *Advertising Age*, vol. 69, June 29, 1998, p. 37. Describes efforts toward the end of the 1990s to develop industry guidelines and systems to protect privacy and head off the drive for regulation. Generally privacy advocates have felt that some efforts (such as TRUSTe) have been modestly successful but insufficient.

Beiser, Vince. "The CyberSnoops: How Internet Gumshoes Breach Personal Privacy." *Maclean's*, vol. 110, June 23, 1997, p. 42. Describes the "data brokers" and online investigators who can find out nearly everything about a person—for a price. Most of the information is publicly available and legal to obtain, but the result of aggregating the information raises privacy issues and has been the subject of concern by the Federal Trade Commission and legislators.

Brinkley, Joel. "Judge Orders a Credit Bureau to Stop Selling Consumer Lists." *New York Times*, vol. 147, August 27, 1998, p. A2ff. Growing federal concern about the misuse of consumer information was signaled by a Federal Trade Commission order forbidding TransUnion Corporation, a major credit-reporting organization, from selling consumer lists generated from its records.

———. "Web Site Agrees to Safeguards in First On-Line Privacy Deal." *New York Times*, vol. 147, August 14, 1998 p. A15. Gives background on the influential online privacy case against GeoCities, a web hosting and customization company. The Federal Trade Commission won a settlement in which the company agreed to seek customer permission before distributing information about users' background, income, and lifestyle.

Buderi, Robert. "E-Commerce Gets Smarter." *Technology Review*, April 2005, n.p. Also available online. URL: http://www.technologyreview.com/articles/05/04/issue/feature_ecommerce.asp. Describes "multichanneling" technologies that are being used to integrate marketing between online and storefront. For example, online retailers are making it easier to review products online than examine and purchase them in a physical store. The key to making it work is an ongoing effort to cultivate and improve relationships with customers, using data-mining technology and research to determine buying habits. However, consumers must be convinced they are receiving extra value through personalization, as well as having their privacy protected.

Annotated Bibliography

Burress, Charles. "Cal Issues Alert About Stolen Laptop Computer." *San Francisco Chronicle*, March 29, 2005, p. B1. The theft of a laptop computer containing 98,000 Social Security numbers from an unlocked office at the University of California, Berkeley, highlights a troublesome privacy threat—theft of highly portable computers containing sensitive data. The data had been downloaded to the laptop but not yet encrypted. Steps are being taken to make sure all data is encrypted at its source.

Dahl, Darren. "New Liability for Hacked Companies." *Inc*, vol. 26, June 2004, p. 28. Many companies that have discovered their computers have been penetrated and customer information compromised have "stonewalled" and not told customers about the situation. However, California passed a law in 2003 requiring that such break-ins be fully disclosed, and Senator Diane Feinstein (D-CA) has introduced similar federal legislation.

"The Data Game: Sophisticated Marketing Wizards Can Track Just About Everything a Consumer Does." *Maclean's*, vol. 111, August 17, 1998, p. 14. Describes the data-mining industry that gathers detailed information from credit cards, supermarket "clubs," and other sources and sells it to marketers who want to target certain kinds of customers.

"Database Firms to Curb What They Sell." *San Francisco Chronicle*, June 11, 1997, p. B1. Reports the results of a major early online privacy dispute: Lexis-Nexis and seven other companies making up the Individual Reference Services Group (including Experian and ChoicePoint) agreed to release private information only to "qualified subscribers" and to limit the scope of the information provided, such as by not including Social Security numbers. (However, new problems with misuse of ChoicePoint data would emerge in 2004–05.)

Engario, Pete, Josey Puliyenthuruthel, and Manjeet Kripalani. "Fortress India? Call Centers and Credit-Card Processors Are Tightening Security to Ease U.S. and European Fears of Identity Theft." *Business Week*, August 30, 2004, p. 28. Reports that the call centers in India that process so many transactions for U.S. and European customers are increasingly taking steps to prevent misuse of personal information. They are responding to the growing pressure seen in dozens of bills in the U.S. Congress and state legislatures that could severely limit the outsourcing of data services.

Garfinkel, Simson. "Privacy and the New Technology: What They Do Know Can Hurt You." *The Nation*, vol. 270, February 28, 2000, p. 11ff. A comprehensive statement of the threat to privacy brought about by the wide accessibility of personal information collected by business and accessible via the Internet, often for illegitimate purposes. Computer security flaws add to the risk of harassment, identity theft, or, worse, intrusions. The author argues for strong federal legislation to restrict the gathering and dissemination of personal information.

———. "The Pure Software Act of 2006." *Technology Review*, April 2004, n.p. Also available online. URL: http://www.technologyreview.com/articles/04/04/wo_garfinkel040704.asp?p=1. Spyware is software that is loaded under false pretenses and surreptitiously records and transmits user information. Spyware is often subtler and harder to fight than viruses and worms. The author suggests that in addition to using technical means, new laws fight spyware by insisting on "truth in labeling" like that required for food and drugs.

Gillmor, Dan. "Violating Privacy Is Bad Business." *Computerworld*, vol. 32, March 23, 1998, p. 38. Argues that it is shortsighted for companies to gather unnecessary information about their customers just to resell it. The result can be lost customers and perhaps onerous regulations.

Hadley, Jane. "'Loyalty' Cards Cause Griping Over Swiping." *Seattle Post-Intelligencer*, May 11, 2002, n.p. Also available online. URL: http://seattlepi.nwsource.com/local/70072_loyal11.asp. Reports on the debate over supermarket loyalty cards. The markets generally say they don't sell or share the data but use it only to create special offers and more effectively market products. Some customers like the convenience of the cards, but others object to the tracking of their shopping habits and worry about the loss of control over their information. Some consumer groups have concluded that there is no real long-term savings for consumers who use the cards.

Hagel, J., and J. F. Rayport. "The Coming Battle for Customer Information." *Harvard Business Review*, January–February 1997, pp. 53–65. Reports on the high stakes for companies that seek to take advantage of the flood of personal information available to be collected online while resisting demands for regulation.

Hulme, George V. "Bills Aim to Block Spyware." *InformationWeek*, June 24, 2004, p. 79. Describes pending California and federal legislation that would require that users give consent before "hidden" programs are installed on their computers. However, that consent, to be effective, would have to be clearly visible rather than being buried in a user license agreement. Existing provisions of the Computer Fraud and Abuse Act also provide ammunition for going after illegal spyware.

———. "Breach of Trust." *InformationWeek*, May 3, 2004, n.p. Also available online. URL: http://www.informationweek.com/story/showArticle.jhtml?articleID=19400012. There is a growing number of data breaches where intruders gain access to customer data in financial institutions. Only a fraction of these incidents is brought to public attention—enough to cause a possible consumer backlash. Various security measures, including firewalls and antivirus software, are discussed. Banks are improving security, but many have not yet done enough.

Kandra, Anne. "The Great American Privacy Makeover: An Exclusive PC World Survey Reveals That Even Savvy Web Users Can Do More to Safeguard Their Privacy and Data." *PC World*, vol. 21, November 2003, p. 144ff. An in-depth feature article surveys 1,500 web users. Even though most of the users surveyed had considerable online experience, for many their actual practices did not match up with their expressed privacy concerns. For example, many users employed a relatively easy to guess password for all their services and never changed it. The article includes case studies ("makeovers") and suggestions for users.

Kelly, Tina. "You Can Search, but Can You Hide? Using the Net, Old Friends, Old Flames and Old Debts May Find You." *New York Times*, vol. 148, November 26, 1998, p. G1. Discusses the mixed blessings that come from the ability to find almost anyone through information in online databases.

Labaton, Steve. "U.S. Cracking Down on Information Brokers." *New York Times*, April 23, 1999, p. 14. Reports on the Federal Trade Commission's crackdown on private investigators who advertise on the Internet that they can obtain confidential information about individuals' bank, credit, and other records. Such investigators often call banks and falsely claim to be the individual being investigated or a relative.

Lamb, Gregory M. "ID Stolen? Call a Privacy Gumshoe." *Christian Science Monitor*, March 9, 2005, p. 12. Describes high-tech private eyes who can secure one's identity and privacy—for a hefty price. The author also summarizes help for ordinary people who face identity theft and online scams.

Lazarus, David. "It's Impressive, Scary to See What a Zaba Search Can Do." *San Francisco Chronicle*, April 15, 2005, pp. C1, C6. Describes a service from ZabaSearch.com that can find just about anyone's current address, phone number, and date of birth. The results even link to a mapping service to provide an aerial photo of the person's house and directions for getting there. The developer argues that the search is just a natural extension of the information capabilities of the Internet and the use of the network to bring people together. However, critics point out that the tool would seem to be an ideal aid for stalkers and other criminals.

———. "Postcards with Data Disturbing." *San Francisco Chronicle*, April 9, 2005, pp. C2, C3. Reports that New Jersey–based Automatic Data Processing sent postcards to more than 1,000 employees of Adecco Employment Services, on which the employees' Social Security numbers had been accidentally printed. The company apologized and provided information resources to the employees but did not offer to pay for monitoring their credit records for signs of identity theft.

———. "SBC's Second Thoughts." *San Francisco Chronicle*, December 12, 2004. p. C1. The giant phone company SBC is reconsidering its plan to charge higher prices to customers who do not agree to let the company share their information with up to 50 affiliates or subsidiaries. State legislatures are considering outlawing the practice.

———. "Shifting Sands in Data Leak." *San Francisco Chronicle*. February 25, 2005, p. C1. A columnist explains the issues involved in the selling of personal information records by companies such as Choice Point, which sold 144,000 records to bogus businesses set up by data thieves. Spokespersons from ChoicePoint and the Electronic Privacy Information Center give contrasting views of whether the industry has shown sufficient responsibility.

———. "Who Else Had Your Bank Account Number?" *San Francisco Chronicle*, January 5, 2005, p. A1. Dennis Yu was surprised when someone else began cashing checks on his account. It turned out that the bank had given him an account number "recycled" from a closed account. Banks claim they are running out of numbers and that it would be too expensive to accommodate longer numbers.

Lifsher, Marc. "State Lawmakers Grill ChoicePoint Over Privacy Concerns, Potential for ID Theft." *Los Angeles Times*, March 31, 2005, p. C1. The revelation that thieves posing as legitimate businesses had gained access to thousands of consumer records has prompted California legislators to demand prompter, fuller disclosure of data breaches. Some have also suggested requiring ChoicePoint to provide consumers with free access to their records.

McCullagh, Dean. "Database Nation: The Upside of 'Zero Privacy.'" *Reason*, June 2004, pp. 26–35. The "assault on privacy" has been highly publicized in the media, and activists raise continual cries of alarm. However, the author argues that the information swapping in the "database society" also has many invisible but important benefits. These include market efficiency (and thus lower prices), enabling consumers to view tailored offerings, and giving better terms to financially responsible consumers. The focus should instead be on preventing genuine privacy threats from government while letting the tort system provide protection against invasions of privacy by businesses and individuals.

Metzger, Miriam J., and Sharon Docter. "Public Opinion and Policy Initiatives for Online Privacy Protection." *Journal of Broadcasting & Electronic Media*, vol. 47, September 2003, p. 350ff. Surveys studies of popular opinion with regard to online privacy issues and compares what the public appears to want with what lawmakers and industry makers may be offering.

Mulligan, Deirdre, and Stephen J. Col. "Should the Federal Government Set Privacy Standards for the Internet?" *CQ Researcher*, November 6, 1998, p. 969. Debates whether a national privacy standard is necessary or if industry can develop effective disclosure and opt-out policies.

O'Hara, Robert, Jr. "Research Firms Weave a Tangled Web to Net Private Information." *San Francisco Chronicle*, June 15, 1998, p. A8. Gives examples of online research and investigation services that will obtain information about anyone for a fee by employing both legal sources and questionable methods such as "pretext calling."

Postrel, Virginia. "The Politics of Privacy." *Forbes*, vol. 161, June 1, 1998, p. S130. Argues that information arising out of transactions is shared by both parties—such as a consumer and a business—and that regulations that make it only the property of its originator should not replace the variety of arrangements offered in the marketplace.

Robischon, Noah. "My Week as an Internet Gumshoe." *Time*, vol. 149, June 2, 1997, p. 65. Confirms Senator Diane Feinstein's contention that lots of personal information is available on the Internet by obtaining Feinstein's own family birth dates, legal records, unlisted phone number, and other information from a succession of free sources and information brokers.

Roth, Mark S. "Beware of Cookies: Do Marketers that Track a User's Online Activities Threaten Privacy?" *National Law Journal*, vol. 23, August 20, 2001, p. C1. Although many Web users are concerned about the privacy implications of using "cookies" to track their browsing activities, litigation has generally upheld their use. The applicability of statutes such as the Federal Wiretap Act, Electronic Communications Privacy Act, and the Computer Fraud and Abuse Act is discussed.

Rothfelder, Jeffrey. "You Are for Sale." *PC World*, vol. 16, September 1998, p. 96. Gives examples of how marketers gather and cross-reference personal data to target consumers in ways that can amount to a startling invasion of privacy.

Schwartz, John. "Guarding Privacy vs. Enforcing Copyrights." *New York Times*, September 29, 2003, p. C1. There are fundamental conflicts between the desire to protect intellectual property by identifying violators and the privacy rights of online users who are caught up in subpoenas. Privacy advocates argue that subpoenas searching for illegal file-swappers are often overbroad and violate privacy.

Spinello, Richard A. "The End of Privacy: Companies That Collect Information for a Specific Purpose Can Resell or Reuse It for Other Purposes with Impunity." *America*, vol. 176, January 4, 1997, p. 9ff. Argues that existing laws are inadequate in protecting consumer, financial, and medical privacy. The issues have changed little since the article was written.

Zeller, Tom. "Breach Points Up Flaws in Privacy Laws." *New York Times*, February 24, 2005, p. C1. Recent cases of unauthorized access to consumer data at firms such as ChoicePoint have revealed the inadequacy of the current "patchwork" of federal and state privacy laws. Senator Diane Feinstein DCA is introducing tough new privacy bills that would require prompt consumer notification of privacy breaches.

Web Documents

"Are You Being Stalked? Tips for Protection." Privacy Rights Clearinghouse. Available online. URL: http://www.privacyrights.org/fs/fs14-stk.htm. Updated in June 2001. Stalking is the ultimate violation of personal privacy. This fact sheet offers an overview of federal and state laws that can be used against stalkers as well as practical tips for hiding from stalkers—many of which are also good strategies for protecting one's general privacy.

Borland, John. "States Join Spyware Battle." CNet News.com Available online. URL: http://news.com.com/2100–1024_3–5170263.html. Posted on March 4, 2004. Utah has passed an anti-spyware bill, and legislation has been introduced in Iowa and California. However, industry groups are concerned that laws that regulate specific technological specifics rather than misuse may hamper the development of legitimate features. There are also different legislative focuses: Utah focuses on "adware," while proposed bills in Iowa and California are more concerned with stopping the transmission of user information. Privacy and industry groups would both prefer a single federal solution, though they disagree on specific provisions.

"California S.B. 27, 'Shine the Light' Law." Electronic Privacy Information Center. Available online. URL: http://www.epic.org/privacy/profiling/sb27. html. Updated January 25, 2005. Describes a 2003 California law that many privacy advocates consider to be a landmark and potential model for the nation. The new law requires that businesses either allow customers to opt out of information sharing or to make a detailed disclosure of how personal information is shared for marketing purposes.

"Caller ID and My Privacy: What Do I Need to Know?" Privacy Rights Clearinghouse. Available online. URL: http://www.privacyrights.org/fs/fs19-cid. htm. Updated in August 2000. Explains how Caller ID can compromise one's privacy and discusses the pros, cons, and options for blocking it. (Some discussion is specific to California.)

"The Census and Privacy." Electronic Privacy Information Center. Available online. URL: http://www.epic.org/privacy/census/. Updated on May 5, 2003. Describes privacy risks, legal issues, and cases relating to the U.S. Census. The site begins with a history of the census, which has steadily expanded the detailed information sought from citizens every 10 years. Historically, various countries have used census data to identify dissenters and other target groups; in the United States, census data helped authorities round up Japanese Americans at the beginning of World War II. Although personal identification information is stripped out of census records before they are made available to businesses or the public, certain data can be used to "reidentify" records. The use of Social Security numbers also raises concerns. The summary includes links to legal cases and news items.

"Choicepoint." Electronic Privacy Information Center. Available online. URL: http://www.epic.org/privacy/choicepoint/default.html. Updated on March 30, 2005. Introduces and summarizes recent developments involving data breaches and questionable practices of ChoicePoint and other commercial data brokers. The site includes extensive links to documents from the Federal Trade Commission and other sources.

"CLUE and You: How Insurers Size You Up." Privacy Rights Clearinghouse. Available online. URL: http://www.privacyrights.org/fs/fs26-CLUE.htm. Updated in October 2003. Explains the use of CLUE (Comprehensive Loss Underwriting Exchange) reports by insurance companies. Because of this and another database called A-PLUS, changes in a person's credit record or claims or even queries made with one insurance company can affect rates charged for other types of insurance. These databases are little known but they are covered by the Fair Credit Reporting Act, so consumers have the right to access their report and to correct errors.

"Cookies." Electronic Privacy Information Center. Available online. URL: http://www.epic.org/privacy/internet/cookies/. Updated on November 5, 2002. Describes the issues in class action lawsuits brought against the Internet firm DoubleClick alleging misuse of cookies, a common method for recording the actions of web browsers. The main problem seen is the combining of browsing information from cookies with consumer information looked up from a commercial database such as Abacus. The article includes links to other resources relating to cookies.

"CPNI (Customer Proprietary Network Information)." Electronic Privacy Information Center. Available online. URL: http://www.epic.org/privacy/cpni/. Updated November 7, 2002. Describes the status of federal requirements about the sharing of customer information by telephone companies. Currently companies are free to share telephone-related information with affiliated businesses but must seek customer permission if the information is not related to phone service or is being shared with unaffiliated companies. The web page also includes opt-out information and resource links.

"Credit Scoring." Electronic Privacy Information Center. Available online. URL: http://www.epic.org/privacy/creditscoring/. Updated on December 11, 2003. Introduces the operation of scoring used by the credit reporting agencies and its implications for consumers. The article explains the potential for inaccuracies and abuse, and provides some links to news stories and other documents.

"Digital Rights Management and Privacy." Electronic Privacy Information Center. Available online. URL: http://www.epic.org/privacy/drm/default. html. Updated on March 29, 2004. Systems that control access to media files to prevent unauthorized copying or sharing can also raise privacy problems. Users may have to reveal their identity without assurance their information will not be misused. The ability to access potentially controversial content anonymously is also lost. In addition to raising these issues, there is also discussion of the Digital Millennium Copyright Act (DMCA) and links to materials from the Electronic Frontier Foundation and other organizations.

"Double Trouble with the DoubleClick/Abacus Merger." Electronic Privacy Information Center. Available online. URL: http://www.epic.org/privacy/doubletrouble/. Updated on March 21, 2000. An introduction to the issues raised by the combining of cookie tracking data with a consumer information database. The site includes materials relating to the Electronic Privacy's Information Center's complaint against DoubleClick/Abacus before the Federal Trade Commission.

"E-Commerce and You: Online Shopping Tips." Privacy Rights Clearinghouse. Available online. URL: http://www.privacyrights.org/fs/fs23-shopping.htm. Updated in September 2002. Introduces the basics of safe online shopping, including identifying secure web sites, obtaining information about unknown companies, understanding privacy policies, use of payment methods, and information that should not be disclosed in web forms.

Edelman, Benjamin. "'Spyware': Research, Testing, Legislation, and Suits." [Personal web site.] Available online. URL: http://www.benedelman.org/spyware/. Updated on July 13, 2005. The author, who has researched spyware issues and served as an expert witness, provides an introduction and links to current issues, research, legislation, and litigation involving software that surreptitiously obtains and transmits user information.

"The Fair Credit Reporting Act (FCRA) and the Privacy of Your Credit Report." Electronic Privacy Information Center. Available online. URL: http://www.epic.org/privacy/fcra/. Updated on December 8, 2004. Provides an introduction, news summary, and links relating to the Fair Credit Reporting Act.

Garon, John M. "New Hampshire's Latest Revolution: Liability for Damage Caused by Selling Personal Information." Interface Tech News. Available online. URL: http://www.interfacenow.com/syndicatepro/displayarticle.asp?ArticleID=565. Posted in April 2003. Discusses the case of the data broker Docusearch being held liable for providing personal information about Amy Boyer to her stalker/killer Liam Youens. The court found that Docusearch had ignored a serious, foreseeable risk of harm to Boyer. Hopefully the decision will have a positive impact on other online investigators.

"Gender and Electronic Privacy." Electronic Privacy Information Center. Available online. URL: http://www.epic.org/privacy/gender/. Updated on July 15, 2004. Introduces and provides news on privacy issues that are particularly relevant to women. These include pretexting as a way to gain personal information, stalking, and high-tech voyeurism.

"The Gramm-Leach-Bliley Act." Electronic Privacy Information Center. Available online. URL: http://www.epic.org/privacy/glba/. Updated January 21, 2005. Summarizes the provisions and shortcomings of the 1999 Gramm-Leach-Bliley Act (GLBA), which provides limited privacy rights to customers of financial institutions. The article includes links to cases and news stories.

Gross, Grant. "U.S. Lawmakers Push for Data Privacy Legislation: Fallout from the ChoicePoint and LexisNexis Data Breaches Continues." IDG.net. Available online. URL: http://www.computerworld.com/printthis/2005/0,4814,100405,00.html (or QuickLink 53198). Posted on March 16, 2005. Reports that Congress has expressed alarm about the compromising of personal data held by the nation's major data brokers, and that new regulations are likely to be passed by the end of the year. Many data brokers support stronger privacy protections but oppose giving consumers control over the use of their Social Security numbers, warning that it might hamper fraud investigations. However, critics say the industry is still "in denial."

Hachman, Mark. "E-Cyclers Embrace Data Destruction." eWeek. Available online. URL: http://www.eweek.com/article2/0,1759,1665275,00.asp. Posted on October 1, 2004. The computer-recycling industry faces a new challenge: Verifiably destroy data on computer drives to comply with new legislation such as HIPAA (the Health Insurance Portability and Accountability Act) and the Gramm-Leach-Blilely Act.

Hicks, Matt. "Wiretap Ruling Could Signal End of E-Mail Privacy." eWeek. Available online. URL: http://www.eweek.com/article2/0,1759,1619520,00.asp. Posted on July 1, 2004. A federal appeals court has ruled that stored e-mail messages are not protected under the federal Wiretap Act. Legal experts are quoted as saying that the decision means that people should not have an expectation of privacy in e-mail stored on disk, and that it may now be harder to prosecute computer crimes involving stolen data.

Honan, Matthew. "Don't Be Afraid of the Big Bad Gmail." Salon.com. Available online. URL: http://www.salon.com/tech/feature/2004/04/26/gmail/index.

html. Posted on April 26, 2004. The author argues that Google's web-based Gmail service does not represent a real privacy threat. E-mail is scanned for keywords that are matched to provide "targeted" advertisements, but the company says that the process is automatic and no human gains access to the users' e-mail.

Hoofnagel, Chris Jay. "Privacy Risks of E-mail Scanning." Electronic Privacy Information Center. Available online. URL: http://epic.org/privacy/gmail/casjud3.15.05.html. Posted on March 15, 2005. The director of the West Coast office of the Electronic Privacy Information Center testifies before the Judiciary Committee of the California State Senate. He argues that Google's system of scanning users' e-mail in order to generate targeted advertising violates the privacy not only of the service's users but also of senders of messages who never consented to the e-mail scanning.

Hoofnagel, Chris Jay, and Emily Honig. "Victoria's Secret and Financial Privacy." Electronic Privacy Information Center. Available online. URL: http://www.epic.org/privacy/glba/victoriassecret.html. Updated on January 25, 2005. Describes how Congress was spurred into high gear in promoting the Gramm-Leach-Bliley Act when a representative's bank sold his personal information to Victoria's Secret. Representative Joe Barton (R-TX) was dismayed when the company's catalogs began to arrive at his home and he did not want his wife to get the idea he was buying lingerie for women in Washington. A bipartisan coalition overcame the opposition of the banking lobby and passed the law in 1999.

"How Private Is My Credit Report?" Privacy Rights Clearinghouse. Available online. URL: http://www.privacyrights.org/fs/fs6-crdt.htm. Revised in November 2004. Explains what is in a credit report, the meaning of credit scores, and how to obtain one's credit report. The article also describes what information should not be included in credit reports, how to correct errors, who can access credit reports, and limitations on use of credit information for marketing.

"'Junk Mail: How Did They Get My Address?" Privacy Rights Clearinghouse. Available online. URL: http://www.privacyrights.org/fs/fs4-junk.htm. Updated in May 2003. Explains how junk mailers obtain peoples' addresses and how to opt out from the national mailing lists through the Mail Preference Service and Abacus, as well as providing other "mail reduction tips."

Kawamoto, Dawn. "Firms Seek to Reassure E-Shoppers Over Security." ZDNet News.com. Available online. URL: http://news.zdnet.com/2100-1009_22-5583047.html?tag=nl. Posted on February 18, 2005. A panel of security experts from the e-commerce industry discusses ways to reassure online consumers that their security and privacy will be protected. The urgency of this issue is reflected in a survey by RSA Security that found that about one-fourth of online shoppers have reduced their use of e-commerce sites because of concerns about identity theft. While services such as eBay are giving consumers more options with escrow and purchase-protection services, the growing unease with e-mail is threatening the ability of companies to communicate legitimately with their customers. Finally, "federation" schemes where one login and password are used by many companies may result in increased vulnerability and consumer concern.

Mark, Roy. "Anti-Spyware Bill Clears Committee Hurdle." Internetnews.com. Available online. URL: http://www.internetnews.com/security/article.php/3373041. Posted on June 24, 2004. Reports the continuing progress of anti-spyware legislation in Congress. The SPY Act would prohibit keystroke logging, computer hijacking, and displaying advertising windows that cannot be closed. The user must opt in before any information is collected or transmitted.

"My Social Security Number: How Secure Is It?" Privacy Rights Clearinghouse. Available online. URL: http://www.privacyrights.org/fs/fs10-ssn.htm. Updated in June 2004. The Social Security number is a key piece of identification that can be used to retrieve a variety of information about a person and even to assume another's identity to create fraudulent bank or credit accounts. There is currently only limited legal protection against being compelled to disclose one's Social Security number to government agencies and businesses. Individuals should resist such disclosure and consider not doing business with companies that insist on it.

"New Survey Reveals Trust Gap Between Consumers and Businesses About Information Exchange." Harris Interactive. Available online. URL: http://www.harrisinteractive.com/news/allnewsbydate.asp?NewsID=260. Posted on April 2, 2001. A survey of consumer attitudes toward online privacy finds that most online users are concerned about misuse of their information and want to see privacy policies and guarantees. About 60 percent do see the "personalization" of web sites (usually involving cookies) to be a good thing. Most consumers are not using privacy protection software.

Olsen, Stefanie. "FTC: All Eyes on Consumer Privacy." ZDNet News.com. Available online. URL: http://news.zdnet.com/2100-3513_22-5230750.html?tag=nl. Posted on June 10, 2004. Reports that the Federal Trade Commission is gearing up for major privacy enforcement actions involving Internet-based companies. Targets may include e-mail providers that scan customers' messages, services that facilitate spam e-mail, and companies whose careless security exposes consumer data to theft.

"The 'Other' Consumer Reports: What You Should Know About 'Specialty' Reports." Privacy Rights Clearinghouse. Available online. URL: http://www.privacyrights.org/fs/fs6b-SpecReports.htm. Posted in December 2004. While most consumers know about the importance of credit reports, there are a number of other reports that can contain erroneous information or represent a potential for misuse. This fact sheet explains insurance claims reports, medical history reports, residential and tenant reports, check-writing history reports, and employment reports. These reports can be obtained by the consumer at no charge and should be reviewed under certain circumstances, such as when seeking insurance coverage or applying for employment.

"Postal Service Privacy." Electronic Privacy Information Center. Available online. URL: http://www.epic.org/privacy/postal/. Updated on January 27,

2005. Gives an overview of privacy issues arising from use of the postal service. Topics covered include required information for opening a private mail box, use of bar codes for sender identification and tracking ("intelligent mail"), and distribution of information from change of address notices. The site includes news and resource links.

"Privacy and Consumer Profiling." Electronic Privacy Information Center. Available online. URL: http://www.epic.org/privacy/profiling/#selfdefense. Updated on October 13, 2004. Provides a comprehensive and rather detailed account of how companies gather a variety of information from consumers' transactions and create profiles for marketing purposes. Consumers are often grouped into a variety of social/demographic groups with names such as "Elite Suburbs" or "Urban Midscale." There are also huge searchable databases that marketers can query to find, for example, subscribers to *Newsweek* who are Catholic, fit a particular socioeconomic class, and have a record of contributing to nonprofit organizations. Other topics include medical profiling, the potential use of supermarket "loyalty card" data by law enforcement agencies, and measures that consumers can take to reduce access to their personal information.

"Protecting Financial Privacy in the New Millennium: The Burden Is on You." Privacy Rights Clearinghouse. Available online. URL: http://www.privacyrights.org/fs/fs24-finpriv.htm. Revised in September 2002. Describes privacy protections for information about account holders in financial institutions. The article explains provisions of the Gramm-Leach-Bliley Act (GLBA) that complicate privacy problems by allowing combinations of companies to more freely exchange customer information, though some kinds of information cannot be sold to unaffiliated companies. It also explains privacy notices and opt-out procedures.

"Put the FAIR Back in Fair Credit Reporting." U.S. Public Interest Research Group. Available online. URL:http://www.pirg.org/consumer/credit/fcrafacts2003new.htm. Posted on April 11, 2003. Argues that the preemption provision of the Fair Credit Reporting Act should expire in order to let stronger privacy provisions take effect. The PIRG also advocates new laws to protect Social Security numbers, ban use of credit scoring for insurance, and provide comprehensive protection against identity theft.

Roberts, Paul. "2004: Good and Bad for Security." PC World/IDG News Service. Available online. URL: http://www.pcworld.com/news/article/0,aid,119031,00.asp. Posted on December 27, 2004. A review of the year 2004 indicates a rough year for computer security and privacy. There were high-profile data crimes and a considerable increase in online schemes, particularly "phishing." Trojans and spyware were also on the rise. On the other hand, police around the world nabbed some notorious computer criminals, and security for operating systems and businesses is gradually improving.

Robinson, Teri. "FCC to Let Carriers Share Customer Data." *E-Commerce Times*. Available online. URL: http://www.ecommercetimes.com/story/18634.html. Posted on July 17, 2002. Reports that the Federal Communications

Commission, promoted by a recent court decision, will now allow telephone companies to share information about customers with related companies that sell phone-related services. Customer permission will only be required for sharing data with unrelated companies or those whose services are not related to telecommunications.

Rosenberg, Scott. "Defending the Cookie Monster." Salon.com. Available online. URL: http://dir.salon.com/tech/col/rose/2001/05/07/cookies/index. html?sid=1028455. Posted on May 7, 2001. Argues that there's nothing wrong with those little web-tracking files in themselves—indeed, they're needed if a web site is to keep track of your personal preferences. Users can easily control which sites are allowed to use cookies and delete any that are unwanted.

Sharma, Dinesh C. "Study: Cookies in Security Crosshairs." ZDNet.News.com. Available online. URL: http://news.zdnet.com/2100–9588_22–5618296.html ?tag=nl.e589. Posted on March 15, 2005. Reports on a study by Jupiter Research that a growing number of Internet users are blocking or deleting "cookie" files that are deposited on their personal computers by many web sites. Thirty-eight percent of the consumers surveyed believe cookies are invasive of their security or privacy. The increasing resistance to cookies may be threatening the accuracy of data needed to measure the effectiveness of online marketing or advertising.

Smith, Richard M. "The Web Bug FAQ." Electronic Frontier Foundation. Available online. URL: http://www.eff.org/Privacy/Marketing/?f=web_ bug.html. Posted on November 11, 1999. Explains the use of a nearly invisible image used as a way to record the address of a person browsing the page. Web bugs can be used legitimately to compile page-usage statistics, but they can also be used to compile user information in connection with cookies.

Taylor, Humphrey. "Do Not Call Registry Is Working Well." Harris Poll. Available online. URL: http://www.harrisinteractive.com/harris_poll/index. asp?PID=439. Posted on February 13, 2004. Reports the results of a poll showing that the Federal Trade Commission's Do Not Call Registry has been remarkably successful. More than half the nation's adults have signed up, and most report they now receive few or no telemarketing calls.

"Telemarketing: How to Have a Quiet Evening at Home." Privacy Rights Clearinghouse. Available online. URL: http://www.privacyrights.org/fs/fs5-tmkt.htm. Revised in September 2003. Explains how to use the National Do Not Call Registry and other agencies to reduce unwanted marketing calls. The article includes discussion of federal and state laws, legal recourse, and other resources.

"Top Ten Consumer Privacy Resolutions." Electronic Privacy Information Center. Available online. URL: http://www.epic.org/privacy/2004tips.html. Updated on December 25, 2004. Offers practical suggestions for protecting privacy in the form of New Year's resolutions. Suggestions include minimizing the disclosure of personal information in transactions, using opt-out and do-not-call lists, protecting personal computers against viruses and spyware, and regularly obtaining credit reports.

Vaas, Lisa. "Old PCs Can Come Back to Haunt You." eWeek. Available online. URL: http://www.eweek.com/article2/0,1759,1624496,00.asp. Posted on July 16, 2004. Major computer makers HP and Dell have announced programs to help users securely dispose of old computers. While the article focuses on the toxic environmental effects of discarded electronics, the danger of having one's personal data "recycled" is also discussed.

Verton, Dan. "Offshore Coding Work Raises Security Concerns." Computerworld.com. Available online. URL: http://www.computerworld.com/managementtopics/outsourcing/story/0,10801,80935, 00.html. Posted on May 5, 2003. The growing outsourcing of software development to countries such as India, Pakistan, Russia, and China brings the risk that programmers may create software with security flaws that compromise assets or privacy. Often there is little oversight of overseas development efforts.

"The Video Privacy Protection Act (VPPA)." Electronic Privacy Information Center. Available online. URL: http://www.epic.org/privacy/vppa/. Updated August 6, 2002. Describes the legislative history of the VPPA and its specific protections, which have been upheld by courts in several cases.

Weiss, Todd R. "New Federal Rules Dictate Bank ID Theft Notifications: The Regulations Are Designed to Protect Consumers." Computerworld.com. Available online. URL: http://www.computerworld.com/printthis/2005/0,4814,100614,00.html (QuickLink 53393). Posted on March 24, 2005. Reports that the Federal Reserve Board has issued new rules that require banks to notify consumers "as soon as possible" if their personal information is stolen or improperly accessed.

"Wireless Communications: Voice and Data Privacy." Privacy Rights Clearinghouse. Available online. URL: http://www.privacyrights.org/fs/fs2-wire.htm. Updated in June 2004. Warns about the lack of privacy inherent in cordless phones, cellular phones, pagers, and wireless data networks. The article offers suggestions for finding and enabling security features and in preventing fraud. It includes links to resources.

PRIVACY AND HEALTH CARE

This section has works that focus on the use of personal medical information (including genetic information) by providers, insurers, researchers, or other groups involved with the health care system.

Books

Annas, George J. *Rights of Patients: The Authoritative ACLU Guide to the Rights of Patients.* 3rd ed. New York: New York University Press, 2004. This comprehensive reference includes sections on how patients can make sure their privacy and the confidentiality of their records is respected.

Chaikind, Hinda R., et al. *The Health Insurance Portability and Accountability Act (HIPAA): Overview and Analysis.* New York: Nova Science Publishers, 2004. The authors discuss all major sections of the HIPAA regulations including privacy rules.

Hubbartt, William S. *HIPAA Privacy Source Book: A Collection of Practical Examples*. Alexandria, Va.: Society for Human Resource Management, 2004. Provides sample policies, procedures, checklists, and other tools for helping employers or managers understand and comply with the Health Insurance Portability and Accountability Act (HIPAA) privacy rules. If nothing else, browsing this work indicates just how complex this area of privacy law is.

Jones, Nancy Lee, and Alison M. Smith, eds. *Genetic Information: Legal and Law Enforcement Issues*. New York: Novinka Publications, 2004. In the wake of the completion of the "rough draft" of the human genome in 2000 by the Human Genome Project, the legal issues surrounding the use of genetic information have come into sharp relief. The contributors discuss federal and state legislation affecting access to and sharing of genetic information, including the Health Insurance Portability and Accountability Act (HIPAA) and the Americans with Disabilities Act.

————. *Genetic Information: Legal Issues Relating to Discrimination and Privacy*. Washington, D.C.: Congressional Research Service, 2003. Also available online. URL: http://www.ilr.cornell.edu/library/downloads/keyWorkplaceDocuments/CRS/CRSGeneticInformation0701.pdf. Gives background on laws and rulings relevant to the disclosure of genetic information. The book includes discussion of the Health Insurance Portability and Accountability Act, the Americans with Disabilities Act, state statutes, and legislation in the 106th and 107th Congresses.

Laurie, Graeme. *Genetic Privacy: A Challenge to Medico-Legal Norms*. New York: Cambridge University Press, 2002. Argues for a comprehensive view of personal privacy and property rights in one's genetic information. Going beyond existing concepts of confidentiality such a view would lead to stronger protection for individuals dealing with medical providers, insurers, or the government.

National Research Council, Board on Biology. *Privacy Issues in Biomedical and Clinical Research*. Washington, D.C.: National Academy Press, 1998. Proceedings of a forum; includes an overview of privacy issues, special concerns involving genetic information, and possible measures to ensure protection of privacy.

Radetzki, Marcus, Marian Radetzki, and Niklas Juth. *Genes and Insurance: Ethical, Legal and Economic Issues*. New York: Cambridge University Press, 2003. The authors explore the fateful collision between the emergence of detailed genetic knowledge giving the ability to predict future health and a private health insurance system that seeks to minimize costs. While genetic privacy laws may be one way to prevent persons with adverse genetic indications from becoming uninsured, the authors argue that publicly funded health care offers the only permanent solution.

Rothstein, Mark A., ed. *Genetic Secrets: Protecting Privacy and Confidentiality in the Genetic Era*. New Haven: Yale University Press, 1997. A collection of essays by legal and medical experts that explore a variety of issues raised by the advent of genetic research and diagnostics. Topics include the effect of genetic knowledge on the doctor-patient relationship, the rights of nonpatient study subjects, specific uses of genetic technology (such as drug research, forensics, gene data banks, and decision-making by insurance companies and health providers), as well as the relevant legal frameworks in the United States and other nations, with recommendations for reform.

Saunders, Janet McGee. *Patient Confidentiality.* 4th ed. Salt Lake City: Medicode, Inc., 1998. Presents basic guidelines for health professionals concerning what patient information can be released and to whom; organized alphabetically by topic. The book is useful but does not cover recent HIPAA and other regulations.

Stevens, Gina Marie. "A Brief Summary of the Medical Privacy Rule." Washington, D.C.: Congressional Research Service 2003. Also available online. URL: http://www.epic.org/privacy/medical/RS20934.pdf. Summarizes the "Standards for the Privacy of Individually Identifiable Health Information" published in August 2002 by the Department of Health and Human Services. This includes the implementation of HIPAA and subsequent rulings. Provisions include individual rights to access to health records and privacy policies as well as the right to file complaints and request restrictions of disclosure of information.

Yount, Lisa. *Biotechnology and Genetic Engineering.* Rev. ed. New York: Facts On File, 2004. This volume in the "Library in a Book" series includes coverage of genetic privacy issues, as well as general background on genetic science and its applications.

———. *Patients' Rights in the Age of Managed Health Care.* New York: Facts On File, 2001. This volume in the Library in a Book series includes coverage of medical privacy issues.

Articles and Papers

Cooper, Christine Godsil. "Your Genes or Your Job: Genetic Testing in the Workplace." *Employee Rights Quarterly,* vol. 3, Fall 2002, p. 1ff. As the capabilities of genetic testing to predict future medical problems grows, so does the threat of discrimination or other adverse impacts against employees. Surveying these emerging issues, the author concludes that current legal protections under varying state laws are insufficient and a new federal statute is required. The Americans with Disabilities Act (ADA) may offer recourse but only after actual damages have been suffered and only if they can be proved to be related to the testing.

Feder, Barnaby J., and Tom Zeller, Jr. "Identity Chip Planted Under Skin Approved for Use in Health Care." *New York Times,* October 14, 2004, p. A1. An implanted identification chip has been approved for medical use. Advocates suggest the chips may provide life-saving information in emergencies and reduce medical errors, but privacy advocates are concerned that it may eventually become a ubiquitous way to track peoples' movements . . . or medical information may be surreptitiously read and misused.

Finkelstein, Katherine Eban. "The Computer Cure: Privacy Isn't Always the Best Medicine." *The New Republic,* vol. 219, September 14, 1998, p. 28ff. Argues that a national medical-records database is worth having despite privacy concerns because it would enable "smart" computer programs to identify drug interactions and other potentially life-threatening situations.

Freudenheim, Milt. "Medicine at the Click of a Mouse: On-Line Health Files Are Convenient. Are They Private?" *New York Times,* August 12, 1998, p. D1. Both health care providers and insurers are rapidly going online and offering patients access to medical information and lab results. However, this can expose sensitive information to the privacy and security risks endemic to the Internet.

Hustead, Joanne L., and Janlori Goldman. "Genetics and Privacy." *American Journal of Law & Medicine,* Summer–Fall 2002, p. 285ff. A detailed overview of the laws and legal issues relating to genetic testing and the use of genetic information. The authors argue for a concept of "genetic privacy" that includes the right against genetic discrimination.

Johnson, Steven. "Trading Privacy for Health." *Discover,* vol. 25, December 2004, n.p. Also available online. URL: http://www.discover.com/issues/dec-04/departments/emerging-technology. Advocates of uniform digital medical records argue that they are far more reliable (and thus safer) than traditional hand-scrawled doctors' notes. When combined with data-mining technology, the records could also be used by the Food and Drug Administration for early detection of serious problems with new drugs. Researchers could also find correlations suggesting risks or benefits for various treatments. The author admits there are concerns with potential breaches of privacy and misuse of the patient data but suggests that most people would be willing to take such risks in exchange for the benefits of safer and more effective medical care.

Kingkead, Gwen. "To Study Disease, Britain Plans a Genetic Census." *New York Times,* December 21, 2002, p. F5. While a proposed detailed survey of the distribution of genes in the British population holds great promise for understanding patterns of disease, it also raises concerns about the potential misuse of individuals' genetic data.

Lebau, Steve, and Richard Neuworth. "Genetic Testing: Balancing Benefits and Abuses." *USA Today Magazine,* vol. 129, July 2000, p. 28. Explains that some employers might use testing for genetic susceptibilities to assign employees to safer work areas. However, other employers might use genetic screening to avoid hiring applicants who have a higher potential for incurring medical expenses. In some cases genetic susceptibilities correlate with race or ethnicity, opening another potential for discrimination. It is up to Congress to pass a Genetic Privacy Act that would prevent such abuses.

Lohr, Steve. "Road Map to a Digital System of Health Records." *New York Times,* January 19, 2005, p. C1. Reports on a government advisory study that urges the creation of a standardized system of digital health records. A common format would allow records to be transferred between hospitals, laboratories, and insurers in the same way that common standards allow for the seamless transfer of e-mail between different types of computer systems. However, privacy would be protected by the lack of a single centralized database and by giving patients control over the use of their records.

MacDonald, Chris, and Bryn Williams Jones. "Ethics and Genetics: Susceptibility Testing in the Workplace." *Journal of Business Ethics*, vol. 35, February 2002, p. 235ff. The growing availability of genetic tests that show disease risks offers both benefits and risks. The author surveys the pros and cons and offers a set of criteria for voluntary (not mandatory) genetic testing.

Melton, L. Joseph, III. "The Threat to Medical Records Research." *New England Journal of Medicine*, vol. 337, November 13, 1997, p. 1,466ff. Argues that the new privacy restrictions being implemented under the federal HIPAA law can deny key data to medical researchers; proposes use of review boards to allow access to records while protecting patients' interests.

Orentlicher, David, and Bob Barr. "Is a 'Unique Health Identifier' for Every American a Good Idea?" *Insight on the News*, vol. 14, August 24, 1998, p. 24ff. Debates the proposed use of a universal health ID number. Orentlicher believes it would improve medical care and even save lives by detecting harmful drug side effects and interactions; on the other hand, Barr warns of massive invasion of privacy and potential ammunition for government meddlers.

Russell, Sabin. "Dispute on Medical Records Settled." *San Francisco Chronicle*, December 7, 2004, p. B1. The University of California agreed to stop restricting access to records of newly diagnosed cancer patients. The university had believed it was bound by the federal Health Insurance Portability and Accountability Act, but the ban was threatening to cripple the Cancer Registry used by many medical researchers.

Smith, Virginia A., and Dawn Fallik. "Doctors, Patients Grapple with Specifics of Privacy Rule." *Philadelphia Inquirer*, March 8, 2005, p. A01. Two years after the federal HIPAA medical privacy act took effect, some doctors are finding that the complicated rules are making it harder to communicate with patients. For example, the condition of one family member cannot be discussed with another unless the appropriate release has been signed. On the other hand, the use of a single consent form for "routine disclosure" may not be meaningfully protecting patients' privacy rights.

Snider, Dixie E. "Patient Consent for Publication and the Health of the Public." *Journal of the American Medical Association*, vol. 278, August 27, 1997, p. 624ff. Argues that procedures for removing information about patients' identities and for obtaining informed consent can be too strict in some cases and can prevent timely warnings about serious disease outbreaks.

Trippe, Bill. "First, Do No Harm: Can Privacy and Advanced Information Technology Coexist?" *EContent*, vol. 26, March 2003, p. 38ff. Argues that in using the growing capabilities of networking and database technology in health care, privacy can be protected by designing systems that provide only the information needed—and no more. Thus a clinician would receive information truly relevant to medical decision making but not extraneous personal information.

Veatch, Robert M. "Consent, Confidentiality, and Research." *New England Journal of Medicine*, vol. 336, March 20, 1997, p. 869ff. Describes a study that shows that many patients who received genetic testing were not asked for consent for use of the information in research studies and that doctors who did the tests may not have been fully aware of the purposes of the study.

Woodward, Beverly R. "The Computer-Based Patient Record and Confidentiality." *New England Journal of Medicine*, vol. 333, November 23, 1995, p. 1,419ff. Introduces the arguments for increased computerization of health records (efficiency, safety, better medical research) and against (misuse of records to discriminate, leading to serious consequences for insurance and employment).

Web Documents

Choy, Angela, et al. "Exposed Online: Why the New Federal Health Privacy Regulation Doesn't Offer Much Protection to Internet Users." Pew Internet & American Life Health Privacy Project. Available online. URL: http://www.pewinternet.org/pdfs/PIP_HPP_HealthPriv_report.pdf. Posted in November 2001. Suggests that the new regulations under the Health Insurance Portability and Accountability Act are insufficiently comprehensive and fail to deal with many online health services. Many web sites don't fit within the "covered entities" affected by the law.

"Examples of Privacy Violations." HIPAAps.com. Available online. URL: http://er.hipaaps.com/examples.html. Posted in 2002. A compilation of recent examples of violations of health privacy by providers, insurers, and others.

"Genetic Privacy." Electronic Privacy Information Center. Available online. URL: http://www.epic.org/privacy/genetic/. Updated on June 23, 2004. Explains how DNA can be used as a unique identifier, the collection of samples and data, its use in law enforcement, and the risks of misuse of genetic information. Some privacy advocates believe that the unique characteristics of genetic information mean that it deserves special and explicit protection beyond that applied to all personal medical information. There are no federal laws explicitly addressing this issue, though laws such as the Health Insurance Portability and Accountability Act (HIPAA) apply in some cases. The article includes links to news, cases, and other resources.

Givens, Beth. "Ten Privacy Principals [sic] for Health Care." Privacy Rights Clearinghouse. Available online. URL: http://www.privacyrights.org/ar/privprin.htm. Posted in November 6, 1998. Describes problems that have rendered the privacy implied in the Hippocratic Oath virtually obsolete. Givens suggests principles including openness; access (by patients to their records); accuracy; limiting collection, use, disclosure, and retention; preventing secondary usage without consent; getting informed consent; and providing for security, compliance, and accountability.

"Health Privacy in the Hands of Government: HIPAA Privacy Regulation—Troubled Process, Troubling Results." Privacilla.org. Available online. URL: http://www.privacilla.org/releases/HIPAA_Report.pdf. Posted in April 2003.

This free market–based critique acknowledges the importance of health privacy but argues that Congress has turned over its responsibilities to a bureaucracy whose complex regulations have spawned an industry of lawyers and other experts. The inflexible regulations will actually block the development of better privacy protections. "True health privacy relies on empowered patients choosing among options made available to them by providers competing to serve them."

"HIPAA Basics: Medical Privacy in the Electronic Age." Privacy Rights Clearinghouse. Available online. URL: http://www.privacyrights.org/fs/fs8a-hipaa. htm. Revised in July 2003. An overview of the new federal medical privacy rules. The article explains what types of records are covered by HIPAA and how the law will affect the use of medical records by employers, the government, credit reporting agencies, and health care providers.

"How Private Is My Medical Information?" Privacy Rights Clearinghouse. Available online. URL: http://www.privacyrights.org/fs/fs8-med.htm. Revised in February 2004. Explains privacy protections for medical records, including the federal Health Insurance Portability and Accountability Act (HIPAA), which covers some but not all types of medical records. The article also explains who has access to medical records and the role of the Medical Information Bureau (MIB). It includes a variety of resources to consult in various situations.

"Kansas AG Presses for Women's Medical Records." Health Privacy Project. Available online. URL: http://www.healthprivacy.org/info-url_nocat2303/ info-url_nocat_show.htm?doc_id=263221. Posted in 2005. Reports on demands by the attorney general of Kansas for the medical records of nearly 90 women who sought late-term abortions at two Kansas clinics in 2003. The AG says the records are needed for an investigation of possible child sexual abuse (presumably of underaged patients) and of violation of the state's laws limiting late-term abortions. Privacy and abortion rights groups have joined the clinics in fighting the subpoenas in court.

"Medical Privacy." Electronic Privacy Information Center. Available online. URL: http://www.epic.org/privacy/medical/. Updated on July 8, 2004. Provides an overview of the principles of medical privacy (starting with the Hippocratic Oath) and surveys federal and state law, health information and employment decisions, use of health information in marketing, and disclosure of health information to law enforcement officers. The overview concludes with advice to consumers about maintaining health privacy and links to source documents and other resources.

Pritts, Joy, et al. "The State of Health Privacy: An Uneven Terrain: A Comprehensive Survey of State Health Privacy Statutes." Health Privacy Project. Available online. URL: http://www.georgetown.edu/research/ihcrp/privacy/ statereport.pdf. Posted on August 8, 1999. Reports that states have enacted a great variety of health privacy regulations at different times and for different purposes, resulting in wide variation in the protections available to citizens. State statutes are generally not comprehensive and do not take recent developments in information technology into account. Nevertheless, detailed protections specified in state laws may be lost if federal law is allowed to preempt them.

Rosencrance, Linda. "Kaiser Permanente Patient Data Exposed Online: The Company Is Pointing a Finger at a Former Employee." Computerworld. com. Available online. URL: http://www.computerworld.com/printthis/2005/0,4814,100420,00.html (or QuickLink 53209). Posted on March 16, 2005. Reports that a former Kaiser employee had posted personal information for 140 Kaiser Permanente patients on her web log. The self-proclaimed "Diva of Disgruntled" is evidently posting the information as a protest against her termination, and she also criticizes the company for its sloppy security.

CORPORATE AND WORKPLACE PRIVACY

Issues covered by works in this section include workplace monitoring and employee privacy, and corporate policies concerning e-mail and other Internet use.

Books

Doubilet, David M., and Vincent I. Polley, eds. *Employee Use of the Internet and E-Mail: A Model Corporate Policy with Commentary on Its Use in the U.S. and Other Countries.* Chicago, Ill.: American Bar Association, 2002. The conflict between the need of employers to protect themselves from legal exposure for employees' misuse of e-mail and the Internet and the privacy interests of employees has created a legal minefield. Further, what is permissible varies greatly between the United States and (for example) the European countries. This model policy attempts to reconcile these conflicting interests. Legal experts from various countries provide their commentary on its provisions.

Hubbartt, William S. *New Battle Over Workplace Privacy: Safe Practices to Minimize Conflict, Confusion and Litigation.* New York: Amacom, 1998. An employers' guide intended to help them avoid pitfalls in dealing with issues such as using health or other records in making employment-related decisions, workplace monitoring, employee testing, and other concerns. Relevant legal cases are cited throughout.

Lane, Frederick S., III. *The Naked Employee: How Technology Is Compromising Workplace Privacy.* New York: Amacom, 2003. A guide to surveillance and monitoring in the workplace, including everything from tracking e-mail and Web use to the development of uniforms that can track employees' location and even personal habits. The author suggests ways employees can act to protect their privacy and to restrain the use of intrusive technologies.

McCloskey, Kevin L. *Workplace Drug Testing: A Handbook for Managers and In-House Counsel.* Horsham, Penn.: LRP Publications, 1995. Provides detailed guidance to managers who want to implement an effective drug-testing program in the workplace. The book includes checklists and sample forms and documents.

Moore, Mark H., Carol V. Petrie, and Anthony A. Braga, eds. *The Polygraph and Lie Detection.* Washington, D.C.: National Academies Press, 2003. Evaluates the usefulness and limitations of so-called lie detectors, which are often used in screening employees for sensitive positions as well as in law enforcement investigations. The general conclusion is that the technology should not be relied upon too heavily since it can be inaccurate or "spoofed" by subjects.

Repa, Barbara Kate. *Your Rights in the Workplace.* Berkeley, Calif.: Nolo, 2005. A comprehensive guide to legal rights written in lay language. It includes a discussion of privacy rights and related issues such as disability and health care.

Weckert, John, ed. *Electronic Monitoring in the Workplace: Controversies and Solutions.* Hershey, Penn.: Idea Group Publishing, 2004. The contributors address a variety of topics and perspectives in which the need for creating an efficient and harassment-free workplace comes into conflict with employees' expectations of privacy and dignity. Topics include employee attitudes toward workplace surveillance and ways for management and employees to negotiate surveillance and monitoring policies.

Articles and Papers

Armendariz, Yvette. "PSST!—Your Boss Can See Your E-mail." *Arizona Republic*, March 20, 2005, p. D1. Consequences of an injudicious e-mail can range from embarrassment to reprimand, firing, or even lawsuits or criminal charges. By 2004, 60 percent of surveyed companies were monitoring employees' e-mail. Some industries such as financial services are required to archive all e-mail, and use of this software has spread to other sectors. Employees must assume that anything they type may be kept indefinitely.

Burson, Pat. "Is Videotaping the Baby Sitter a Good Idea? And Should You Tell Her She's on 'Candid Camera'?" *Fort Worth Star-Telegram*, January 4, 2005, p. 1E. A variety of interested parties and experts are asked where they stand on the use of cameras (hidden or disclosed) to monitor babysitters. Some see it as a sensible way to protect one's children and cite cases where serious abuse was uncovered. However, most ethicists suggest that monitoring creates a problematic working relationship and that parents need to do a better job of finding a trustworthy nanny in the first place. A compromise point of view suggests using the cameras but giving the nanny fair notice.

Persson, Anders, and Sven Ove Hansson. "Privacy at Work—Ethical Criteria." *Journal of Business Ethics*, vol. 42, January 2003, p. 59ff. Proposes ethical criteria for adopting drug or genetic testing or surveillance programs in the workplace. Employees have a prima facie right to privacy, but this can be balanced against other interests of the employer, the business's clientele, or the employees themselves.

Townsend, Anthony M., and James T. Bennett. "Privacy, Technology, and Conflict: Emerging Issues and Action in Workplace Privacy." *Journal of Labor Research*, vol. 24, Spring 2003, p. 195ff. Summarizes the current status of workplace issues and the use of e-mail interception, Web monitoring, cameras, and other technologies. Although the law is generally on the side of the employer, the author warns that the public climate may be moving toward more support for worker privacy. Farsighted companies should develop attractive privacy policies.

Web Documents

"2004 Workplace E-Mail and Instant Messaging Summary." American Management Association. Available online. URL: http://www.amanet.org/research/pdfs/IM_2004_Summary.pdf (free registration required). Posted in 2004. Surveys the use of e-mail and instant messaging in corporate America, including experiences with litigation and elements of existing policies.

"A Checklist of Responsible Information-Handling Practices." Privacy Rights Clearinghouse. Available online. URL: http://www.privacyrights.org/fs/fs12-ih2.htm. Updated in May 2002. Gives guidelines for businesses and other organizations for handling personal information, including case studies illustrating potential problems. The first section focuses on privacy policies for various modes of communication and data storage. The second part focuses on policies in relationship to employees' use of e-mail and voice mail, as well as electronic monitoring systems.

Dichter, Mark S. "Electronic Interaction in the Workplace: Monitoring, Retrieving, and Storing Employee Communications in the Internet Age." Morgan, Lewis & Bockius LLP. Available online. URL: http://www.morganlewis.com/PDFs/A5C845ED-575B-4ADC-8A47F2801DC3594C_PUBLICATION.PDF. Posted in June 1999. After a brief (and now outdated) introduction, this report explains the legal basis (upheld in many court cases) for employer monitoring of workplace e-mail and other communications. Cases relating to racial and sexual harassment and defamation are also noted.

"Employee Background Checks: A Jobseeker's Guide." Privacy Rights Clearinghouse Available online. URL: http://www.privacyrights.org/fs/fs16-bck.htm. Updated in June 2004. Explains how background checks for employment or promotion are conducted, including what is typically included and what cannot legally be included. The article also discusses the use of credit and consumer information reports. There are tips for preparing for a background check by "preemptively" making sure the relevant records are correct.

"Employee Monitoring: Is There Privacy in the Workplace?" Privacy Rights Clearinghouse. Available online. URL: http://www.privacyrights.org/fs/fs7-work.htm. Revised in September 2002. Explains what employers can and cannot do in terms of surveillance and monitoring, including phone calls, e-mail, and computer use. The article includes discussion of applicable laws and possible legal recourse.

"Employment Background Checks: A Guide for Small Business Owners." Privacy Rights Clearinghouse. Available online. URL: http://www.privacyrights.org/fs/fs16b-smallbus.htm. Updated in September 2004. Discusses the process of checking applicant's backgrounds from the point of view of small business owners. Acknowledges the difficult position of small businesses that must face potential legal liability both for negligent hiring and for improper investigation procedures. The article explains how to use legitimate sources of information or screening services while avoiding dubious ones (such as many Internet-based information brokers).

"Online Job Search Web Sites: Tips to Safeguard Your Privacy." Privacy Rights Clearinghouse. Available online. URL: http://www.privacyrights.org/fs/fs25-JobSeekerPriv.htm. Updated in November 2003. Many people now use web-based services to search for jobs or post résumés online. However, the privacy given to information posted on these sites can vary greatly and privacy statements must be read carefully. The article also includes discussion of how to evaluate the practices of résumé writing services.

"Workplace Privacy." Electronic Privacy Information Center. Available online. URL: http://www.epic.org/privacy/workplace/. Updated on August 3, 2004. An overview of workplace privacy issues including applicable principles, the limited protections afforded by federal and state law, and issues surrounding specific types of surveillance and monitoring. The article includes resource and news links.

PRIVACY AND YOUNG PEOPLE

This section's works involve the particular privacy needs and vulnerabilities faced by young people from elementary school through college age, and the response of institutions to these concerns.

Books

Bakst, Daren, and Sylvia Burgess, eds. *Privacy in the 21st Cenutury.* Palm Beach Gardens, Fla.: Council on Law in Higher Education, 2004. Provides cases and commentary on legal issues affecting privacy of students and faculty in higher education.

Durrett, Deanne. *Teen Privacy Rights: A Hot Issue.* Berkeley Heights, N.J.: Enslow, 2001. Written at a junior high school level but also useful for adults, this account uses vivid anecdotes to illustrate situations where school policies may conflict with rights under the Fourth and Fifth Amendments. There is also a chapter on how teens can protect their privacy, particularly online.

Federal Trade Commission. *Protecting Children's Privacy Under COPPA: A Survey on Compliance.* Washington, D.C.: Federal Trade Commission, April 2002. Also available online. URL: http://www.ftc.gov/os/2002/04/coppasurvey.pdf. Survey results suggest that the passage of federal legislation requiring active steps for protecting the privacy of children has had a partial effect. Most of the sites surveyed had privacy notices that explained what information could be collected from children and how it might be shared with other companies or used for marketing purposes. However, only about half the sites explained that parents could review or delete information about their children or refuse its further use.

Hawke, Constance S. *Computer and Internet Use on Campus: A Legal Guide to Issues of Intellectual Property, Free Speech, and Privacy.* San Francisco: Jossey-Bass, 2000. A guide to a variety of legal issues raised by the use of computers in universities. The book includes discussion of relevant cases.

Persico, Deborah A. *New Jersey vs. T.L.O.: Drug Searches in Schools.* Springfield, N.J.: Enslow, 1998. Written for high school students, this account explains the issues in the landmark Supreme Court case that determined that students had only limited Fourth Amendment rights against searching their possessions for drugs or contraband. The author suggests that the outcome of the case has disturbing implications for students' privacy in other areas.

Russo, Charles J., and Ralph D. Mawdsley. *Searches, Seizures and Drug Testing Procedures: Balancing Rights and School Safety.* Horsham, Penn.: LRP Publications, 2004. Written primarily for school administrators, this handbook provides detailed guidance on how schools can develop procedures for drug testing and student searches that will withstand constitutional challenges.

Turow, Joseph. *Privacy Policies on Children's Websites: Do They Play by the Rules?* Washington, D.C.: Annenberg Public Policy Center, 2001. Analyzes compliance with the privacy protection rules for children's web sites announced by the Federal Trade Commission in 2000. According to the report, the biggest problem is that although most sites followed rules about the placement of links, the privacy policies were typically not clear and understandable to parents.

Articles and Papers

Cai, Xiaomei, et al. "Children's Website Adherence to the FTC's Online Privacy Protection Rule." *Journal of Applied Communications Research*, vol. 31, November 2003, p. 346ff. Studies the extent to which online marketers comply with the Children's Online Privacy Protection Act (COPPA). Only four of 162 popular children's web sites analyzed fully complied with the law. Practical considerations in obtaining parental permission to receive information about children may be part of the problem.

Carissimo, Karen. "Adoption Law Reform: Finding Jennifer." *San Francisco Chronicle*, January 23, 2005, p. C5. A contributor to a public opinion column describes the dilemma facing adopted children who want to learn the identity of their birth parents. She argues that California's laws that preserve adoption secrecy frustrate adoptee's attempts to come to terms with their identity. Legal restrictions can also prevent access to vital medical information such as a history of mental illness or other possibly hereditary conditions.

Flynn, Laurie J. "New Efforts Are Being Made to Keep Online Merchants from Collecting Personal Information from Children." *New York Times*, May 12, 2003, p. C4. Describes efforts by advocates of children's privacy who are not satisfied with existing protections under the federal Children's Online Privacy Protection Act. For example, Amazon.com has been accused of allowing children under 13 to post information in product reviews. Amazon replied that the information had been removed and that the site was not intended for children. (The FTC later ruled in favor of Amazon.)

Jabs, Carolyn. "Why Children Need Privacy." *Working Mother*, vol. 20, October 1997, p. 99ff. Describes the psychological importance of providing children with appropriate privacy.

Annotated Bibliography

Kandra, Anne. "Should Parents Become Big Brother? New Software Allows Parents to Control Virtually Everything Children Do Online." *PC World*, vol. 22, January 2004, p. 59ff. Describes software that parents can use to monitor children's online activities, including the contents of chat sessions. Some parents used the software to discover evidence of drug and alcohol abuse or inappropriate sexual relationships, enabling early intervention. Critics worry that the monitoring invades the privacy of young people and may well undermine their trust and willingness to cooperate with parents. Some child experts favor the judicious use of monitoring as part of a clearly articulated agreement with children.

Merritt, George. "Colleges Easy Prey to Hackers." *Denver Post*, November 17, 2004, p. B01. University campuses are a "target rich" environment for hackers, and the ease of use and free communication that foster a rich campus environment are often at odds with the need for better security. Thousands of students are vulnerable to having their private information compromised or used for identity theft.

Nevius, C. W. "New Arsenal for Army Recruiters." *San Francisco Chronicle*, January 29, 2005, p. B1. The columnist describes how his son, a high school senior, was phoned by an army recruiter. To the latter's dismay, the young man's main interest was not in joining the military but in finding out how the army had gotten his name and phone number. The answer turns out to be in an obscure provision of the No Child Left Behind Act that requires schools to provide student contact information to the military unless the person specifically opts out. With no end in sight in the war in Iraq, the military has stepped up its advertising and recruiting efforts.

Roberts, Richard L., Larry Rogers, and Sara M. Fier. "Duty-to-Warn: Implications for School Administrators." *The Clearing House*, vol. 71, September–October 1997, p. 53ff. Describes court cases that explore the legal conflict between school counselors' and administrators' duty to warn potential victims of threatening behavior or deadly diseases like AIDS and their obligation to protect the confidentiality of their student clients. While court decisions have often been unclear or contradictory, administrators can take steps to create better policies.

Salzman, Avi. "On Campus, a Security Card and More." *New York Times*, October 5, 2003, Section 14CN, p. 3. Describes a security system installed at Quinnipiac University in Hamden, Connecticut. It is so comprehensive that it requires students to swipe ID cards for access to all facilities thus giving university officials access to detailed records of students' movements. The card is also used as a debit card.

Schemo, Diana Jean. "A Federal Proposal to Keep Data on All College Students Raises Questions of Privacy." *New York Times*, November 29, 2004, p. 19. Privacy advocates are alarmed by a proposal to require that information about all students entering college be stored in a new central database. Previously colleges have provided only aggregate statistical data, except with regard to financial aid.

Teinowitz, Ira. "FTC Proposal on Kids' Privacy Raises Ire of Watchdog Groups." *Advertising Age*, vol. 76, March 14, 2005, p. 35. Many privacy and

201

consumer advocates are angry at the decision of the Federal Trade Commission to allow merchants to use a "sliding scale" of ways to obtain parental permission to receive information from children. The policy is supposed to match the stringency of the requirements to the sensitivity and risk involved in the information. However, critics believe the new system may not have adequate safeguards and that it fails to carry out the intent of the federal Children's Online Privacy Protection Act.

Web Documents

"The Children's Online Privacy Protection Act (COPPA)." Electronic Privacy Information Center. Available online. URL: http://www.epic.org/privacy/kids/. Updated April 28, 2003. Introduces the historical background and provisions of the COPPA legislation, which resulted from increasing concern that children were being targeted for information and marketing without parental consent. A number of problematic aspects of the law are also discussed, including the problem of determining which users of a site are underage and the use of credit card numbers for age verification, which introduces privacy risks of its own. The Electronic Privacy Information Center and a coalition of 11 consumer organizations has sued Amazon.com, alleging that the giant online bookstore has disclosed children's personal information in violation of the COPPA.

"Children's Privacy and Safety on the Internet: A Resource Guide for Parents." Electronic Privacy Information Center. Available online. URL: http://www. privacyrights.org/fs/fs21-children.htm. Updated in August 2004. Gives tips for parents on how to protect children from problematic online marketing practices and objectionable material. Discusses the use, limitation, and legal issues surrounding the use of web-filtering software. The article also discusses safe use of chat and instant message services and gives suggestions for better communication between parents and kids concerning Internet use.

"For Parents: Keeping Kids Privacy-Safe Online." Consumer PrivacyGuide.org. Available online. URL: http://www.consumerprivacyguide.org/kids/forparents. shtml. Downloaded on August 31, 2004. Helps parents understand the danger of children giving out personal information online and provides tips from the Federal Trade Commission, including how to identify and parse a web site's privacy policy.

Newitz, Annalee. "Don't Look Now, but the Dean Is Watching." Salon.com. Available online. URL: http://www.salon.com/tech/feature/2003/11/12/ campus_surveillance/index.html. Posted on November 12, 2003. Reports that university administrators are increasingly monitoring student e-mail, citing concerns about terrorism and pressure to crack down on copyright violations.

"Play It Safe." Bonus.com. Available online. URL: https://www.wiredsafety.org (click link). Downloaded on August 13, 2004. An interactive game that helps children recognize when they may be revealing too much personal information about themselves or their activities.

"Privacy in Education: A Guide for Parents and Adult-Age Students." Privacy Rights Clearinghouse. Available online. URL: http://www.privacyrights.org/

fs/fs29-education.htm. Posted in October 2004. Explains the rights that parents and adult students have under the Family Educational Rights and Privacy Act. Parents have the rights to access their children's student records. They also have some rights to opt out of disclosure of some student information or its use in certain surveys or studies. There is also a discussion of issues specific to students in colleges and universities.

"Student Privacy." Electronic Privacy Information Center. Available online. URL: http://www.epic.org/privacy/student/. Updated on June 29, 2005. Provides introduction and news links relating to privacy issues affecting students. Describes the provisions of the Family Educational Rights and Privacy Act (FERPA), which restricts sharing of student records without parental permission, subject to a variety of exceptions. There is also discussion of the federal No Child Left Behind Act, which places some restrictions on surveying and profiling students.

"Tips for Privacy-smart Kids!" Consumer Privacy Guide.org. Available online. URL: http://www.consumerprivacyguide.org/kids/forkids.shtml. Downloaded on August 30, 2004. In kid-friendly language, provides brief tips for avoiding giving too much information online. It notes that "Just like in the schoolyard, at the store or on the telephone, kids need to be careful about who they give information to."

Vijayan, Jaikumar. "First Online Privacy Law Looms: But Most Companies Already Follow Requirements of California's AB 68, Experts Say." Computerworld.com. Available online. URL: http://www.computerworld.com/securitytopics/security/privacy/story/0,10801,94061, 00.html. Posted on June 24, 2004. The California's Online Privacy Act of 2003 will soon be in effect. It requires that online sites post privacy policies, explain what information is collected and how it will be used, as well as how individuals can correct errors in their information. Unlike another California law that requires prompt notification of database breaches, the Online Privacy Act's provisions are already being met by most companies.

THE SURVEILLANCE SOCIETY

Many observers believe that the many separate privacy issues found today must be viewed in a larger context of pervasive surveillance and information gathering. Works in this section explore this "big picture," including the growing use of cameras and other technology by individuals. For works on specific monitoring, surveillance, or data-gathering technologies, see the sections on "Identification Systems and Biometrics" and "Surveillance, Screening, and Tracking Systems."

Books

Garfinkel, Samson. *Database Nation: The Death of Privacy in the 21st Century.* Cambridge, Mass: O'Reilly, 2000. Vividly describes the massive data-gathering and analysis systems that are now being used by corporations and the government to sift through personal information for marketing, insurance and employment decisions, and law enforcement. As consumers and citizens, individuals have effectively lost control over this information and usually have no idea how it is being used—and misused.

Hunter, Richard. *World Without Secrets: Business, Crime, and Privacy in the Age of Ubiquitous Computing.* New York: Wiley, 2002. A whirlwind tour of the vanishing privacy in everyday life. Examples include streets with 24 hour/day video surveillance, cars that record detailed information about their movements, houses that may be too "smart" for their owners' good, and software that quietly collects information from consumers. The last chapter views the aftermath of September 11 as "a Digital Pearl Harbor" launching a final assault on privacy.

Norris, Clive, and Gary Armstrong. *The Maximum Surveillance Society: The Rise of CCTV.* New York: Berg, 1999. Describes the use of closed-circuit television (CCTV) in public places, which grew substantially during the 1990s. The authors' study of CCTV use in Britain raises questions of whether it has any real effect on crime and the possibility that the actual motivations behind it reflect class structures and the desire for social control.

O'Harrow, Robert, Jr. *No Place to Hide.* New York: Free Press, 2005. A vivid and chilling account of the explosion in database and surveillance technology in the wake of the September 11, 2001, terrorist attacks. The author focuses on the emergence of a "security-industrial complex" in which government security agencies team up with commercial firms that have huge databases of personal information at their disposal. The roles of key individuals are featured throughout.

Parenti, Christian. *The Soft Cage: Surveillance in America.* New York: Basic Books, 2003. Argues that pervasive modern threats of government surveillance and corporate information collection threaten to undermine the freedom and self-confidence that citizens must have in an effective democracy.

Stanley, Jay. *The Surveillance-Industrial Complex: How the American Government Is Conscripting Businesses and Individuals in the Construction of a Surveillance Society.* New York: American Civil Liberties Union, 2004. Also available online. URL: http://www.aclu.org/Files/OpenFile.cfm?id=16225. A critical look at a number of government efforts that combine resources from government and business in the name of fighting terrorism. Although such efforts were also used during the cold war, the scope and variety of current programs is much greater. It includes "watch" programs, some of which survived the demise of TIPS (Terrorist Information and Prevention System), as well as new public-private efforts for data gathering and analysis, profiling, and surveillance. The ACLU describes some litigation areas and urges public vigilance.

Sykes, Charles L. *The End of Privacy: Personal Rights in the Surveillance Society.* New York: St. Martin's Press, 1999. The author, a journalist and policy analyst who has tackled education and legal issues, turns his attention to the threat to privacy of intrusive government, media, and corporations. He suggests a variety of measures to protect or regain privacy.

Annotated Bibliography

Whitaker, Reg. *The End of Privacy: How Total Surveillance Is Becoming a Reality*. New York: New Press, 1999. Describes in great detail the systems of surveillance and monitoring that now involve nearly every aspect of Americans' lives. Whitaker suggests that many people may accept such intrusions as the price of consumer convenience.

Articles and Papers

Berman, Jerry, and Paula Bruening. "Is Privacy Still Possible in the Twenty-first Century?" *Social Research*, vol. 68, Spring 2001, pp. 306–317. The authors argue that while new technologies such as cell phones (with their location information) and the Internet have shrunk the sphere of personal privacy somewhat, new legislation and technical tools (such as encryption) have strengthened privacy in other respects.

Clarke, Roger. "While You Were Sleeping . . . Surveillance Technologies Arrived." *Australian Quarterly*, vol. 73, January–February 2001, n.p. Available online. URL: http://www.anu.edu.au/people/Roger.Clarke/DV/AQ2001.html. Updated on February 2, 2001. The "surveillance society" is quietly becoming a reality as new technologies are developed for digital capture of images and data ("dataveillance"). Related areas discussed include identification and tracking and the effects of surveillance systems on behavior.

Kornblum, Janet. "Prying Eyes Are Everywhere." *USA Today*, April 14, 2005, p. 1D. A variety of pundits and activists view with alarm the growing commercial availability of high-tech spying tools such as unobtrusive cameras, GPS devices, and software for monitoring computer activity. These devices may be extending the natural human desire to snoop on one's neighbors into a dangerous degree of intrusiveness and invasion of privacy.

Napolitano, Jo. "Hold It Right There, and Drop That Camera." *New York Times*, December 11, 2003, p. G1. Ubiquitous camera-equipped phones are bringing a new threat to privacy in places such as locker rooms, showers, and restrooms. Chicago is considering a ban on using the phones in places where an average person would expect a reasonable right to privacy. The phones are also potential tools for voyeurs and fetishists.

Web Documents

Bentham, Jeremy. "Panopticon: Or the Inspection-House." Cartome.org. Available online. URL: http://cartome.org/panopticon2.htm. Posted on June 16, 2001. Transcription of Jeremy Bentham's writings on the Panopticon surveillance prison, originally written in 1787. Efficient surveillance is seen as an essential ingredient in prisons, reformatories, and all other institutions holding individuals for "safe custody, confinement, solitude, forced labor, and instruction." In the late 20th century the Panopticon began to be used as a metaphor for an emerging society of pervasive surveillance.

"Theory of Surveillance: The Panopticon." Cartome.org. Available online. URL: http://cartome.org/panopticon1.htm. Posted June 16, 2001. An architectural plan and description of the Panopticon, a prison designed by Jeremy Bentham in which prisoners are continually subject to being viewed by unseen observers. The site also includes an interpretation by philosopher Michel Foucault.

Zettner, Kim. "Brave New Era for Privacy Fight." Wired News. Available online. URL: http://www.wired.com/news/privacy/0,1848,66242,00.html. Posted on January 13, 2005. Looking at the next few years, privacy advocates (both liberal and conservative) see threats from the continuing expansion of government power in the "war on terrorism," in the use of data mining and other technologies in the private sector, and in a growing convergence of government programs and commercial databases. Other emerging concerns include standardized driver's licenses that amount to a de facto national ID, DNA databases, and radio frequency (RFID) tags.

PRIVACY ISSUES

Works in this section provide resources or discussion of both legal and technical aspects of privacy issues and privacy protection.

GENERAL AND INTERNATIONAL PRIVACY LAW

This section includes general resources on privacy law that include more than one subtopic, as well as background and discussion of international and comparative privacy laws and policies.

Books

Bennett, Colin J., and Charles D. Raab. *The Governance of Privacy: Policy Instruments in Global Perspective.* Burlington, Vt.: Ashgate Publishing, 2000. Describes and analyzes the development of privacy policy in modern industrial states. In each case the policies reflect the interaction of social values and the perception of the risks and benefits of different forms of commerce. However, because of the global nature of commerce, the degree of privacy protection ultimately provided will depend on whether a common regulatory standard or pervasive deregulation prevails.

Berthold, Mark, and Raymond Wacks. *Hong Kong Data Privacy Law: Territorial Regulation in a Borderless World.* 2d ed. Hong Kong: Sweet & Maxwell Asia, 2003. While most students of international privacy law focus on the United States, Great Britain, and the European Union, one of the most comprehensive and innovative data privacy laws emerged in Hong Kong in the late 1990s. The authors explain how the Personal Data Privacy Ordinance addresses many of the concerns about data protection and international data transfer that have vexed experts in Western countries.

Cornelius, Vita, ed. *Personal Privacy.* New York: Novinka Publications, 2002. Provides perspectives on the constitutional and legislative protection of privacy in the United States, including federal legislation and Fourth Amendment cases, with a recent trend that suggests a diminishing sphere of personal privacy.

Electronic Privacy Information Center. *The Public Voice WSIS Sourcebook: Perspectives on the World Summit on the Information Society.* Washington, D.C.: Electronic Privacy Information Center, 2004. Describes the upcoming international conference and includes official documents, regional statements, and perspectives on various issues.

Herold, Rebecca, ed. *The Privacy Papers: Managing Technology, Consumer, Employee and Legislative Actions.* Boca Raton, Fla.: CRC Press, 2001. A collection of papers discussing privacy issues arising from new technologies and corporate practices. Topics include employee monitoring, privacy of employee records, the need to protect consumer information, and threats such as computer break-ins, identity theft, and corporate espionage. The book includes sample policies.

Imparato, Nicholas, ed. *Public Policy and the Internet: Privacy, Taxes, and Contract.* Stanford, Calif.: Hoover Institution Press, 2000. The authors discuss three major areas of legal disputes in the online world: privacy and e-commerce, taxation of online commerce, and the need for new forms of contracts to deal with digital goods and services.

Jasper, Margaret C. *Privacy and the Internet: Your Expectations and Rights Under the Law.* Dobbs Ferry, N.Y.: Oceana Publications, 2003. Designed for students, this work provides an overview of what the law protects, the role of federal and state laws and agencies, and practical advice for dealing with cookies, viruses, identity theft, and other threats. The book includes appendixes summarizing laws and cases as well as suggested readings.

Kahin, Brian, and Charles Nessen, eds. *Borders in Cyberspace: Information Policy and the Global Information Infrastructure.* Cambridge: MIT Press, 1997. Discusses how differences in national laws make it difficult to cope with privacy issues in a network that ignores national boundaries. It includes discussion of commerce, security, and personal privacy.

Keynes, Edward. *Liberty, Property, and Privacy: Toward a Jurisprudence of Substantive Due Process.* University Park: Pennsylvania State University Press, 1996. Discusses privacy concepts in relation to assertion of individual rights in encounters with the power of the state.

Kuner, Christopher. *European Data Privacy Law and Online Business.* New York: Oxford University Press, 2003. Written for e-commerce business professionals, this guide explains the principles behind European Union data privacy regulations and applies them to commercial transactions and employee data both within Europe and between European and outside companies. The book includes the texts of relevant laws.

Lessig, Lawrence. *Code and Other Laws of Cyberspace.* New York: Basic Books, 1999. An accessible account of the emerging issues in Internet regulation, including surveillance, privacy, and ownership of intellectual property. A continuing theme is the tension between the inherent characteristics of cyberspace and the attempts of traditional special interests and policymakers to impose their will on the new medium. The author suggests the ultimate solutions must be "coded" into the architecture of the net.

Li, Joyce H-S. *The Center for Democracy and Technology and Internet Privacy in the U.S.: Lessons of the Last Five Years.* Lanham, Md.: Scarecrow Press, 2003. Describes the issues that the Center for Democracy and Technology and Privacy has tackled in recent years, including ownership and access to personal data such as identifying information.

Loader, Brian D. *The Governance of Cyberspace: Politics, Technology and Global Restructuring.* New York: Routledge, 1997. A variety of contributors tackle the question of how the Internet can be governed without being stifled. The intersection between law enforcement, marketing, and privacy protection plays an important part in this debate. Some contributors opt for creating international legal structures, while others look primarily to self-regulation and engineering solutions.

Marcella, Albert J., Jr., and Carol Stucki. *Privacy Handbook: Guidelines, Exposures, Policy Implementation, and International Issues.* New York: Wiley, 2003. A comprehensive and well-organized privacy handbook for businesses, professionals, and anyone concerned with the current state of privacy laws, policies, and issues. The book includes suggested readings and other useful resources.

McCarthy, J. Thomas. *The Rights of Publicity and Privacy.* 2d ed. St. Paul, Minn.: West Group, 2000. A systematic analysis of the rights of the individual to control the commercial or media use of his or her personal identity. Although not generally applicable to routine use of consumer information, "privacy torts" can sometimes be brought in certain cases.

Satterwhite, Robert A., et al. *Privacy Matters: Leading CTOs and Lawyers on What Every Business Professional Should Know About Privacy, Technology, and the Internet.* Boston, Mass.: Aspatore Books, 2003. A survey of emerging issues in Internet-related privacy as it affects the employment and marketing practices of businesses. It focuses on the impact of the changing legal and technological environment.

Schachter, Madeleine. *Informational and Decisional Privacy.* Durham, N.C.: Carolina Academic Press, 2003. This handbook provides excerpts and analysis of legal decisions in the most relevant cases involving both the protection of personal information and the protection of the right to make personal decisions about matters such as reproduction.

Smith, Marcia S. *Internet Privacy: Overview and Pending Legislation.* Washington, D.C.: Congressional Research Service, 2004. Also available online. URL: http://www.usembassy.it/pdf/other/RL31408.pdf. Surveys current issues involving privacy of Internet users, including law enforcement access to online subscriber records under the USA PATRIOT Act and the growing use of intrusive "spyware" and "adware." The book includes summary of legislation pending in the 108th Congress.

Smith, Robert Ellis. *The Law of Privacy Explained.* Providence, R.I.: Privacy Journal, 1993. Although needing to be supplemented by more recent cases, this is a useful overview of the principles of privacy law, including both constitutional law and common law (civil torts).

——. *War Stories: Accounts of Persons Victimized by Invasions of Privacy.* Providence, R.I.: Privacy Journal, 2004. Describes actual incidents of invasion of privacy, including a table of categories (such as bank records and drug testing). Sources and legal citations are included.

Swire, Peter P., and Robert E. Litan. *None of Your Business: World Data Flows, Electronic Commerce, and the European Privacy Directive.* Washington, D.C.: Brookings Institution Press, 1998. Discusses the European Union Directive on Data Protection of 1998 and its implications, some of which have been addressed by later "Safe Harbor" provisions.

Articles and Papers

Armstrong, Jonathan. "Privacy in Europe: The New Agenda." *Journal of Internet Law*, vol. 8, November 2004, p. 3ff. Surveys the current status of privacy laws in Europe. There is still considerable variation between countries, partly because of the addition of more countries to the European Union. Laws about data transfer and security are also discussed.

Branscomb, Anne Wells. "Public and Private Domains of Information: Defining the Legal Boundaries." *Bulletin of the American Society for Information Science*, vol. 21, December–January 1994, p. 14ff. Discusses property rights as they apply to information, ranging from copyright to privacy law.

Clymer, Adam. "Protection of Privacy by States Is Ranked." *New York Times*, October 20, 2002, p. 31. According to a study by *Privacy Journal*, California and Minnesota have the best state privacy protections. California has a special privacy office and its courts have expansively interpreted privacy rights in the state constitution. Minnesota considers disclosure of private facts to be a civil tort. Texas is currently in the lowest of the study's five tiers but is improving, while the federal government itself would fall into the fourth tier.

Crump, Catherine. "Data Retention: Privacy, Anonymity, and Accountability Online." *Stanford Law Review*, vol. 56, October 2003, p. 191ff. A systematic introduction and analysis of how the Fourth Amendment privacy and First Amendment anonymous speech and association rights are being applied in court cases involving access to stored data and communications. If the Internet is redesigned to force identity disclosure, then the rights based on anonymity are lost.

Kuttner, Robert. "The U.S. Could Use a Dose of Europe's Privacy Medicine." *Business Week*, November 16, 1998, p. 22. Argues that the United States should adopt tougher privacy and junk e-mail/fax laws similar to those already in force in Europe.

Lessig, Lawerence. "The Law of the Horse: What Cyberlaw Might Teach." *Harvard Law Review*, vol. 113, December 1999, pp. 501–546. Also available online. URL: http://www.lessig.org/content/articles/works/finalhls.pdf. This paper responds to a challenge from a conference where a judge insisted that there was no more "a law of cyberspace" than there was "a law of the horse." The author replies that while not all special concerns require fundamental rethinking of the law, computers and the development of cyberspace do. The "architecture" of cyberspace interacts with law, customary norms, and other forces to shape online behavior. For example, the attempts to protect privacy and regulate obscenity, although very different in objectives, both run up against the structure of cyberspace. In the long run regulating that structure itself would be the most effective approach.

Rosen, Jeffrey. "A Watchful State: After a Terrorist Attack in 1993, Britain Installed Cameras Everywhere." *New York Times Magazine*, October 7, 2001, p. 38. Describes the use of surveillance cameras in London, which were installed in 1993 and promoted as a tool against IRA terrorists. The cameras' main success, however, has been against auto thieves and traffic offenders.

———. "Nothing to Hide, Nothing to Fear; Europeans Stand to Lose More of Their Privacy and Civil Liberties than Americans." *Newsweek International*, March 8, 2004, p. 47. The author of *The Naked Crowd* says that Europeans appear even more willing than Americans to trade privacy for security and the war on terrorism. For example, the British have little objection to the widespread use of public surveillance cameras. Western Europeans are also used to centralized government databases and the use of fingerprints and biometrics. On the other hand, the Europeans do have protections against commercial use of personal data that are tougher and more comprehensive than those afforded to Americans.

Swire, Peter P. "Trustwrap: The Importance of Legal Rules to Electronic Commerce and Internet Privacy." *Hasting Law Journal*, vol. 54 (2003), p. 847ff. Argues that an effective approach to privacy involves companies using legal commitments and appropriate transaction procedures to create a "trustwrap" that builds consumer assurance. The author cites a number of developments that already embody the trustwrap concept and leverage existing structures into the e-commerce realm. These include online credit card payments and PayPal, the development of online extensions of traditional stores, and eBay's development of enhanced buyer protections. Recent legislation is discussed in this context, with the suggestion that with a mature industry, one has time to craft appropriate legislation.

Web Documents

Cline, Jay. "U.S. Should Welcome EU Drive for Short Privacy Notices." Computerworld.com. Available online. URL: http://www.computerworld.com/printthis/2005/0,4814,99941,00.html (or QuickLink 52731). Posted on February 23, 2005. The author of this opinion piece praises the European initiative that would have businesses use brief privacy notices in plain language that spells out information policies and consumer rights. There would be three increasingly detailed "layers" with the full policy in the last layer. Two American companies, Expedia and Bank of America, already use similar notices.

Charts summarize the strengths and weaknesses of privacy policies of these and other companies.

"Data Retention." Electronic Privacy Information Center. Available online. URL: http://www.epic.org/privacy/intl/data_retention.html. Updated on March 25, 2004. Notes, documents, and links relating to the provisions of the European Union's Directive on Privacy and Electronic Communications that deal with the storage of data by telecommunications and e-mail providers.

"Directive 95/46/EC of the European Parliament and of the Council of 24 October 1995 on the Protection of Individuals with Regard to the Processing of Personal Data and on the Free Movement of Such Data." European Union. Available online. URL: http://aspe.os.dhhs.gov/datacncl/eudirect.htm. Text of the European Union's data protection and privacy regulations.

"Fourth Amendment." 'Lectric Law Library. Available online. URL: http://www.lectlaw.com/def/f081.htm. Downloaded on April 3, 2005. A succinct summary of how various types of search and seizure procedures have been interpreted with regard to the Fourth Amendment of the U.S. Constitution.

"The Privacy Act of 1974." Electronic Privacy Information Center. Available online. URL: http://www.epic.org/privacy/1974act/. Updated on August 26, 2003. An overview of the fundamental law (5 U.S.C. § 552a) that gives citizens the right to examine government records pertaining to them and requires agencies to follow "fair information practices" when gathering and handling personal data, as well as placing restrictions on data sharing. The book includes links to news, resources, and cases.

"Privacy Preemption Watch." Electronic Privacy Information Center. Available online. URL: http://www.epic.org/privacy/preemption/. Updated on December 1, 2004. Gives an overview of the issue of preemption. With regard to federal privacy laws, preemption generally refers to the question of whether states or localities are precluded from enacting laws covering the same subject matter. Preemption can either set a "floor" that states are free to exceed, or establish a "ceiling." Recent developments are discussed and relevant links are provided.

"Right to Financial Privacy Act." Electronic Privacy Information Center. Available online. URL: http://www.epic.org/privacy/rfpa/. Updated on September 5, 2003. Explains the federal law passed in response to a Supreme Court decision that refused to acknowledge a privacy interest in bank transaction records. The RFPA generally requires that account holders be notified and have the opportunity to contest disclosure of account information to law enforcement officials. The site includes a discussion of the legislative history, exceptions specified in the law, and links to relevant cases and news stories.

"Safe Harbor Overview." International Trade Administration. Available online. URL: http://www.ita.doc.gov/td/ecom/SafeHarborOverviewAug00.htm. Posted in August 2000. Summarizes and answers questions about the agreement on procedures for U.S. firms for compliance with European privacy standards. Principles in the Safe Harbor include consumer notice and choice about information sharing, consumer access to their information, and the ability to change erroneous information.

Privacy in the Information Age

PRIVACY, LAW ENFORCEMENT, AND NATIONAL SECURITY

The wars on crime and terrorism have led to an unprecedented use of surveillance, data-gathering, analysis, and screening tools. Works in this section discuss these activities and their perceived privacy threats.

Books

Adams, Helen R., et al. *Privacy in the 21st Century: Issues for Public, School, and Academic Libraries.* Westport, Conn.: Libraries Unlimited, 2005. Focuses on privacy issues as they affect libraries and their users, with an emphasis on the effects of technology. Topics include the USA PATRIOT Act and searches of library borrowing records and privacy of Internet and online database access. The book includes sample privacy and confidentiality policies.

Ball, Kirstie, and Frank Webster, eds. *Intensification of Surveillance: Crime, Terrorism and Warfare in the Information Age.* Sterling, Va.: Pluto Press, 2003. Describes the now pervasive use of surveillance technologies that have expanded greatly since September 11, 2001. The contributors discuss the advantages of various surveillance tools for fighting crime and terrorism in relation to their potential costs, including the impact on personal privacy. The book includes an extensive bibliography.

Bamford, James. *Body of Secrets: Anatomy of the Ultra-Secret National Security Agency: From the Cold War Through the Dawn of a Century.* New York: Anchor Books, 2002. In discussions about government monitoring of communications, the shadowy presence of the National Security Agency inevitably looms. While the amount of current information is necessarily limited, this account vividly portrays the culture and some of the past activities of the spy agency in this sequel to the earlier book *The Puzzle Palace.*

Bazan, Elizabeth B. *The Foreign Intelligence Surveillance Act.* New York: Novinka Books, 2002. Provides a detailed overview of the controversial law that has been expanded in the post–September 11 environment to provide for secret investigations and surveillance. Bazan explores the connection with detentions and arrests outside the normal legal system, such as with "enemy combatants."

Dash, Samuel. *The Intruders: Unreasonable Searches and Seizures from King John to John Ashcroft.* New Brunswick, N.J.: Rutgers University Press, 2004. Describes the gradual development of protection from arbitrary government searches and seizures. The text describes the background in English law (starting with the Magna Charta), how American revolutionaries added a critical new component (the prohibition against nonspecific or "general" warrants), and how the courts have elaborated the interpretation of the Fourth and Fifth amendments in recent years.

Doyle, Charles. *Libraries and the USA PATRIOT Act.* Washington, D.C.: Congressional Research Service, 2003. Also available online. URL: http://www.ala.org/ala/washoff/WOissues/civilliberties/theusapatriotact/

Annotated Bibliography

CRS215LibrariesAnalysis.pdf. A provision of the USA PATRIOT Act would apparently allow federal authorities to access library borrowing records using secret FISA subpoenas. While the library community has considerable concern based on past experience, the FBI has said it has not sought such subpoenas.

Fodor, Margie Druss. *Megan's Law: Protection or Privacy?* Berkeley Heights, N.J.: Enslow Publishers, 2001. Written for junior-high or older students, this "Issues in Focus" book discusses the development of laws that require the disclosure of the presence of registered sex offenders in the community. Particular activists and cases are profiled to give a picture of how the values of safety and privacy are brought into conflict and (sometimes) resolved. Other ways of keeping children safe from predators are also discussed.

Foerstel, Herbert. *Surveillance in the Stacks: The FBI's Library Awareness Program.* New York: Greenwood Press, 1991. Describes an early (and controversial) program that enlisted the aid of librarians in identifying suspected terrorists.

Henderson, Harry. *The Terrorist Challenge to America.* New York: Facts On File, 2003. This volume in the "Library in a Book" series includes considerable coverage of the civil liberties implications of expanded surveillance powers under the USA PATRIOT Act, as well as the use of secret warrants.

McWhirter, Darien A. *Search, Seizure, and Privacy.* Westport, Conn.: Greenwood Publishing, 1994. Designed for high school students through college undergraduates, this clearly written and well-organized exposition covers the principles and case law involving searches and seizures under the Fourth Amendment. The privacy protection for different locations (home vs. business, for example) and circumstances (inside a car or inside baggage) are also explained and illustrated with examples.

Raul, Alan Charles. *Privacy and the Digital State: Balancing Public Information and Personal Privacy.* Boston: Kluwer Academic Publishers, 2002. The author, a scholar with the Progress and Freedom Foundation, begins with the premise that privacy rights have always been, and must always be, balanced against the security of society. The events of September 11, 2001, have necessarily made security the first priority, and concepts of privacy will have to be modified to allow the government to protect citizens from attack. However, the author also acknowledges the importance of honoring constitutional guarantees of privacy, and he shows how court decisions have weighed them against other considerations such as freedom of the press and also maintained limits on the intrusive powers of law enforcement.

Rosen, Jeffrey. *The Naked Crowd: Reclaiming Security and Freedom in an Anxious Age.* New York: Random House, 2004. The author approaches the tradeoffs between privacy and security by looking at the ambivalent popular attitudes toward the many measures and systems adopted since September 11, 2001, such as the USA PATRIOT Act, the Total Information Awareness program, the US-VISIT program, and proposals for a national ID card. The challenge is to allow targeted surveillance for specific threats (such as weapons or explosives) without a "coalescing" of data that would strip away virtually all personal information privacy.

Privacy in the Information Age

Shane, Peter M., John Podesta, and Richard C. Leone, eds. *A Little Knowledge: Privacy, Security and Public Information after September 11.* New York: Century Foundation Press, 2004. Selected proceedings of the Security, Technology and Privacy Conference focusing on ways in which new restrictions on access to scientific information can be counterproductive, while weak privacy protections in the United States may promote dubious invasions of privacy.

Smith, Marcia S., et al. *The Internet and the USA PATRIOT Act: Potential Implications for Electronic Privacy, Security, Commerce, and Government.* Washington, D.C.: Congressional Research Service, 2002. Also available online. URL: http://www.epic.org/privacy/terrorism/usapatriot/RL31289.pdf. Summarizes the application of the USA PATRIOT Act with regard to electronic commerce, security, and privacy.

Articles and Papers

Andrews, Paul. "Keeping Watch Now Goes Both Ways." *Seattle Times*, April 14, 2005, n.p. Also available online. URL: http://seattletimes.nwsource.com/html/businesstechnology/2002240978_spyware14.html. Reports a talk by Steve Mann at the Computers, Freedom and Privacy conference in which he suggests ubiquitous cameras in cell phones and even lapel pins might enable people to protect themselves from law enforcement abuses by recording activities in real time—a process he calls "sousveillance," or watching from below. Cameras could even send their data directly over a wireless link to the Internet to preserve evidence even if the equipment is confiscated or destroyed.

Baard, Erik. "Buying Trouble: Your Grocery List Could Spark a Terror Probe." *The Village Voice*, July 24, 2002, n.p. Also available online. URL: http://www.villagevoice.com/news/0230,baard,36760,1.html. Describes how an overzealous marketing official gave authorities supermarket "loyalty card" records following the September 11 attacks. Although not typical, the incident may be just the tip of an iceberg of commercial data that is becoming available to government investigators. Although new data-mining algorithms for identifying potential terrorists show promise, rash and ill-considered decisions by agents may lead to grief for innocent shoppers.

Egelko, Bob. "Supreme Court Expands Police Search Powers: Drug-Sniffing Dogs Now Have Access to Any Car Stopped." *San Francisco Chronicle*, January 23, 2005, p. A4. Reports a Supreme Court decision that allows use of drug-sniffing dogs during any lawful traffic stop. The Court's two dissenters and privacy advocates warn that the decision will encourage police to undertake more stops and "sweeps" in order to search for drugs.

Epstein, Edward. "Left and Right Unite to Challenge Patriot Act Provisions: Group Wants Limits on Access Allowed Law Enforcement." *San Francisco Chronicle*, March 23, 2005, p. A3. Reports the growing efforts of an unusual left-right coalition that is seeking to change provisions of the USA PATRIOT Act. The proposed new wording would require that authorities show a judge specific evidence of terrorist links before someone's library, medical, or firearms records could be examined.

214

———. "White House Willing to Scale Back Patriot Act." *San Francisco Chronicle*, April 6, 2005, pp. 1, 11. As Congress considers whether to renew 16 provisions of the USA PATRIOT Act, Attorney General Alberto Gonzales expressed his willingness to consider modifications provided they do not compromise the ability to fight terrorism. Critics seek to remove provisions that allow searching of library and bookstore records and that allow for undisclosed "sneak and peak" warrants. A coalition of liberal and conservative activists has been promoting a SAFE (Security and Freedom Enhancement) Act to strengthen protections for civil liberties.

Goo, Sara Kehaulani. "Secret Rule Requiring ID for Flights at Center of Court Battle." *Washington Post*. October 7, 2004, p. A13. This account of John Gilmore's challenge to airport ID requirements focuses on the government's contention that its rules must be kept secret for security reasons. Media organizations have also joined the fight to make the documents a part of the public court record.

Hoffnagel, Chris Jay. "Big Brother's Little Helpers: How ChoicePoint and Other Commercial Data Brokers Collect and Package Your Data for Law Enforcement." *North Carolina Journal of International Law and Commercial Regulation*, vol. 29, Summer 2004, p. 595ff. Also available online. URL: http://www.epic.org/privacy/choicepoint/cp_article.pdf. ChoicePoint and other commercial data brokers allow law enforcement agencies to obtain extensive information about suspects. The author used the Freedom of Information Act to obtain information about the relationship between data brokers and government agencies. He concludes that while obtaining information to aid criminal investigations can be appropriate, there is little regulation of its use or training of law enforcement officers about privacy issues. As a result the balance of power between individuals and the government has been upset.

James, Barry. "Internet Crime-Fighting Plan May Open Door for Snoopers." *International Herald Tribune*, March 23, 2001, p. 25. Describes the controversial Convention on Cybercrime that is being adopted by the European Union. While proponents see the convention as providing necessary tools for going after child pornographers and hackers who work across national boundaries, critics are concerned about the law's lack of privacy protection and the outlawing of anonymity, which can help protect political dissidents. Further, provisions designed to protect copyrights may deprive disadvantaged users of access to important information.

Lichtblau, Eric. "U.S. Seeks Access to Bank Records to Deter Terror." *New York Times*, April 10, 2005, p. A1. Reports that the Bush administration is preparing to create a database containing perhaps hundreds of millions of records of international banking transactions. Promoted as a way to identify the financial activities of terrorist groups as well as criminal money laundering, the plan is opposed by a banking industry that feels itself already overburdened by reporting requirements. Meanwhile, there are also questions about how the privacy of customers will be ensured.

Timberg, Craig. "Virginia Lists Sex Offenders on Internet." *Washington Post*, December 30, 1998, p. A1. A state's web site listing names and other information about convicted sex offenders leads to conflict between security and privacy. Advocates say the list will help parents protect their children from violent predators, but opponents fear the program may lead to vigilantism and loss of employment for ex-offenders who may be trying to reform.

Web Documents

"The Attorney General's Guidelines." Electronic Privacy Information Center. Available online. URL: http://www.epic.org/privacy/fbi/. Updated on March 17, 2003. Describes the guidelines used by the FBI in criminal and antiterrorist investigations. The latest guidelines were released in 2002; they have changed several times since the abuses in the 1960s and congressional investigations in the 1970s. The site includes links to historical documents relating to COINTELPRO (domestic counter-dissident activities), as well as to discussion of the new guidelines.

Borland, John. "A Global Assault on Anonymity." CNET News.com. Available online. URL: http://news.com.com/2009–1009_3–5405947.html. Posted on October 20, 2004. Initiatives such as Total Information Awareness (TIA) and the Computer Assisted Passenger Prescreening System (CAPPS I and II), as well as the use of data mining and search tools by government agencies, are threatening privacy. Resistance to such efforts is seen in the withdrawal of 11 of the original 16 states participating in the Multistate Anti-Terrorism Information Exchange (MATRIX) program. However, there seems to be a shortage of people sincerely seeking to reconcile security and privacy concerns.

"Counter-Terrorism Proposals." Electronic Privacy Information Center. Available online. URL: http://www.epic.org/privacy/terrorism/. Updated on November 12, 2002. Provides news and views on the USA PATRIOT Act and other laws passed in the wake of September 11, 2001 and that threaten privacy through a substantial loosening of restrictions on surveillance.

"Fear of Online Crime: Americans Support FBI Interception of Criminal Suspects' Email and New Laws to Protect Online Privacy." Pew Internet and American Life. Available online. URL: http://www.pewinternet.org/pdfs/PIP_Fear_of_crime.pdf. Posted on April 2, 2001. This survey shows a familiar tension between privacy and security. Large majorities of respondents are deeply worried about various forms of Internet crime (particularly child pornography) and 54 percent favor giving law enforcement authorities the right to intercept criminal suspects' e-mail and other communications. However, opinion is more evenly divided about Carnivore, the rather mysterious software used by the FBI to intercept communications. On the other hand, 62 percent of respondents say that new laws are needed to protect online privacy.

Hall, Mimi. "Privacy Czar Balances Needs of Nation, Citizens." USA Today. Available online. URL: http://www.usatoday.com/news/washington/2004-06-13-privacy-czar_x.htm. Updated on July 9, 2004. Nuala O'Connor Kelly, the official in charge of privacy policies for the Department of Homeland Security, faces a daunting challenge: to create a system "that allows for people to pass through their ordinary life in the way they want to but still has some level of security for all of us." Civil libertarians say they respect Kelly but that the jury is still out on whether she can be effective in protecting privacy in the face of programs such as the CAPPS II airline passenger screening system.

"The USA PATRIOT Act." Electronic Privacy Information Center. Available online. URL: http://www.epic.org/privacy/terrorism/usapatriot/default.html. Updated on March 21, 2005. Gives an overview of provisions of the USA PATRIOT Act that raised new privacy issues in the wake of the "war on terrorism." For example, there are expanded powers to install telephone and data communications tracing devices. Internet service providers must provide additional information about subscribers, and the use of secret warrants is expanded. The web page includes news and resource links.

"Wiretapping/Eavesdropping on Telephone Conversations: Is There Cause for Concern?" Privacy Rights Clearinghouse. Available online. URL: http://www.privacyrights.org/fs/fs9-wrtp.htm. Revised in March 2004. Explains what to do if one thinks one is being illegally wiretapped and explains the circumstances under which law enforcement agencies or private individuals can legally monitor phone conversations. The article also explains pen registers, "trap and trace" devices, and interception of digital or data communications.

IDENTIFICATION SYSTEMS AND BIOMETRICS

Works in this first of more technical sections of this bibliography discusses the use of identification cards (including the possibility of a national identification system) as well as "smart cards" and the use of physical (biometric) forms of identification.

Books

Eaton, Joseph W. *The Privacy Card: A Low Cost Strategy to Combat Terrorism.* Lanham, Md.: Rowman & Littlefield Publishers, 2003. This revision of a book first published in the 1980s suggests that a tamper-proof universal ID card combining information and biometrics is a necessity in the age of terrorism. The challenge is to implement such a system while protecting privacy and preventing abuses. A variety of possible implementations are presented, each with advantages and drawbacks.

Kent, Stephen T., and Lynette I. Millett, eds. *Who Goes There? Authentication Through the Lens of Privacy.* Washington, D.C.: National Academies Press, 2003. Also available online. URL: http://www.nap.edu/books/0309088968/html/. A report by the Committee on Authentication Technologies and Their Privacy Implications of the Research Council of the National Academies.

Smith, Alison M. *National Identification Cards: Legal Issues.* Washington, D.C.: Congressional Research Service, 2002. Summarizes the legal background and controversy over the proposed use of some form of uniform national identification, perhaps incorporating biometric data.

Smith, Robert Ellis. *A National ID Card: A License to Live.* Providence, R.I.: Privacy Journal, 2000. A concise summary of the arguments for and against a proposed national mandatory identification card. Smith opposes national ID cards, both because of the great potential for abuse and the chilling effect on peoples' sense of freedom and autonomy in their daily lives.

———. *Social Security Numbers: Uses and Abuses.* Providence, R.I.: Privacy Journal, 2002. Includes a brief history of the use of Social Security numbers since their inception in the 1930s and discusses court cases involving the compelled use of the numbers. The book also includes practical advice on how to keep one's Social Security number private or to use alternative means of identification.

Woodward, John D., Jr. *Biometrics: Identity Assurance in the Information Age.* Berkeley, Calif.: McGraw Hill-Osborne, 2003. A guide to the design, selection, and deployment of biometric identification systems. Describes the accuracy, vulnerability, and cost of each major type of system—fingerprints, hand geometry, facial and voice recognition, and eye structure (iris and retinal scanning). There is a discussion of privacy and legal issues, as well as a variety of case studies of biometric systems in use today.

Articles and Papers

Brill, Steven. "The Biggest Hole in the Net." *Newsweek,* December 30, 2002, p. 48. Proposes a voluntary national ID card for persons who have been pre-screened against criminal and antiterrorist records. The card would have biometric identifiers and would allow screened persons to have quick, easy access to airports and other public facilities.

Feder, Barnaby J. "Face-Recognition Technology Improves." *New York Times,* March 14, 2003, p. C2. A test of 10 facial recognition systems by four federal agencies shows that the technology has improved in its ability to match face scans with stored images in a database. However, performance is still poor in outdoor settings (about 50 percent accuracy).

Garfinkel, Simson. "An RFID Bill of Rights." *Technology Review,* October 2002, n.p. Wireless identification tags are soon going to show up on everything. The author believes that now is the time to establish consumer rights, such as the right to know whether RFID tags are in use and to have them removed or deactivated when an item is purchased. Consumers should not be forced to accept RFID in order to receive services.

Kirn, Walter. "The Mother of Reinvention: The Real Reason Americans Detest the Idea of a National ID Card." *Atlantic Monthly,* vol. 289, May 2002, p. 28ff. Although many Americans are worried about the potential abuse of government power, there are also deeply rooted philosophical and psychological reasons for opposition to a national ID card. Americans cherish their ability to reinvent themselves, in effect changing their identity. There is also the American tradition, bolstered somewhat by the Bill of Rights, that says that people should not have to prove their identity or explain themselves to authorities.

Annotated Bibliography

Leach, Susan Llewelyn. "A Driver's License as a National ID?" *Christian Science Monitor*, January 24, 2005, p. 11. The newly passed National Intelligence Reform Act includes a provision for standardized information in driver's licenses. The standards are to be developed by federal and state officials working together with technical experts. However, the standards are expected to focus mainly on tightening and standardizing license applications procedures; the licenses themselves will not be required to include electronic or biometric information. Nevertheless privacy advocates are concerned that standardization plus a central database will in effect create a national ID system.

Rice-Oxley, Mark. "Britain's Latest Security Bid: A National ID Card." *Christian Science Monitor*, November 14, 2003, p. 6. Reports that the British government is preparing to issue national identity cards containing personal and biometric information. While the cards are being touted as an effective new weapon against terrorism, critics oppose them as expensive, unnecessary, and as contributing to a "surveillance society."

Robertson, Jack. "U.S. Transportation Chief Pushes Biometrics Adoption—Report Urges Airports to Install Equipment, Screen Passengers Entering Country." *EBN*, October 15, 2001, p. 1. In a report issued by the transportation secretary, Norman Mineta, just after the September 11 attacks, airports were urged to install biometric passenger-screening systems. Such systems, which have been in limited use by the Immigration and Naturalization Service, match physical characteristics (such as fingerprints, the retina, or facial features) to identification information. The system could also be used to check in "preapproved" passengers who have been investigated and certified as "safe flyers." Such a passenger would carry a card that would be verified against his or her physical characteristics.

Willing, Richard. "Airline ID Requirement Faces Legal Challenge." *USA Today*, October 10, 2004, n.p. Also available online. URL: http://www.usatoday.com/news/nation/2004–10–10-privacy_x.htm. Reports on activist John Gilmore's probably doomed efforts to overturn requirements for providing identification before boarding a plane. Gilmore is appealing the dismissal of his 2002 suit against the federal government. Gilmore does not oppose baggage screening and other measures directed at keeping weapons and bombs off aircraft.

Web Documents

Agre, Philip E. "Your Face Is Not a Bar Code: Arguments Against Automatic Face Recognition in Public Places." University of California, Los Angeles. Department of Information Studies. Available online. URL: http://polaris.gseis.ucla.edu/pagre/bar-code.html. Posted on September 10, 2003. The author argues that face recognition systems have legitimate uses, such as for providing access to secure areas or matching suspects against a "mug shot" database. However, using face recognition systems routinely in public places (such as at the Super Bowl) is likely to result in misuse of the data or at least an unacceptably high rate of "false positives."

Biba, Erin. "Biometric Passports Set to Take Flight: Your Next Passport May Be Electronic, but Will It Be Any More Secure?" PC World.com. Available online. URL: http://www.pcworld.com/news/article/0,aid,120112,00.asp. Posted on March 21, 2005. The State Department has announced that it is ready to start issuing biometric passports containing radio frequency identification (RFID) chips. Privacy experts are concerned that because the information stored in the new passports is unencrypted, it could be easily read from 30–65 feet away by anyone who has a suitable scanner.

"Biometric Identifiers." Electronic Privacy Information Center. Available online. URL: http://www.epic.org/privacy/biometrics/. Updated on March 18, 2005. Describes the use of devices to scan, store, and identify physical characteristics. The site identifies the major areas of concern: storage, vulnerability, confidence/accuracy, authenticity, linking to other information, and ubiquity. The page also includes links to related news stories.

Clarke, Roger. "Smart Card Technical Issues Starter Kit." Department of Computer Science, Australian National University. Available online. URL: http://www.anu.edu.au/people/Roger.Clarke/DV/SCTISK.html. Posted April 8, 1998. Provides background on the use of "smart cards," originally intended as a briefing for privacy advocates. Clarke describes the types of cards, authentication, security, cryptography, applications, and related privacy issues.

"Face Recognition." Electronic Privacy Information Center. Available online. URL: http://www.epic.org/privacy/facerecognition/. Updated on August 21, 2003. Introduces the use of automatic face-recognition systems (which most people first heard about in the context of the 2001 Super Bowl in Tampa, Florida). The web page includes news and resource links.

Gilmore, John. "Gilmore v. Ashcroft—FAA ID Challenge FAQ." Available online. URL: http://cryptome.org/gilmore-v-usa-faq.htm. Posted on July 18, 2002. Gilmore explains the reasons for his 2002 lawsuit demanding the right to travel without having to provide identification. He argues that the focus on identification and profiling not only violates fundamental constitutional rights and involves secret, unaccountable procedures but also diverts resources and attention from measures that might actually enhance security.

Harper, Jim. "A National ID: Government Initiatives and the Private Sector." Privacilla.org. Available online. URL: http://www.privacilla.org/releases/CDIA_Remarks_01-27-05.html. Posted on January 27, 2005. The editor of the Privacilla.org web site discusses the national ID effort in remarks to the annual conference of the Consumer Data Industry Association. He argues that the issue is not whether to have a national ID card. Driver's licenses are already going to be turned into the effective equivalent of a national ID. The focus should be on developing ID systems that authorize access without conveying unnecessary information or engaging in pervasive surveillance.

McCullagh, Declan. "Scanning the Future of Privacy." CNet News.com. Available online. URL: http://news.com.com/2100-1029-994080.html. Posted on March 25, 2003. A report from the National Research Council suggests guidelines for using authentication systems such as passwords, identification and "smart cards," and biometrics. The report warns that developers must be particularly careful about systems that link identification and databases that record personal data and information about activities. There must be strong regard for constitutional rights of privacy and freedom of association.

"National ID Cards." Electronic Privacy Information Center. Available online. URL: http://www.epic.org/privacy/id_cards/. Updated on April 1, 2005. Gives an overview and links to news and events relating to proposals for a national ID card.

Scheeres, Julia. "Support for ID Cards Waning." Wired News. Available online. URL: http://www.wired.com/news/print/0,1294,51000,00.html. Posted on March 13, 2002. Reports that recent surveys show a decline in support for proposed National ID cards. Support had peaked in the wake of the September 11 terrorist attacks at 70 percent according to a Pew Center poll. However, a Gartner poll showed only 26 percent support, though a majority supported the use of uniform IDs for specific purposes, such as tracking airline passengers.

Singel, Ryan. "Passport Safety, Privacy Face Off." Wired News. Available online. URL: http://www.wired.com/news/privacy/0,1848,62876,00.html. Posted on March 31, 2004. Reports on new passport standards to be promulgated by the International Civil Aviation Organization. The standards include standard face-recognition biometrics, with optional use of fingerprints or iris scans. An international coalition of privacy groups has asked that the standards not be finalized until privacy concerns are fully addressed and strict standards for the collection and use of data are developed.

"Social Security Numbers." Electronic Privacy Information Center. Available online. URL: http://www.epic.org/privacy/ssn/. Updated September 28, 2004. Describes the history of the use of Social Security numbers (SSNs) for identification, the notification requirements in the 1974 Privacy Act, the SSN as a tool of identity theft, and requirements for legislation that would effectively prevent misuse of the SSN. The web page includes resource and news links.

"VeriChip." Electronic Privacy Information Center. Available online. URL: http://www.epic.org/privacy/rfid/verichip.html. Updated October 20, 2004. Describes the VeriChip, a radio frequency identification device implanted under the skin. The FDA has approved its use as a medical identification device, but it has also been used for tracking purchases in a nightclub. Use as an access device raises privacy concerns.

"VeriChip Personal Identification System—Frequently Asked Questions." Applied Digital Corp. Available online. URL: http://www.adsx.com/faq/verichipfaq.html. Describes an identification chip intended to be inserted just under a person's skin, potentially for use in identifying persons for access to secure environments or for verifying transactions. Users' data then is stored in a central database.

Williams, Sam. "The Curse of the Biometric Future." Salon.com. Available online. URL: http://www.salon.com/tech/feature/2004/02/26/biometric/index.html. Posted on February 26, 2004. Describes the development of facial biometrics. The author builds on the developer's characterization of the technology as being both a blessing and a sort of curse. Although there are concerns about the misuse of the technology, the author also notes that the accuracy of the available technology falls well short of popular conceptions fostered by the media.

Zetter, Kim. "Great Taste, Less Privacy." *Wired News*. Available online. URL: http://www.wired.com/news/privacy/0,1848,62182,00.html. Posted on February 6, 2004. Bars, stores, and other venues often swipe patron's driver's licenses in order to verify age and authenticity. However, they can also combine the information they obtain with commercial databases to find out a lot more than customers might want them to know. An exhibit (now a web site) called Swipe is helping people learn just what can be learned about them.

SURVEILLANCE, SCREENING, AND TRACKING SYSTEMS

This section includes works on a variety of systems for surveillance (such as cameras and face-recognition systems), automatic screening or profiling systems, and technology such as radio frequency ID (RFID) and the use of GPS devices for monitoring the location of persons or things.

Books

Corwall, Agnes S. *Telecommunications Issues in Focus.* New York: Nova Science Publishers, 2002. Describes recent regulatory and technical developments in telecommunications, including a number of areas relating to surveillance and privacy, such as unwanted telemarketing calls, digital surveillance, remote sensing, and encryption.

Krouse, William J. *The Multi-State Anti-Terrorism Information Exchange (MATRIX) Pilot Project.* Washington, D.C.: Congressional Research Service, 2004. Also available online. URL: http://www.mipt.org/pdf/CRS_RL32536. pdf. Provides an overview of a federal pilot project involving the use of data-mining techniques with public records to help generate leads for antiterrorism investigations. Many states soon dropped out of the project and privacy concerns continued.

Monmonier, Mark. *Spying with Maps: Surveillance Technologies and the Future of Privacy.* Chicago: University of Chicago Press, 2002. The author, a professor of geography, provides details about surveillance, mapping, and geographic analysis systems used by the military, law enforcement, and even private businesses. He believes many of these systems can be useful but can also represent a new and growing threat to privacy. The concept of privacy may need to be expanded to include "locational privacy"—the ability to not have people track where one is or has been.

Peters, Thomas A. *Computerized Monitoring and Online Privacy.* Jefferson, N.C.: McFarland, 1999. While perhaps containing too much detail for many readers, this overview provides a broad perspective on how a variety of types of software have included functions that monitor and record user interactions. Much of this functionality may be benign and even useful—for example, in helping developers to create educational or library software that is easier and more rewarding to use. Understanding this pervasive feature of software can be a starting point for identifying potential privacy issues or threats.

Petersen, Julie K. *Understanding Surveillance Technologies: Spy Devices, Their Origins and Applications.* Grand Rapids, Mich.: CRC Press, 2000. A well-illustrated guide to the operation and use of a wide variety of surveillance and monitoring technologies. These include bugs, hidden cameras, aerial surveillance, radar, infrared, wiretapping, and electronic eavesdropping techniques. The author also discusses the many contexts in which such systems may be used, including the media, employers, law enforcement, and intelligence agencies, as well as outlining the privacy issues that often arise.

Schneier, Bruce, and David Banisar. *The Electronic Privacy Papers: Documents on the Battle for Privacy in the Age of Surveillance.* New York: Wiley, 1997. A collection of documents obtained under the Freedom of Information Act. Topics of these previously classified or restricted documents include proposed telecommunications surveillance systems, wiretapping, cryptography (including the Clipper Chip), and key escrow systems. Each document is annotated to explain its significance.

Stevens, Gina Marie. *Privacy: Total Information Awareness Programs and Latest Developments.* Washington, D.C.: Congressional Research Service, 2003. Also available online. URL: http://www.fas.org/irp/crs/RL31730.pdf. Describes the controversial Defense Research Projects Agency (DARPA) "Total Information Awareness" program. This five-year project, eventually renamed and then abandoned, would have used data-mining techniques to analyze a vast number of personal transactions to uncover patterns that might be associated with terrorist group activity. The privacy and civil liberties concerns that led to the curtailment of the program are also explored.

Stevens, Gina Marie, and Charles Doyle. *Privacy: Wiretapping and Electronic Eavesdropping.* Washington, D.C.: Congressional Research Service, 2003. Also available online. URL: http://www.epic.org/privacy/wiretap/98-326.pdf. Provides an overview of federal law governing wiretapping and electronic eavesdropping, including the impact of the USA PATRIOT Act and other post–September 11 developments.

United States Department of Homeland Security. *US-VISIT Program, Increment 1, Privacy Impact Assessment.* Washington, D.C.: Department of Homeland Security, December 18, 2003. Also available online. URL: http://www.epic.org/privacy/us-visit/us-visit_pia.pdf. Describes the new program for collecting data and biometric scans from non-immigrant visitors to the United States. The report also describes how information will be used, shared, and safeguarded.

United States General Accounting Office. *Data Mining: Federal Efforts Cover a Wide Range of Uses.* Washington, D.C.: GAO, 2004. Also available online.

URL: http://www.gao.gov/new.items/d04548.pdf. A survey of federal agencies and departments showed that 52 of 128 are using or are planning to use data mining. Reasons cited included improving efficiency and service, analyzing intelligence, and detecting waste, fraud, and abuse.

Articles and Papers

Barber, Grayson. "Public Video Surveillance Erodes Our Integrity." *New Jersey Law Journal*, vol. 165, July 30, 2001, p. 23ff. Argues that although anonymity on the Internet and in the street can make it hard to hold people accountable for their actions (such as defamation or harassment), it is necessary for the protection of liberty. The United States has a long history of anonymous political activity.

Biever, Celeste. "The Phone that Knows You Better Than You Do." *New Scientist*, vol. 184, November 27, 2004, p. 21. Describes work toward the development of an "assistive cell phone" by MIT researchers. The phone can keep track of the destination and timing of calls and even map "socialization patterns" through gauging the proximity of other phone users. However, little concern is expressed about the privacy implications of such technology.

Colker, David. "Go Ahead, Just Try to Disappear." *Los Angeles Times*, December 27, 2004, p. A1. Reports the growing use of Global Positioning System (GPS)–equipped mobile phones and other devices to track children, workers, even pets. But while knowing the location of one's children can be comforting to a parent, workers and travelers may experience an oppressive sense of always being monitored and tracked.

Cooper, Simon. "Who's Spying on You?" *Popular Mechanics*, vol. 182, January 5, 2005, p. 56. Reports several emerging privacy threats. As a result of a federal mandate, GPS-enabled cell phones can now be used as tracking devices, sometimes without the consent of the owner. Required event data recorders in vehicles could be used by insurance companies to deny coverage based on driving habits. Radio frequency ID devices (including implantable VeriChips) could allow people themselves to be tracked.

Dobson, Jerome E. "Every Step You Take, Every Move You Make: It's Time for an Explicit National Debate on Human-Tracking that Goes Far Beyond Privacy Issues." *Chicago Tribune*, February 25, 2005, p. 21. For $200 plus a small monthly fee anyone can obtain a device and use it to track a child, a forgetful parent, or perhaps a spouse suspected to be unfaithful. But while the privacy issues are obvious, psychological and sociological consequences of pervasive tracking of people also need to be considered and debated.

Eggen, Dan. "FBI Misused Secret Wiretaps, According to Memo." *Washington Post*, October 10, 2002, p. A14. Reports that an internal memo obtained by a member of Congress reveals that the FBI had illegally videotaped suspects, recorded telephone calls, and intercepted e-mails in secret investigations under the FISA (Foreign Intelligence Surveillance Act). Remarkably these abuses occurred a year and a half before the September 11 attacks. The FBI

says it has fully investigated the problems and reformed the related procedures, but critics worry about the ongoing lack of accountability.

Eggen, Dan, and Jonathan Krim. "Easier Internet Wiretaps Sought." *Washington Post*, March 13, 2004, p. A1. Reports that the U.S. Justice Department is
seeking to require Internet service providers to be subject to the same wiretap access requirements as other telecommunications providers. Officials
argue that they must have the capability to decode data packets that represent
voice-over-Internet phone calls. Industry attorneys oppose the request because of significant costs that would be imposed on providers, while some privacy advocates believe the government would be interfering too much in the
architecture of the Internet.

Farivar, Cyrus. "When Shots Ring Out, a Listening Device Acts as Witness."
New York Times, December 16, 2004, p. E9. The Center for Neural Engineering at the University of Southern California has developed a system that
combines cameras, microphones, and software to identity gunshots and pin-
point their location. The system uses a neural network that is "trained" to
recognize sounds. The time it takes for the sound to be received at various locations allows for triangulation and switching to an appropriately placed surveillance camera. (Although most people would consider it desirable to be
able to find shooters, use of such a system to identify other types of sounds
might represent a privacy threat.)

Garfinkel, Simson. "I See You." *Technology Review*, March 5, 2003, n.p. The author recounts his installation of an inexpensive webcam surveillance system in
his new home. Afterward, he reflects that he, like most people, is concerned
with being spied on in public but comfortable with the idea of keeping an eye
on his own property.

Geracimos, Ann. "Walking 'Signature.'" *Washington Times*, March 4, 2004, n.p.
Also available online. URL: http://www.washingtontimes.com/functions/
print.php?StoryID=20040303-094727-4753r. Computer scientists are working
on a system that can uniquely identify individuals based on finding distinctive,
invariant characteristics of gait (the way of walking). Although variations in
lighting, shadows, and terrain complicate the effort, such a system could be
used to help diagnose motion disorders or to gauge the progress of physical
therapy. However, the system could also be used for surveillance, where it
might identify persons whose face is obscured or out of the camera field.

Goold, Benjamin J. "Public Area Surveillance and Police Work: The Impact of
CCTV on Police Behaviour and Autonomy." *Surveillance & Society*, vol. 1, pp.
191–203. Also available online. URL: http://www.surveillance-and-society.
org/articles1(2)/publicpolice.pdf. The pervasive use of public surveillance
cameras in the United Kingdom may be reducing crime and changing public
behavior. However, it may also be changing the behavior of the police, some
of whom fear that surveillance footage taken out of context might be used to
support complaints against them.

Jackson, William. "To Share Is Human: Anonymous Data-Mining Technology
Protects Privacy." *Government Computer News*, vol. 23, December 13, 2004,

p. 21ff. Describes a system where items from different databases can be "hashed" and compared for matches without revealing the actual information. For example, airport ticketing information could be compared against a "No Fly List." The advantage is that the privacy of personal information would not be exposed to the persons doing the matching.

Kandra, Anne. "National Security vs. Online Privacy: The New Antiterrorism Law Steps Up Electronic Surveillance of the Internet." *PC World*, vol. 20, January 2002, p. 37ff. The author expresses concern about provisions of the new USA PATRIOT Act as they apply to Internet use. E-mail and Web activities of persons unrelated to a particular investigation might be "swept up," and the secret technology for Internet surveillance (formerly known as Carnivore) remains obscure but troubling.

Lee, Jennifer 8. "Welcome to the Database Lounge." *New York Times*, March 21, 2002, p. G1. Recounts how driver's license scanners now used at some bars to verify age can also be used to surreptitiously gather personal information about customers. As more licenses become machine readable, the privacy concerns about such scanning are likely to grow.

Markoff, John, and Eric Lichtblau. "Gaps Seen in 'Virtual Border' Security System." *New York Times*, May 31, 2004, p. C1. The expansion of the US-VISIT border screening program has been challenged by computer scientists and engineers. The critics point to a history of government boondoggles in information technology. They suggest that as with missile defense systems, the inherent difficulty of the task is far greater than usually admitted.

McGee, Jim. "Fighting Terror with Databases; Domestic Intelligence Plans Stir Concern." *Washington Post*, February 16, 2002, p. A27. Federal authorities are building powerful new investigative tools by linking databases containing information about, for example, immigrants and resident aliens. Local police are being given increased access to information from federal agencies, and often carrying out interviews on their behalf. As a sort of pilot program, 5,000 Middle Eastern men who share some characteristics with the September 11 hijackers have been "voluntarily" interviewed. Some civil libertarians believe that an open-ended database system may suck in thousands of innocent citizens and subject them to harassment and employment difficulties, and serve to deter legitimate political dissent, as happened in the 1950s and 1970s.

Miller, Leslie. "Air Passenger ID Screening Called Inadequate on Privacy." *San Francisco Chronicle*, March 29, 2005, p. A5. The Government Accountability Office has reported that the Secure Flight passenger-screening program now in development has failed to meet nine of 10 conditions required for further funding. Officials with the program admit that there have been delays with implementing privacy protection and notification. Further, the program does not provide any recourse for passengers whose names may have been put on "no fly" lists erroneously.

"Move Over, Big Brother." *The Economist*. vol. 373, December 2, 2004, p. 31. Security expert Bruce Schneier argues that the widespread availability of inexpensive camera phones, webcams, and other devices is enabling ordinary people to catch criminals and hold institutions accountable for their actions. A "photographically armed" society may become more polite, but the ubiquitous surveillance of all by all could inhibit free expression and nonconformity.

Newitz, Annalee. "They've Got Your Number . . ." *Wired Magazine*, vol. 12, December 2004, n.p. Also available online. URL: http://www.wired.com/wired/archive/12.12/phreakers.html. A modern wireless "phone phreaker" demonstrates how easy it is to intercept cell phone calls with a hidden antenna, a Bluetooth wireless device, and software. Phones can even be manipulated or taken over without the owner's knowledge. Today's legions of cell phone users are shown to be vulnerable to hackers and industrial spies.

O'Harrow, Robert, Jr. "Tiny Sensors that Can Track Anything." *Washington Post*, September 24, 2004, p. E1. Coming soon: tiny networked sensors called "smart dust" that can be used to monitor environmental conditions and detect problems . . . but that could also track people and their activities.

Schwartz John. "Privacy Fears Erode Support for a Network to Fight Crime." *New York Times*, March 15, 2004, p. C1. Reports that 11 of the 16 states that had signed up for the Multistate Anti-Terrorism Information Exchange (Matrix) have withdrawn from the project. While most of the states cited financial issues, some officials have also cited privacy concerns.

———. "Snoop Software Gains Power and Raises Privacy Concerns." *New York Times*, October 10, 2003, p. A1. Describes software designed specifically for monitoring or spying on a person's computer activities, often recording keystrokes. Some software can even turn on a person's webcam and transmit pictures of him or her. Mark Rotenberg of the Electronic Privacy Information Center says that the makers of such software should not be allowed to disclaim responsibility for its use.

———. "This Car Can Talk. What It Says May Cause Concern." *New York Times*, December 29, 2003, p. C1. The growing use of systems such as OnStar that keep track of a car's location offers motorists effective emergency help, such as by routing responders to the scene even when the driver does not know his or her location. However, privacy advocates such as Beth Givens of the Privacy Rights Clearinghouse worry that law enforcement or even hackers may use the system to track a target's location. Data stored in "black box" recorders that record driving behavior also raises issues.

Taslitz, Andrew E. "The Fourth Amendment in the Twenty-First Century: Technology, Privacy, and Human Emotions." *Law and Contemporary Problems*, vol. 65, Spring 2002, p. 125ff. The author argues that the traditional standard of a reasonable expectation of privacy should be supplanted by a standard that looks at the emotional experience of privacy. A review of Supreme Court decisions shows that the current narrow conception of privacy would allow for a great deal of intrusive surveillance and monitoring in public places. Peoples' need to feel they have a choice over what they reveal to others and how, and merely being in a public place, should not mean that one cannot have a sense of privacy.

Van Voris, Bob. "Black Box Car Idea Opens Can of Worms: Litigation Advantages Seen. But Privacy Issues Are Big Worry." *National Law Journal*, vol. 21,

June 14, 1999, p. A1. New technology similar to aircraft data recorders can now track a driver's speed and even whether the seat belt was fastened. This data could be important testimony in traffic accident cases, but it has also raised concerns from privacy advocates.

Verton, Dan. "Postal Service Pursues 'Intelligent Mail' Despite Privacy Concerns." *Computerworld*, August 11, 2003. n.p. Also available online. URL: http://www.computerworld.com/securitytopics/security/privacy/story/0,10801,83866,00.html. An advisory commission has recommended that the U.S. Postal Service pursue "personalized" mail options that would include identification of the sender of mail. Bar codes would uniquely identify each mail piece. Originally such systems were developed to make mail processing more efficient, but now they are being touted as an antiterrorism measure. However, they threaten the anonymity of the mail, which is linked to a First Amendment right to speak freely.

Volokh, Eugene. "Big Brother Is Watching—Be Grateful!" *Wall Street Journal*, March 26, 2002, p. A2. The author, a First Amendment scholar, argues that the use of public surveillance cameras can be effective for deterring crime. Because they are used only in public areas, there is no "expectation of privacy" and thus no constitutional violation. The risk of abuse of such systems by law enforcement officials can be minimized.

Walker, Leslie. "Balancing Data Needs and Privacy." *Washington Post*, May 8, 2003, p. E1. Even as the Defense Department worked on the Total Information Awareness program, it also financed research to develop a "privacy appliance." This software would screen out personal data unrelated to a specific query and would also track all requests to prevent unauthorized use of the system. Similar techniques will be needed if any comprehensive database and data-mining systems are to be trusted with individuals' privacy.

Wong, May. "Online Data Conflict with Desire for Privacy." *Washington Post*, December 26, 2003, p. A15. The combination of online phone directories and mapping services has created a new privacy threat: Stalkers cannot only find out where someone lives (without having to know the city), but can also see how to get there.

Web Documents

"Air Travel Privacy." Electronic Privacy Information Center. Available online. URL: http://www.epic.org/privacy/airtravel/. Updated on March 29, 2005. Discusses recent measures and proposals for analyzing passenger data to profile or identify potential terrorists. This includes the CAPPS (Computer Assisted Passenger Pre-screening System).

Baard, Erik. "Smile, You're on In-Store Camera." Wired News. Available online. URL: http://www.wired.com/news/print/0,1294,54078,00.html. Posted on August 8, 2002. Describes a near-future system that will track the movements of shoppers in a way similar to the way Web users are tracked today. A camera captures the shopper's face, then his or her file is updated with information about purchases that can be used later for targeted marketing.

Annotated Bibliography

Baard, Mark. "Balancing Utility with Privacy." Wired News. Available online. URL: http://www.wired.com/news/technology/0,1282,60871,00.html. Posted on October 21, 2003. The coming world of "ubiquitous computing" will use networks of tiny wireless sensors, and "smart" appliances and software to enable people to track and control many aspects of their environment. However, the more the system is "aware" of, the greater the potential loss of privacy.

Black, Jane. "Roll up Your Sleeve—for a Chip Implant." BusinessWeek Online. Available online. URL: http://www.businessweek.com/bwdaily/dnflash/mar2002/nf20020321_1025.htm. Posted on March 21, 2002. Describes a family that has volunteered to have radio frequency identification chips implanted in their bodies as part of a trial program. The Jacobs family (dubbed the "Chipsons") and chip supporters believe the VeriChip devices can save lives by giving emergency personnel information about a person's current prescriptions and allergies. The chips may also be used for tracking paroled convicts and even children, but these and other potential privacy issues are still in the future.

Chakrabarti, Samidh, and Aaron Strauss. "Carnival Booth: An Algorithm for Defeating the Computer-Assisted Airline Passenger Screening System." Massachusetts Institute of Technology. Available online. URL: http://swissnet.ai.mit.edu/6805/student-papers/spring02-papers/caps.htm. Posted on May 16, 2002. Uses mathematical models and computer simulation to show that the Computer-Assisted Airline Passenger Screening System (CAPS) or any other system that uses profiles to select passengers for intensive screening will be less secure than a system that randomly selects passengers for thorough screening. The flaw is that once a passenger has received special treatment, he or she can use the details to deduce the profile being applied in that particular case and create an "anti-profile," allowing for subsequent bypassing of the screening. A terrorist cell could systematically probe the system to find out how to get its operatives onboard. Finally, if the use of profiles does not increase security, it cannot be justified on legal grounds.

"Documents Show Errors in TSA's 'No Fly' Watchlist." Electronic Privacy Information Center. Available online. URL: http://www.epic.org/privacy/airtravel/foia/watchlist_foia_analysis.html. Posted in April 2003. Describes how Freedom of Information Act (FOIA) litigation by the Electronic Privacy Information Center revealed heavily edited documents that suggest that the Transportation Security Agency's "No-Fly" watch list has many errors and problems. In addition, it is not clear who is responsible for maintaining the list and evaluating its accuracy and effectiveness.

Fisher, Dennis. "RSA Seeks to Fix RFID Worries." eWeek. Available online. URL: http://www.eweek.com/article2/0,1759,1655594,00.asp. Posted on August 25, 2003. Researchers at RSA Security Inc. have developed a technique that uses "blocker tags" to control which reading devices could read which tags. This could prevent, for example, a department store reader from identifying personal items being carried by a shopper.

Harper, Jim. "RFID Tags and Privacy: How Bar-Codes-on-Steroids Are Really a 98-Lb. Weakling." Competitive Enterprise Institute. Available online. URL: http://www.cei.org/pdf/4080.pdf. Posted on June 21, 2004. Gives a good summary of the use and benefits of radio frequency identification (RFID) technology with consumer products. Although privacy concerns have been raised about the surreptitious tracking of consumers and their goods, the author suggests that privacy will be adequately protected by a combination of pressure from consumers, existing laws, and technologies that can block unwanted scanning.

Krazit, Tom. "Intel: Home Sensors Could Monitor Seniors, Aid Diagnosis." Computerworld/IDG News Service. Available online. URL: http://www.computerworld.com/printthis/2005/0,4814,98801,00.html (QuickLink 51815). Posted January 7, 2005. Intel Corporation is working on a project that would install a network of home sensors that could help monitor the location and health of seniors and detect emergency conditions. Integrated communications could also help people keep in touch with aging parents. Such a product may ease the problem of caring for a rapidly growing senior population. Strict regulations under HIPAA (Health Insurance Portability and Accountability Act) may allay privacy concerns.

Manjoo, Farhad. "Brave New Skies." Salon.com. Available online. URL: http://www.salon.com/tech/feature/2003/09/04/plane_surveillance/index.html. Posted on September 4, 2003. Describes the ongoing plans to obtain information about all passengers before they board airliners. Manjoo discusses the CAPPS II initiative and the controversial gathering of passenger data from several cooperating airlines without telling the public. Some conservatives are joining civil libertarians in sounding the alarm about a system that might be used for ordinary law enforcement as well as antiterrorism efforts.

———. "Everything Is Watching You." Salon.com. Available online. URL: http://www.salon.com/tech/feature/2003/07/24/rfid/index.html. Posted on July 24, 2003. Describes the development of radio tracking (RFID) devices that may soon be embedded in a wide variety of products. The systems are likely to be used at first only for inventory control in warehouses and distributions channels, and critics believe there will be consumer resistance if individual packages purchased in stores are tracked.

Matthews, William. "FBI to Build Data Warehouse." FCW.com. Available online. URL: http://www.fcw.com/fcw/articles/2002/0603/news-fbi-06-03-02.asp. Posted on June 3, 2002. Reports that the FBI made "investigative data warehousing" one of its key strategies in the war against terrorism. In addition to centralizing its major databases and making them available for systematic data mining and analysis, the effort is part of the agency's overall push to modernize its information technology. Most of the software to be employed is already in commercial use.

"Metropolitan Police: General Order, Draft: Closed-Circuit Television Cameras (CCTV)." DC Watch. Available online. URL: http://www.dcwatch.com/police/020404.htm. Posted on April 4, 2002. Gives the policy and guidelines for use of the Washington, D.C., closed-circuit television surveillance system. Cameras are not to be used in an area where there is a "reasonable expectation of privacy" and they are to be used only for gathering information on specific incidents.

Mieszkowski, Katharine. "The Checkout Line—Or the Check-You-Out Line?" Salon.com. Available online. URL: http://www.salon.com/tech/feature/2004/07/26/rfid_library/index.html. Posted on July 26, 2004. Describes the growing use of RFID (radio frequency identification) chips in library books. The system allows people to check their own books out, relieving tight library labor budgets. Civil libertarians are concerned that hackers or law enforcement agents using scanners might be able to read the chips and learn what books patrons are reading. Librarians, however, say they are protecting user privacy by using only internal identification numbers, not book titles or ISBNs.

"Protestor Privacy and Free Expression Rights." Electronic Privacy Information Center. Available online. URL: http://www.epic.org/privacy/protest/. Updated on October 17, 2004. Links the screening and surveillance of protestors to threats to the rights of assembly and free expression under the First Amendment. Gives historical and post–September 11 examples of government surveillance of protestors. The web page includes news and resource links.

"Radio Frequency Identification: Applications and Implications for Consumers." Federal Trade Commission. Available online. URL: http://www.ftc.gov/bcp/workshops/rfid/index.htm. Posted June 21, 2004. Provides the agenda and transcripts from a conference on the implications of emerging radio frequency identification (RFID) technology for businesses, consumers, and policymakers.

"Radio Frequency Identification (RFID) Systems." Electronic Privacy Information Center. Available online. URL: http://www.epic.org/privacy/rfid/. Updated February 18, 2005. Describes the growing use of radio frequency identification (RFID) tags, which are used to remotely and automatically identify merchandise, pets, and even people. The greatest privacy threat is the potential ability to link RFID information with a specific consumer. The web page includes news and resource links.

"Scientists Can Now Read Your Eyes—Literally!" ExpressIndia. Available online. URL: http://www.expressindia.com/fullstory.php?newsid=37622#compstory. Posted on October 25, 2004. Columbia University scientists have developed a computer system that can capture images mirrored on the surface of a human eye. This may make it possible for surveillance systems not only to see people but also to see what those people are seeing, even though it is outside the direct field of the camera.

"Secure Flight." Electronic Privacy Information Center. Available online. URL: http://www.epic.org/privacy/airtravel/secureflight.html. Updated on March 29, 2005. Provides news and links relating to the federal airline passenger screening program formerly known as CAPPS II.

Steinhardt, Barry. "Testimony by ACLU's Barry Steinhardt on Surveillance System before DC City Council." American Civil Liberties Union. Available online. URL: http://www.aclu.org/Privacy/Privacy.cfm?ID=13505&c=130. Posted on December 12, 2002. The director of the ACLU's Program on Technology and Liberty argues that there is no real evidence of the efficacy of public surveillance cameras for reducing crime, and that such systems might easily be abused through unauthorized access or even by police agencies that could use them to intimidate political dissidents. On balance the risks of this technology outweigh any slight benefits.

Tanner, Robert. "Pressure Builds for U.S. More Surveillance Cameras." Information Week (AP article). Available online. URL: http://informationweek.com/story/showArticle.jhtml?articleID=166402011. Posted on July 25, 2005. Describes growing advocacy for use of public video surveillance in the aftermath of the London transit bombings. Advocates include Senator Hillary Clinton, but critics argue that cameras can only detect attackers afterward, not deter them.

"United States Visitor and Immigrant Status Indicator Technology (US-VISIT)." Electronic Privacy Information Center. Available online. URL: http://www.epic.org/privacy/us-visit/default.html. Updated on March 21, 2005. Describes the ongoing program to scan, collect, and use biometric identifiers and databases to screen persons entering the United States. Questions remain about completion of privacy assessments and about use of the information outside the entry process. The web page includes news links.

"Video Surveillance." Electronic Privacy Information Center. Available online. URL: http://www.epic.org/privacy/surveillance/. Updated March 15, 2005. Describes issues raised by the growing use of public surveillance cameras in Britain and, to a lesser degree, in U.S. cities such as Washington, D.C. Such surveillance can have a chilling effect on movement, free association, and the right to protest. Includes news links.

White, James C. "People, Not Places: A Policy Framework for Analyzing Location Privacy Issues." Terry Sanford Institute of Public Policy, Duke University. Available online. URL: http://www.epic.org/privacy/location/jwhitelocationprivacy.pdf. Posted in spring 2003. This student "master's memo" argues that the use of tracking devices providing "locational information" requires a broader look at what expectation of privacy people might have even in a public place. The combination of locational information with databases and data mining has the potential of rendering the anonymous exercise of movement, association, and other rights impossible.

Zetter, Kim. "A CAPPS by Any Other Name." Wired News. Available online. URL: http://www.wired.com/news/privacy/0,1848,67015,00.html. Posted on May 25, 2005. Reports that a group of civil libertarians and security experts have called on the federal government to delay the planned August rollout of its Secure Flight program, the latest incarnation of CAPPS (computer-assisted passenger prescreening system). Critics warn that the system may use commercial databases that often contain incorrect information, and the system still lacks procedures by which innocent passengers can clear their names.

Annotated Bibliography

GOVERNMENT ACCOUNTABILITY
AND FREEDOM OF INFORMATION

Privacy advocates often see the necessity of making government transparent and accountable as being essential for robust protection of privacy. Works in this section discuss the Freedom of Information Act, the Privacy Act, and the attempt to obtain information about government activities or to review and correct information about individuals held by government agencies.

Books

Birkinshaw, Patrick. *Freedom of Information: The Law, the Practice and the Ideal.* 3rd ed. Evanston, Ill.: Northwestern University Press, 2001. Provides political, social, and cultural context for the development of British laws regulating access to information, including the Official Secrets Act, the UK Code of Practice on Access to Information, and European Union regulations.

Committee on Government Reform, House of Representatives. "A Citizen's Guide on Using the Freedom of Information Act and the Privacy Act of 1974 to Request Government Records." Washington, D.C.: U.S. Government Printing Office, 1999. Also available online. URL: http://frwebgate. access.gpo.gov/cgi-bin/getdoc.cgi?dbname=106_cong_reports& docid=f:hr050.106.pdf. Explains the roles of the Freedom of Information and Privacy acts in making government information available to citizens. It also explains exemptions and exclusions.

Dickson, Donald T. *Confidentiality and Privacy in Social Work: A Guide to the Law for Practitioners and Students.* New York: Free Press, 1998. Describes privacy issues and procedures social workers should use to comply with relevant laws and protect both the agency and its clients.

Drapeau, Michel, and Marc-Aurèle Racicot. *Federal Access to Information and Privacy Legislation Annotated 2004.* Toronto: Thomson Carswell, 2004. A very detailed guide and reference to Canadian freedom of information and privacy protection legislation. The book includes guidelines for citizens and business.

Duncan, George T., Thomas B. Jabine, and Virginia A. de Wolf, eds. *Private Lives and Public Policies: Confidentiality and Accessibility of Government Statistics.* Washington, D.C.: National Academy Press, 1993. Discusses privacy issues involving collection of statistical data by government agencies and recommends appropriate practices. The book is useful as an overview and historical background to the topic.

Duning, Natilee, ed. *Freedom of Information in the Digital Age.* Nashville, Tenn.: First Amendment Center and Reston, Va.: ASNE, 2001. Also available online. URL: http://www.freedomforum.org/publications/first/foi/foiinthedigitalage. pdf. Presents surveys on the American public's and newspaper editors' attitudes toward access to government information and urges the newspaper industry to actively promote freedom of information. Reports that six in 10 Americans see public access as "crucial" to good government. However, the public is mistrustful of both government and the private sector as stewards of information and 56 percent support stronger privacy laws.

Foerstel, Herbert N. *Freedom of Information and the Right to Know: The Origins and Applications of the Freedom of Information Act.* Westport, Conn.: Greenwood Publishing, 1999. Describes the development of the idea that freedom of information is crucially important to a democracy, its embodiment in the federal Freedom of Information Act, and the continuing conflicts between government agencies and citizens seeking more information about their operation.

Hammitt, Harry A., ed. *Litigation Under the Federal Open Government Laws, 2004.* Washington, D.C.: Electronic Privacy Information Center, 2004. A manual for lawyers, journalists, researchers, and activists. The book provides full discussion and guidelines for litigation under the federal Freedom of Information Act, Privacy Act, Federal Advisory Committee Act, and Government in the Sunshine Act. New editions of the book are issued annually.

Henry, Christopher L. *Freedom of Information Act.* New York: Novinka Publications, 2004. Explains the 1996 Freedom of Information Act (U.S. Code Title 5, Section 552), including procedures for requesting information from government agencies and the nine exceptions and three exclusions that can be used to refuse disclosure of certain types of records.

Hudson, David L., Jr. *Open Government: An American Tradition Faces National Security, Privacy, and Other Challenges.* Langhome, Penn.: Chelsea House, 2005. Written for high school students and adults, this overview looks at how in the post–September 11 world the government is both threatening privacy and often concealing the nature and extent of its actions. The book includes discussion questions and suggestions for further reading.

Vaughn, Robert G., ed. *Freedom of Information.* Burlington, Vt.: Ashgate Publishing, 2000. Contributors discuss the background and significance of the United States Freedom of Information Act of 1966, the Whistleblower Protection Act of 1989, and the Electronic Freedom of Information amendments of 1996 as well as the British Freedom of Information law.

Articles and Papers

Dolan, Maura. "Justices Overturn Privacy Decision: State High Court Rules that the Media's Use of Information Taken from Public Records Does Not Violate 1st Amendment Protections." *Los Angeles Times,* December 7, 2004, p. B1. Reports a California state supreme court decision saying that the media can disclose any information from public records. In this case a person with a 12-year-old felony conviction had reformed and was living a quiet, lawful life. The media's First Amendment rights were held to outweigh the person's privacy interests.

Marquess, Kate. "Open Court?" *ABA Journal,* April 1, 2001, p. 54. Reports that though the growing trend to make all court filings available online is a boon to researchers and the media, such documents may expose sensitive material or infringe on privacy rights.

Mendoza, Martha. "Freedom of Information Restrictions Rising." *Los Angeles Times,* March 20, 2005, p. A17. The trend to tighten or resist access to government information began even before September 11, 2001, and security concerns are usually the reason given. The Associated Press reviewed statistics on request under the Freedom of Information Act since 1988 and found that most federal agencies, with the exception of the Social Security and Veterans administations, were fulfilling a considerably smaller proportion of queries. In addition more documents are being classified and thousands of previously public documents have been pulled off government web sites.

Richelson, Jeffrey T. "Holding Back: How Agencies Thwart the Freedom of Information Act." *Bulletin of the Atomic Scientists,* vol. 59, December 2003, pp. 26–32. The Freedom of Information Act has been a considerable success with thousands of news stories each year being dependent on information retrieved pursuant to the law. However, varying interpretations by different agencies have sometimes improperly blocked access to the requested information, as shown in several case studies involving access to information about nuclear activities and historical information from the CIA.

Robertson, Geoffrey. "A Triumph for Sir Humphrey." *New Statesman,* vol. 127, March 6, 1998, p. 24ff. Describes the British lawmaker's Sir Humphrey Appleby's campaign to pass the nation's first real Freedom of Information Act; criticizes some shortcomings, such as the exceptions given for files on individuals from security agencies.

Wilson, Des. "The Fact that Britain Is Finally Getting a Freedom of Information Act Is Almost Entirely Due to the Single-Mindedness of One Great Reformer." *New Statesman,* vol. 127, April 24, 1998, p. 19. Describes the efforts of reformer Maurice Frankel that have contributed to the coming enactment of Great Britain's new freedom of information law.

Web Documents

"The Driver's Privacy Protection Act (DPPA) and the Privacy of Your State Motor Vehicle Record." Electronic Privacy Information Center. Available online. URL: http://www.epic.org/privacy/drivers/. Updated on August 14, 2004. Explains the background and provisions of the 1994 federal law that prevents state motor vehicles departments from distributing personal information used in connection with driver's licenses and related records without the license holder's permission.

"From Cradle to Grave: Government Records and Your Privacy." Privacy Rights Clearinghouse. Available online. URL: http://www.privacyrights.org/fs/fs11-pub.htm. Updated in February 2004. Describes the government records generated by many different activities during a person's lifetime. Some records are public (and thus publicly accessible), while others are confidential. A number of federal and state laws restrict the release of certain kinds of records and information, such as medical information and Social Security numbers.

Koontz, Linda D. "Internet Privacy: Comparison of Federal Agency Practices with Fair Information Principles." General Accounting Office. Availabile online. URL: http://www.gao.gov/new.items/ai00296r.pdf. Posted September 11, 2000. Testimony before the Commerce Committee of the House of

Representatives summarizes a survey of the privacy practices of federal agency web sites in terms of implementing the Federal Trade Commission's four Fair Information Principles. Eighty-five percent of the sites have posted privacy notices. The four principles were implemented by the following percentages of the sites: Notice (69 percent), Choice (45 percent), Access (17 percent), and Security (23 percent).

Ravnitzky, Michael. "A Selected Bibliography on the Freedom of Information Act, 1980–2004." LLRX.com. Available online. URL: http://www.llrx.com/features/foiabiblio.htm. Posted on March 15, 2004. Presents selected books and articles on the U.S. Freedom of Information Act and related issues.

TOOLS AND STANDARDS FOR PRIVACY AND ANONYMITY

This final section lists resources that discuss software tools and services that allow online users to protect their privacy (such as through encryption) or to remain anonymous. There are also works discussing the pros and cons of allowing anonymous use of e-mail and web domains.

Books

Brands, Stefan A. *Rethinking Public Key Infrastructures and Digital Certificates: Building in Privacy.* Cambridge: MIT Press, 2000. Although digital certificates are already widely used in certain sensitive applications, the author argues that the development of powerful surveillance tools by governments and hackers will eventually require that virtually all communications and transactions be protected by building a public key infrastructure into the Internet. Such a system could verify the validity of the participants and data in a transaction without leaving information that can be used by snoopers and profilers. The details, however, will be understandable only to technical readers.

Caloyannides, Michael A. *Privacy Protection and Computer Forensics.* 2d ed. Boston: Artech House, 2004. Gives detailed how-to guidance on how to remove or protect sensitive stored information that could be vulnerable to hackers, spies, or other intruders. The book includes discussion of spyware and other forms of malicious software, as well as the special vulnerabilities of wireless connections, PDAs, and even cell phones.

Cannon, J. C. *Privacy: What Developers and IT Professionals Should Know.* Upper Saddle River, N.J.: Pearson Education, 2004. A guide for information industry professionals on how to develop applications and practices that ensure data privacy. The book includes a CD with sample source code and additional privacy resources.

Competitive Enterprise Institute. *The Future of Financial Privacy: Private Choices Versus Political Rules.* Washington D.C.: Competitive Enterprise

Institute, 2000. A variety of experts of generally libertarian inclination suggest ways in which new technologies might promote privacy while allowing commerce to avoid politically imposed boundaries.

Diffie, Whitfield, and Susan Landau. *Privacy on the Line: The Politics of Wiretapping and Encryption.* Cambridge: MIT Press, 1998. Surveys the development of encryption and wiretapping technologies and explores their impact on public policy. (Diffie is a coinventor of public key cryptography.)

Dingledine, Roger, and Paul Syverson, eds. *Privacy-Enhancing Technologies: Third International Workshop, PET 2003, Dresden, Germany, March 26–28, Revised Papers.* New York: Springer-Verlag, 2003. Latest in an annual series of papers on technological methods of enhancing anonymity and privacy in Web activities and transactions. The material is rather technical and best suited for readers with some background in computer networking and security.

Electronic Privacy Information Center. *Cryptography and Liberty: An International Survey of Encryption Policy.* Washington, D.C.: Electronic Privacy Information Center, 2004. An annual survey of government policies on cryptography around the world, including export controls on cryptographic software. This is of importance because cryptography is a powerful tool for protecting privacy but can also be viewed as a threat to the ability of law enforcement agencies to gather evidence.

Feghhi, Jalal, and Peter Williams. *Digital Certificates: Applied Internet Security.* Reading, Mass.: Addison-Wesley, 1998. Describes the design and implementation of digital certificates that use cryptography to authenticate and secure transactions.

Garfinkel, Simson. *PGP: Pretty Good Privacy.* Sebastapol, Calif.: O'Reilly, 1994. The classic introduction to the public-domain encryption system that is used by millions of computer users to keep their data safe from prying eyes. The book includes a historical account of the development of public key cryptography.

Gilmore, John, ed. *Cracking DES: Secrets of Encryption Research, Wiretap Politics and Chip Design.* Sebastapol, Calif.: O'Reilly, 1998. Describes in technical detail how computer code-crackers built a relatively inexpensive computer system that "cracked" the government's supposedly secure 56-bit DES code; explores the politics of encryption that has tended to prevent the adoption of stronger legal encryption technologies.

Hoffman, Lance J. *Building in Big Brother: The Cryptographic Policy Debate.* New York: Springer-Verlag, 1995. Provides a wide-ranging discussion of the controversy caused in the early 1990s by the federal Clipper Chip proposal, which pitted privacy against law enforcement and national security interests.

Kahn, David. *The Codebreakers: The Comprehensive History of Secret Communication from Ancient Times to the Internet.* Rev. ed. New York: Scribner, 1996. Describes the wide variety of codes, ciphers, and other systems for secret messages used throughout history; includes coverage of computer cryptography and the Internet.

Levy, Steven. *Crypto: How the Code Rebels Beat the Government—Saving Privacy in the Digital Age.* New York: Viking, 2001. A fascinating account of how maverick computer scientists and programmers such as Whitfield Diffie and Philip Zimmerman developed powerful encryption algorithms and software despite the opposition of government spy agencies. Their work offered the possibility of creating a bulwark to protect privacy in the digital age.

Loshin, Peter. *Personal Encryption Clearly Explained.* San Diego, Calif.: AP Professional, 1998. Introduces encryption concepts and then explains hands-on procedures for using encryption for security.

Ludlow, Peter, ed. *High Noon on the Electronic Frontier: Conceptual Issues in Cyberspace.* Cambridge: MIT Press, 1996. Contains a variety of writings from the first years of the World Wide Web, ranging from academic papers to provocative manifestos. The book discusses issues such as privacy, encryption, copyright, and the development of virtual communities.

Mel, H. X., and Doris Baker. *Cryptography Decrypted.* Reading, Mass.: Addison-Wesley, 2000. An exceptionally well-presented introduction and tutorial in public key cryptography that can provide an understanding of its nuances without the reader knowing advanced mathematics or computer science. The book thus provides a good grounding for researchers focusing on the public policy issues surrounding cryptography today.

Neumann, Peter. *Computer-Related Risks.* Reading, Mass.: Addison-Wesley, 1995. Introduces the study of the risks and unforeseen consequences of complex computer systems, including threats to privacy. (Current examples can be found in the comp.risks online newsgroup and digest.)

Prins, J. E. J., and M. J. M. Van Dellen. *Digital Anonymity and the Law: Tensions and Dimensions.* New York: Cambridge University Press, 2003. Anonymity is often viewed as a way to protect privacy, and the Internet makes anonymous (or nearly anonymous) interactions quite possible. A legal conflict arises between anonymity and the need of law enforcement and judicial authorities to fix the identity of persons so as to be able to hold them accountable for their actions. However, laws that can be used to force persons to reveal their identity can also be used to invade privacy or chill freedom of expression. Relevant U.S. and European regulations are discussed.

Rahn, Richard W. *The End of Money and the Struggle for Financial Privacy.* Seattle, Wash.: Discovery Institute, 1999. Argues that money (currency and checks) is rapidly being replaced by transactions that can be controlled by individuals largely outside the purview of government authorities. Encryption and other mechanisms can allow for any desired degree of anonymity. However, governments will resist this trend, arguing the need to ensure safety and to ensure tax revenue.

Singh, Simon. *The Code Book: The Evolution of Secrecy from Mary Queen of Scots to Quantum Cryptography.* New York: Doubleday, 1999. An accessible account of the development of secret writing and cryptosystems over the past five centuries. The book includes good explanations of basic principles as well as of the modern debate over access to strong cryptography and the potential threat (or promise) of incredibly powerful quantum computing systems.

Stallings, William. *Protect Your Privacy: The PGP User's Guide.* Englewood Cliffs, N.J.: Prentice Hall, 1995. Probably the best and most accessible technical guide to the PGP encryption software. As with the other PGP books, Internet sources should be consulted for updated information.

Van Der Lubbe, Jan C. *Basic Methods of Cryptography.* New York: Cambridge University Press, 1998. Describes the application of cryptography in a variety of information systems, including banking, medical, and telecommunications.

Wayner, Peter. *Digital Cash: Commerce on the Net.* 2nd ed. Boston: AP Professional, 1997. Provides a detailed overview of various systems for digital payment that can allow for secure and possibly anonymous online transactions.

Zimmermann, Philip R. *The Official PGP User's Guide.* Cambridge: MIT Press, 1995. The developer of Pretty Good Privacy (PGP) explains how to use his software while recounting his struggles with government authorities who sought to block its distribution.

Articles and Papers

Armstrong, H. L., and P. J. Forde. "Internet Anonymity Practices in Computer Crime." *Information Management & Computer Security*, vol. 11, October 22, 2003, pp. 209–215. Considers the role that the ability to be anonymous plays in Internet crimes such as money laundering, drug dealing, hacking, fraud, and distribution of child pornography. Because anonymity gives criminals a considerable advantage both in cooperating with one another and in committing crimes, society must determine what restrictions should be placed upon it.

Clarke, Roger. "Introducing PITs and PETs: Technologies Affecting Privacy." *Privacy Law & Policy Reporter,* March 2001, p. 181ff. Also available online. URL: http://www.anu.edu.au/people/Roger.Clarke/DV/PITsPETs.html. Updated on February 28, 2001. Describes and classifies Privacy-Invasive Technologies (PITs) and Privacy-Enhancing Technologies (PETs). These include a variety of devices, software tools, and standards. Some PETs are "gentle" and allow for pseudonymity rather than total anonymity.

Granger, M., and Elaine Newton. "Protecting Public Anonymity." *Issues in Science and Technology*, vol. 21, October 2004, p. 83. In addition to legal measures, attention to design is needed in order to minimize the potential for privacy abuse in emerging technologies. System design standards should include a clear understanding of a system's intended function and only the data needed for that purpose should be collected. Protection of privacy and anonymity should be part of "best practices" in industry, and there should be legal consequences for failure to meet such standards.

Grossman, Wendy M. "Anonymous Trust." *Scientific American*, vol. 291, August 2004, p. 20ff. Describes a proposed computer security scheme called direct anonymous attestation (DAA). This would allow computers to verify that software was certified safe before running it, without allowing the computer to be identified or tracked by the certification authority. This would provide security without opening a privacy loophole.

Henderson, Rick. "Clipping Encryption." *Reason*, vol. 30, May 1998, p. 7ff. Presents the libertarian side of the classic debate over the Clipper Chip proposal. Henderson argues that providing the government with access to decryption keys would make it too easy for agencies to violate privacy without the normal requirements for search warrants.

Machrone, Bill. "Trust Me?" *PC Magazine*, vol. 17, June 9, 1998, p. 85. Describes the TRUSTe privacy policy disclosure program, using the example of the Land's End catalog company.

Markoff, John. "A Safer System for Home PC's Feels Like Jail to Some Critics." *New York Times*, June 30, 2003, p. C1. IBM and Hewlett-Packard are introducing new personal computers that have integrated hardware and software designed to protect data privacy as well as prevent the use of the computer to reproduce copyrighted material illegally. This concept of "trusted computing" aims to be a way to deal with privacy and security concerns in a way that is more transparent to the user, but critics argue that the control of such technology by large companies may stifle innovation and competition.

Matlis, Jan. "P3P: The Platform for Privacy Preferences (P3P) Is a Voluntary Protocol that Sets Standards for Web Providers to Publish Their Privacy Policies and Allows Web Users to Automatically Match Those Policies to Their Privacy Preferences." *Computerworld*, vol. 36, October 28, 2002, p. 28. Explains how P3P uses standardized descriptions of elements in privacy policies combined with web browser plug-in software. The article also lists the basic questions about a web site that a user should be able to answer using P3P.

Noguchi, Yuki. "Online Search Engines Help Lift Cover of Privacy." *Washington Post*, February 9, 2004, p. A1. Google and other search engines systematically "crawl" through the Internet, making content searchable and accessible. Unfortunately some web sites do not properly exclude sensitive personal information from such automatic indexing. As a result private investigators or spies can then use Google to retrieve the confidential data. All webmasters should be warned how to follow the technical procedures needed to keep their data away from search engines.

Ricadela, Aaron. "Quantum's Next Leap." *InformationWeek*, May 10, 2004, n.p. Also available online. URL: http://www.informationweek.com/story/showArticle.jhtml?articleID=20000170. Discusses Defense Department proposals to accelerate the development of quantum computers that can vastly increase the amount of data that can be processed using the same number of bits. Although a practical quantum computer probably lies 20 or more years in the future, such a machine may make present methods of cryptography useless, exposing information to intruders.

Sanger, David E., and Jeri Clausing. "U.S. Removes More Limits on Encryption." *New York Times*, January 13, 2000, p. 1. The federal government, perhaps bowing to recent court decisions, has made it possible to sell most encryption software to foreign countries after submitting the product for a one-time review. (Countries listed as terrorist-sponsoring states would still be excluded.) However, some critics complain that the regulations are still too complicated and don't protect the rights of U.S. computer scientists to share ideas with foreign counterparts.

Schwartz, John. "Dispute on Electronic Message Encryption Takes on New Urgency." *New York Times*, September 25, 2001, p. C1. The debate over control of encryption software took on new urgency after September 11—but Philip Zimmermann, developer of Pretty Good Privacy, is sticking to his guns. He believes the availability of encryption is essential for human rights groups. Other experts believe that with the software widely available and impossible to uninvent, the time for debate is past.

Thibodeau, Patrick. "P3P Supporters Struggle to Increase Adoption of Data Privacy Standard; Backers Look for Ways to Overcome Obstacles that Are Slowing Deployments." *Computerworld*, vol. 36, November 18, 2002, p. 20. Reports that the Platform for Privacy Preferences (P3P) is being slowly adopted by major web sites. The system uses software to match elements of privacy policies with users' settings indicating the amount and types of privacy required. However, technical problems and legal uncertainties are making many big firms reluctant to implement the system.

Turner, Eric C., and Subhasish Dasgupta. "Privacy on the Web: An Examination of User Concerns, Technology, and Implications for Business Organizations and Individuals." *Information Systems Management*, vol. 20, Winter 2003, p. 8ff. Individual privacy concerns are an increasingly important factor in consumers' willingness to deal with web sites and in their overall satisfaction. Privacy concerns can be managed systematically using the "information technology privacy cycle" and by using tools such as the Platform for Privacy Preferences (P3P).

Web Documents

Bacard, André. "Anonymous Remailer FAQ." [Author's web site.] Available online. URL: http://www.andrebacard.com/remail.html. Updated on March 28, 2005. Describes services that provide privacy for e-mail and newsgroup postings by removing information that could be used to identify the sender (some services provide encryption as well). Bacard distinguishes between pseudonymous remailers that require trusting the provider and true anonymous remailers. He also discusses pros and cons of use, acknowledging the tremendous growth in spam and other abuses since this FAQ was first published.

Callas, Jon, and Jim Reavis. "The Dawn of Pervasive Encryption." SearchSecurity. com. Available online. URL: http://download.pgp.com/pdfs/whitepapers/Pervasive_encryption_040214.pdf. Posted in 2004. Argues that encryption (as embodied in software such as Pretty Good Privacy) is moving from a function used ad hoc by individuals to an integral part of the network infrastructure. This movement is being driven by government and regulatory pressures, the continuing growth in computing power, and developments in distributed computing architecture.

Cisneros, Oscar. "Unmasking the Anonymous Posters." Wired News. Available online. URL: http://www.wired.com/news/politics/0,1283,20983,00.html. Posted on July 29, 1999. Reports suggest that the ability to file civil lawsuits and obtain subpoenas against anyone is being used to unmask the identity of anonymous online posters. Sometimes the service provider (such as Yahoo!) does not notify the poster, who is then unable to contest the release of his or her identity. Plaintiffs defend the subpoenas as being necessary to identify persons involved with defamation and other torts.

Fried, Ina. "Finding a Replacement for Passwords." CNet News.com. Available online. URL: http://news.com.com/Finding+a+replacement+for+passwords/2100-1029_3- 5586249.html. Posted on February 23, 2003. Bill Gates and other industry leaders are beginning to say that passwords used to access on-line services are ineffective, vulnerable, and obsolete. However, adopting hardware authentication devices, biometrics, and other systems could prove too expensive for most businesses.

Froomkin, A. Michael. "Anonymity and Its Enmities." Journal of Online Law. Available online. URL: http://www.wm.edu/law/publications/jol/95_96/froomkin.html. Posted in June 1995. A classic article describing the mechanics of anonymous communication on the Internet and exploring the legal doctrines applicable to it. Anonymity can facilitate criminal activity and evade accountability, but it can also protect essential freedom of speech and association.

"Internet Anonymity." Electronic Privacy Information Center. Available online. URL: http://www.epic.org/privacy/anonymity/. Posted in 2000. Describes the value of anonymity, particularly for the protection of dissidents and whistleblowers. The web page includes news and notable cases.

Kanellos, Michael. "Random Answers Retain Privacy." ZDNet News.com. Available online. URL: http://news.zdnet.com/2100-1009_22-5469837.html. Posted on November 29, 2004. Describes an interesting technique being explored by IBM researchers. Personal customer data such as age would be replaced with randomly generated numbers before being stored in the database. Users of the database could determine the randomization algorithm and recover the pattern or shape of the data but not the exact numbers. The result might be a way to protect privacy while allowing for profiling or data mining.

McCullagh, Declan. "Privacy Reduction's Next Act." News.com. Available online. URL: http://news.com/2010-1028-5155054.html. Posted on February 9, 2004. A proposed federal law would add stiff penalties for persons who put false or misleading information in their Internet domain registration records (which are accessed by the WHOIS database). The idea is to make it easier to go after spammers, intellectual property thieves, and other miscreants. However, political dissidents and whistleblowers have a legitimate need to disguise their identity.

McGuire, David. "Ruling On '.us' Domain Raises Privacy Issues." Washingtonpost.com. Available online. URL: http://www.washingtonpost.com/wp-dyn/articles/A7251-2005Mar4.html. Posted on March 4, 2005. Reports that the Commerce Department has ruled that people who own Internet addresses ending in .us will have to provide their phone numbers and addresses for a publicly searchable database. Privacy advocates oppose the ruling, arguing that it prevents the privacy and anonymity of free speech and that the measure is not necessary, since under the existing "proxy" registration system law enforcement officers can still obtain identifying information through a court order.

Wagner, Jim. "EFF Throws Support to 'Anonymous' Internet Project." Internet News.com. Available online. URL: http://www.internetnews.com/security/article.php/3454521. Posted on January 4, 2005. Reports that the Electronic Frontier Foundation is supporting and distributing open-source software called Tor that routes Internet traffic through anonymous, encrypted surfers, preventing tracking of online activity. However, users must still deal with cookies and avoid indiscreet use of web forms.

"WHOIS." Electronic Privacy Information Center. Available online. URL: http://www.epic.org/privacy/whois/. Updated March 31, 2005. Describes privacy problems raised by the WHOIS database, which contains names and contact information for owners of Web domains. It is suggested that existing international privacy guidelines be used and that provisions must be made to allow for anonymous ownership of domains. The site includes resource and news links.

CHAPTER 8

ORGANIZATIONS AND AGENCIES

There are many organizations that are devoted in whole or in part to privacy issues. The following entries include consumer advocacy and education groups, trade organizations, professional and technical organizations, and government agencies.

American Civil Liberties Union (ACLU)
URL: http://www.aclu.org
E-mail: Web form
Phone: (888) 567-ACLU
125 Broad Street, 18th Floor
New York, YN 10004-2400
Originally founded in 1920, the ACLU conducts extensive litigation on constitutional issues including privacy and free speech.

American Health Information Management Association (AHIMA)
URL: http://www.ahima.org
E-mail: info@ahima.org
Phone: (800) 335-5535
233 North Michigan Avenue
Suite 2150
Chicago, IL 60681-5800
An industry/professional organization; offers "white papers" on patient privacy.

Association for Computing Machinery (ACM)
URL: http://www.acm.org
E-mail: acmhelp@acm.org
Phone: (800) 342-6626
One Astor Plaza
1515 Broadway
New York, NY 10036
Premier organization for computer scientists and professionals. Has many educational and technical publications (some online) including those dealing with security and privacy issues.

Biometric Consortium
URL: http://www.biometrics.org
E-mail: info@biometrics.org
(for LISTSERV)
A group of biometrics research and industry organizations. Provides links and references on biometric identification systems.

Center for Democracy and Technology (CDT)
URL: http://www.cdt.org
E-mail: Web form
Phone: (202) 637-9800
1634 Eye Street, W
Suite 1100
Washington, DC 20006

A nonprofit public-interest organization that promotes technology policies and legislation that maximize constitutional principles of free speech and individual privacy.

Center for Media Literacy (CML)
URL: http://www.medialit.org
E-mail: cml@medialit.org
Phone: (310) 581-0260
3101 Ocean Park Building
Suite 200
Santa Monica, CA 90405
General media and critical-thinking skills are important tools for helping children protect their privacy and security online. This nonprofit organization develops media education projects and materials and provides training and resources to teachers and others.

Computer Emergency Response
  Team (CERT)
URL: http://www.cert.org
E-mail: cert@cert.org
Phone: (412) 268-7090
CERT Coordination Center
Software Engineering Institute
Carnegie Mellon University
Pittsburgh, PA 15213-3890
An organization that attempts to respond quickly to disruptions of computer networks such as those caused by hacker attacks. Issues technical advisories on newly discovered vulnerabilities of computer operating systems.

Computer Professionals for Social
  Responsibility (CPSR)
URL: http://www.cpsr.org/cpsr
E-mail: cpsr@cpsr.org
Phone: (650) 322-3778
P.O. Box 717
Palo Alto, CA 94302

CPSR sponsors an annual conference and maintains numerous mailing lists on computer-related issues and a large Internet site of information. It also publishes a journal and a newsletter. CPSR sponsors working groups on civil liberties, working in the computer industry, and other topics.

Computer Security Institute
URL: http://www.gocsi.com
E-mail: csi@cmp.com
Phone: (415) 947-6320
600 Harrison Street
San Francisco, CA 94107
An organization for training computer security professionals, dealing with encryption, secure transaction systems, and other issues.

Computing Technology Industry
  Association (CompTIA)
URL: http://www.comptia.org
E-mail: Web form
Phone: (630) 678-8300
1815 S. Meyers Road
Suite 300
Oak brook Terrace, IL 60181-5228
A major computer industry association; certifies computer professionals and becomes involved in policy issues.

Consumer Action
URL: http://www.
  consumeraction.org
E-mail: Web forms
Phone: (415) 777-9635
717 Market Street
Suite 310
San Francisco, CA 94103
A nonprofit consumer advocacy group founded in 1971. Advocates and lobbies for consumer rights, offers multilingual educational material

through its National Consumer Resources Center. Its Credit and Finance Project provides links to agencies that can resolve personal credit problems.

Consumer Data Industry Organization
URL: http://www.cdiaonline.org
E-mail: Web form
1090 Vermont Avenue, NW
Suite 200
Washington, DC 20005-4905
A trade organization representing companies that work with consumer information for fraud prevention and risk management, credit and mortgage reports, employment screening, and other purposes.

Consumer Project on Technology (CPT)
URL: http://www.cptech.org
Phone: (202) 387-8030
P.O. Box 19367
Washington, DC 20036
CPT was created by Ralph Nader in spring 1995 to focus on a variety of issues, including telecommunications regulation; pricing of ISDN services; fair use under the copyright law; issues relating to the pricing, ownership, and development of pharmaceutical drugs; and impact of technology on personal privacy. Their web site provides links to a number of e-mail lists.

Consumers Against Supermarket Privacy Invasion and Numbering (CASPIAN)
URL: http://www.nocards.org
E-mail: Web form
Advocacy organization opposing the use of supermarket discount cards, RFID chips, and other methods for tracking and obtaining information from customers.

Department of Health and Human Services (DHHS)
URL: http://www.dhhs.gov
Phone: (202) 619-0257
200 Independence Avenue, SW
Washington, DC 20201
Has a number of policies and efforts relating to patient privacy; see web site for search forms.

Department of Homeland Security (DHS)
URL: http://www.dhs.gov
E-mail: Web form
Washington, DC 20528
The DHS was established in 2002 as a single, coordinated effort for protecting the territory of the United States from terrorists. The new department has incorporated a number of existing agencies (such as the Coast Guard, U.S. Immigration, and the Secret Service) and new agencies (such as the Transportation Security Administration), as well as coordinating efforts with intelligence agencies such as the FBI and CIA. Many activities of component agencies can have an impact on privacy.

Direct Marketing Association
URL: http://www.the-dma.org
E-mail: customer service@ the-dma.org
Phone: (212) 768-7277
1120 Avenue of the Americas
New York, NY 10036-6700
Organization for the promotion of direct marketing. Also runs the Telephone Preference Service (P.O. Box 9014, Farmingdale, NY 11735-9014) that consumers can use to prevent

telemarketing calls as well as the Mail Preference Service.

Electronic Frontier Foundation (EFF)
URL: http://www.eff.org
E-mail: information@eff.org
Phone: (415) 436-9333
654 Shotwell Street
San Francisco, CA 94110
Organization formed in 1990 to maintain and enhance intellectual freedom, privacy, and other values of civil liberties and democracy in networked communications. Publishes newsletters, Internet guidebooks, and other documents; provides mailing lists and other online forums; and hosts a large electronic document archive.

Electronic Privacy Information Center (EPIC)
URL: http://www.epic.org
E-mail: Web form
Phone: (202) 483-1140
1718 Connecticut Avenue, NW
Suite 200
Washington, DC 20009
EPIC was established in 1994 to focus public attention on emerging privacy issues relating to the National Information Infrastructure, such as the Clipper Chip, the Digital Telephony proposal, medical records privacy, and the sale of consumer data. EPIC conducts litigation, sponsors conferences, produces reports, publishes the *EPIC Alert*, and leads campaigns on privacy issues.

Equifax
URL: http://www.equifax.com/
Phone: 1-800 685-1111 (to order copy of credit report)

Equifax Credit Information Services
P.O. Box 740241
Atlanta, GA 30374-0241
One of the three major credit bureaus. A person can order credit reports at their web site.

Experian
URL: http://www.experian.com/
Phone: (888) 397-3742
(to order credit report)
175 Anton Building
Costa Mesa, CA 92626
One of three major credit bureaus. A person can order credit reports at its web site or remove name from mailing lists.

Federal Bureau of Investigation (FBI)
URL: http://www.fbi.gov
Phone: (202) 324-5520
FBI
Freedom of Information Privacy Section
935 Pennsylvania Avenue, NW
Washington, DC 20535
Citizens can find out if the FBI has records about them by writing to this address and including their complete name, address, place of birth, and notarized signature.

Federal Communications Commission (FCC)
URL: http://www.fcc.gov
E-mail: fccinfo@fcc.gov
Phone: (888) CALL-FCC (general info)
445 12th Street, NW
Washington, DC 20554
The principal federal regulatory agency for all interstate communications by wire, cable, radio, etc.

Federal Trade Commission (FTC)
URL: http://www.ftc.gov
Phone: (202) 326-2222
600 Pennsylvania Avenue, NW
Room 130, FTC
Washington, DC 20580
Federal regulatory agency that regulates many aspects of commerce, including regulations dealing with privacy and information disclosure.

Federation of American Scientists (FAS)
Project on Government Secrecy
URL: http://www.fas.org/sgp/
E-mail: Web form
Phone: (202) 546-3300
1717 K Street, NW
Suite 209
Washington, DC 2003b
"Works to challenge excessive government secrecy and to promote public oversight."

Global Internet Liberty Campaign (GILC)
URL: http://www.gilc.org
E-mail: gilc@gilc.org
International coalition of more than 60 privacy, free speech, and human rights groups dedicated to fighting international threats to privacy and to free speech on the Internet.

Information Systems Security Association
URL: http://www.issa.org/
E-mail: Web form
Phone: (800) 370-ISSA
Technical Enterprises, Inc.
7044 South 13th Street
Oak Creek, WI 53154
Trade and professional group involved in computer security and privacy issues.

Institute of Electrical and Electronics Engineers (IEEE) Computer Society
URL: http://www.computer.org
E-mail: membership@computer.org
Phone: (202) 371-0101
1730 Massachusetts Avenue, NW
Washington, DC 200369-1992
The IEEE Computer Society is the largest component of the Institute of Electrical and Electronics Engineers. Its conferences, journals, and other resources are aimed mainly at computer and information professionals but have considerable impact on policy debates. Compared to the other leading computer society (the Association for Computing Machinery), the IEEE is more engineering-oriented, although there is considerable overlap.

International Association for Cryptologic Research
URL: http://www.iacr.org
E-mail: webmaster@iacr.org
Santa Rosa Administrative Center
University of California—
Santa Barbara
Santa Barbara, CA 93106-6120
International organization to further the study and development of cryptography. Runs conferences and publishes a journal.

Internet Society
URL: http://www.isoc.org
E-mail: isoc@isoc.org
Phone: (703) 648-9880
1770 Wiehle Avenue
Suite 102
Reston, VA 20190
A wide-ranging professional organization devoted to shaping the future of the Internet. Deals with issues

such as privacy and free expression that are important to keeping the Internet viable and growing.

Medical Information Bureau (MIB)
URL: http://www.mib.com
E-mail: infoline@mib.com
Phone: (866) 692-6901
MIB, Inc.
P.O. Box 105
Essex Station
Boston, MA 02112
Central clearinghouse for medical records information; designed primarily to fight insurance fraud. Attempts to deal with privacy concerns that arise in its distribution of medical records.

Medical Privacy Coalition
URL: http://www.
  medicalprivacycoalition.org
E-mail: Web form
A coalition of groups involved with medical privacy and other patients' rights issues. Advocates for stronger privacy protections.

National Workrights Institute
URL: http://www.workrights.org
E-mail: info@workrights.org
Phone: (609) 683-0313
166 Wall Street
Princeton, NJ 08540
Worker's rights organization that focuses on a number of privacy issues, including drug testing, electronic monitoring, genetic discrimination, and medical privacy.

**Organization for Economic
  Cooperation and Development
  (OECD)**
URL: http://www.oecd.org
E-mail: webmaster@oecd.org
Phone: +33 (0)1.45.24.82.00
2, rue André-Pascal

F-75775 Paris Cedex 16
FRANCE
Organization of 30 nations in Europe and Asia (and the United States and Mexico). It promotes development of the market economy. Includes policies and proposals relating to privacy, data security, and electronic commerce.

PGP Users' Mailing List
URL: http://cryptorights.org/lists/
  pgp-users
To subscribe follow the link to the Mailman subscribe page. This is an Internet mailing list covering all aspects of using the Pretty Good Privacy encryption program.

Privacy International
URL: http://www.
  privacyinternational.org
E-mail: pi@privacy.org
Phone: +44 7947 778247
6-8 Amwell Street
Clerkenwell London
ECIR 1UQ UK
International organization that monitors both government and private surveillance and threats to privacy.

Privacy Rights Clearinghouse
URL: http://www.privacyrights.org
E-mail: Web form
Phone: (619) 298-3396
3100 5th Avenue
Suite B
San Diego, CA 92103
Produces useful fact sheets and an annual report, and maintains a tollfree hotline to provide advice to consumers about their rights.

Private Citizen
URL: http://www.private-citizen.
  com

E-mail: pci@private-citizen.com
Phone: (630) 393-2370
P.O. Box 233
Naperville, IL 60566
Gives consumers help for fighting junk mail, junk calls, including a *Sue a Telemarketer* book.

RISKS Digest
URL: http://catless.ncl.ac.uk/
  Risks
To receive current postings, use web browser or news reader to access newsgroup: comp.risks
A Usenet newsgroup devoted to exploring the hidden risks and consequences that can arise from the computer systems upon which so much of our society now depends. Moderated by the ACM Committee on Computers and Public Policy.

**State Public Interest Research
  Groups (PIRGs)**
URL: http://www.pirg.org
The state PIRGs are nonprofit, nonpartisan consumer and environmental watchdog groups that advocate for better consumer privacy laws, preventing identity theft, and correcting credit reports. Fact sheets and reports available on the Web. Site provides links to state PIRGs. See also U.S. Public Interest Group.

TransUnion
URL: http://www.tuc.com
E-mail: Web form
Phone: (800) 916-8800
(Credit questions)
P.O. Box 2000
Chester, PA 19022
One of three major credit bureaus. A person can order credit reports on the web site, as well as see information about privacy rights and policies and "opting out" of mailing lists.

**Transportation Security
  Administration (TSA)**
URL: http://www.tsa.dot.gov
Email: 9-AWA-TELLFAA@
  faa.gov
400 Seventh Street, SW
Washington, DC 20590
The TSA has taken over responsibility for airport security from the Federal Aviation Administration (FAA). It is also responsible for developing security programs for ground transportation.

TRUSTe
URL: http://www.truste.org/
Phone: (415) 520-3400
E-mail: Web form
685 Market Street
Suite 560
San Francisco, CA 94105
Organization seeking to create policies and mechanisms for safe commerce on the Internet, including protection of privacy. Certifies privacy policies.

**U.S. Public Interest Research
  Group (U.S. PIR6)**
E-mail: uspirg@pirg.org
URL: http://www.uspirg.org
Phone: (202) 546-9707
218 D Street, SE
Washington, DC 20003-1900
The national public interest group; watchdog for environment and consumer rights. Has become more involved with privacy interests. See also State Public Interest Groups.

World Wide Web Consortium
URL: http://www.w3.org

E-mail: Web form
Phone: (617) 253-2613
U.S. Office:
Massachusetts Institute
  of Technology
32 Vassal Street
Room 32-G515
Cambridge, MA 02139
International industry consortium for development of protocols and other standards to "lead the Web to its full potential." Includes a section for privacy and is developing the Platform for Privacy Preferences, a way to have web sites uniformly disclose privacy practices and to allow users (or their software) to negotiate with them. See URL: http://www.w3.org/P3P/.

PART III

APPENDICES

APPENDIX A

FREEDOM OF INFORMATION ACT (5 U.S.C. 552), 1966

-CITE-
5 USC Sec. 552
-EXPCITE-
TITLE 5—GOVERNMENT ORGANIZATION AND EMPLOYEES
PART I—THE AGENCIES GENERALLY
CHAPTER 5—ADMINISTRATIVE PROCEDURE
SUBCHAPTER II—ADMINISTRATIVE PROCEDURE
-HEAD-
Sec. 552. Public information; agency rules, opinions, orders, records, and proceedings
-STATUTE-
(a) Each agency shall make available to the public information as follows:

(1) Each agency shall separately state and currently publish in the Federal Register for the guidance of the public —

(A) descriptions of its central and field organization and the established places at which, the employees (and in the case of a uniformed service, the members) from whom, and the methods whereby, the public may obtain information, make submittals or requests, or obtain decisions;

(B) statements of the general course and method by which its functions are channeled and determined, including the nature and requirements of all formal and informal procedures available;

(C) rules of procedure, descriptions of forms available or the places at which forms may be obtained, and instructions as to the scope and contents of all papers, reports, or examinations;

(D) substantive rules of general applicability adopted as authorized by law, and statements of general policy or interpretations of general applicability formulated and adopted by the agency; and

(E) each amendment, revision, or repeal of the foregoing.

Except to the extent that a person has actual and timely notice of the terms thereof, a person may not in any manner be required to resort to, or be adversely affected by, a matter required to be published in the Federal

Register and not so published. For the purpose of this paragraph, matter reasonably available to the class of persons affected thereby is deemed published in the Federal Register when incorporated by reference therein with the approval of the Director of the Federal Register.

(2) Each agency, in accordance with published rules, shall make available for public inspection and copying —

(A) final opinions, including concurring and dissenting opinions, as well as orders, made in the adjudication of cases;

(B) those statements of policy and interpretations which have been adopted by the agency and are not published in the Federal Register;

(C) administrative staff manuals and instructions to staff that affect a member of the public;

(D) copies of all records, regardless of form or format, which have been released to any person under paragraph (3) and which, because of the nature of their subject matter, the agency determines have become or are likely to become the subject of subsequent requests for substantially the same records; and

(E) a general index of the records referred to under subparagraph (D); unless the materials are promptly published and copies offered for sale. For records created on or after November 1, 1996, within one year after such date, each agency shall make such records available, including by computer telecommunications or, if computer telecommunications means have not been established by the agency, by other electronic means. To the extent required to prevent a clearly unwarranted invasion of personal privacy, an agency may delete identifying details when it makes available or publishes an opinion, statement of policy, interpretation, staff manual, instruction, or copies of records referred to in subparagraph (D). However, in each case the justification for the deletion shall be explained fully in writing, and the extent of such deletion shall be indicated on the portion of the record which is made available or published, unless including that indication would harm an interest protected by the exemption in subsection (b) under which the deletion is made. If technically feasible, the extent of the deletion shall be indicated at the place in the record where the deletion was made. Each agency shall also maintain and make available for public inspection and copying current indexes providing identifying information for the public as to any matter issued, adopted, or promulgated after July 4, 1967, and required by this paragraph to be made available or published. Each agency shall promptly publish, quarterly or more frequently, and distribute (by sale or otherwise) copies of each index or supplements thereto unless it determines by order published in the Federal Register that the publication would be unnecessary and impracticable, in which case the agency shall nonetheless provide copies of such index on request at a cost not to exceed the direct cost of duplication. Each agency shall make the index referred to in subparagraph

(E) available by computer telecommunications by December 31, 1999. A final order, opinion, statement of policy, interpretation, or staff manual or instruction that affects a member of the public may be relied on, used, or cited as precedent by an agency against a party other than an agency only if —

(i) it has been indexed and either made available or published as provided by this paragraph; or

(ii) the party has actual and timely notice of the terms thereof.

(3) (A) Except with respect to the records made available under paragraphs (1) and (2) of this subsection, each agency, upon any request for records which (i) reasonably describes such records and (ii) is made in accordance with published rules stating the time, place, fees (if any), and procedures to be followed, shall make the records promptly available to any person.

(B) In making any record available to a person under this paragraph, an agency shall provide the record in any form or format requested by the person if the record is readily reproducible by the agency in that form or format. Each agency shall make reasonable efforts to maintain its records in forms or formats that are reproducible for purposes of this section.

(C) In responding under this paragraph to a request for records, an agency shall make reasonable efforts to search for the records in electronic form or format, except when such efforts would significantly interfere with the operation of the agency's automated information system.

(D) For purposes of this paragraph, the term "search" means to review, manually or by automated means, agency records for the purpose of locating those records which are responsive to a request.

(4) (A) (i) In order to carry out the provisions of this section, each agency shall promulgate regulations, pursuant to notice and receipt of public comment, specifying the schedule of fees applicable to the processing of requests under this section and establishing procedures and guidelines for determining when such fees should be waived or reduced. Such schedule shall conform to the guidelines which shall be promulgated, pursuant to notice and receipt of public comment, by the Director of the Office of Management and Budget and which shall provide for a uniform schedule of fees for all agencies.

(ii) Such agency regulations shall provide that —

(I) fees shall be limited to reasonable standard charges for document search, duplication, and review, when records are requested for commercial use;

(II) fees shall be limited to reasonable standard charges for document duplication when records are not sought for commercial use and the request is made by an educational or noncommercial scientific institution, whose purpose is scholarly or scientific research; or a representative of the news media; and

(III) for any request not described in (I) or (II), fees shall be limited to reasonable standard charges for document search and duplication.

(iii) Documents shall be furnished without any charge or at a charge reduced below the fees established under clause (ii) if disclosure of the information is in the public interest because it is likely to contribute significantly to public understanding of the operations or activities of the government and is not primarily in the commercial interest of the requester.

(iv) Fee schedules shall provide for the recovery of only the direct costs of search, duplication, or review. Review costs shall include only the direct costs incurred during the initial examination of a document for the purposes of determining whether the documents must be disclosed under this section and for the purposes of withholding any portions exempt from disclosure under this section. Review costs may not include any costs incurred in resolving issues of law or policy that may be raised in the course of processing a request under this section. No fee may be charged by any agency under this section —

(I) if the costs of routine collection and processing of the fee are likely to equal or exceed the amount of the fee; or

(II) for any request described in clause (ii) (II) or (III) of this subparagraph for the first two hours of search time or for the first one hundred pages of duplication.

(v) No agency may require advance payment of any fee unless the requester has previously failed to pay fees in a timely fashion, or the agency has determined that the fee will exceed $250.

(vi) Nothing in this subparagraph shall supersede fees chargeable under a statute specifically providing for setting the level of fees for particular types of records.

(vii) In any action by a requester regarding the waiver of fees under this section, the court shall determine the matter de novo: Provided, That the court's review of the matter shall be limited to the record before the agency.

(B) On complaint, the district court of the United States in the district in which the complainant resides, or has his principal place of business, or in which the agency records are situated, or in the District of Columbia, has jurisdiction to enjoin the agency from withholding agency records and to order the production of any agency records improperly withheld from the complainant. In such a case the court shall determine the matter de novo, and may examine the contents of such agency records in camera to determine whether such records or any part thereof shall be withheld under any of the exemptions set forth in subsection (b) of this section, and the burden is on the agency to sustain its action. In addition to any other matters to which a court accords substantial weight, a court shall accord substantial weight to an affidavit of an agency concerning the agency's determination as to technical feasibility under paragraph (2) (C) and subsection (b) and reproducibility under paragraph (3) (B).

(C) Notwithstanding any other provision of law, the defendant shall serve an answer or otherwise plead to any complaint made under this subsection within thirty days after service upon the defendant of the pleading in which such complaint is made, unless the court otherwise directs for good cause shown.

Appendix A

(D) Repealed. Pub. L. 98-620, title IV, Sec. 402(2), Nov. 8, 1984, 98 Stat. 3357.

(E) The court may assess against the United States reasonable attorney fees and other litigation costs reasonably incurred in any case under this section in which the complainant has substantially prevailed.

(F) Whenever the court orders the production of any agency records improperly withheld from the complainant and assesses against the United States reasonable attorney fees and other litigation costs, and the court additionally issues a written finding that the circumstances surrounding the withholding raise questions whether agency personnel acted arbitrarily or capriciously with respect to the withholding, the Special Counsel shall promptly initiate a proceeding to determine whether disciplinary action is warranted against the officer or employee who was primarily responsible for the withholding. The Special Counsel, after investigation and consideration of the evidence submitted, shall submit his findings and recommendations to the administrative authority of the agency concerned and shall send copies of the findings and recommendations to the officer or employee or his representative. The administrative authority shall take the corrective action that the Special Counsel recommends.

(G) In the event of noncompliance with the order of the court, the district court may punish for contempt the responsible employee, and in the case of a uniformed service, the responsible member.

(5) Each agency having more than one member shall maintain and make available for public inspection a record of the final votes of each member in every agency proceeding.

(6) (A) Each agency, upon any request for records made under paragraph (1), (2), or (3) of this subsection, shall —

(i) determine within 20 days (excepting Saturdays, Sundays, and legal public holidays) after the receipt of any such request whether to comply with such request and shall immediately notify the person making such request of such determination and the reasons therefor, and of the right of such person to appeal to the head of the agency any adverse determination; and

(ii) make a determination with respect to any appeal within twenty days (excepting Saturdays, Sundays, and legal public holidays) after the receipt of such appeal. If on appeal the denial of the request for records is in whole or in part upheld, the agency shall notify the person making such request of the provisions for judicial review of that determination under paragraph (4) of this subsection.

(B) (i) In unusual circumstances as specified in this subparagraph, the time limits prescribed in either clause (i) or clause (ii) of subparagraph (A) may be extended by written notice to the person making such request setting forth the unusual circumstances for such extension and the date on which a determination is expected to be dispatched. No such notice shall specify a date that would result in an extension for more than ten working days, except as provided in clause (ii) of this subparagraph.

259

(ii) With respect to a request for which a written notice under clause (i) extends the time limits prescribed under clause (i) of subparagraph (A), the agency shall notify the person making the request if the request cannot be processed within the time limit specified in that clause and shall provide the person an opportunity to limit the scope of the request so that it may be processed within that time limit or an opportunity to arrange with the agency an alternative time frame for processing the request or a modified request. Refusal by the person to reasonably modify the request or arrange such an alternative time frame shall be considered as a factor in determining whether exceptional circumstances exist for purposes of subparagraph (C).

(iii) As used in this subparagraph, "unusual circumstances" means, but only to the extent reasonably necessary to the proper processing of the particular requests —

(I) the need to search for and collect the requested records from field facilities or other establishments that are separate from the office processing the request;

(II) the need to search for, collect, and appropriately examine a voluminous amount of separate and distinct records which are demanded in a single request; or

(III) the need for consultation, which shall be conducted with all practicable speed, with another agency having a substantial interest in the determination of the request or among two or more components of the agency having substantial subject-matter interest therein.

(iv) Each agency may promulgate regulations, pursuant to notice and receipt of public comment, providing for the aggregation of certain requests by the same requestor, or by a group of requestors acting in concert, if the agency reasonably believes that such requests actually constitute a single request, which would otherwise satisfy the unusual circumstances specified in this subparagraph, and the requests involve clearly related matters. Multiple requests involving unrelated matters shall not be aggregated.

(C) (i) Any person making a request to any agency for records under paragraph (1), (2), or (3) of this subsection shall be deemed to have exhausted his administrative remedies with respect to such request if the agency fails to comply with the applicable time limit provisions of this paragraph. If the Government can show exceptional circumstances exist and that the agency is exercising due diligence in responding to the request, the court may retain jurisdiction and allow the agency additional time to complete its review of the records. Upon any determination by an agency to comply with a request for records, the records shall be made promptly available to such person making such request. Any notification of denial of any request for records under this subsection shall set forth the names and titles or positions of each person responsible for the denial of such request.

(ii) For purposes of this subparagraph, the term "exceptional circumstances" does not include a delay that results from a predictable agency workload of requests under this section, unless the agency demonstrates reasonable progress in reducing its backlog of pending requests.

(iii) Refusal by a person to reasonably modify the scope of a request or arrange an alternative time frame for processing a request (or a modified request) under clause (ii) after being given an opportunity to do so by the agency to whom the person made the request shall be considered as a factor in determining whether exceptional circumstances exist for purposes of this subparagraph.

(D) (i) Each agency may promulgate regulations, pursuant to notice and receipt of public comment, providing for multitrack processing of requests for records based on the amount of work or time (or both) involved in processing requests.

(ii) Regulations under this subparagraph may provide a person making a request that does not qualify for the fastest multitrack processing an opportunity to limit the scope of the request in order to qualify for faster processing.

(iii) This subparagraph shall not be considered to affect the requirement under subparagraph (C) to exercise due diligence.

(E) (i) Each agency shall promulgate regulations, pursuant to notice and receipt of public comment, providing for expedited processing of requests for records —

(I) in cases in which the person requesting the records demonstrates a compelling need; and

(II) in other cases determined by the agency.

(ii) Notwithstanding clause (i), regulations under this subparagraph must ensure —

(I) that a determination of whether to provide expedited processing shall be made, and notice of the determination shall be provided to the person making the request, within 10 days after the date of the request; and

(II) expeditious consideration of administrative appeals of such determinations of whether to provide expedited processing.

(iii) An agency shall process as soon as practicable any request for records to which the agency has granted expedited processing under this subparagraph. Agency action to deny or affirm denial of a request for expedited processing pursuant to this subparagraph, and failure by an agency to respond in a timely manner to such a request shall be subject to judicial review under paragraph (4), except that the judicial review shall be based on the record before the agency at the time of the determination.

(iv) A district court of the United States shall not have jurisdiction to review an agency denial of expedited processing of a request for records after the agency has provided a complete response to the request.

(v) For purposes of this subparagraph, the term "compelling need" means —

(I) that a failure to obtain requested records on an expedited basis under this paragraph could reasonably be expected to pose an imminent threat to the life or physical safety of an individual; or

(II) with respect to a request made by a person primarily engaged in disseminating *information*, urgency to inform the public concerning actual or alleged Federal Government activity.

(vi) A demonstration of a compelling need by a person making a request for expedited processing shall be made by a statement certified by such person to be true and correct to the best of such person's knowledge and belief.

(F) In denying a request for records, in whole or in part, an agency shall make a reasonable effort to estimate the volume of any requested matter the provision of which is denied, and shall provide any such estimate to the person making the request, unless providing such estimate would harm an interest protected by the exemption in subsection (b) pursuant to which the denial is made.

(b) This section does not apply to matters that are —

(1) (A) specifically authorized under criteria established by an Executive order to be kept secret in the interest of national defense or foreign policy and (B) are in fact properly classified pursuant to such Executive order;

(2) related solely to the internal personnel rules and practices of an agency;

(3) specifically exempted from disclosure by statute (other than section 552b of this title), provided that such statute (A) requires that the matters be withheld from the public in such a manner as to leave no discretion on the issue, or (B) establishes particular criteria for withholding or refers to particular types of matters to be withheld;

(4) trade secrets and commercial or financial information obtained from a person and privileged or confidential;

(5) inter-agency or intra-agency memorandums or letters which would not be available by law to a party other than an agency in litigation with the agency;

(6) personnel and medical files and similar files the disclosure of which would constitute a clearly unwarranted invasion of personal privacy;

(7) records or information compiled for law enforcement purposes, but only to the extent that the production of such law enforcement records or information (A) could reasonably be expected to interfere with enforcement proceedings, (B) would deprive a person of a right to a fair trial or an impartial adjudication, (C) could reasonably be expected to constitute an unwarranted invasion of personal privacy, (D) could reasonably be expected to disclose the identity of a confidential source, including a State, local, or foreign agency or authority or any private institution which furnished information on a confidential basis, and, in the case of a record or information compiled by criminal law enforcement authority in the course of a criminal investigation or by an agency conducting a lawful national security intelligence investigation, information furnished by a confidential source, (E) would disclose techniques

and procedures for law enforcement investigations or prosecutions, or would disclose guidelines for law enforcement investigations or prosecutions if such disclosure could reasonably be expected to risk circumvention of the law, or (F) could reasonably be expected to endanger the life or physical safety of any individual;

(8) contained in or related to examination, operating, or condition reports prepared by, on behalf of, or for the use of an agency responsible for the regulation or supervision of financial institutions; or

(9) geological and geophysical information and data, including maps, concerning wells.

Any reasonably segregable portion of a record shall be provided to any person requesting such record after deletion of the portions which are exempt under this subsection. The amount of information deleted shall be indicated on the released portion of the record, unless including that indication would harm an interest protected by the exemption in this subsection under which the deletion is made. If technically feasible, the amount of the information deleted shall be indicated at the place in the record where such deletion is made.

(c) (1) Whenever a request is made which involves access to records described in subsection (b) (7) (A) and —

(A) the investigation or proceeding involves a possible violation of criminal law; and

(B) there is reason to believe that (i) the subject of the investigation or proceeding is not aware of its pendency, and (ii) disclosure of the existence of the records could reasonably be expected to interfere with enforcement proceedings, the agency may, during only such time as that circumstance continues, treat the records as not subject to the requirements of this section.

(2) Whenever informant records maintained by a criminal law enforcement agency under an informant's name or personal identifier are requested by a third party according to the informant's name or personal identifier, the agency may treat the records as not subject to the requirements of this section unless the informant's status as an informant has been officially confirmed.

(3) Whenever a request is made which involves access to records maintained by the Federal Bureau of Investigation pertaining to foreign intelligence or counterintelligence, or international terrorism, and the existence of the records is classified information as provided in subsection (b) (1), the Bureau may, as long as the existence of the records remains classified information, treat the records as not subject to the requirements of this section.

(d) This section does not authorize withholding of information or limit the availability of records to the public, except as specifically stated in this section. This section is not authority to withhold information from Congress.

(e) (1) On or before February 1 of each year, each agency shall submit to the Attorney General of the United States a report which shall cover the preceding fiscal year and which shall include —

(A) the number of determinations made by the agency not to comply with requests for records made to such agency under subsection (a) and the reasons for each such determination;

(B) (i) the number of appeals made by persons under subsection (a) (6), the result of such appeals, and the reason for the action upon each appeal that results in a denial of information; and

(ii) a complete list of all statutes that the agency relies upon to authorize the agency to withhold information under subsection (b) (3), to withhold information under each such statute, and a concise description a description of whether a court has upheld the decision of the agency to withhold information under each such statute, and a concise description of the scope of any information withheld;

(C) the number of requests for records pending before the agency as of September 30 of the preceding year, and the median number of days that such requests had been pending before the agency as of that date;

(D) the number of requests for records received by the agency and the number of requests which the agency processed;

(E) the median number of days taken by the agency to process different types of requests;

(F) the total amount of fees collected by the agency for processing requests; and

(G) the number of full-time staff of the agency devoted to processing requests for records under this section, and the total amount expended by the agency for processing such requests.

(2) Each agency shall make each such report available to the public including by computer telecommunications, or if computer telecommunications means have not been established by the agency, by other electronic means.

(3) The Attorney General of the United States shall make each report which has been made available by electronic means available at a single electronic access point. The Attorney General of the United States shall notify the Chairman and ranking minority member of the Committee on Government Reform and Oversight of the House of Representatives and the Chairman and ranking minority member of the Committees on Governmental Affairs and the Judiciary of the Senate, no later than April 1 of the year in which each such report is issued, that such reports are available by electronic means.

(4) The Attorney General of the United States, in consultation with the Director of the Office of Management and Budget, shall develop reporting and performance guidelines in connection with reports required by this subsection by October 1, 1997, and may establish additional requirements for such reports as the Attorney General determines may be useful.

(5) The Attorney General of the United States shall submit an annual report on or before April 1 of each calendar year which shall include for the prior calendar year a listing of the number of cases arising under this section, the exemption involved in each case, the disposition of such case, and the cost, fees, and penalties assessed under subparagraphs (E), (F), and (G) of subsec-

tion (a) (4). Such report shall also include a description of the efforts under-taken by the Department of Justice to encourage agency compliance with this section.

(f) For purposes of this section, the term —

(1) "agency" as defined in section 551(1) of this title includes any executive department, military department, Government corporation, Government controlled corporation, or other establishment in the executive branch of the Government (including the Executive Office of the President), or any independent regulatory agency; and

(2) "record" and any other term used in this section in reference to information includes any information that would be an agency record subject to the requirements of this section when maintained by an agency in any format, including an electronic format.

(g) The head of each agency shall prepare and make publicly available upon request, reference material or a guide for requesting records or information from the agency, subject to the exemptions in subsection (b), including —

(1) an index of all major information systems of the agency;

(2) a description of major information and record locator systems maintained by the agency; and

(3) a handbook for obtaining various types and categories of public *information* from the agency pursuant to chapter 35 of title 44, and under this section.

-SOURCE-

(Pub. L. 89–554, Sept. 6, 1966, 80 Stat. 383; Pub. L. 90–23, Sec. 1, June 5, 1967, 81 Stat. 54; Pub. L. 93–502, Sec. 1–3, Nov. 21, 1974, 88 Stat. 1561–1564; Pub. L. 94–409, Sec. 5(b), Sept. 13, 1976, 90 Stat. 1247; Pub. L. 95–454, title IX, Sec. 906(a)(10), Oct. 13, 1978, 92 Stat. 1225; Pub. L. 98–620, title IV, Sec. 402(2), Nov. 8, 1984, 98 Stat. 3357; Pub. L. 99–570, title I, Sec. 1802, 1803, Oct. 27, 1986, 100 Stat. 3207–48, 3207–49; Pub. L. 104–231, Sec. 3–11, Oct. 2, 1996, 110 Stat. 3049–3054.)

APPENDIX B

U.S. SUPREME COURT RULING: *KATZ V. UNITED STATES*, 1967

KATZ V. UNITED STATES CERTIORARI TO THE UNITED STATES COURT OF APPEALS FOR THE NINTH CIRCUIT. NO. 35.

Argued October 17, 1967.
Decided December 18, 1967.

Petitioner was convicted under an indictment charging him with transmitting wagering information by telephone across state lines in violation of 18 U.S.C. 1084. Evidence of petitioner's end of the conversations, overheard by FBI agents who had attached an electronic listening and recording device to the outside of the telephone booth from which the calls were made, was introduced at the trial. The Court of Appeals affirmed the conviction, finding that there was no Fourth Amendment violation since there was "no physical entrance into the area occupied by" petitioner. Held:

1. The Government's eavesdropping activities violated the privacy upon which petitioner justifiably relied while using the telephone booth and thus constituted a "search and seizure" within the meaning of the Fourth Amendment. Pp. 350–353.

(a) The Fourth Amendment governs not only the seizure of tangible items but extends as well to the recording of oral statements. Silverman v. United States, 365 U.S. 505, 511. P. 353.

(b) Because the Fourth Amendment protects people rather than places, its reach cannot turn on the presence or absence of a physical intrusion into any given enclosure. The "trespass" doctrine of Olmstead v. United States, 277 U.S. 438, and Goldman v. United States, 316 U.S. 129, is no longer controlling. Pp. 351, 353.

2. Although the surveillance in this case may have been so narrowly circumscribed that it could constitutionally have been authorized in advance, it was

not in fact conducted pursuant to the warrant procedure which is a constitutional precondition of such electronic surveillance. Pp. 354–359. 369 F.2d 130, reversed.

Burton Marks and Harvey A. Schneider argued the cause and filed briefs for petitioner. [389 U.S. 347, 348]

John S. Martin, Jr., argued the cause for the United States. With him on the brief were Acting Solicitor General Spritzer, Assistant Attorney General Vinson and Beatrice Rosenberg.

MR. JUSTICE STEWART delivered the opinion of the Court.

The petitioner was convicted in the District Court for the Southern District of California under an eight-count indictment charging him with transmitting wagering information by telephone from Los Angeles to Miami and Boston, in violation of a federal statute. At trial the Government was permitted, over the petitioner's objection, to introduce evidence of the petitioner's end of telephone conversations, overheard by FBI agents who had attached an electronic listening and recording device to the outside of the public telephone booth from which he had placed his calls. In affirming his conviction, the Court of Appeals rejected the contention that the recordings had been obtained in violation of the Fourth Amendment, [389 U.S. 347, 349] because "[t]here was no physical entrance into the area occupied by [the petitioner]." We granted certiorari in order to consider the constitutional questions thus presented.

The petitioner has phrased those questions as follows:
"A. Whether a public telephone booth is a constitutionally protected area so that evidence obtained by attaching an electronic listening recording device to the top of such a booth is obtained in violation of the right to privacy of the user of the booth. [389 U.S. 347, 350]
"B. Whether physical penetration of a constitutionally protected area is necessary before a search and seizure can be said to be violative of the Fourth Amendment to the United States Constitution."

We decline to adopt this formulation of the issues. In the first place, the correct solution of Fourth Amendment problems is not necessarily promoted by incantation of the phrase "constitutionally protected area." Secondly, the Fourth Amendment cannot be translated into a general constitutional "right to privacy." That Amendment protects individual privacy against certain kinds of governmental intrusion, but its protections go further, and often have nothing to do with privacy at all. Other provisions of the Constitution protect personal privacy from other forms of governmental invasion. But the protection of a person's general right to privacy—his right to be let alone by other people—is, like the [389 U.S. 347, 351] protection of his property and of his very life, left largely to the law of the individual States.

Privacy in the Information Age

Because of the misleading way the issues have been formulated, the parties have attached great significance to the characterization of the telephone booth from which the petitioner placed his calls. The petitioner has strenuously argued that the booth was a "constitutionally protected area." The Government has maintained with equal vigor that it was not. But this effort to decide whether or not a given "area," viewed in the abstract, is "constitutionally protected" deflects attention from the problem presented by this case. For the Fourth Amendment protects people, not places. What a person knowingly exposes to the public, even in his own home or office, is not a subject of Fourth Amendment protection. See Lewis v. United States, 385 U.S. 206, 210; United States v. Lee, 274 U.S. 559, 563. But what he seeks to preserve as private, even in an area accessible to the public, may be constitutionally protected. [389 U.S. 347, 352] See Rios v. United States, 364 U.S. 253; Ex parte Jackson, 96 U.S. 727, 733.

The Government stresses the fact that the telephone booth from which the petitioner made his calls was constructed partly of glass, so that he was as visible after he entered it as he would have been if he had remained outside. But what he sought to exclude when he entered the booth was not the intruding eye—it was the uninvited ear. He did not shed his right to do so simply because he made his calls from a place where he might be seen. No less than an individual in a business office, in a friend's apartment, or in a taxicab, a person in a telephone booth may rely upon the protection of the Fourth Amendment. One who occupies it, shuts the door behind him, and pays the toll that permits him to place a call is surely entitled to assume that the words he utters into the mouthpiece will not be broadcast to the world. To read the Constitution more narrowly is to ignore the vital role that the public telephone has come to play in private communication.

The Government contends, however, that the activities of its agents in this case should not be tested by Fourth Amendment requirements, for the surveillance technique they employed involved no physical penetration of the telephone booth from which the petitioner placed his calls. It is true that the absence of such penetration was at one time thought to foreclose further Fourth Amendment inquiry, Olmstead v. United States, 277 U.S. 438, 457, 464,466; Goldman v. United States, 316 U.S. 129,134–136, for that Amendment was thought to limit only searches and seizures of tangible [389 U.S. 347, 353] property. But "[t]he premise that property interests control the right of the Government to search and seize has been discredited." Warden v. Hayden, 387 U.S. 294, 304. Thus, although a closely divided Court supposed in Olmstead that surveillance without any trespass and without the seizure of any material object fell outside the ambit of the Constitution, we have since departed from the narrow view on which that decision rested. Indeed, we have expressly held that the Fourth Amendment governs not only the seizure of tangible items, but extends as well to the recording of oral statements, overheard without any "technical trespass under . . . local property law." Silverman v. United States, 365 U.S. 505, 511. Once this much is acknowledged, and once it is recognized that the Fourth

Amendment protects people—and not simply "areas"—against unreasonable searches and seizures, it becomes clear that the reach of that Amendment cannot turn upon the presence or absence of a physical intrusion into any given enclosure.

We conclude that the underpinnings of Olmstead and Goldman have been so eroded by our subsequent decisions that the "trespass" doctrine there enunciated can no longer be regarded as controlling. The Government's activities in electronically listening to and recording the petitioner's words violated the privacy upon which he justifiably relied while using the telephone booth and thus constituted a "search and seizure" within the meaning of the Fourth Amendment. The fact that the electronic device employed to achieve that end did not happen to penetrate the wall of the booth can have no constitutional significance. [389 U.S. 347, 354]

The question remaining for decision, then, is whether the search and seizure conducted in this case complied with constitutional standards. In that regard, the Government's position is that its agents acted in an entirely defensible manner: They did not begin their electronic surveillance until investigation of the petitioner's activities had established a strong probability that he was using the telephone in question to transmit gambling information to persons in other States, in violation of federal law. Moreover, the surveillance was limited, both in scope and in duration, to the specific purpose of establishing the contents of the petitioner's unlawful telephonic communications. The agents confined their surveillance to the brief periods during which he used the telephone booth, and they took great care to overhear only the conversations of the petitioner himself.

Accepting this account of the Government's actions as accurate, it is clear that this surveillance was so narrowly circumscribed that a duly authorized magistrate, properly notified of the need for such investigation, specifically informed of the basis on which it was to proceed, and clearly apprised of the precise intrusion it would entail, could constitutionally have authorized, with appropriate safeguards, the very limited search and seizure that the Government asserts in fact took place. Only last Term was sustained the validity of [389 U.S. 347, 355] such an authorization, holding that, under sufficiently "precise and discriminate circumstances," a federal court may empower government agents to employ a concealed electronic device "for the narrow and particularized purpose of ascertaining the truth of the . . . allegations" of a "detailed factual affidavit alleging the commission of a specific criminal offense." Osborn v. United States, 385 U.S. 323, 329–330. Discussing that holding, the Court in Berger v. New York, 388 U.S. 41, said that "the order authorizing the use of the electronic device" in Osborn "afforded similar protections to those . . . of conventional warrants authorizing the seizure of tangible evidence." Through those protections, "no greater invasion of privacy was permitted than was necessary under the circumstances." Id., at 57. Here, too, a similar [389 U.S. 347, 356] judicial order could have accommodated "the legitimate needs of law enforcement" by authorizing the carefully limited use of electronic surveillance.

The Government urges that, because its agents relied upon the decisions in Olmstead and Goldman, and because they did no more here than they might properly have done with prior judicial sanction, we should retroactively validate their conduct. That we cannot do. It is apparent that the agents in this case acted with restraint. Yet the inescapable fact is that this restraint was imposed by the agents themselves, not by a judicial officer. They were not required, before commencing the search, to present their estimate of probable cause for detached scrutiny by a neutral magistrate. They were not compelled, during the conduct of the search itself, to observe precise limits established in advance by a specific court order. Nor were they directed, after the search had been completed, to notify the authorizing magistrate in detail of all that had been seized. In the absence of such safeguards, this Court has never sustained a search upon the sole ground that officers reasonably expected to find evidence of a particular crime and voluntarily confined their activities to the least intrusive [389 U.S. 347, 357] means consistent with that end. Searches conducted without warrants have been held unlawful "notwithstanding facts unquestionably showing probable cause," Agnello v. United States, 269 U.S. 20, 33, for the Constitution requires "that the deliberate, impartial judgment of a judicial officer . . . be interposed between the citizen and the police . . ." Wong Sun v. United States, 371 U.S. 471, 481–482. "Over and again this Court has emphasized that the mandate of the [Fourth] Amendment requires adherence to judicial processes," United States v. Jeffers, 342 U.S. 48, 51, and that searches conducted outside the judicial process, without prior approval by judge or magistrate, are per se unreasonable under the Fourth Amendment—subject only to a few specifically established and well-delineated exceptions.

It is difficult to imagine how any of those exceptions could ever apply to the sort of search and seizure involved in this case. Even electronic surveillance substantially contemporaneous with an individual's arrest could hardly be deemed an "incident" of that arrest. [389 U.S. 347, 358] Nor could the use of electronic surveillance without prior authorization be justified on grounds of "hot pursuit." And, of course, the very nature of electronic surveillance precludes its use pursuant to the suspect's consent.

The Government does not question these basic principles. Rather, it urges the creation of a new exception to cover this case. It argues that surveillance of a telephone booth should be exempted from the usual requirement of advance authorization by a magistrate upon a showing of probable cause. We cannot agree. Omission of such authorization "bypasses the safeguards provided by an objective predetermination of probable cause, and substitutes instead the far less reliable procedure of an after-the-event justification for the . . . search, too likely to be subtly influenced by the familiar shortcomings of hindsight judgment." Beck v. Ohio, 379 U.S. 89, 96.

And bypassing a neutral predetermination of the scope of a search leaves individuals secure from Fourth Amendment [389 U.S. 347, 359] violations "only in the discretion of the police." Id., at 97.

These considerations do not vanish when the search in question is transferred from the setting of a home, an office, or a hotel room to that of a telephone booth. Wherever a man may be, he is entitled to know that he will remain free from unreasonable searches and seizures. The government agents here ignored "the procedure of antecedent justification . . . that is central to the Fourth Amendment," a procedure that we hold to be a constitutional precondition of the kind of electronic surveillance involved in this case. Because the surveillance here failed to meet that condition, and because it led to the petitioner's conviction, the judgment must be reversed. It is so ordered.

MR. JUSTICE MARSHALL took no part in the consideration or decision of this case.

[All Footnotes and Footnote references have been omitted.]

APPENDIX C

PRIVACY ACT OF 1974

-CITE-
5 USC Sec. 552a
-EXPCITE-
TITLE 5—GOVERNMENT ORGANIZATION AND EMPLOYEES
PART I—THE AGENCIES GENERALLY
CHAPTER 5—ADMINISTRATIVE PROCEDURE
SUBCHAPTER II—ADMINISTRATIVE PROCEDURE
-HEAD-
Sec. 552a. Records maintained on individuals
-STATUTE-
(a) Definitions.—For purposes of this section —

(1) the term "agency" means agency as defined in section 552(e) (FOOT-NOTE 1) of this title;

(FOOTNOTE 1) See References in Text note below.

(2) the term "individual" means a citizen of the United States or an alien lawfully admitted for permanent residence;

(3) the term "maintain" includes maintain, collect, use, or disseminate;

(4) the term "record" means any item, collection, or grouping of information about an individual that is maintained by an agency, including, but not limited to, his education, financial transactions, medical history, and criminal or employment history and that contains his name, or the identifying number, symbol, or other identifying particular assigned to the individual, such as a finger or voice print or a photograph;

(5) the term "system of records" means a group of any records under the control of any agency from which information is retrieved by the name of the individual or by some identifying number, symbol, or other identifying particular assigned to the individual;

(6) the term "statistical record" means a record in a system of records maintained for statistical research or reporting purposes only and not used in whole or in part in making any determination about an identifiable individual, except as provided by section 8 of title 13;

(7) the term "routine use" means, with respect to the disclosure of a record, the use of such record for a purpose which is compatible with the purpose for which it was collected;

Appendix C

(8) the term "matching program" —

(A) means any computerized comparison of —

(i) two or more automated systems of records or a system of records with non-Federal records for the purpose of —

(I) establishing or verifying the eligibility of, or continuing compliance with statutory and regulatory requirements by, applicants for, recipients or beneficiaries of, participants in, or providers of services with respect to, cash or in-kind assistance or payments under Federal benefit programs, or

(II) recouping payments or delinquent debts under such Federal benefit programs, or

(ii) two or more automated Federal personnel or payroll systems of records or a system of Federal personnel or payroll records with non-Federal records,

(B) but does not include —

(i) matches performed to produce aggregate statistical data without any personal identifiers;

(ii) matches performed to support any research or statistical project, the specific data of which may not be used to make decisions concerning the rights, benefits, or privileges of specific individuals;

(iii) matches performed, by an agency (or component thereof) which performs as its principal function any activity pertaining to the enforcement of criminal laws, subsequent to the initiation of a specific criminal or civil law enforcement investigation of a named person or persons for the purpose of gathering evidence against such person or persons;

(iv) matches of tax information (I) pursuant to section 6103(d) of the Internal Revenue Code of 1986, (II) for purposes of tax administration as defined in section 6103(b)(4) of such Code, (III) for the purpose of intercepting a tax refund due an individual under authority granted by section 404(e), 464, or 1137 of the Social Security Act; or (IV) for the purpose of intercepting a tax refund due an individual under any other tax refund intercept program authorized by statute which has been determined by the Director of the Office of Management and Budget to contain verification, notice, and hearing requirements that are substantially similar to the procedures in section 1137 of the Social Security Act;

(v) matches —

(I) using records predominantly relating to Federal personnel, that are performed for routine administrative purposes (subject to guidance provided by the Director of the Office of Management and Budget pursuant to subsection (v)); or

(II) conducted by an agency using only records from systems of records maintained by that agency; if the purpose of the match is not to take any adverse financial, personnel, disciplinary, or other adverse action against Federal personnel;

(vi) matches performed for foreign counterintelligence purposes or to produce background checks for security clearances of Federal personnel or Federal contractor personnel; or

(vii) matches performed incident to a levy described in section 6103(k)(8) of the Internal Revenue Code of 1986;

(9) the term "recipient agency" means any agency, or contractor thereof, receiving records contained in a system of records from a source agency for use in a matching program;

(10) the term "non-Federal agency" means any State or local government, or agency thereof, which receives records contained in a system of records from a source agency for use in a matching program;

(11) the term "source agency" means any agency which discloses records contained in a system of records to be used in a matching program, or any State or local government, or agency thereof, which discloses records to be used in a matching program;

(12) the term "Federal benefit program" means any program administered or funded by the Federal Government, or by any agent or State on behalf of the Federal Government, providing cash or in-kind assistance in the form of payments, grants, loans, or loan guarantees to individuals; and

(13) the term "Federal personnel" means officers and employees of the Government of the United States, members of the uniformed services (including members of the Reserve Components), individuals entitled to receive immediate or deferred retirement benefits under any retirement program of the Government of the United States (including survivor benefits).

(b) Conditions of Disclosure.—No agency shall disclose any record which is contained in a system of records by any means of communication to any person, or to another agency, except pursuant to a written request by, or with the prior written consent of, the individual to whom the record pertains, unless disclosure of the record would be —

(1) to those officers and employees of the agency which maintains the record who have a need for the record in the performance of their duties;

(2) required under section 552 of this title;

(3) for a routine use as defined in subsection (a)(7) of this section and described under subsection (e)(4)(D) of this section;

(4) to the Bureau of the Census for purposes of planning or carrying out a census or survey or related activity pursuant to the provisions of title 13;

(5) to a recipient who has provided the agency with advance adequate written assurance that the record will be used solely as a statistical research or reporting record, and the record is to be transferred in a form that is not individually identifiable;

(6) to the National Archives and Records Administration as a record which has sufficient historical or other value to warrant its continued preservation by the United States Government, or for evaluation by the Archivist of the United States or the designee of the Archivist to determine whether the record has such value;

(7) to another agency or to an instrumentality of any governmental jurisdiction within or under the control of the United States for a civil or criminal law enforcement activity if the activity is authorized by law, and if the head of the agency or instrumentality has made a written request to the agency which main-

tains the record specifying the particular portion desired and the law enforcement activity for which the record is sought;

(8) to a person pursuant to a showing of compelling circumstances affecting the health or safety of an individual if upon such disclosure notification is transmitted to the last known address of such individual;

(9) to either House of Congress, or, to the extent of matter within its jurisdiction, any committee or subcommittee thereof, any joint committee of Congress or subcommittee of any such joint committee;

(10) to the Comptroller General, or any of his authorized representatives, in the course of the performance of the duties of the General Accounting Office;

(11) pursuant to the order of a court of competent jurisdiction; or

(12) to a consumer reporting agency in accordance with section 3711(e) of title 31.

(c) Accounting of Certain Disclosures.—Each agency, with respect to each system of records under its control, shall —

(1) except for disclosures made under subsections (b)(1) or (b)(2) of this section, keep an accurate accounting of —

(A) the date, nature, and purpose of each disclosure of a record to any person or to another agency made under subsection (b) of this section; and

(B) the name and address of the person or agency to whom the disclosure is made;

(2) retain the accounting made under paragraph (1) of this subsection for at least five years or the life of the record, whichever is longer, after the disclosure for which the accounting is made;

(3) except for disclosures made under subsection (b)(7) of this section, make the accounting made under paragraph (1) of this subsection available to the individual named in the record at his request; and

(4) inform any person or other agency about any correction or notation of dispute made by the agency in accordance with subsection (d) of this section of any record that has been disclosed to the person or agency if an accounting of the disclosure was made.

(d) Access to Records.—Each agency that maintains a system of records shall —

(1) upon request by any individual to gain access to his record or to any information pertaining to him which is contained in the system, permit him and upon his request, a person of his own choosing to accompany him, to review the record and have a copy made of all or any portion thereof in a form comprehensible to him, except that the agency may require the individual to furnish a written statement authorizing discussion of that individual's record in the accompanying person's presence;

(2) permit the individual to request amendment of a record pertaining to him and —

(A) not later than 10 days (excluding Saturdays, Sundays, and legal public holidays) after the date of receipt of such request, acknowledge in writing such receipt; and

(B) promptly, either —

(i) make any correction of any portion thereof which the individual believes is not accurate, relevant, timely, or complete; or

(ii) inform the individual of its refusal to amend the record in accordance with his request, the reason for the refusal, the procedures established by the agency for the individual to request a review of that refusal by the head of the agency or an officer designated by the head of the agency, and the name and business address of that official;

(3) permit the individual who disagrees with the refusal of the agency to amend his record to request a review of such refusal, and not later than 30 days (excluding Saturdays, Sundays, and legal public holidays) from the date on which the individual requests such review, complete such review and make a final determination unless, for good cause shown, the head of the agency extends such 30-day period; and if, after his review, the reviewing official also refuses to amend the record in accordance with the request, permit the individual to file with the agency a concise statement setting forth the reasons for his disagreement with the refusal of the agency, and notify the individual of the provisions for judicial review of the reviewing official's determination under subsection (g)(1)(A) of this section;

(4) in any disclosure, containing information about which the individual has filed a statement of disagreement, occurring after the filing of the statement under paragraph (3) of this subsection, clearly note any portion of the record which is disputed and provide copies of the statement and, if the agency deems it appropriate, copies of a concise statement of the reasons of the agency for not making the amendments requested, to persons or other agencies to whom the disputed record has been disclosed; and

(5) nothing in this section shall allow an individual access to any information compiled in reasonable anticipation of a civil action or proceeding.

(e) Agency Requirements.—Each agency that maintains a system of records shall —

(1) maintain in its records only such information about an individual as is relevant and necessary to accomplish a purpose of the agency required to be accomplished by statute or by executive order of the President;

(2) collect information to the greatest extent practicable directly from the subject individual when the information may result in adverse determinations about an individual's rights, benefits, and privileges under Federal programs;

(3) inform each individual whom it asks to supply information, on the form which it uses to collect the information or on a separate form that can be retained by the individual —

(A) the authority (whether granted by statute, or by executive order of the President) which authorizes the solicitation of the information and whether disclosure of such information is mandatory or voluntary;

(B) the principal purpose or purposes for which the information is intended to be used;

(C) the routine uses which may be made of the information, as published pursuant to paragraph (4)(D) of this subsection; and

(D) the effects on him, if any, of not providing all or any part of the requested information;

(4) subject to the provisions of paragraph (11) of this subsection, publish in the Federal Register upon establishment or revision a notice of the existence and character of the system of records, which notice shall include —

(A) the name and location of the system;

(B) the categories of individuals on whom records are maintained in the system;

(C) the categories of records maintained in the system;

(D) each routine use of the records contained in the system, including the categories of users and the purpose of such use;

(E) the policies and practices of the agency regarding storage, retrievability, access controls, retention, and disposal of the records;

(F) the title and business address of the agency official who is responsible for the system of records;

(G) the agency procedures whereby an individual can be notified at his request if the system of records contains a record pertaining to him;

(H) the agency procedures whereby an individual can be notified at his request how he can gain access to any record pertaining to him contained in the system of records, and how he can contest its content; and

(I) the categories of sources of records in the system;

(5) maintain all records which are used by the agency in making any determination about any individual with such accuracy, relevance, timeliness, and completeness as is reasonably necessary to assure fairness to the individual in the determination;

(6) prior to disseminating any record about an individual to any person other than an agency, unless the dissemination is made pursuant to subsection (b)(2) of this section, make reasonable efforts to assure that such records are accurate, complete, timely, and relevant for agency purposes;

(7) maintain no record describing how any individual exercises rights guaranteed by the First Amendment unless expressly authorized by statute or by the individual about whom the record is maintained or unless pertinent to and within the scope of an authorized law enforcement activity;

(8) make reasonable efforts to serve notice on an individual when any record on such individual is made available to any person under compulsory legal process when such process becomes a matter of public record;

(9) establish rules of conduct for persons involved in the design, development, operation, or maintenance of any system of records, or in maintaining any record, and instruct each such person with respect to such rules and the requirements of this section, including any other rules and procedures adopted pursuant to this section and the penalties for noncompliance;

(10) establish appropriate administrative, technical, and physical safeguards to insure the security and confidentiality of records and to protect against any anticipated threats or hazards to their security or integrity which could result in substantial harm, embarrassment, inconvenience, or unfairness to any individual on whom information is maintained;

(11) at least 30 days prior to publication of information under paragraph (4)(D) of this subsection, publish in the Federal Register notice of any new use or intended use of the information in the system, and provide an opportunity for interested persons to submit written data, views, or arguments to the agency; and

(12) if such agency is a recipient agency or a source agency in a matching program with a non-Federal agency, with respect to any establishment or revision of a matching program, at least 30 days prior to conducting such program, publish in the Federal Register notice of such establishment or revision.

(f) Agency Rules.—In order to carry out the provisions of this section, each agency that maintains a system of records shall promulgate rules, in accordance with the requirements (including general notice) of section 553 of this title, which shall —

(1) establish procedures whereby an individual can be notified in response to his request if any system of records named by the individual contains a record pertaining to him;

(2) define reasonable times, places, and requirements for identifying an individual who requests his record or information pertaining to him before the agency shall make the record or information available to the individual;

(3) establish procedures for the disclosure to an individual upon his request of his record or information pertaining to him, including special procedure, if deemed necessary, for the disclosure to an individual of medical records, including psychological records, pertaining to him;

(4) establish procedures for reviewing a request from an individual concerning the amendment of any record or information pertaining to the individual, for making a determination on the request, for an appeal within the agency of an initial adverse agency determination, and for whatever additional means may be necessary for each individual to be able to exercise fully his rights under this section; and

(5) establish fees to be charged, if any, to any individual for making copies of his record, excluding the cost of any search for and review of the record.

The Office of the Federal Register shall biennially compile and publish the rules promulgated under this subsection and agency notices published under subsection (e)(4) of this section in a form available to the public at low cost.

(g) (1) Civil Remedies.—Whenever any agency

(A) makes a determination under subsection (d)(3) of this section not to amend an individual's record in accordance with his request, or fails to make such review in conformity with that subsection;

(B) refuses to comply with an individual request under subsection (d)(1) of this section;

(C) fails to maintain any record concerning any individual with such accuracy, relevance, timeliness, and completeness as is necessary to assure fairness in any determination relating to the qualifications, character, rights, or opportunities of, or benefits to the individual that may be made on the basis of such record, and consequently a determination is made which is adverse to the individual; or

(D) fails to comply with any other provision of this section, or any rule promulgated thereunder, in such a way as to have an adverse effect on an individual, the individual may bring a civil action against the agency, and the district courts of the United States shall have jurisdiction in the matters under the provisions of this subsection.

(2) (A) In any suit brought under the provisions of subsection (g)(1)(A) of this section, the court may order the agency to amend the individual's record in accordance with his request or in such other way as the court may direct. In such a case the court shall determine the matter de novo.

(B) The court may assess against the United States reasonable attorney fees and other litigation costs reasonably incurred in any case under this paragraph in which the complainant has substantially prevailed.

(3) (A) In any suit brought under the provisions of subsection (g)(1)(B) of this section, the court may enjoin the agency from withholding the records and order the production to the complainant of any agency records improperly withheld from him. In such a case the court shall determine the matter de novo, and may examine the contents of any agency records in camera to determine whether the records or any portion thereof may be withheld under any of the exemptions set forth in subsection (k) of this section, and the burden is on the agency to sustain its action.

(B) The court may assess against the United States reasonable attorney fees and other litigation costs reasonably incurred in any case under this paragraph in which the complainant has substantially prevailed.

(4) In any suit brought under the provisions of subsection (g)(1)(C) or (D) of this section in which the court determines that the agency acted in a manner which was intentional or willful, the United States shall be liable to the individual in an amount equal to the sum of —

(A) actual damages sustained by the individual as a result of the refusal or failure, but in no case shall a person entitled to recovery receive less than the sum of $1,000; and

(B) the costs of the action together with reasonable attorney fees as determined by the court.

(5) An action to enforce any liability created under this section may be brought in the district court of the United States in the district in which the complainant resides, or has his principal place of business, or in which the agency records are situated, or in the District of Columbia, without regard to the amount in controversy, within two years from the date on which the cause of action arises, except that where an agency has materially and willfully misrepresented any information required under this section to be disclosed to an individual and the information so misrepresented is material to establishment of the liability of the agency to the individual under this section, the action may be brought at any time within two years after discovery by the individual of the misrepresentation. Nothing in this section shall be construed to authorize any civil action by reason of any injury sustained as the result of a disclosure of a record prior to September 27, 1975.

(h) Rights of Legal Guardians.—For the purposes of this section, the parent of any minor, or the legal guardian of any individual who has been declared to be incompetent due to physical or mental incapacity or age by a court of competent jurisdiction, may act on behalf of the individual.

(i) (1) Criminal Penalties.—Any officer or employee of an agency, who by virtue of his employment or official position, has possession of, or access to, agency records which contain individually identifiable information the disclosure of which is prohibited by this section or by rules or regulations established thereunder, and who knowing that disclosure of the specific material is so prohibited, willfully discloses the material in any manner to any person or agency not entitled to receive it, shall be guilty of a misdemeanor and fined not more than $5,000.

(2) Any officer or employee of any agency who willfully maintains a system of records without meeting the notice requirements of subsection (e)(4) of this section shall be guilty of a misdemeanor and fined not more than $5,000.

(3) Any person who knowingly and willfully requests or obtains any record concerning an individual from an agency under false pretenses shall be guilty of a misdemeanor and fined not more than $5,000.

(j) General Exemptions.—The head of any agency may promulgate rules, in accordance with the requirements (including general notice) of sections 553(b)(1), (2), and (3), (c), and (e) of this title, to exempt any system of records within the agency from any part of this section except subsections (b), (c)(1) and (2), (e)(4)(A) through (F), (e)(6), (7), (9), (10), and (11), and (i) if the system of records is —

(1) maintained by the Central Intelligence Agency; or

(2) maintained by an agency or component thereof which performs as its principal function any activity pertaining to the enforcement of criminal laws, including police efforts to prevent, control, or reduce crime or to apprehend criminals, and the activities of prosecutors, courts, correctional, probation, pardon, or parole authorities, and which consists of (A) information compiled for the purpose of identifying individual criminal offenders and alleged offenders and consisting only of identifying data and notations of arrests, the nature and disposition of criminal charges, sentencing, confinement, release, and parole and probation status; (B) information compiled for the purpose of a criminal investigation, including reports of informants and investigators, and associated with an identifiable individual; or (C) reports identifiable to an individual compiled at any stage of the process of enforcement of the criminal laws from arrest or indictment through release from supervision.

At the time rules are adopted under this subsection, the agency shall include in the statement required under section 553(c) of this title, the reasons why the system of records is to be exempted from a provision of this section.

(k) Specific Exemptions.—The head of any agency may promulgate rules, in accordance with the requirements (including general notice) of sections 553(b)(1), (2), and (3), (c), and (e) of this title, to exempt any system of records within the agency from subsections (c)(3), (d), (e)(1), (e)(4)(G), (H), and (I) and (f) of this section if the system of records is —

Appendix C

(1) subject to the provisions of section 552(b)(1) of this title;

(2) investigatory material compiled for law enforcement purposes, other than material within the scope of subsection (j)(2) of this section: Provided, however, That if any individual is denied any right, privilege, or benefit that he would otherwise be entitled by Federal law, or for which he would otherwise be eligible, as a result of the maintenance of such material, such material shall be provided to such individual, except to the extent that the disclosure of such material would reveal the identity of a source who furnished information to the Government under an express promise that the identity of the source would be held in confidence, or, prior to the effective date of this section, under an implied promise that the identity of the source would be held in confidence;

(3) maintained in connection with providing protective services to the President of the United States or other individuals pursuant to section 3056 of title 18;

(4) required by statute to be maintained and used solely as statistical records;

(5) investigatory material compiled solely for the purpose of determining suitability, eligibility, or qualifications for Federal civilian employment, military service, Federal contracts, or access to classified information, but only to the extent that the disclosure of such material would reveal the identity of a source who furnished information to the Government under an express promise that the identity of the source would be held in confidence, or, prior to the effective date of this section, under an implied promise that the identity of the source would be held in confidence;

(6) testing or examination material used solely to determine individual qualifications for appointment or promotion in the Federal service the disclosure of which would compromise the objectivity or fairness of the testing or examination process; or

(7) evaluation material used to determine potential for promotion in the armed services, but only to the extent that the disclosure of such material would reveal the identity of a source who furnished information to the Government under an express promise that the identity of the source would be held in confidence, or, prior to the effective date of this section, under an implied promise that the identity of the source would be held in confidence.

(1) At the time rules are adopted under this subsection, the agency shall include in the statement required under section 553(c) of this title, the reasons why the system of records is to be exempted from a provision of this section.

(l) Archival Records.—Each agency record which is accepted by the Archivist of the United States for storage, processing, and servicing in accordance with section 3103 of title 44 shall, for the purposes of this section, be considered to be maintained by the agency which deposited the record and shall be subject to the provisions of this section. The Archivist of the United States shall not disclose the record except to the agency which maintains the record, or under rules established by that agency which are not inconsistent with the provisions of this section.

(2) Each agency record pertaining to an identifiable individual which was transferred to the National Archives of the United States as a record which has

sufficient historical or other value to warrant its continued preservation by the United States Government, prior to the effective date of this section, shall, for the purposes of this section, be considered to be maintained by the National Archives and shall not be subject to the provisions of this section, except that a statement generally describing such records (modeled after the requirements relating to records subject to subsections (e)(4)(A) through (G) of this section) shall be published in the Federal Register.

(3) Each agency record pertaining to an identifiable individual which is transferred to the National Archives of the United States as a record which has sufficient historical or other value to warrant its continued preservation by the United States Government, on or after the effective date of this section, shall, for the purposes of this section, be considered to be maintained by the National Archives and shall be exempt from the requirements of this section except subsections (e)(4)(A) through (G) and (e)(9) of this section.

(m) (1) Government Contractors.—When an agency provides by a contract for the operation by or on behalf of the agency of a system of records to accomplish an agency function, the agency shall, consistent with its authority, cause the requirements of this section to be applied to such system. For purposes of subsection (i) of this section any such contractor and any employee of such contractor, if such contract is agreed to on or after the effective date of this section, shall be considered to be an employee of an agency.

(2) A consumer reporting agency to which a record is disclosed under section 3711(e) of title 31 shall not be considered a contractor for the purposes of this section.

(n) Mailing Lists.—An individual's name and address may not be sold or rented by an agency unless such action is specifically authorized by law. This provision shall not be construed to require the withholding of names and addresses otherwise permitted to be made public.

(o) Matching Agreements.—(1) No record which is contained in a system of records may be disclosed to a recipient agency or non-Federal agency for use in a computer matching program except pursuant to a written agreement between the source agency and the recipient agency or non-Federal agency specifying —

   (A) the purpose and legal authority for conducting the program;

   (B) the justification for the program and the anticipated results, including a specific estimate of any savings;

   (C) a description of the records that will be matched, including each data element that will be used, the approximate number of records that will be matched, and the projected starting and completion dates of the matching program;

   (D) procedures for providing individualized notice at the time of application, and notice periodically thereafter as directed by the Data Integrity Board of such agency (subject to guidance provided by the Director of the Office of Management and Budget pursuant to subsection (v)), to —

      (i) applicants for and recipients of financial assistance or payments under Federal benefit programs, and

Appendix C

(ii) applicants for and holders of positions as Federal personnel, that any information provided by such applicants, recipients, holders, and individuals may be subject to verification through matching programs;

(E) procedures for verifying information produced in such matching program as required by subsection (p);

(F) procedures for the retention and timely destruction of identifiable records created by a recipient agency or non-Federal agency in such matching program;

(G) procedures for ensuring the administrative, technical, and physical security of the records matched and the results of such programs;

(H) prohibitions on duplication and redisclosure of records provided by the source agency within or outside the recipient agency or the non-Federal agency, except where required by law or essential to the conduct of the matching program;

(I) procedures governing the use by a recipient agency or non-Federal agency of records provided in a matching program by a source agency, including procedures governing return of the records to the source agency or destruction of records used in such program;

(J) information on assessments that have been made on the accuracy of the records that will be used in such matching program; and

(K) that the Comptroller General may have access to all records of a recipient agency or a non-Federal agency that the Comptroller General deems necessary in order to monitor or verify compliance with the agreement.

(2) (A) A copy of each agreement entered into pursuant to paragraph (1) shall —

(i) be transmitted to the Committee on Governmental Affairs of the Senate and the Committee on Government Operations of the House of Representatives; and

(ii) be available upon request to the public.

(B) No such agreement shall be effective until 30 days after the date on which such a copy is transmitted pursuant to subparagraph (A)(i).

(C) Such an agreement shall remain in effect only for such period, not to exceed 18 months, as the Data Integrity Board of the agency determines is appropriate in light of the purposes, and length of time necessary for the conduct, of the matching program.

(D) Within 3 months prior to the expiration of such an agreement pursuant to subparagraph (C), the Data Integrity Board of the agency may, without additional review, renew the matching agreement for a current, ongoing matching program for not more than one additional year if —

(i) such program will be conducted without any change; and

(ii) each party to the agreement certifies to the Board in writing that the program has been conducted in compliance with the agreement.

(p) Verification and Opportunity to Contest Findings.—(1) In order to protect any individual whose records are used in a matching program, no recipient agency, non-Federal agency, or source agency may suspend, terminate, reduce, or make a final denial of any financial assistance or payment under a Federal benefit program to such individual, or take other adverse action against such individual, as a result of information produced by such matching program, until —

    (A) (i) the agency has independently verified the information; or

        (ii) the Data Integrity Board of the agency, or in the case of a non-Federal agency the Data Integrity Board of the source agency, determines in accordance with guidance issued by the Director of the Office of Management and Budget that —

            (I) the information is limited to identification and amount of benefits paid by the source agency under a Federal benefit program; and

            (II) there is a high degree of confidence that the information provided to the recipient agency is accurate;

    (B) the individual receives a notice from the agency containing a statement of its findings and informing the individual of the opportunity to contest such findings; and

    (C) (i) the expiration of any time period established for the program by statute or regulation for the individual to respond to that notice; or

        (ii) in the case of a program for which no such period is established, the end of the 30-day period beginning on the date on which notice under subparagraph (B) is mailed or otherwise provided to the individual.

(2) Independent verification referred to in paragraph (1) requires investigation and confirmation of specific information relating to an individual that is used as a basis for an adverse action against the individual, including where applicable investigation and confirmation of —

    (A) the amount of any asset or income involved;

    (B) whether such individual actually has or had access to such asset or income for such individual's own use; and

    (C) the period or periods when the individual actually had such asset or income.

(3) Notwithstanding paragraph (1), an agency may take any appropriate action otherwise prohibited by such paragraph if the agency determines that the public health or public safety may be adversely affected or significantly threatened during any notice period required by such paragraph.

(q) Sanctions.—(1) Notwithstanding any other provisions of law, no source agency may disclose any record which is contained in a system of records to a recipient agency or non-Federal agency for a matching program if such source agency has reason to believe that the requirements of subsection (p), or any matching agreement entered into pursuant to subsection (o), or both, are not being met by such recipient agency.

(2) No source agency may renew a matching agreement unless —

    (A) the recipient agency or non-Federal agency has certified that it has complied with the provisions of that agreement; and

    (B) the source agency has no reason to believe that the certification is inaccurate.

(r) Report on New Systems and Matching Programs.—Each agency that proposes to establish or make a significant change in a system of records or a matching program shall provide adequate advance notice of any such proposal (in duplicate) to the Committee on Government Operations of the House of Representatives, the Committee on Governmental Affairs of the Senate, and the Office of Management and Budget in order to permit an evaluation of the probable or potential effect of such proposal on the *privacy* or other rights of individuals.

(s) Biennial Report.—The President shall biennially submit to the Speaker of the House of Representatives and the President pro tempore of the Senate a report —

(1) describing the actions of the Director of the Office of Management and Budget pursuant to section 6 of the Privacy Act of 1974 during the preceding 2 years;

(2) describing the exercise of individual rights of access and amendment under this section during such years;

(3) identifying changes in or additions to systems of records;

(4) containing such other information concerning administration of this section as may be necessary or useful to the Congress in reviewing the effectiveness of this section in carrying out the purposes of the Privacy Act of 1974.

(t) (1) Effect of Other Laws.—No agency shall rely on any exemption contained in section 552 of this title to withhold from an individual any record which is otherwise accessible to such individual under the provisions of this section.

(2) No agency shall rely on any exemption in this section to withhold from an individual any record which is otherwise accessible to such individual under the provisions of section 552 of this title.

(u) Data Integrity Boards.—(1) Every agency conducting or participating in a matching program shall establish a Data Integrity Board to oversee and coordinate among the various components of such agency the agency's implementation of this section.

[Footnotes omitted]

APPENDIX D

PRIVACY PROVISIONS OF THE GRAMM-LEACH-BLILEY ACT, 1999

GRAMM-LEACH-BLILEY ACT 15 USC, SUBCHAPTER 1, SEC. 6801–6809 DISCLOSURE OF NONPUBLIC PERSONAL INFORMATION

SEC. 6801. PROTECTION OF NONPUBLIC PERSONAL INFORMATION

(a) Privacy obligation policy

It is the policy of the Congress that each financial institution has an affirmative and continuing obligation to respect the privacy of its customers and to protect the security and confidentiality of those customers' nonpublic personal information.

(b) Financial institutions safeguards

In furtherance of the policy in subsection (a) of this section, each agency or authority described in section 6805(a) of this title shall establish appropriate standards for the financial institutions subject to their jurisdiction relating to administrative, technical, and physical safeguards —

(1) to insure the security and confidentiality of customer records and information;

(2) to protect against any anticipated threats or hazards to the security or integrity of such records; and

(3) to protect against unauthorized access to or use of such records or information which could result in substantial harm or inconvenience to any customer. . . .

Appendix D

Sec. 6802. Obligations with Respect to Disclosures of Personal Information

(a) Notice requirements

Except as otherwise provided in this subchapter, a financial institution may not, directly or through any affiliate, disclose to a nonaffiliated third party any nonpublic personal information, unless such financial institution provides or has provided to the consumer a notice that complies with section 6803 of this title.

(b) Opt out

(1) In general

A financial institution may not disclose nonpublic personal information to a nonaffiliated third party unless —

(A) such financial institution clearly and conspicuously discloses to the consumer, in writing or in electronic form or other form permitted by the regulations prescribed under section 6804 of this title, that such information may be disclosed to such third party;
(B) the consumer is given the opportunity, before the time that such information is initially disclosed, to direct that such information not be disclosed to such third party; and

(C) the consumer is given an explanation of how the consumer can exercise that nondisclosure option.

(2) Exception

This subsection shall not prevent a financial institution from providing nonpublic personal information to a nonaffiliated third party to perform services for or functions on behalf of the financial institution, including marketing of the financial institution's own products or services, or financial products or services offered pursuant to joint agreements between two or more financial institutions that comply with the requirements imposed by the regulations prescribed under section 6804 of this title, if the financial institution fully discloses the providing of such information and enters into a contractual agreement with the third party that requires the third party to maintain the confidentiality of such information.

(c) Limits on reuse of information

Except as otherwise provided in this subchapter, a nonaffiliated third party that receives from a financial institution nonpublic personal information under this section shall not, directly or through an affiliate of such receiving third party, disclose such information to any other person that is a nonaffiliated third party of both the financial institution and such receiving third party, unless such disclosure would be lawful if made directly to such other person by the financial institution.

(d) Limitations on the sharing of account number information for marketing purposes

A financial institution shall not disclose, other than to a consumer reporting agency, an account number or similar form of access number or access code for a credit card account, deposit account, or transaction account of a consumer to any nonaffiliated third party for use in telemarketing, direct mail marketing, or other marketing through electronic mail to the consumer.

(e) General exceptions

Subsections (a) and (b) of this section shall not prohibit the disclosure of non-public personal information —

(1) as necessary to effect, administer, or enforce a transaction requested or authorized by the consumer, or in connection with —

(A) servicing or processing a financial product or service requested or authorized by the consumer;

(B) maintaining or servicing the consumer's account with the financial institution, or with another entity as part of a private label credit card program or other extension of credit on behalf of such entity; or

(C) a proposed or actual securitization, secondary market sale (including sales of servicing rights), or similar transaction related to a transaction of the consumer;

(2) with the consent or at the direction of the consumer;

(3)(A) to protect the confidentiality or security of the financial institution's records pertaining to the consumer, the service or product, or the transaction therein; (B) to protect against or prevent actual or potential fraud, unauthorized transactions, claims, or other liability; (C) for required institutional risk control, or for resolving customer disputes or inquiries; (D) to persons holding a legal or beneficial interest relating to the consumer; or (E) to persons acting in a fiduciary or representative capacity on behalf of the consumer;

(4) to provide information to insurance rate advisory organizations, guaranty funds or agencies, applicable rating agencies of the financial institution, persons assessing the institution's compliance with industry standards, and the institution's attorneys, accountants, and auditors;

(5) to the extent specifically permitted or required under other provisions of law and in accordance with the Right to Financial Privacy Act of 1978 (12 U.S.C. 3401 et seq.), to law enforcement agencies (including a Federal functional regulator, the Secretary of the Treasury with respect to subchapter II of chapter 53 of title 31, and chapter 2 of title I of Public Law 91-508 (12 U.S.C. 1951–1959), a State insurance authority, or the Federal Trade Commission), self-regulatory organizations, or for an investigation on a matter related to public safety;

(6) (A) to a consumer reporting agency in accordance with the Fair Credit Reporting Act (15 U.S.C. 1681 et seq.), or (B) from a consumer report reported by a consumer reporting agency;

(7) in connection with a proposed or actual sale, merger, transfer, or exchange of all or a portion of a business or operating unit if the disclosure of nonpublic personal information concerns solely consumers of such business or unit; or

(8) to comply with Federal, State, or local laws, rules, and other applicable legal requirements; to comply with a properly authorized civil, criminal, or regulatory investigation or subpoena or summons by Federal, State, or local authorities; or to respond to judicial process or government regulatory authorities having jurisdiction over the financial institution for examination, compliance, or other purposes as authorized by law. . . .

SEC. 6803. DISCLOSURE OF INSTITUTION PRIVACY POLICY

(a) Disclosure required

At the time of establishing a customer relationship with a consumer and not less than annually during the continuation of such relationship, a financial institution shall provide a clear and conspicuous disclosure to such consumer, in writing or in electronic form or other form permitted by the regulations prescribed under section 6804 of this title, of such financial institution's policies and practices with respect to —

(1) disclosing nonpublic personal information to affiliates and nonaffiliated third parties, consistent with section 6802 of this title, including the categories of information that may be disclosed;

(2) disclosing nonpublic personal information of persons who have ceased to be customers of the financial institution; and

(3) protecting the nonpublic personal information of consumers.

Such disclosures shall be made in accordance with the regulations prescribed under section 6804 of this title.

(b) Information to be included

The disclosure required by subsection (a) of this section shall include —
(1) the policies and practices of the institution with respect to disclosing nonpublic personal information to nonaffiliated third parties, other than agents of the institution, consistent with section 6802 of this title, and including —

(A) the categories of persons to whom the information is or may be disclosed, other than the persons to whom the information may be provided pursuant to section 6802(e) of this title; and

(B) the policies and practices of the institution with respect to disclosing of nonpublic personal information of persons who have ceased to be customers of the financial institution;

(2) the categories of nonpublic personal information that are collected by the financial institution;

(3) the policies that the institution maintains to protect the confidentiality and security of nonpublic personal information in accordance with section 6801 of this title; and

(4) the disclosures required, if any, under section 1681a(d)(2) (A)(iii) of this title. . . .

SEC. 6804. RULEMAKING

(a) Regulatory authority

(1) Rulemaking

The Federal banking agencies, the National Credit Union Administration, the Secretary of the Treasury, the Securities and Exchange Commission, and the Federal Trade Commission shall each prescribe, after consultation as appropriate with representatives of State insurance authorities designated by the National Association of Insurance Commissioners, such regulations as may be necessary to carry out the purposes of this subchapter with respect to the financial institutions subject to their jurisdiction under section 6805 of this title.

(2) Coordination, consistency, and comparability

Each of the agencies and authorities required under paragraph (1) to prescribe regulations shall consult and coordinate with the other such agencies and authorities for the purposes of assuring, to the extent possible, that the regulations prescribed by each such agency and authority are consistent and comparable with the regulations prescribed by the other such agencies and authorities.

(3) Procedures and deadline

Such regulations shall be prescribed in accordance with applicable requirements of title 5 and shall be issued in final form not later than 6 months after November 12, 1999.

(b) Authority to grant exceptions

The regulations prescribed under subsection (a) of this section may include such additional exceptions to subsections (a) through (d) of section 6802 of this title as are deemed consistent with the purposes of this subchapter. . . .

SEC. 6805. ENFORCEMENT

(a) In general

This subchapter and the regulations prescribed thereunder shall be enforced by the Federal functional regulators, the State insurance authorities, and the Federal Trade Commission with respect to financial institutions and other persons subject to their jurisdiction under applicable law, as follows:

Appendix D

(1) Under section 1818 of title 12, in the case of —

(A) national banks, Federal branches and Federal agencies of foreign banks, and any subsidiaries of such entities (except brokers, dealers, persons providing insurance, investment companies, and investment advisers), by the Office of the Comptroller of the Currency;

(B) member banks of the Federal Reserve System (other than national banks), branches and agencies of foreign banks (other than Federal branches, Federal agencies, and insured State branches of foreign banks), commercial lending companies owned or controlled by foreign banks, organizations operating under section 25 or 25A of the Federal Reserve Act (12 U.S.C. 601 et seq., 611 et seq.), and bank holding companies and their nonbank subsidiaries or affiliates (except brokers, dealers, persons providing insurance, investment companies, and investment advisers), by the Board of Governors of the Federal Reserve System;

(C) banks insured by the Federal Deposit Insurance Corporation (other than members of the Federal Reserve System), insured State branches of foreign banks, and any subsidiaries of such entities (except brokers, dealers, persons providing insurance, investment companies, and investment advisers), by the Board of Directors of the Federal Deposit Insurance Corporation; and

(D) savings associations the deposits of which are insured by the Federal Deposit Insurance Corporation, and any subsidiaries of such savings associations (except brokers, dealers, persons providing insurance, investment companies, and investment advisers), by the Director of the Office of Thrift Supervision.

(2) Under the Federal Credit Union Act (12 U.S.C. 1751 et seq.), by the Board of the National Credit Union Administration with respect to any federally insured credit union, and any subsidiaries of such an entity.

(3) Under the Securities Exchange Act of 1934 (15 U.S.C. 78a et seq.), by the Securities and Exchange Commission with respect to any broker or dealer.

(4) Under the Investment Company Act of 1940 (15 U.S.C. 80a-1 et seq.), by the Securities and Exchange Commission with respect to investment companies.

(5) Under the Investment Advisers Act of 1940 (15 U.S.C. 80b-1 et seq.), by the Securities and Exchange Commission with respect to investment advisers registered with the Commission under such Act.

(6) Under State insurance law, in the case of any person engaged in providing insurance, by the applicable State insurance authority of the State in which the person is domiciled, subject to section 6701 of this title.

(7) Under the Federal Trade Commission Act (15 U.S.C. 41 et seq.), by the Federal Trade Commission for any other financial institution or other person that is not subject to the jurisdiction of any agency or authority under paragraphs (1) through (6) of this subsection.

(b) Enforcement of section 6801

(1) In general

Except as provided in paragraph (2), the agencies and authorities described in subsection (a) of this section shall implement the standards prescribed under section 6801(b) of this title in the same manner, to the extent practicable, as standards prescribed pursuant to section 1831p-1(a) of title 12 are implemented pursuant to such section.

(2) Exception

The agencies and authorities described in paragraphs (3), (4), (5), (6), and (7) of subsection (a) of this section shall implement the standards prescribed under section 6801(b) of this title by rule with respect to the financial institutions and other persons subject to their respective jurisdictions under subsection (a) of this section.

(c) Absence of State action

If a State insurance authority fails to adopt regulations to carry out this subchapter, such State shall not be eligible to override, pursuant to section 1831x(g)(2)(B)(iii) of title 12, the insurance customer protection regulations prescribed by a Federal banking agency under section 1831x(a) of title 12.

(d) Definitions

The terms used in subsection (a)(1) of this section that are not defined in this subchapter or otherwise defined in section 1813(s) of title 12 shall have the same meaning as given in section 3101 of title 12. . . .

SEC. 6806. RELATION TO OTHER PROVISIONS

Except for the amendments made by subsections (a) and (b), nothing in this chapter shall be construed to modify, limit, or supersede the operation of the Fair Credit Reporting Act (15 U.S.C. 1681 et seq.), and no inference shall be drawn on the basis of the provisions of this chapter regarding whether information is transaction or experience information under section 603 of such Act (15 U.S.C. 1681a). . . .

SEC. 6807. RELATION TO STATE LAWS

(a) In general

This subchapter and the amendments made by this subchapter shall not be construed as superseding, altering, or affecting any statute, regulation, order, or interpretation in effect in any State, except to the extent that such statute, regulation, order, or interpretation is inconsistent with the provisions of this subchapter, and then only to the extent of the inconsistency.

(b) Greater protection under State law

For purposes of this section, a State statute, regulation, order, or interpretation is not inconsistent with the provisions of this subchapter if the protection such statute, regulation, order, or interpretation affords any person is greater than the protection provided under this subchapter and the amendments made by this subchapter, as determined by the Federal Trade Commission, after consultation with the agency or authority with jurisdiction under section 6805(a) of this title of either the person that initiated the complaint or that is the subject of the complaint, on its own motion or upon the petition of any interested party. . . .

SEC. 6808. STUDY OF INFORMATION SHARING AMONG FINANCIAL AFFILIATES

(a) In general

The Secretary of the Treasury, in conjunction with the Federal functional regulators and the Federal Trade Commission, shall conduct a study of information sharing practices among financial institutions and their affiliates. Such study shall include —

(1) the purposes for the sharing of confidential customer information with affiliates or with nonaffiliated third parties;

(2) the extent and adequacy of security protections for such information;

(3) the potential risks for customer privacy of such sharing of information;

(4) the potential benefits for financial institutions and affiliates of such sharing of information;

(5) the potential benefits for customers of such sharing of information;

(6) the adequacy of existing laws to protect customer privacy;

(7) the adequacy of financial institution privacy policy and privacy rights disclosure under existing law;

(8) the feasibility of different approaches, including opt-out and opt-in, to permit customers to direct that confidential information not be shared with affiliates and nonaffiliated third parties; and

(9) the feasibility of restricting sharing of information for specific uses or of permitting customers to direct the uses for which information may be shared.

(b) Consultation

The Secretary shall consult with representatives of State insurance authorities designated by the National Association of Insurance Commissioners, and also with financial services industry, consumer organizations and privacy groups, and other representatives of the general public, in formulating and conducting the study required by subsection (a) of this section.

(c) Report

On or before January 1, 2002, the Secretary shall submit a report to the Congress containing the findings and conclusions of the study required under subsection (a) of this section, together with such recommendations for legislative or administrative action as may be appropriate. . . .

SEC. 6809. DEFINITIONS

As used in this subchapter:

(1) Federal banking agency

The term "Federal banking agency" has the same meaning as given in section 1813 of title 12.

(2) Federal functional regulator

The term "Federal functional regulator" means —

(A) the Board of Governors of the Federal Reserve System;

(B) the Office of the Comptroller of the Currency;

(C) the Board of Directors of the Federal Deposit Insurance Corporation;

(D) the Director of the Office of Thrift Supervision;

(E) the National Credit Union Administration Board; and

(F) the Securities and Exchange Commission.

(3) Financial institution

(A) In general

The term "financial institution" means any institution the business of which is engaging in financial activities as described in section 1843(k) of title 12.

(B) Persons subject to CFTC regulation

Notwithstanding subparagraph (A), the term "financial institution" does not include any person or entity with respect to any financial activity that is subject to the jurisdiction of the Commodity Futures Trading Commission under the Commodity Exchange Act (7 U.S.C. 1 et seq.).

(C) Farm credit institutions

Notwithstanding subparagraph (A), the term "financial institution" does not include the Federal Agricultural Mortgage Corporation or any entity chartered and operating under the Farm Credit Act of 1971 (12 U.S.C. 2001 et seq.).

Appendix D

(D) Other secondary market institutions

Notwithstanding subparagraph (A), the term "financial institution" does not include institutions chartered by Congress specifically to engage in transactions described in section 6802(e)(1)(C) of this title, as long as such institutions do not sell or transfer nonpublic personal information to a nonaffiliated third party.

(4) Nonpublic personal information

(A) The term "nonpublic personal information" means personally identifiable financial information —

(i) provided by a consumer to a financial institution;

(ii) resulting from any transaction with the consumer or any service performed for the consumer; or

(iii) otherwise obtained by the financial institution.

(B) Such term does not include publicly available information, as such term is defined by the regulations prescribed under section 6804 of this title.

(C) Notwithstanding subparagraph (B), such term —

(i) shall include any list, description, or other grouping of consumers (and publicly available information pertaining to them) that is derived using any nonpublic personal information other than publicly available information; but

(ii) shall not include any list, description, or other grouping of consumers (and publicly available information pertaining to them) that is derived without using any nonpublic personal information.

(5) Nonaffiliated third party

The term "nonaffiliated third party" means any entity that is not an affiliate of, or related by common ownership or affiliated by corporate control with, the financial institution, but does not include a joint employee of such institution.

(6) Affiliate

The term "affiliate" means any company that controls, is controlled by, or is under common control with another company.

(7) Necessary to effect, administer, or enforce

The term "as necessary to effect, administer, or enforce the transaction" means —

(A) the disclosure is required, or is a usual, appropriate, or acceptable method, to carry out the transaction or the product or service business of which the transaction is a part, and record or service or maintain the consumer's account in the ordinary course of providing the financial service or financial product, or to administer or service benefits or claims relating to the transaction or the product or service business of which it is a part, and includes —

(i) providing the consumer or the consumer's agent or broker with a confirmation, statement, or other record of the transaction, or information on the status or value of the financial service or financial product; and

(ii) the accrual or recognition of incentives or bonuses associated with the transaction that are provided by the financial institution or any other party;

(B) the disclosure is required, or is one of the lawful or appropriate methods, to enforce the rights of the financial institution or of other persons engaged in carrying out the financial transaction, or providing the product or service;

(C) the disclosure is required, or is a usual, appropriate, or acceptable method, for insurance underwriting at the consumer's request or for reinsurance purposes, or for any of the following purposes as they relate to a consumer's insurance: Account administration, reporting, investigating, or preventing fraud or material misrepresentation, processing premium payments, processing insurance claims, administering insurance benefits (including utilization review activities), participating in research projects, or as otherwise required or specifically permitted by Federal or State law; or

(D) the disclosure is required, or is a usual, appropriate or acceptable method, in connection with —

(i) the authorization, settlement, billing, processing, clearing, transferring, reconciling, or collection of amounts charged, debited, or otherwise paid using a debit, credit or other payment card, check, or account number, or by other payment means;

(ii) the transfer of receivables, accounts or interests therein; or

(iii) the audit of debit, credit or other payment information.

(8) State insurance authority

The term "State insurance authority" means, in the case of any person engaged in providing insurance, the State insurance authority of the State in which the person is domiciled.

(9) Consumer

The term "consumer" means an individual who obtains, from a financial institution, financial products or services which are to be used primarily for personal, family, or household purposes, and also means the legal representative of such an individual.

(10) Joint agreement

The term "joint agreement" means a formal written contract pursuant to which two or more financial institutions jointly offer, endorse, or sponsor a financial product or service, and as may be further defined in the regulations prescribed under section 6804 of this title.

(11) Customer relationship

The term "time of establishing a customer relationship" shall be defined by the regulations prescribed under section 6804 of this title, and shall, in the case of a financial institution engaged in extending credit directly to consumers to finance purchases of goods or services, mean the time of establishing the credit relationship with the consumer. . . .

INDEX

Locators in **boldface** indicate main topics. Locators followed by *c* indicate chronology entries. Locators followed by *b* indicate biographical entries. Locators followed by *g* indicate glossary entries.

Index

Index

Index

Index